The Economy
in the 1980s:
A Program for
Growth and Stability

THE ECONOMY IN THE 1980s:

A PROGRAM FOR GROWTH

AND STABILITY

Michael J. Boskin, *Editor*

George F. Break

John T. Cuddington

Patricia Drury

Alain Enthoven

Laurence J. Kotlikoff

Ronald I. McKinnon

John H. Pencavel

Henry S. Rowen

John L. Scadding

John B. Shoven

James L. Sweeney

David J. Teece

Institute for Contemporary Studies
San Francisco, California

Transaction Books
New Brunswick (U.S.A.) and London (U.K.)

Inquiries, book orders, and catalog requests should be addressed to the Institute for Contemporary Studies, Suite 811, 260 California Street, San Francisco, California 94111—415—398—3010.

Library of Congress Catalog Number 80—80647.
ISBN 0—917616—39—1 (paper).
ISBN 0—87855—399—1 (cloth). Available through Transaction Books, Rutgers—The State University, New Brunswick, NJ 08903.

CONTENTS

V

The International Economy

VI

The Role of Government in the Economy

VII

Potential Policy Problems of the 1980s

VIII

Summary and Conclusion

CONTRIBUTORS

MICHAEL J. BOSKIN
Professor of Economics, Stanford University;
Director, Program on Social Insurance Research,
National Bureau of Economic Research

GEORGE F. BREAK
Professor of Economics, University of California—Berkeley

JOHN T. CUDDINGTON
Assistant Professor of Economics, Stanford University

PATRICIA DRURY
Research Associate, Graduate School of Business,
Stanford University

ALAIN ENTHOVEN
Marriner S. Eccles Professor of Public and Private Management,
Graduate School of Business; Professor of Health Care
Economics, School of Medicine, Stanford University

LAURENCE J. KOTLIKOFF
Assistant Professor of Economics, Yale University

RONALD I. McKINNON
Professor of Economics, Stanford University

JOHN H. PENCAVEL
Professor of Economics, Stanford University

HENRY S. ROWEN
Professor of Public Management, Graduate School of Business;
Director, Stanford International Energy Program,
Stanford University

JOHN L. SCADDING
Economist, Federal Reserve Bank of San Francisco

JOHN B. SHOVEN
Professor of Economics, Stanford University

JAMES L. SWEENEY
Professor, Engineering-Economic Systems; Director,
Energy Modeling Forum, Stanford University

DAVID J. TEECE
Associate Professor of Business Economics, Graduate School
of Business and Department of Economics,
Stanford University

PREFACE

In the decade of the 1970s the U.S. economy experienced its worst performance in four decades. Rising U.S. inflation and stagnant productivity growth were responsible for the worst economic performance of any Western country.

The institute has published a number of studies on specific economic problems—on energy, planning, health care, tax reform, international trade, and other subjects. This is our first attempt to present an integrated view of the economy as a whole, looking back at serious problems experienced in the 1970s as part of fashioning a systematic statement of what reforms are necessary to restore to the U.S. economy the growth and stability of prior decades.

Michael J. Boskin was the logical choice to organize this project, having edited two previous institute studies, *The Crisis in Social Security* (1977) and *Federal Tax Reform* (1978). For the purpose he recruited a number of past contributors—George F. Break, John T. Cuddington, Alain Enthoven, Laurence J. Kotlikoff, Ronald I. McKinnon, Henry S. Rowen, John B. Shoven, and James L. Sweeney, in addition to new institute authors John L. Scadding, John H. Pencavel, Patricia Drury, and David J. Teece.

As part of the project, we organized a conference—following a format developed in our recent national security study—at which the authors could exchange ideas about chapters and topics; these discussions, elaborating and refining the issues considered, appear at the end of most of the chapters and provide interesting supplementary material.

In addition to the formal authors, we would like to thank A. Lawrence Chickering (Executive Director of the institute), Leif Olsen (Chairman of the Economic Policy Committee of Citibank), and Caspar W. Weinberger (formerly Secretary of Health, Education, and Welfare and head of the Office of Management and Budget) who also participated in the discussions.

The economy will almost certainly be the central issue in the coming presidential election. It is clear—and in fact, universally acknowledged—that the U.S. economy is going through its most severe test since the Great Depression. Restoring growth and stability to the economy must be a top priority for the next administration. We think this book presents a compelling statement of reforms that are necessary to prevent continuing economic distress and to restore the long-term growth which the United States has enjoyed for most of its history.

> H. Monroe Browne
> President,
> Institute for Contemporary Studies

June 1980
San Francisco, California

I

U.S. Performance in Historical and International Perspective

1

MICHAEL J. BOSKIN

U.S. Economy at the Crossroads

Economic growth rate and the 1970s. Changes in the labor force. Problems with inflation. Saving and investment. Overseas investment incentives. Government and economics. The discontented.

The U.S. economy is at a crossroads in its history. In the decade ahead a myriad of interrelated private and public policies will shape the future of our economy and society for the decades to come. Perhaps unknowingly, we will shape an economic environment which either will continue to take us down the road of high inflation, sluggish real economic growth, and periodic disruption—with all the dangerous social consequences such a situation implies—or we will begin to unravel the disincentives which obstruct steady economic progress and will restore an environment in which a continuously expanding ability to produce goods and services will allow most of our citizens continuous gains in their standard of living while meeting the needs of the less fortunate in our society with minimum social disruption. Following is a summary of the recent performance of the U.S. economy together with a statement of emerging issues, policies, and problems which it is likely to confront in the coming decade and beyond.

THE RAPIDLY CHANGING ECONOMY

By any yardstick, the performance of the U.S. economy in the 1970s was abysmal. It was our worst decade since the 1930s. While this is revealed in a variety of commonly used statistics to describe the overall performance, many of these statistics have a very different interpretation when placed against the backdrop of a rapidly changing economy.

Income Growth and the Standard of Living

The most basic yardsticks of an economy's performance are the level and growth rate of its people's standard of living, normally measured by average income per person. We frequently quote real gross national product (GNP) per capita as a measure of our economic well-being. Real GNP per capita measures the total value, adjusted for inflation, of all goods and services provided in our society, per person. Over the last century the United States, as well as such other societies as France and Germany, have seen their real GNP per capita grow at an average of almost 2.0 percent per year. While substantial temporary fluctuations have occurred in this rate, such an average not only was maintained over the last century but, if we look at the two and a half decades after World War II—the period 1947 to 1973—real GNP per capita grew at 2.4 percent per year. At such a rate GNP per capita will approximately *double between generations;* that is, each successive generation will be approximately twice as wealthy over its lifetime as the generation which preceded it.

Since the early 1970s our rate of real GNP per capita growth has slowed markedly. Real GNP per capita since 1973 has grown at about 1.2 percent per year, about half the rate for the bulk of the post−World War II period. The other usual measure of economic well-being, real disposable personal income—income after taxes—followed a similar pattern; it grew at about 2.5 percent per year from 1947 through 1973 and only at about 1.3 percent per year since then. But such measures dramatically *understate* the decline in our economic performance for the period.

The 1970s were a decade of unprecedented labor force expansion. The combination of the post−World War II baby boom generation moving into the labor force in unprecedented numbers and the enormous increase in labor force participation of married women leave us today with the largest ratio of workers to total population in U.S. history. That is, our GNP per person has been growing very slowly, even though we have many more workers than ever before. Were we to look at the growth of real GNP per employed worker, we would note that in the period 1963 through 1973, this grew at 1.9 percent per year, but in the period 1973 through 1979, at a horrendous 0.1 percent per year. The latter figure compares to about 2.7 percent for France, 3.2 percent for Germany, 3.4 percent for Japan, 1.6 percent for Italy, and 0.3 percent for the United Kingdom. To put these rates into perspective, if they continue, average income in the United States will soon fall behind that in France and Germany, and eventually that in Japan. We did terribly—

not only relative to our own history, but relative to our major trading competitors and to other advanced economies. Why has our growth rate slowed so markedly? As we examine other factors and changes in our economy, the answers become obvious.

Labor Force, Unemployment, Retirement, Poverty

In the postwar period, and especially in the 1970s, there has been a major change in the U.S. labor force. As noted above, female labor force participation rates soared in the 1970s. Shortly after World War II less than one in three women worked in the marketplace; today well over half of them do. Combined with the dramatic increase in young workers entering the labor force in the 1970s, caused primarily by the post–World War II baby boom generation finishing school and going to work for the first time, this large increase in the proportion of adults seeking employment placed particular strain on the ability of our economy rapidly to find meaningful employment for all of them. As a result, unemployment rates rose on average in the 1970s relative to the 1950s and 1960s. Indeed, because of this changing composition of the labor force, most economists now place the so-called natural unemployment rate—that compatible with stable prices, normal entry and reentry, and job turnover in the labor force—*at about 5.5 percent to 6.0 percent.* Even. President Carter's own Council of Economic Advisors defines this full employment level of unemployment at 4.9 percent, substantially larger than the 4.0 percent which was commonly quoted in the 1960s. At this level we have been very close to full employment of the labor force for the last two years.

Nowhere has a change in our economy been more dramatic than in the relative importance of unemployment in our society. In 1933 the unemployment rate was about 25 percent—at a time when few families had two potential earners, when average wages were much lower and average unemployment longer than they are today, when there was no social security system and other government programs to aid the unemployed and the poor were extremely limited.

The nature of unemployment in the postwar economy, particularly in the 1970s, has changed markedly. Since World War II the unemployment rate has exceeded an annual 6 percent only five times. In the last couple of years the average duration of unemployment has been three to four months. Coverage under unemployment insurance has been expanded to well over 80 percent of the labor force, while in 1947 only slightly over one-half of the labor force was covered. Finally, last year most spells of unemployment were due either to entry or reentry into the labor force, or to persons quitting their job or being placed on *temporary* furlough from their firm (for example, due to seasonal factors). That is, much unemployment was not involuntary; it was not due to insufficient demand for labor in our economy. While unemployment will undoubtedly rise in the next twelve to eighteen months as our current recession worsens, it is still important to note that we have largely controlled unemployment in the postwar period and have provided substantial income security to those who become unemployed. (Indeed, in cushioning with unemployment insurance the full economic harm done to those who become unemployed, many have suggested that we reduce the incentive to seek and find new work.)

A substantial problem remains, however, in what might be called the structural unemployment of particular population subgroups. Minorities, women, and teenagers all have much higher unemployment rates than prime-age white males. While the official statistics probably overstate unemployment among minority teenagers, the very high rate—which for minority teenagers has been about 35 percent or more in recent years—is a serious social problem. The unemployment rate of such groups is not easily reduced by broad-brushed traditional fiscal and monetary policy measures to heat up the economy. Instead, policy must deal with such groups more directly.

A major achievement of our economy in the 1970s was its ability rapidly, albeit not instantly, to expand employment at an astounding rate. Thus, despite the rapid influx of new people into the labor force, in the last decade employment increased by some 18 million persons, 80 percent of whom were in the private sector of the economy.

As incomes have grown, unemployment has been kept more or less under control, and government transfer programs have grown extensively, the percentage of the population living below the poverty line has declined markedly. This reduction has been a great success story. Twenty-two percent of Americans in 1962 lived in families below the poverty line as measured by the official poverty index. Although that group is today about 11 percent, the poverty index is now badly and seriously biased because it is based only on cash income and does not include in-kind government transfer payment programs (subsidized housing, medical care, food stamps) which have shown major growth since 1962. If we include such transfer payments, the number living below the official poverty line would be slightly under 5 percent (see Anderson 1979). We have largely eliminated poverty in the United States, but our official statistics reveal only part of this accomplishment.

Another set of rather remarkable changes in the post —World War II labor force has been the explosion of those seeking earlier retirement, the decline in the average workweek, and the changing age structure of our population and labor force. In 1948 about half the men over age 65 were still in the labor force; today only one in five are. More people now claim their first social security benefit at age 62 than at age 65. The average workweek has declined in the same interval from slightly over 40 hours to about 36 hours per week. At the same time, the life expectancy of the elderly has increased substantially, by about three years for elderly women and one and a half years for elderly men since 1960. These two factors—earlier retirement and longer life expectancy—combine to increase the average length of the retirement period by an astounding 30 percent. Even with the stable age structure of our population, the elderly would still need substantially more resources to maintain their retirement income for this longer retirement period.

The longer retirement period will eventually combine with a dramatic increase in the ratio of retirees to workers in our society. Even if birthrates return to normal levels for the balance of this century, the post–World War II baby boom and recent baby bust imply an increase in the ratio of retirees to workers of roughly 70 percent by shortly after the turn of the century. This will place heavy pressure on our fiscal institutions, social security, labor market, and on intrafamily relations. The best estimate of the trustees of the Social Security Administration is that early in the next century the current ratio of one retiree for every three and a quarter workers will increase to approximately one retiree for every two workers.

Inflation

While we have controlled the unemployment problem in the postwar period and cushioned its effect, we have not done nearly so well with inflation. In the two decades from 1947 to 1967 the inflation rate averaged only 1.6 percent per year. At such levels, inflation was not a major social issue. From 1967 to 1977, however, inflation averaged 7.0 percent. When President Ford left office in early 1977 inflation was down to 4.8 percent. Today it is averaging about 12.0 percent.* This compares to inflation rates in 1978 of 4.0 percent in Japan, 3.0 percent in Germany, 9.0 percent in France, and 9.0 percent in the United Kingdom.

*Alternative inflation measures are discussed in Chapter 3.

There is no greater challenge facing the U.S. economy than gradually controlling inflation and restoring real economic growth to its historical level. Inflation is damaging for a number of reasons, two of them especially crucial. First, it reduces incentives to save and invest. As the inflation rate rises, uncertainty about the return to investment also rises substantially. It is now well documented that the variance of prices rises with inflation. It is also well documented that investors are quite risk-averse (note the substantial interest premium paid by issuers of risky bonds). Inflation also insidiously interreacts with our unindexed tax system, substantially reducing the after-tax, after-inflation rate of return to saving and investment. As a simple example, in a world with no inflation, a 4 percent return on investment and a 50 percent tax rate (chosen for convenience) will produce an after-tax, after-inflation return of 2 percent. Interest rates tend to rise roughly point for point with inflation (see Feldstein and Summers 1978); therefore, 12 percent inflation will push interest rates up to about 16 percent. Even ignoring movement into higher tax brackets—at the 50 percent tax rate—the after-tax return of 8 percent represents a 4 percent *loss* after tax in relation to the 12 percent inflation rate. Inflation has reduced the rate of return after taxes and inflation from 2 percent to minus 4 percent. Given evidence that both saving and investment increase with the after-tax, after-inflation returns (Boskin 1978), our inflation and unindexed tax system have seriously retarded saving and investment.

The second major problem caused by inflation is a substantial redistribution of income. When inflation is not perfectly anticipated—which, into the distant future, is impossible—a major redistribution of income occurs between creditors and debtors. When the inflation accelerates, debtors gain and creditors lose, and vice versa. Indeed, in economies with high and widely vacillating inflation rates—such as many countries in Latin America, the United Kingdom for several years in the 1970s, Israel today, etc.—a huge fraction of the population has more at stake in speculating against the rate of inflation than it does in its own wages, in terms of its ultimate standard of living. In such societies a substantial fraction of economic activity is devoted to beating inflation rather than to producing goods and services.

Inflation also redistributes income because commodities which are consumed disproportionately by certain groups show greater price increases than other commodities; also because many government programs which redistribute income adjust or index for inflation in a particular way. Although social security benefits are indexed, such benefits amount to only one-third of the income of the elderly; the other two-thirds of their income are often hit brutally by inflation. For example, an elderly couple retiring in 1976 on an unindexed benefit from accumulated savings and pensions would have lost almost 20 percent of the purchasing power of their retirement nest egg thanks to increased inflation since they retired. If current inflation rates continue for another four years, this elderly couple would lose between one-third and one-half of the purchasing power of their assets.

It is important to note that the inflation rate measures average—not particular—price increases. Beside energy, the most rapidly rising prices in the last decade have been for food and medical care, commodities consumed disproportionately by (and often subsidized for) the poor and elderly, respectively. Indeed, we will see that many government spending programs designed to help these people may have contributed to the inflation that harms them so much.

By now it should be abundantly clear that our major economic problem has shifted from insufficient demand and high unemployment to substantial sustained inflation and sluggish economic growth. What causes inflation? Why has it accelerated so much recently? Popular discussion has exaggerated the role of energy price increases in our inflation. Although they played an important part both in the

1974–1975 recession and in the current inflation, even accounting for the indirect pass through of oil price increases to other commodities, energy price increases cannot account for more than 3 percent of our 13+ percent inflation rate.

There is substantial consensus among economists that the current acceleration of inflation, like the acceleration in the late 1960s, was due to a massive expansion of the money supply by the Federal Reserve. Although in previous bursts of inflation the Federal Reserve often appeared to "monetize" federal government deficits (buying government bonds issued to finance the deficit), it is less clear that the most recent acceleration of inflation can be so blamed. The causes of the recent monetary explosion are a subject of some dispute. While part of the blame must go to rapid, deficit-financed, federal budget expansion, a balanced budget would not immediately reduce the inflation rate to minimal levels. Recent federal budgets, however, have basically abdicated the role of fiscal policy and required exclusive reliance on monetary policy in the attempt to combat inflation. Not only is it unlikely that this will be as successful as a combined fiscal and monetary policy approach, but particular sectors of the economy—housing, automobiles, and consumer durables—will be hit much harder in a credit crunch than would otherwise be necessary (Heller and Boskin 1979).

Among the administration's policies to combat inflation, voluntary wage and price guidelines offer little hope except in those cases in which the government has substantial leverage—for example, where it can bargain with import quotas or the threat of dumping excess government supplies on the market. Indeed, *mandatory* wage and price controls have never been successful other than temporarily. The best evidence suggests that the Nixon controls, once removed, led to an inflation rate 1.5 percentage points *higher* than we otherwise would have had. Controls lead to black markets, quality deterioration, service delay, and ultimately to more inflation when they are removed. Guidelines have led to excessive costs and unfounded expectations that fly in the face of budgetary and monetary policy realities.

Saving, Investment, Productivity, Capital Formation and Ownership

Saving is important for two reasons: it is a major form of funding available to finance new investments, and it is *the* way in which our citizens transfer resources from one part of their lifetime to another, especially from their peak earning years to retirement. In the 1973 through 1977 period the average rate of *personal* saving in the United States was 6.7 percent. By 1978 it had fallen to 5.3 percent. The first quarter of 1980 it fell to a thirty-year low of 3.3 percent. This compares to personal saving rates in the same period of almost 25 percent in Japan, over 15 percent in France, and almost 18 percent in West Germany.

Our *national* saving rate has three components: personal, corporate, and government saving. Our personal saving rate has fallen substantially, and our corporate saving rate has remained relatively constant. Government investment has also fallen substantially as a share of GNP, from 3.5 percent in 1965 to less than 2.0 percent today. Further, government spending on research and development has also declined markedly.

If our low rate of private saving continues, an essential problem concerns the confluence of that possibility with a drastic increase in the ratio of retirees to workers shortly after the turn of the century and the large, and possibly greater, increase in the length of the retirement period. When we try to finance the baby boom generation's retirement early in the next century, government will have to absorb a greatly increased burden in supporting the elderly. The problem is aggravated by the fact that even at *current* relative levels of promised benefits, the social security system faces an immense long-term deficit.

Investment has not fallen as much as saving, because the outflow of U.S. capital has declined substantially; we have also seen a substantial increase in the inflow of foreign capital to the United States in recent years. The U.S. gross invesment rate in physical tangible capital has fallen slightly. But of our $386 billion of gross private investment in 1979, the bulk went into housing and replacement of worn-out capital as well as into pollution abatement and safety programs; real net addition to plant and equipment was about $40 billion, less than 2 percent of GNP. Since government disinvestment is substantial, we are adding very little to our capacity to produce (nonhousing, nonpollution abatement) goods and services.

This very low investment rate is important for several reasons: (1) by adding so little to our capital stock, we are seriously impairing productivity growth and hence future wages and standards of living; (2) by investing at a much lower rate than our major trading partners, even when we produce new technology they embody it in their capital stock much more rapidly than we do. Put simply, beginning to restore incentives to save and invest in the United States is one major avenue to expanding our real income growth. The decline in our saving and investment rates has been matched by declining productivity growth, noted earlier. The more important likely causes include inflation, increased taxation, increased government regulation, the changing experience and age structure of the labor force and its changing occupational mix, and the changing composition of output toward nontraditional goods and services such as pollution control and safety and services relative to manufactured goods.

To those who are concerned that encouraging saving and investment will benefit only the wealthy, it is important that we correct certain misconceptions about capital, its form and ownership. In general, the share of total capital in the United States owned by individuals has declined rapidly over the past half century. Government capital and the capital owned by the nonprofit sector also represent a much greater proportion of U.S. capital than in the past. Further, labor's share of national income has risen sharply—from less than two-thirds of GNP a quarter century ago to about 80 percent today.

If we think of the capitalized value of earnings as the stock of human capital—the knowledge and skill embodied in the labor force—this too has been growing as a fraction of total capital in the United States. My own estimates suggest that about 80 percent of the total capital owned in the United States is due to people accumulating savings in pension funds and other forms over their lifetimes rather than inheriting it. Some estimates suggest that pension funds own approximately a fifth of the value of shares on the New York Stock Exchange. Put simply, the usual division of labor and capital is no longer very relevant to a large fraction of our population: workers old enough to have accumulated a substantial stake in a pension have as much to gain in an increased rate of return on the capital owned by their pension as they do on increased wages for the remainder of their working lives.

International Trade

Declining saving and investment in the United States has been matched by an abysmal international economic performance. While *we* helped engineer an enormous expansion of world trade in the last decade and a half, our share of world manufacturing exports declined from 29 percent in 1958 to 19 percent in 1978. While we've been running large trade deficits, other advanced countries such as Germany and Japan, which rely still more heavily (relatively) on imported oil than we do, export enough more manufactured goods than they import to run trade surpluses—about $20 billion each in 1978 for Japan and Germany. Obviously, as the domestic value of the dollar has fallen and as our inflation has deteriorated relative to that of many of our trading partners, the average value of the dollar versus other currencies has fallen as well from a 1972 index of 100 to around 82 today. Indeed, one of the most important institutional features of the postwar economy was the abandonment of fixed exchange rates in the 1971–1972 period. This was the last nail in the coffin of the gold standard, and is perhaps partially to blame for our subsequently worsened internal money supply control.

The Economic Role of Government

Nowhere has change in the U.S. economy been more evident than in the growth of government spending and taxes. A half century ago, in 1929, only 10 percent of GNP passed through the public sector; today that figure is about 37 percent. In 1929 only a quarter of the then much smaller absolute and relative amounts of government spending was done at the federal level; today that figure exceeds two-thirds.

Just as government spending has grown and the level at which it is spent has shifted from state and local governments to Washington in recent years, so the composition of federal spending has been drastically altered. In 1952 transfer payments accounted for only 15 percent of the then much smaller federal government spending. Today more than half of total federal spending is on transfer payments such as unemployment insurance, welfare, Medicare, social security, food stamps, and housing allowances. In fact, the growth of transfer payments has been so great that they now account for 14 percent of personal income—as opposed to 2 percent in 1929. Obviously, the growth of transfer payments has been one of the major reasons for the reduction of poverty in the United States. That growth has made almost irrelevant the usual measure of fiscal stimulus due to government spending—the current deficit. Even in Keynesian theory, government spending stimulates the economy when the spending is on *good and services,* not on transfer payments.

As government spending has grown, so have taxes. The most important change over the last twenty years has been the great increase in the relative importance of the social security tax, which is now the largest tax paid by a majority of American families. It is also the second largest item on the federal budget and is gaining rapidly on the income tax. Further, while we have largely excused lower-income people from paying personal income taxes and have reduced personal income tax rates on the very rich, the rapid increase of government spending and inflation has increased the combined (i.e., federal, state, and local) *marginal* tax rate additional earnings or interest income to an all-time high for the typical American family. High tax rates are no longer the exclusive right of the rich. The median earner faces a combination of taxes which exceeds 40 percent on additional earnings. The adverse incentives embodied in high tax rates to work, save, invest, and/or report income for tax purposes have thus spread to the general population.

The national debt has also risen greatly in recent years. In 1978 the federal deficit was about $60 billion, and it is projected to be about $40 billion this year. At the same time, state and local governments were running a very large surplus (while federal grants to state and local governments approximated $80 billion). While the federal government has issued more and more debt in recent years, very high inflation rates have reduced the real value of the outstanding debt previously issued. Hence, the ratio of government debt to GNP in recent years has actually fallen.

However, substantial implicit debt remains in the social security system. Taking the present value of currently legislated benefits in social security and subtracting the present value of currently legislated taxes (including those passed in the 1977 amendments, not due to take effect until the 1980s and 1990s), social security still has a long-term deficit of about three-quarters of a trillion dollars—about the size of the privately held national debt of the United States.

Implicit taxes via regulation add substantially to the true U.S. tax burden. When the government requires private individuals to adopt certain activities—however desirable—it is similar to the government levying a tax on those activities and spending the funds (the tax proceeds) to achieve the desired goals. For example, requiring five hundred dollars of pollution and safety control equipment on automobiles is similar to levying a five hundred dollar tax on automobiles and paying auto companies to install the equipment out of the proceeds. Under current statistical practice, this shows up as gross auto sales, not as government spending and taxes. While estimates of the compliance cost of regulation vary widely, it is safe to conclude that they are substantial and that they add several percentage points to total government spending and "revenues."

A related problem concerns off-budget government activity. To the estimated $40 billion deficit for fiscal year 1980 on the books, we must add an estimated $18 billion deficit for off-the-books government economic activity and about $20 to $25 billion for federally sponsored agencies. A substantial number of quasi-governmental agencies such as the Federal Financing Bank are not included in the official budget but will run substantial deficits this year.

We do a poor job of projecting future costs of current programs, choosing instead to rely almost exclusively on current-year or very short-term estimates. And the failure to keep a separate capital account at a time when government investment is quite low may have the effect of disguising billions more in deficits on current account being made up by drawing down government capital. These are some of the major reasons why so many spending programs have grown much more rapidly than originally forecast.

THE RESTLESS TAXPAYER

All of these problems—slower economic growth, high inflation, high and rising taxes, increased private mandated activity, and declining international competitiveness—combine with demographic changes to create an enormous discontent with government spending and budgetary policy.
Some have argued that this discontent—like the hoola
hoop—will soon fade away, that it is largely the aftermath of
Watergate and related activities. I believe it is deeply rooted
in our economic problems of the last decade. Following two
and a half decades of steady economic growth, in the last half
dozen years the typical taxpaying, working family has seen
no gain in its standard of living. Its earnings have barely
kept pace with inflation and rising taxes, and *what little real
economic growth has occurred has gone into increased transfer
payments which the working, taxpaying population does not
receive.* With the substantial progress made by government
policies in mitigating unemployment and reducing poverty,
the major goal for such programs in the future must be to
make them more cost effective, not to expand them.

The rapid growth of government spending, by transfering
resources from the private sector to the government—including those taken from private saving and investment to
government transfer payment programs, along with high tax
rates, government deficits, and the concomitant inflation
they may help induce—has seriously impaired private incentives in the economy along with our ability to provide a
steadily rising standard of living for the general population.
A growing percentage of the U.S. population now *blames the
government* for these economic ills, just as it once thanked
the government for serving as a buffer against unemployment and poverty. Combined with the dramatic changes in
the age structure of our population, these economic changes

render the "tax revolt" much easier to understand. Nineteen seventy-eight was the first year since the depression to see a majority of the voting age population of the United States that was born since the depression. Hence, these voters had personally experienced, as their major economic problems, high taxes, inflation, and sluggish growth rather than unemployment and inadequate social programs. As their percentage increases in ensuing years, discontent with government is likely to increase in the years ahead and not to decrease—unless serious steps are soon taken to solve these problems.

II

Productivity and Economic Growth

2

MICHAEL J. BOSKIN

Economic Growth and Productivity

Measures of economic growth. Changes in economies here and elsewhere. U.S. saving and investment, inflation and taxes. The slowdown in productivity. Structural reforms and reduced tax rates.

The mere mention of the term "economic growth" conjures up different images, hopes, and complaints to different people. To the mass of mankind struggling at the margin of subsistence in the world's less-developed economies, the prospect of economic growth is literally the most important issue facing those individuals and societies. For most persons living in advanced, predominantly free-enterprise, economies such as those of North America and Western

Europe, substantial economic progress over the last two centuries has lifted the bulk of the population well above subsistence so that they have come to experience—indeed, to expect—relatively steady increases in their standard of living. Economic growth implies to some people a variety of untoward consequences that occasionally accompany growth, such as environmental pollution and congestion. Hence, we see at the same time movements to halt growth and desperate attempts to increase it; conflicting concerns for growth, appreciation of the need for it, and alternative measures to achieve it pervade what has now become a heated debate. While most would concede that some economic growth is desirable for the less-developed economies of the world, debates rage in most advanced economies over the desirability of growth per se, and especially of the form that growth takes.

The most traditional measure of economic growth is the rate of increase of gross national product (GNP) per capita, per employed worker, or per worker hour. For an entire economy this measure obviously is only an average and conceals variations in the growth rate across industries, regions, and population subgroups. Further, since the growth rate reflects the increase in output over and above its original level, rapid increases in growth rates are statistically more likely when the base from which the growth is measured is quite small. But GNP is not by any stretch of the imagination a perfect measure of economic well-being. For example, it fails to include an evaluation of work performed in the household without explicit pay such as caring for and raising children, of changes in the value of leisure time consumed, and of a variety of illegal or off-the-books activities. It also fails to net out the costs embodied in such phenomena as environmental pollution and congestion. Indeed, the oft-quoted example of valuing the output of a factory which belches smoke into the air, and then adding to that output the value of the resources used to clean up the air so dirtied, indicates how misleading traditional income measures can be.

Perhaps as important as these traditional concerns is the difficulty in measuring the value of nontraditional goods and services such as increased safety on the job, the pleasantness of surroundings, and so on.

Finally, since economic growth is often a heavily politicized issue—for example, between centrally planned and private enterprise economies—political manipulation of the economy and even of the growth statistics themselves is possible.

Against this background, the debate over the desirability of economic growth seems vacuous. The debate is merely a matter of defining appropriate growth concepts; different people use different measures of growth, reflecting their different valuations of nontraditional goods and services and/or environmental decay. Even the most vehement opponent of traditional economic growth cannot object to economic growth which includes the value of these nontraditional goods and services and which nets out the cost of environmental and other factors. The primary beneficiaries of economic growth are the workers whose wages increase as their productivity advances. It is likely, moreover, as we get wealthier, that we will demand more leisure, safety, and cleaner air along with traditional goods and services.

Another dimension of the decisions which influence economic growth, one which supercedes these measurement problems, is the concept of the optimal rate of economic growth. At first glance, it may seem rather silly to argue that there is an optimal rate of economic growth. After all, if the economy can grow faster, it will produce more and more goods and services, or more leisure time, or more nontraditional services in the future; it is difficult to see why this is not desirable in and of itself. Were other things equal, we would certainly prefer to have more goods and services or more leisure time, etc. The trouble is that in order for an economy to promote its economic growth, it must take resources away from current consumption of goods and services and devote them to investment and innovation. There is thus a more direct cost of economic growth than that mentioned above: the foregone consumption from which increased investment can occur. So, however, appropriately measured, the growth "problem" is to balance the gains in future standards of living against the costs of today's reduced standards.[1]

This growth problem has dimensions within and between generations. Each generation might be willing to refrain from additional consumption today, and thereby to generate increased saving and investment in order to expand their consumption later in life, perhaps during retirement. This would raise the rate of capital formation, even if none of the additional capital were bequeathed to future generations.

But with capital formation and economic growth, substantial intergenerational bequests of capital occur both privately, within families, and publicly, because of the passing of ownership of government capital through time. Decisions we make today about private saving and investment and about government investment thus potentially affect not only our own well-being—that of people currently alive later in their lives—but that of unborn generations.

Since unborn generations are represented only as their parents and grandparents take their economic opportunities into account, future generations may not be appropriately represented in decisions concerning investment policy. It may be that if they were, we would save and invest more than we do today. While this is a matter for conjecture, especially since each generation will be wealthier than its predecessor in a growing economy, there are a variety of reasons to suspect that our present growth rate is far below its optimal level. This occurs because of a variety of distortions in incentives to save, invest, and innovate, most of which are created by government policies designed to achieve other ends. The stagnant recent performance of the U.S. economy will become evident by looking at the recent record.

THE RECENT GROWTH PERFORMANCE

Rapid economic growth over long periods is a relatively recent phenomenon and a blessing for mankind. Often traced to the Industrial Revolution or to the period immediately preceding it, the previous very minor gains in living standards of average persons throughout the world accelerated substantially in many countries in the last two centuries. While this progress was not spread uniformly across all individuals within any given country, or evenly across all countries, by historical standards the growth performance of what are now called the advanced economies over the last two centuries is indeed impressive.

While exact statistics for any given economy are hard to come by and a comparison across countries runs into difficulties of comparability, real income per person in the United States grew at about 2 percent per year over the last century, and almost at that rate in France and Germany. The United Kingdom, which was the wealthiest society on earth at the end of the nineteenth century, has grown about 1 percentage point per year more slowly than the United States since then and is now a relatively poor member of the Common Market.

While such numbers might appear to be very small, at a growth rate of 2 percent per year real incomes will almost double between generations. The economic and social environment created by that rate of economic progress across generations is vastly different from that in a slowly growing economy, where the tensions over the division of a stagnant pie are greatly magnified.

Table 1 presents an estimate of the annual growth rate in GNP per employed worker in some of the major industrialized countries for the last two decades. It is abundantly clear that growth in many of these countries has slowed substantially, but nowhere has the recent performance been as abysmal as in the United States. While we should not expect the rate of economic progress of the other industrialized countries or the United States to continue at its extra rapid rate in the immediate post−World War II period and we should not be surprised that these other countries—starting from a lower base—were able to grow somewhat more rapidly than we, the size of the recent decline in our rate of economic progress is alarming. Put simply, there has been virtually no growth in GNP per employed worker in the United States since 1973, whereas economies like Japan, Germany, and France were able to grow at about 3 percent per year.[2] Were such a growth rate to continue, we would soon see our standard of living falling rapidly behind that of these countries.

This rapid decline in our economic growth in recent years, especially when compared to our historical experience and to the recent experience of other countries, suggests that restoration of economic growth to something like its historic level should be and will be a major economic policy goal in the immediate future. Is the United States capable of reverting to its historical growth? Or have we reached a stage where our economy will continue to stagnate? Are developed and imposed constraints on our economic growth so great as to prevent a general increase in the overall standard of living? Before returning to these issues, let us consider the sources of income and productivity growth and their relative contributions.

Table 1
Annual Growth Rate in GNP
per Employed Worker

Country	1963 to 1973	1973 to 1979
United States	1.9	0.1
Japan	8.7	3.4
Germany	4.6	3.2
France	4.6	2.7

Source: *Economic Report of the President, 1980.*

SOURCES OF INCOME AND PRODUCTIVITY GROWTH

There are several basic ways in which an economy can improve the standard of living for its population — which means an increase in real incomes per capita. First, the available labor force can be made more productive by providing them with more capital per worker. Over a very long period, the average annual increase in the capital/labor ratio in the U.S. economy was 2.5 percent; since 1973 there has been no increase whatsoever in this ratio. This implies not only that workers are not getting more capital with which to work; it also implies that production methods are changing more slowly. Hence the second potential vehicle for promoting economic growth: technical change. Just as providing workers with more capital will make them more productive, so providing them with better-quality capital will do the same. High-speed computers, for example, make many workers much more productive than they were with old-style computational capabilities. In turn, this reduces the cost of producing certain goods or services, enables existing workers to increase their production, or frees part of the work force to produce other goods and services.

Our understanding of technical change is somewhat limited. We can point to many important historical episodes, ranging from the reformation of crop rotation systems in agriculture several centuries ago through a series of important transportation advances (rail, air, etc.) to the recent explosion in high-speed electronics. But while these innovations played an important role in economic growth, many improvements in product lines, production techniques, and in the quality of the capital stock are also important. Further, there is a widely held view that such innovation often must be financed by venture capital which is forthcoming for such risky investments only at the possibility of very large returns on investment. This conclusion was a major impetus toward the reduction in capital gains taxes in 1978.

Two important issues with respect to technical change concern, first, the extent to which the investment process itself leads to "learning by doing" and hence opens opportunities for new types of investment, further lowers production costs, and frees resources for other purposes; and second, the extent to which new technology is embodied in new capital as opposed to converting old. These measures are important for several reasons, especially in light of the much lower investment rate in the United States than in other advanced economies (see Table 2).

The third major method to promote economic growth involves improving the knowledge and skills of the labor force itself, so-called human capital. Economists have long believed, and have attempted to document, that much economic activity can be regarded as investment by workers in an attempt to increase their future earnings. While it is perhaps most common to think of formal higher education in

Table 2

Rates of Gross National Saving and Investment
(average 1960–1974 share of GNP)

Country	Saving	Investment
France	25.4	26.0
Germany	27.1	26.4
Japan	37.2	36.8
Sweden	24.1	24.2
Switzerland	29.7	29.7
United States	18.6	18.6

Source: Organization for Economic Cooperation and Development.

this regard, there are many other important forms of such investment: in health, nutrition, mobility, and experience and training on the job. There are substantial difficulties in measuring investment in human capital and its rate of return, yet many recent commentators have suggested that in the United States the investment in human capital is perhaps as large as the investment in ordinary capital (see Kendrick 1979). Certainly we spend a much higher fraction of our income on advanced education than do most other societies.

Other factors may influence economic growth for short periods. For example, improvements in resource allocation toward more efficient uses can increase the level of income over a short period and hence accelerate the growth rate temporarily. But such advances cannot increase the rate of economic progress indefinitely, because opportunities to improve the resource allocation will eventually be exhausted.

There is much debate among economists about the relative contribution of these different sources of economic growth.

Perhaps the most widely quoted study is Denison's (1974) on the sources of growth of national income per person employed. In the postwar period through 1969, Denison attributes about half of an adjusted growth rate of 2.6 percent to advances in knowledge and about half to changes in capital and land per person employed, to improved resource allocation, and to the economies of scale of larger markets. Denison's large "residual" of advances to knowledge has been subject to attack from a number of sources. While the debate continues over precise contributions to growth, it is clear that technical change and capital formation are extremely important vehicles for promoting economic growth and rising standards of living. Let us turn to a more detailed discussion of capital formation and its determinants.

CAPITAL FORMATION AND ITS DETERMINANTS IN THE UNITED STATES

There are many types of capital and many sectors in which capital formation may take place. On the most basic level, our capital stock consists of land, structures, inventories, and knowledge; it may be invested in the household, business, or government sectors of our economy. As a rough generalization, we can decompose our notions about capital formation into our knowledge about the determinants of each of the major types of capital formation.

Table 3 presents a description of gross saving and investment as a percentage of the U.S. GNP in recent years. Saving in society serves two purposes: it provides us with a source of funds for new capital investment, and it provides the savers with claims to future consumption when they eventually sell off those claims—for example, during retirement. Our national saving rate consists of personal saving, corporate saving, and government saving. Business saving comprises a substantial fraction of the total; government saving or dis-saving is rather minor, whereas about a quarter of our saving comes from the household sector. Further, funds may be made available for U.S. investment by foreigners, and conversely, U.S. saving may go abroad to help finance investment overseas. In recent years the personal saving rate has declined precipitously and now is at a forty-year low, slightly over 3 percent of disposable income and only about 2 percent of GNP. Business saving has remained at roughly the same percentage of GNP, on average, for many years.

Table 3

U.S. Gross Saving and Investment by Source and Type (as percent of GNP)

	1965–1969	1978–1979
Gross Saving	15.8	15.3
Personal	4.4	3.2
Business	11.6	11.8
Government:	− 0.2	0.3
Federal	− 0.3	− 0.8
State and local	0	1.2
Gross Investment		
Nonresidential	10.5	10.6
Residential	4.0	4.0
Inventories	1.3	0.9
Net foreign	0.1	− 0.9

Source: *Economic Report of the President, 1980.*

Of our gross investment, a substantial fraction goes into residential construction, much more than in other economies. The overwhelming bulk of this gross investment in recent years has been in replacement of the depreciating and obsolescing capital stock and in increased expenditures on pollution abatement and safety. Only about $40 billion or so of our total gross investment last year, or well under 2.0 percent of GNP, was real net investment in additional plant and equipment. In addition to the decline in the personal saving rate and our very low rate of real net investment in business plant and equipment, our investment rate in research and development, while still higher than that of most other economies, has also fallen from 2.75 percent to 2.25 percent of GNP in the last two decades and therefore will likely lead to slower advances in knowledge and technical change in the future.[3]

Our human capital expenditures are substantial. The real issue is how much of these expenditures should be treated as investment as opposed to consumption, and how to get reasonable estimates of the rates of return to such expenditures. It was long argued that the return to educational investment was substantially higher than that accruing to regular capital, and that therefore society was underinvesting in education. But it is now clear from a number of studies that, as we have educated a much larger fraction of our potential labor force to a higher level than ever before, the marginal return to such investment is not as great today as it once was, and it is still declining.

What factors influence the incentives of household, corporations, and other businesses to save and to invest? As with most other economic activities, economists have now well documented the fact that the flow of resources into investment, and to a lesser extent into saving, are substantially influenced by the expected returns—net of taxes and inflation—of engaging in these activities relative to alternative opportunities. These activities also involve substantial risks, and hence the degree of risk involved combines with the degree of risk-aversion of the populace in influencing incentives to save and to invest. Finally, the uneven flow of income over the lifetime of a typical worker creates still an additional motive to save and then to dissave later in life—to make consumption more even over the lifetime. If the consumption of each family exactly matched its income every year, there would not only be substantial fluctuations in midlife, but extreme destitution late in life and early in life. To partially adjust for this, families typically save some of their income during their peak earning years in order to accrue claims to future consumption, especially during retirement or when they have to finance their children's education.

Our tax system affects the expected returns and risks involved in saving and investment in myriad ways, particularly when combined with the fact that it is unindexed, taxing nominal returns to saving and investment even in a world of high inflation rates (see the discussion in Chapters 3 and 7). Consider an investment made in the corporate sector financed by the issue of equity. The return from this investment is first subject to corporate taxes at a marginal rate of about 46 percent. Of the after-tax profits, some are paid out as dividends which are immediately subject to personal income taxes, and some become retained earnings of the corporation—the vehicle for corporate saving—and ultimately will be reflected, on average, in higher share prices and a future capital gain for the owner. Thus, on this portion of after-tax corporate profit, personal taxes will be paid at the lower capital gains rate and also will be deferred until the capital gains are realized (see Chapter 7). In any event, a large gap exists between the before-tax and after-tax rate of return to investment in our economy. Although the deductibility of interest payments combines with debt finance partially to ameliorate this problem, economists believe overall that the tax system substantially reduces the expected net-of-tax-and-inflation returns to investment (see Feldstein and Summers 1978). Worse yet, these effective tax rates have been rising substantially through time, particularly because of inflation. While the exact magnitudes are subject to many technical disagreements, there is now substantial evidence that private investment is quite responsive to such tax-induced reductions in net returns to investment. Therefore, the pure return effect of the tax system has substantially reduced private investment.

Further, the taxes collected are a transfer of resources from the private sector to the government. In recent times, virtually all of increased government spending has gone for transfer payments, not for purchases of goods and services. The mere transfer of the resources to the government, therefore, over and above the tax-induced rate of return reduction effect, substantially lowered the rate of national capital formation. Worse yet, the substantial risks involved, especially in long-term investment, are exacerbated in our current inflation context. There is now substantial documentation that the variance of inflation increases as the inflation rate increases, and this increases risk and uncertainty about expected future returns (see Fischer and Modigliani 1978).

Similar effects occur on the private saving side. An individual considering putting funds aside to save for future purposes—for example, a child's education or one's own retirement—is partly affected by the terms at which he or she can do so, i.e., the after-tax, after-inflation rate of return to saving. Again, our tax system operates to reduce the return to saving. There are many tax-exempt vehicles for saving (certain types of life insurance, private pensions, IRA accounts, etc.), yet overall our tax system puts a very heavy penalty on saving and encourages current consumption. My own studies suggest that this substantially retards private saving in our economy (Boskin 1978). This result needs to be further elaborated and reconfirmed; it appears, however, that our current tax system has substantially reduced the supply of capital available for investment purposes. Worse yet, our unindexed tax system interacts with our inflation rate in an insidious manner to reduce substantially the after-tax, after-inflation rate of return.[4] There is also substantial evidence that this reduction in the real net rate of return discourages investment demand.

Other government policies affect saving and investment decisions—as, for example, the potential reduction of private saving because of the availability of certain types of government programs as a substitute. A case in point is the social security system, which is financed on a pay-as-you-go basis with current taxes used to finance current benefits. It is plausible to assume that prospective retirees think of their potential benefits as an asset in their retirement income portfolio and therefore face reduced pressure to save for their retirement. Their own private saving would have made its way into capital markets and been available for private investment; social security, however, creates no real capital. If savers indeed save less because of the promise of future social security benefits, our national saving rate is much lower than it would be otherwise. One commentator has suggested that this decrease is so large as to have substantially decreased national income (see Feldstein 1974).

Monetary policy and credit availability affect incentives to save and to invest. They influence the climate of risk and uncertainty in which those decisions are made and the nominal interest rates which affect expected real net returns. Government regulations substantially increase the costs of investment and the uncertainty concerning future returns. At the most extreme, a long-term investment project can be rendered highly uncertain by current and prospective growth of regulatory programs. Indeed, it is often alleged that businesses are not even certain they will be allowed to finish building a plant because of the prospect of substantial changes in regulation and private litigation that may occur.

A variety of fallacies are popularly mentioned concerning our lack of need for increased saving and investment. The first is the argument that since our saving and investment rates are not very different from what they were many years ago, they need not be increased. This assumes both that past saving and investment rates were at appropriate levels, and that nothing has changed in the interim to alter our appropriate level of saving and investment. But much has changed in our economy in the last two deades. The enormous increase in employment in the 1970s requires substantial capital formation just to preserve the historic growth in the capital/labor ratio. Further, substantial increases in life expectancy and earlier retirement (see Chapter 1) should be leading people to save more for their retirement rather than less. If we do not increase our saving rate, we face the awkward prospect of a larger fraction of our population retired for longer periods, having saved too little of its income to finance that retirement. These people will be thrown in still greater proportion upon public transfer payment programs to help finance their retirement.

Further, if there is anything to the learning-by-doing and/or embodiment hypotheses discussed above, our very low investment rate by international standards means that other economies are embedding the new technology in their capital stock much more quickly than are we, and hence will be increasing the productivity of their workers relative to those in the United States.

In addition to the changes in life expectancy and age structure of the population, substantial changes in the household structure of the population have also occurred in the last several decades. These have an important bearing on the consumption/saving choice and on the appropriate investment rate in our economy. For example, average household size has declined from 3.4 to 2.8, and the proportion of households headed by women has increased from 15 percent to 24 percent in the last three decades.

Finally, it might be noted that while the government, especially the federal government, was doing a large amount of investing—in everything from roads to automobiles, from typewriters to submarines—in the 1950s and 1960s, our rate of government investment has now fallen markedly. The national investment rate has thus declined, even though our private investment rate has not fallen very much. Moreover, in recent years the declining personal saving rate has required that we finance an increasing fraction of our private investment by importing foreign capital. While this is a useful short-term solution to the problem, the convincing examples of sustaining investment and economic growth financed by importing foreign capital all involve economies that at the time were not well developed—for example, the United States and Canada in the nineteenth century, and many less-developed countries today. A recent study (Feldstein and Horioka 1979) suggests that the flow of international capital is predominantly a short-term phenomenon, and that investment ultimately must be financed from domestic sources. While this remains a matter of contention (and our international capital markets are changing rapidly), it would be unwise to predicate the future course of our economy's investment and economic progress on heavy reliance on importing foreign capital.

THE RECENT PRODUCTIVITY SLOWDOWN

Several studies have been completed which examine the causes of the recent productivity slowdown. Unfortunately, they reach conflicting conclusions. Denison (1979*a*), for example, attributes over one-third of the productivity slowdown to such factors as accelerated reduction in average hours of work, a more rapid shift in the age/sex composition of the labor force, a slower increase in capital per worker, changes in the legal environment, and a slowdown in the gains from scale economies. He leaves over two-thirds of the slowdown in the unexplained "residual" series for advances in knowledge. Robin Siegel (1979) claims the single largest element in the productivity slowdown was the stagnation in the capital/labor ratio after 1973; his study also confirms the importance of the shifting demographic composition of the labor force. Finally, Lester Thurow (1978) argues that substantial sectoral shifts in the economy, especially toward services — a traditionally below-average sector for productivity — have been very important.

While we cannot be certain about the precise causes of the recent decline in our productivity growth, a general consensus exists that the following have been major contributors:

1. High and rising inflation and marginal tax rates on the returns to saving and investment, and hence a declining rate of private capital formation.

2. The displacement of private economic activity by government economic activity.

3. The changing age, experience, and occupational mix of the labor force.

4. The shift in output away from manufacturing toward services.

5. The growth of government regulatory policies.

Despite debate over reasons for the current slowdown, economists are in much greater agreement about the causes of long-term growth rate trends. Concerning those, there is a consensus that, there is a consensus that the declining growth rate of our standard of living is primarily caused by an *erosion of incentives to produce income and wealth.* These incentives take a variety of forms in the U.S. economy. The most important, of course, are the returns, net of taxes and inflation, of engaging in alternative activities. The combination of inflation, an unindexed tax system, and compared to other advanced economies a much heavier relative reliance on taxes on investment as opposed to those on consumption, contribute to reduce the after-tax, after-inflation return to saving, investing, innovating, working, and even reporting taxable income.[5]

Many economists have long believed that such private incentives were quite unresponsive to tax or inflation-induced reductions in their real net rates of return. This view has pervaded economic policymaking, including the information given to Congress and the executive branch in analyzing most tax and budget proposals. But considerable evidence has now accumulated that many economic decisions do respond substantially to such incentives. This growing documentation of the disincentives of high and rising tax rates and high inflation rates lead me to believe that private incentives to work, save, and invest are being seriously eroded by our current tax system and government spending. However, there is little evidence to suggest that the responses of these incentives would be so large and so rapid as to recoup any tax revenues potentially lost from a large tax rate cut, without corresponding cuts in government spending.[6] While it is useful to distinguish between the view that incentives are responsive to taxes and inflation and the view that they are not, the available evidence suggests that it will take some time before the cumulative impact becomes felt.

Since the growth of many types of government regulatory policies have increased both the cost and the uncertainty concerning future returns on private investment, it is generally believed that they have substantially reduced long-range investment plans in our economy and have shifted funds from investment in plant and equipment to investment in pollution abatement and safety control. Such investment amounted to some $30 billion in 1979.

With the growth of government spending almost exclusively on transfer payments in recent years, it is fair to say that as the federal government has taken a larger and larger tax bite, resources are being transferred from the private sector, which has a much higher propensity to save and invest, to the government, which is disinvesting. Therefore, our *national* rate of capital formation is not growing at all, and the long-run productivity outlook will not improve until this trend is reversed.

POTENTIAL REMEDIES

What can be done about these disincentives? Obviously, the most important moves toward redressing the imbalance against private incentives to work, save, and invest are the three interrelated policies of slowing the rate of inflation, slowing the growth rate of government spending, and reducing marginal tax rates. The adverse incentives embodied in high tax rates have now spread to the general population. The *only* way to reduce such tax rates in the long run is to slow the growth rate of government spending.

Federal government spending, including spending on transfer payments (see Chapter 9), is approximately 23 percent of GNP. Over the next five years the federal government is scheduled to accrue revenues of *several hundred billion dollars in excess of that necessary to keep the share of federal government spending constant even at this historically high level*. There is therefore going to be a battle between those who favor expansion of existing government spending programs or development of new ones, and those who believe that the overwhelming bulk of these revenues, and perhaps additional revenues if we can lower the ratio of federal spending to GNP, should be returned to the private sector to help promote private incentives. The primary sources of these additional revenues are:

1. The inflation "kicker" in the income taxes, which operates to increase revenues much more rapidly than income.

2. Previously legislated increases in social security tax rates and base.

3. The "windfall profits" tax.

4. Increased federal royalties from leasing of land for oil drilling.

It will thus be possible to run a balanced budget or modest surplus while gradually phasing in substantial tax cuts over the next few years. The size of these tax cuts depends very heavily on how soon and to what extent control can be achieved over government spending (see Chapter 9).

The tax reductions made possible by controlling government spending should include a safe and predictable program of phased-in tax cuts, *announced in advance,* which would still leave modest estimated surpluses, together with contingency plans for further tax cuts as spending is controlled or as economic growth (partly spurred by the tax cuts themselves) allows. *It is crucial that the tax cuts be heavily weighted towards increasing incentives to save, invest, and work, and this would imply tax policies which reduce marginal tax rates.* I would favor, for example, a combination of the following: (1) gradual reduction of the corporate tax rate (perhaps 1 percentage point per year for several years); (2) simplification and acceleration of depreciation allowances;[7] (3) in the context of gradually phased-in reductions in marginal tax rates in the personal income tax, I would expand the option for accruing interest tax free that now exists in such vehicles as IRA and Keogh accounts. For example, we might allow a universal IRA account irrespective of whether an individual had self-employment income or a pension plan on their own regular job. This package would substantially increase saving and investment in the next few years.

These gradually phased-in reductions in tax rates and structural reforms should be consistent with movement towards a longer-term goal of tax reform, which in my view ought to integrate the corporate and personal income taxes and gradually shift the tax base from income to expenditure, thereby removing double taxation of saving. While most European countries have moved substantially in this direction (and this is part of the cause of their higher saving and investment rates), the United States has done so only very slowly (see Chapter 7). ,

Thus my spending control and tax reduction and reform proposals would be the immediate beginning of what hopefully would be a longer-term basic structural reform designed to stabilize—and eventually reduce somewhat— the share of government spending in GNP. These reforms would also make government transfer payments more cost and target effective and would remove many disincentives in our tax system to save and invest.

These proposals obviously must take place in a climate of moderate and predictable rate of growth of the money supply by the Federal Reserve, designed eventually to reduce inflation to a level where it no longer seriously affects economic decisions. It also must be complemented by a regulatory reform which requires government regulations to look at economic costs and benefits. Such reform might involve a brief moratorium on new regulations during reevaluation of existing ones, a scrapping or redesign of regulations which are seen to impair economic progress without serving some other desirable goal efficiently, and improvement of socially useful regulation.

This combination of proposals will enable the United States gradually to restore private incentives in the economy. The speed with which we can increase after-tax real rates of return to different activities and reduce the uncertainty engendered by inflation and government regulation will largely determine the time pattern of our future income growth.

CONCLUSION

While a widespread consensus exists among economists that such policies would substantially improve the climate for economic progress in the 1980s and beyond, substantial obstacles to implementation stand in the way. Our recent past has been dominated by a short-run bias in government decision-making toward increasing government spending in the hope of temporary reductions in unemployment, with little regard for inflationary consequences. Anti-growth groups continue to play an important role in the political process. Worse yet, the very nature of policies to promote economic growth makes them difficult for politicians to adopt. Such policies invariably take a considerable period of time before they have a noticeable payoff. Even if we increased our investment by 20 percent per year, it would be some time before the new investment was a large enough fraction of a greater capital stock to make a significant difference in income. Recall our discussion of the opportunity costs of promoting growth—i.e., foregoing current consumption. In the political process, which is geared to payoffs which have a short time horizon—certainly not much longer than the politician's term in office at best—it is difficult to adopt policies to promote a long-term growth whose benefits will accrue after those who vote for the policies are out of office. On the other hand, the failure to do so will have dramatic consequences. We are already witnessing the reverse phenomenon as the U.S. economy's economic growth has slowed to a crawl compared to that of most other advanced economies.

Will the American voter and taxpayer and worker sit idly while the rest of the world passes us by? I doubt this very much. It will take astute political planning, a massive educational campaign, and a certain amount of political courage to begin to reverse the discincentives that are retarding our economic progress. The fact is, we *can* restore our relatively rapid historical growth; and doing so is essential not only to provide income growth for most American families, but *especially to ameliorate the hardship suffered by the less fortunate in our society.*

The political obstacles to reform are severe; but the consequences of continuing as we have, in stagnation, are potentially catastrophic. The cost of not solving these problems extends well beyond slowing economic progress for our citizens to the threatened loss of political, diplomatic, and military leadership in the free world. That threat may destroy the example we set for the mass of mankind, living on the brink of subsistence, of the relationship between free political institutions and economic progress.

DISCUSSION

McKINNON: I agree about the importance of generating a higher savings rate, but there is a side benefit of increasing the rate of capital formation and productivity growth that is often not emphasized, and that concerns the state of the current account of the American balance of payments. The lack of saving in the United States, the fall of the saving rate in the 1970s, has been reflected in the current account deficit in the balance of goods which we export and import. Since we have had inadequate saving to finance our own capital accumulation, we have essentially drawn on savings of foreigners. This has shown up as a deficit. We misinterpret those deficits. We tell ourselves that we are no longer competitive in the world, and we should be more protectionist. But in fact these deficits are nothing more than reflections of inadequate domestic savings. So if we take steps to correct domestic savings, as Michael outlined, then our balance of trade problem will correct itself.

CUDDINGTON: This question of the desirability of growth, whether slower growth is desirable in some sense, even if properly defined, has important ramifications for the U.S. relationship with other countries. We can't look at the problem or the issue of growth in the closed economy context. If the United States were to slow its growth rate dramatically—for domestic reasons—our relationships with less-developed countries, in particular, would deteriorate dramatically. If our growth slows, the growth of LDCs who depend heavily on our markets will slow much more significantly. And so when we look at the issue of whether the United States should grow more slowly or more rapidly, we have to realize that this has implications for world income, its distribution, and also for our relationship with other countries.

The saving and investment question also has international implications. Really, savings and investments should be looked at in a global context as a question of international financial intermediation. To obtain an efficient allocation of world resources, we have to match borrowers and lenders across national boundaries. Consequently, we should always be cautious or leery of setting up barriers which prevent savings of one country from being transformed into investment in another country.

Michael points out that growth prospects from improved resource allocations might provide a one-time benefit, but no continuing effect on the economy. I would suggest that government distortions—both on a domestic level and in the international economy—are increasing and that the efficiency of resource allocation, if anything, is probably deteriorating rather than improving. I would put much more emphasis on policy directed towards improving the international allocation of resources and not just resource allocation at a domestic level.

McKINNON: I think it is important to be neutral regarding the role of the government. We are a fairly wealthy society. It wouldn't seem to me to be socially optimal to plan to grow at 10 percent per year and sort of rev up the government surplus to generate the savings, which would give us that level of growth. What we really want to strive for is that the government be neutral in what it does itself. That is, its own budget is roughly balanced on current accounts; it doesn't make any decision either to dissave or save net; and secondly, it throws out the right signal to the social security system—that is, that if it is going to promise people pensions when they retire that the social security system should be fully funded in order to pay those pensions. But once it does that, its job is done.

Whether the social rate of saving is high or low will come out of the private financial markets and private decision-making. And I don't think the public sector has then a further role to play in trying to monitor that rate of saving. It is particularly important that the government should be neutral and should not subsidize one class of industry over another. It certainly should provide general support for R&D, which is not in the interests of any one individual to finance, but it should not pick out industries A, B, C, and D for special treatment.

BOSKIN: On the politics of the issue, I think eventually that a large enough portion of the population will get upset about our policies on saving, and that a political constituency is emerging. For example, a much higher percentage of elected (recently elected) Democrats, Democratic House members, who would think of themselves as relatively liberal in the old way of defining liberal and conservative, are actively pursuing tax reforms that promote saving and investment and are actively concerned about changing the way cost-of-living adjustments are made in social security benefits. These are liberal Democrats from liberal states, where such a thing was unthinkable several years ago. Basically, it takes time for these problems to be impressed on politicians.

One basic fundamental problem exists in talking about the
concept of the optimal rate of growth, and that is the problem
of trying to measure parameters which are conceptually not
measurable—which is how people's marginal evaluation of
increased income changes as income changes. My own numbers suggest, in what I consider plausible scenarios, that the
national rate of capital formation ought to be in the low 20
percent, that this would be an optimal rate, and that the actual rate is now running well below that—maybe 6 to 8 percentage points below that, in a broadly defined measure of
capital formation. There is a problem about how one treats
housing. We have to be careful in comparing ourselves, say,
to Japan because people live in different kinds of housing in
Japan and a lot of our savings are embodied in housing.
When I have been talking in general about this, I have
spoken about trying to increase our rate of private investment on the order of a quarter or a third from the current
level over the span of a couple of decades.

KOTLIKOFF: Well, I guess I would like to see some hard
numbers on the subject. My own kind of brief looking at some
investment numbers and some compounding numbers within the last few months, which was fairly casual, just did not
suggest to me any dramatic findings. There was a big recession in the 1970s, but I saw investment rates pop back up in
the late 1970s.

I think in terms of talking about growth we should also be
interested in the distribution of the pie as well as how fast
the pie increases. It may be that we are seeing some international equalization of wage rates and that that process involves a reduction in the real wage in the United States relative to the real rate of return.

If we really look at some long-run evidence about U.S. savings behavior, the Japanese savings behavior, the German
savings behavior, it may be that American citizens just have
completely different types of preferences and that we may
just not be all that savings-crazy. If so, in the long run we will

be consuming relatively less in our old age so that we can consume relatively more when we are young than, perhaps, the Japanese. But that's an efficient outcome if that's what we want.

III

Problems of Short-Term
Economic Stability

3

JOHN L. SCADDING

Inflation: A Perspective from the 1970s

Supply-side economics. Inflation as a tax, not as erosion. Costs and benefits of inflation. The Phillips curve trade-off. Use of the unemployment rate. The funds rate technique. Inflation and social tensions.

Economists traditionally have viewed government spending and taxes as operating on macroeconomic activity through their effects on total spending, or aggregate demand. In recent years a growing body of opinion has come to question whether this can be the entire story, and to inquire whether fiscal policy does not also have an effect on the capacity of the economy to produce—on aggregate supply, in other words. This supply-side economics, as it has come to be

Table 1
Quinquennial Average of Inflation: 1954—1979

Period	Percentage
1954—1959	2.49
1960—1964	1.47
1965—1969	3.52
1970—1974	5.82
1975—1979	7.10

called, focuses on the question of whether rising marginal tax rates have blunted incentives to work and produce sufficiently to have reduced the level of output that is consistent with full employment.

Raising these supply-side considerations implicitly poses the question of whether there is a trade-off between short-run stabilization objectives and long-run goals of promoting growth and efficiency. The framework of a trade-off provides a useful way of analyzing why inflation has gotten progressively worse over the past fifteen years (see Table 1).[1] The analogy with taxation is not as strained as it might at first appear. Inflation represents an excise tax on money, and it has been used consciously by governments (including the U.S. government on occasion) as a source of revenue. Moreover, starting in the early 1960s inflation came to be viewed as a tool that could be used to achieve higher levels of output and employment. In that sense, the inflation tax had become one of the policy tools used to achieve the government's stabilization objectives.

This chapter takes the view that the inflation we have experienced over the past fifteen years represents a more or less conscious choice by policymakers based on their assessments of the relative benefits and costs of inflation. Unfortunately, for reasons we shall go into, they erred in underestimating the costs and in exaggerating the benefits. As a result, the rate of inflation from 1965 on turned out in retrospect to be too high in the sense that the costs accompanying it outweighed the benefits. Moreover, insufficient attention was paid to the costs of reducing inflation. For that reason, once policy erred on the side of inflation it appeared impossible to undo the mistake because the costs were perceived as being too high. Consequently, inflation racheted up from 1965 on. Policy was best capable of temporarily stabilizing the rate of inflation, but it obviously lacked the will to reverse it permanently. This state of affairs is still with us today.

THE INFLATION TAX

The sense in which the economist views inflation as a tax differs from the layman's view. The latter perceives the tax in terms of the erosion in the purchasing power of his income. He failed to appreciate that much of this erosion represents a transfer to others in the private sector, not to the government; it therefore does not represent a tax in the traditional sense of the word. Moreover, for the economy as a whole the purchasing power of incomes must keep pace with inflation because higher prices must represent a revenue to someone. Nevertheless, it is still true that the private sector pays a tax. It does so because, with inflation, it finds the purchasing of its money balances continuously eroding. To offset that erosion, households and firms must divert a larger share of their income to saving in the form of cash balances, which effectively reduces their income for consumption and other forms of saving. This diversion represents the inflation tax they pay.

The ability of the government to capture the inflation tax revenue depends on its power to create money. In earlier times this connection was direct and obvious. The Continental Congress during the Revolutionary War, and the Union and Confederate governments during the Civil War, literally printed paper money to finance their war efforts. In the twentieth century this process has become less direct, with the Federal Reserve indirectly providing the U.S. Treasury with revenue by monetizing government debt. But the ultimate effect is the same.

Outside of wartime, the inflation tax has never contributed a significant share of government revenue in the United States. One measure of the size of the tax is the amount of government money issued. For the United States, this consists of the monetary base—currency in the hands of the public and bank reserves. In 1979 the increase in the monetary base amounted to $11.6 billion; not trivial, but still a relatively small 2 percent of total federal government revenues.

MONEY AND INFLATION

Excessive money growth is both a necessary and a sufficient condition for inflation. It is necessary because no sustained growth in prices is possible unless spending keeps pace, and spending in turn cannot continue to grow unless fueled by successive rounds of money creation. It is sufficient because excessive expansion of money causes unwanted money balances to accumulate, balances which people attempt to get rid of by spending more. Higher spending in turn ultimately shows up in higher prices.

It is for these two reasons that it is legitimate to speak of inflation as essentially a monetary phenomenon. The validity of this proposition is attested to by the evidence. Figure 1 charts the course of inflation over the past quarter-century against the backdrop of the history of monetary expansion. Inflation in Figure 1 is measured by the average rate of growth of prices over four successive quarters. Thus the inflation rate shown for 1979/Q4 is the rate of growth of prices from 1978/Q4 to 1979/Q4. The most broadly based index of prices is used—the gross national product (GNP) price deflator. Monetary growth is represented by the average rate of growth of M_1 (currency plus demand deposits) over the previous three years. Both theory and evidence suggest that prices react slowly to changes in money growth, with most estimates indicating that full adjustment takes three to four years. The use of a three-year average of past money growth captures in a rough way this lagged relationship between money and prices.

It is clear from Figure 1 that every sustained rise in the inflation rate has been accompanied by an increase in money growth. Conversely, there has not been an instance in which a sustained rise in monetary expansion was not followed by a jump in the average rate of inflation. Over shorter intervals the inflation rate obviously can deviate from the rate predicted by monetary expansion. The sharp run up in inflation rates after the quadrupling of oil prices in 1973—1974 is the most dramatic instance in Figure 1. But even in that case inflation soon subsided to the rate that monetary growth could sustain. In the same way, the steep rise in oil prices that occurred in 1979 probably accounts for some of the recent divergence between inflation rates and monetary growth. However, most of this difference is attributable to a break in the way people and firms have managed their money since 1974. Households to some extent, and firms to a much greater degree, have reduced their average cash holdings relative to their transactions needs.[2] Consequently, the

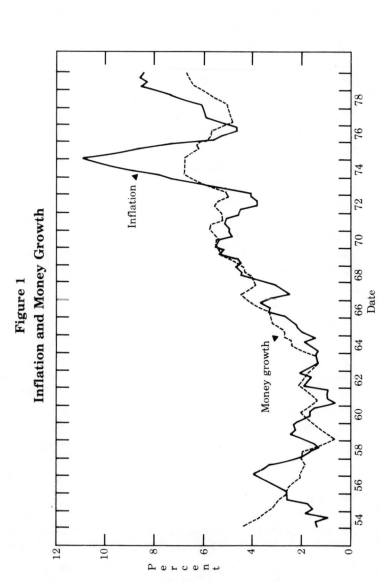

Figure 1
Inflation and Money Growth

velocity of money has increased, adding its own contribution to inflation. It has been estimated that this phenomenon has caused velocity to grow about 1.5 percentage points faster than it would have otherwise. If this difference is added to the monetary growth figures in Figure 1 starting in 1975, the monetary growth curve again more or less coincides with the inflation curve.

To say that inflation is basically a monetary phenomenon means that there is a legitimate sense in which money can be said to cause inflation. Because this is a very precise sense of the meaning of cause, economists modify it by saying that money is the *proximate* cause of inflation. The more interesting question, however, is what causes excessive money— what are the fundamental causes of inflation, in other words? Since there is little disagreement that the Federal Reserve has the technical ability to control money growth, the question of fundamental causes boils down to a question of policy choices, inadvertent or intended. The focus of this chapter is on these policy choices.[3]

THE VIETNAM WAR AND THE PHILLIPS CURVE

Until the 1970s U.S. experience with sustained major bouts of inflation was confined to wartimes and their aftermaths. The amount of inflation in each of these episodes was systematically related to the proportion of government expenditure financed by money creation, and hence implicitly reflected a weighing of its costs and benefits against the alternatives of explicit taxation and government borrowing.

In this respect, the experience of accelerating prices during the Vietnam war represented a continuation of previous experience. The failure of Congress and the administration to raise taxes until 1968, well after the war effort had been stepped up, reflected an implicit decision to finance part of the Vietnam war through the inflation tax. Ironically, economic thinking of the time provided support for this judgment. In the first place, the distorting effects of inflation on economic activity were perceived to be slight. Economic theory argued that inflation was likely to be largely *neutral* in the long run, in the sense that it would have little permanent impact on economic choices once markets had fully adjusted. These market adjustments would take the form of nominal, or dollar, returns being revised upwards so that *real* (i.e., inflation-adjusted) returns were exchanged. In financial markets, for example, yields would be revised upwards by the full increase in inflation, thus preserving the real returns on securities. This phenomenon is often called the *Fisher effect* after the economist Irving Fisher (1867–1947), who extensively examined it beginning in the 1920s.

Only where prices on yields could not adjust was it expected that inflation would have a noticeable effect. This meant that its effects would be confined largely to its role as a tax on cash balances—on currency and, to a lesser extent, on demand deposits.

A higher inflation tax causes people to reduce the amount of cash balances they keep on hand. From society's point of view, this is inefficient. Money costs little to produce, and it is highly useful because it provides society with an extremely efficient way of making transactions. When people economize on cash balances they must resort to less efficient ways of making transactions (barter is an extreme example); alternatively, they must devote resources to managing their cash balances more carefully so that they can be stretched, so to speak, to do the same work as before. Inflation therefore is wasteful because it causes society to use up resources to do work that money could do more cheaply.

All available evidence suggested, however, that this inefficient economizing on money would be relatively slight because the public's demand for cash balances appeared to be relatively insensitive to changes in interest rates and inflation. Even a generous estimate of the cost of this distortion indicates that the loss to an entire generation from a 1.0 percentage point increase in inflation would amount to only 2.5 percent of one year's GNP (Feldstein 1979).

Unlike the costs of inflation, the benefits were perceived as substantial. A significant innovation in macroeconomic theory available to policymakers in the early 1960s was the idea of the Phillips curve. The curve started out simply as an empirical observation that rates of inflation and unemployment appeared to be inversely related. From this observation it was perhaps inevitable that policymakers would come to view this relation as a trade-off—as representing a menu of alternative combinations of unemployment and inflation available to the policymaker. Stimulatory policy thus could "buy" a reduction in unemployment at the expense of a higher inflation rate. Conversely, policy could choose to have a lower inflation rate if it was willing to accept higher unemployment.

The experience of the late 1950s and early 1960s suggested a relatively favorable trade-off between inflation and unemployment (Figure 2 and Table 2). In the 1954–1957 recovery, for example, unemployment had fallen by 1.2 percentage points, while inflation rose by less than 1.0 percentage point. The fall in the unemployment rate during the 1958–1960 recovery was almost identical, and in this case inflation did not measurably accelerate. Moreover, the gains in terms of aggregate output that resulted from these reductions in unemployment were significant. In the middle 1960s Arthur Okun had calculated that a 1.0 percentage point decline in the unemployment rate was associated with an additional 3.0 percentage points of GNP growth. When compared to the relatively trivial costs of inflation mentioned earlier, these gains clearly slanted the choice in favor of less unemployment.

Table 2

The Trade-Off between Inflation and Unemployment

Business Cycle	Unemployment (percentage points)	Inflation Rate (percentage points)
Expansions	*Decline*	*Increase*
1954–1957	1.2	0.74
1958–1960	1.3	−0.03
1961–1969	3.2	4.20
1971–1973*	1.0	2.62
1976–1979*	1.9	3.84
Contractions	*Increase*	*Decline*
1957–1958	2.5	2.65
1960–1961	1.2	1.67
1969–1971*	2.4	1.75
1973–1976*	2.1	2.62

*In the 1970s the lag of inflation behind business activity lengthened, so that the peak inflation rate typically occurs in the year of a business cycle trough. To correct for this, the contraction phase of the cycle is extended one year.

REVISING THE TRADE-OFF

In retrospect it is clear that the benefits of inflation were clearly oversold while its costs were slighted. On the costs side, there was a failure to appreciate the full scope for the distorting effects of inflation. The implicit assumption (noted earlier) had been that financial markets could adjust for inflation, adding an inflation premium to nominal rates of interest that would protect the lender against the decline in the purchasing power of money. Considerable evidence was accumulated to demonstrate that in fact interest rates had ultimately adjusted by approximately the full increase in in-

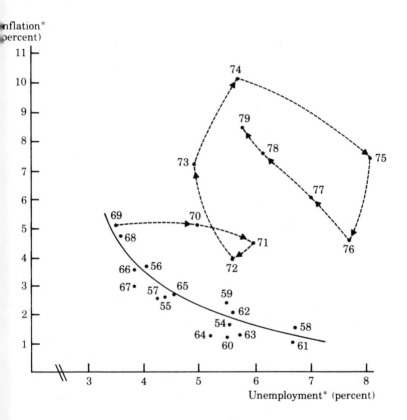

Figure 2
The Phillips Curve

*Unemployment is the unemployment rate for all workers; annual average infla
tion is measured by the rate of change of the GNP deflator, fourth quarter, over
fourth quarter of previous year.

flation. However, this evidence and underlying theory neglected the effect of income taxes. Part of this can be attributed to the fact that when the great inflation began in the mid-1960s, marginal income tax rates were relatively low. If nothing else, this mistake illustrates the danger of extrapolating from relatively limited experience.

The problem here has to do with the fact that from the lender's point of view what matters is his real (i.e., inflation-adjusted) *after-tax* rate of return. Since taxes are levied on nominal interest rates, however, an inflation premium equal to the rate of inflation does not protect the lender's real after-tax return. To illustrate, suppose an investor earns 5.0 percent when inflation is zero. If his marginal tax rate is 30 percent, he earns 3.5 percent in real after-tax terms. Suppose, then, that inflation becomes 3.0 percent and that interest rates adjust to 8.0 percent. The real yield gross of tax is still 5.0 percent as before. But since the lender must pay tax on the full 8.0 percent, his real after-tax return is 2.6 percent, compared to 3.5 percent in the no-tax situation.

The moral is that in a world of income taxes, nominal rates of interest must adjust by more than the rate of inflation if lenders are to be fully protected. As we noted above, contemporary evidence suggests that market rates have more or less kept pace with inflation, implying that after-tax real yields have fallen. Figure 3 uses some skilled calculations to make the same point. The top curve plots Moody's Aaa corporate bond rate. The second curve shows the yield after the expected inflation rate is subtracted; in a world with no taxes, this would be the expected *real* yield on corporate bonds. The bottom curve calculates the expected net-of-tax real yield assuming a 30 percent marginal tax rate. In both cases, a three-year average of past rates of inflation is used to approximate the expected rate of inflation.

Since 1959 nominal interest rates have roughly kept pace with inflation, with both increasing by about 5.3 percentage points. Consequently, real yields before tax have been

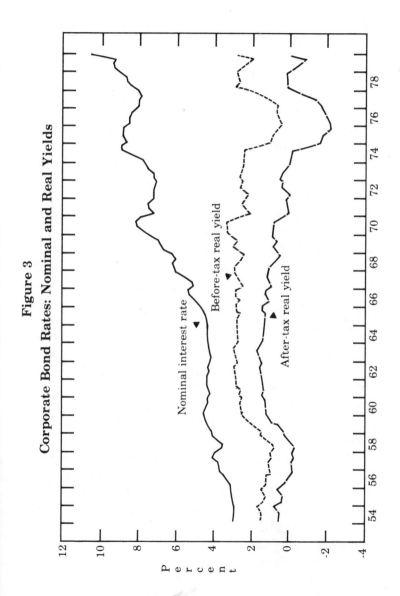

Figure 3

Corporate Bond Rates: Nominal and Real Yields

roughly unchanged, hovering around 2.0 to 2.5 percent except during the severe 1973–1975 recession. In contrast,
after-tax real yields have never recovered from the decline
that set in after 1965 when inflation began to accelerate. As
a result, real after-tax yields have averaged close to zero over
the decade of the 1970s.

On first reflection, it is not obvious why nominal rates
could not have adjusted by more than the increase in inflation rates. Since borrowing costs are tax-deductible, a bor-
rower can afford to pay more than the increase in the inflation rate without affecting his real net-of-tax cost. A corporate tax rate of 48 percent, for example, means that firms
could pay approximately 2 percentage points more for every
1 percentage point increase in inflation without increasing
their real cost of borrowed funds. Apparently the reason why
firms have not been able to do so is due to the tax treatment
of depreciation. Depreciation for tax purposes is calculated
on the basis of historical costs of assets. When prices are rising, these costs understate the cost of replacing assets and
consequently overstate profits. Hence the effective tax rate
on true profits rises. One of the effects of this reduced rate of
after-tax profitability has been to reduce the amount of real
after-tax rates that firms can pay lenders. Calculations made
by Feldstein and Summers (1978), for example, show that
under present tax and depreciation rules an increase in inflation of 6 percentage points (roughly, the increase from
1959 to 1979) would, under the best of circumstances, only
allow firms to raise the rate they could pay on borrowed
money by 10 percentage points. Even that increase, however,
would reduce the real yield earned by any bondholder whose
marginal income tax rate was over 35 percent.

Two unfavorable outcomes have been ascribed to the
decline in real yields. First, savings have been diverted from
financing acquisitions of business plant and equipment to
the purchase of homes and consumer durables. The latter
are perceived by households as providing a hedge against in-

flation which financial assets (including equity) cannot do for the reason described above. At the same time, the decline in the real costs of borrowing have reduced the burden of financing these purchases. Second, the decline in real yields has reduced total saving, as evidenced by the decline in the personal saving rate during the past three years. Both of these effects—the shift away from plant and equipment expenditures and the decline in saving—in turn are blamed for contributing to the decline in productivity growth in the present business cycle.

It is difficult, however, to find any compelling evidence for either of these effects (Table 3). To begin with, the proportion of investment spending going to residential construction has not significantly risen in the 1970s. The proportion for 1974–1979 is about the same as it was from 1961 to 1969 and is lower than it was in the late 1950s. As Cagan and Lipsey (1978) have shown, households have saved more in the form of housing in the last few years, but most of this has taken the form of capital gains on existing housing rather than that of acquiring new housing.

Table 3

Cycle Averages of Saving and Investment: 1954–1979

Cycle (trough to peak)	Personal Savings Rate	Private Savings Rate	Investment Rate	Housing Share of Investment
1954–1957	6.1%	15.8%	16.0%	34%
1958–1960	5.8	15.7	15.0	34
1961–1969	6.0	15.8	15.4	29
1970–1973	7.3	15.8	15.6	30
1974–1979	5.9	15.6	15.1	28

In the second place, the decline in the personal saving rate must be placed in context. A large part of this is cyclical, reflecting the usual behavior near a business cycle peak. Moreover, what matters for providing resources for capital accumulation is private saving—personal (household) saving plus business saving. Table 3 shows that the ratio of private saving to GNP from 1974 to 1979 is only marginally lower than it has been in previous business cycles. It is true that investment relative to GNP is lower, but this is because the government deficit has absorbed a large share of saving, not because saving has declined.[4]

THE SHIFTING PHILLIPS CURVE

The other shock that the experiences of the 1970s delivered to received wisdom was evidence that the Phillips curve trade-off had deteriorated dramatically. Figure 1 shows what happened. The recession of 1969–1970 led to a substantial increase in unemployment but scarcely made a dent in inflation. The experience of the late 1950s and early 1960s had indicated that unemployment rates of over 5.0 percent should have produced a rate of inflation of approximately 2.0 percent. Instead, in 1971 unemployment of 6.0 percent was accompanied by a 4.7 percent rate of inflation.

This new phenomenon of high inflation *and* high unemployment was dubbed stagflation. Developments in the theory underlying the Phillips curve led ultimately to an understanding of what had happened. The key concept in this new theory was the idea of a *natural unemployment rate*. The terminology was perhaps unfortunate, but the idea was illuminating. Essentially, the argument was that there was a normal (natural) level of labor market tightness that was consistent with wages and prices neither accelerating nor decelerating. The rate of unemployment consistent with this degree of labor utilization was called the natural rate. Levels of economic activity that generated tighter labor markets led to rising rates of price and wage inflation, while slacker conditions moderated inflation—thus, the observed inverse relationship between unemployment and inflation.

This was not the full story, however. The other key ingredient of the natural rate hypothesis was that the gains in employment and output were temporary and would disappear, but the rise in inflation would persist. The reason was that as wage and price inflation became pervasive and fully appreciated, firms and households would recognize that the gains in their individual prices and wages, which had prompted them to produce more and work more, were illusory. Economic activity therefore would revert to its normal level. At the same time, however, market participants, in order to protect themselves against inflation, would continue to build previous wage and price increases into their current demands. Consequently, inflation would build up a momentum which would only slowly subside.

Three important conclusions follow from the natural rate hypothesis. First, keeping unemployment below the natural rate necessitates accelerating inflation. Second, because of the momentum built in by past inflation, the trade-off is not reversible. The change in inflation is smaller when unemployment is rising than when it is falling. (Graphically, this means that the Phillips curve is flatter when the movement is downward to the right.) Third, as markets become sensitized to an environment of high inflation, the temporary gains in employment from more expansionary policy are likely to shrink. A more accurate and rapid perception of the inflationary consequences of expansionary policy would lead market participants to mark up prices and wages accordingly, rather than to expand work and output. This effect need not be symmetric. If markets perceive a predisposition to overexpansionary policy on the part of the authorities, they are likely to be quick to react to any evidence of stimulation but prone to discount indications that policy has turned firmer.

As Figure 2 shows, the experience of the 1970s is consistent with all three predictions. Declines in unemployment in each business expansion thus carried the inflation rate to successive new highs, and the rate of inflation tended to become lodged there as intervening recessions erased the gains in output and employment but left little mark on prices. And finally, inflation began to accelerate sooner and worsen more rapidly in the expansions of the 1970s compared to the expansions of the 1950s and 1960s.

In sum, the picture is one of diminishing returns to inflation benefits coupled with rising costs of reversing it. Nevertheless, the inflation rate at the end of the 1970s was more than twice what it had been at the beginning. This happened in part because policy failed to appreciate that the experience of the 1950s and 1960s was not reproducible—that once the temporary demands of the Vietnam war disappeared and output and employment fell back to more sustainable levels, price behavior would *not* revert to the stability of the early 1960s. Also at fault was an inadequate appreciation that labor markets had changed so that the traditional measure of labor market tightness underestimated the degree of inflationary buildup. The inflationary bias of these errors was compounded by the unsuitability of the Federal Reserve's traditional technique for controlling money.

THE PERSISTENCE OF INFLATION

The inflationary momentum that distinguished the 1970s from the two previous decades sprang from a growing conviction among business and labor that the rules of the game had fundamentally changed. Some economists identify this change with the collapse in 1971—1972 of fixed exchange rates, a collapse that they interpret as marking the final abandonment of the gold standard. The gold standard provided a country with a simple means of automatically imposing a high measure of discipline on its domestic monetary policy. In so doing, it effectively promoted internal price stability. The U.S. commitment under the postwar Bretton Woods agreement to buy and sell gold at a fixed price preserved this aspect of the gold standard for the United States. Policy up to 1965 was broadly consistent with this commitment, and therefore with a reasonable degree of price stability. The market apparently interpreted the commitment this way, with the result that inflation did not build up momentum but subsided fairly rapidly once policy turned restrictive.

Despite the Vietnam war, inflation, and the jettisoning of fixed exchange rates, the momentum of inflation that carried into 1970 and 1971 might ultimately have been cured if the authorities had clearly signalled their intention to reduce inflation and had made credible efforts to do so. Instead, the second error mentioned earlier—underestimating the amount of labor market tightness—led them to do the opposite.

The natural rate of unemployment is a valuable analytic tool, but it is a dangerous guide to policy. It is not directly observable and therefore must be inferred from other data. This reduces its usefulness as a policy target. For example, suppose policy attempts to keep unemployment close to the natural rate in an effort to prevent an acceleration in wages and prices. If the natural rate falls, the error will show up in accelerating inflation, which means that the damage has already been done.

There is now a general consensus in the economics profession that the natural rate was higher in the 1970s than it had been earlier. Semiofficial estimates place the contemporary rate somewhere around 5.0 to 5.5 percent compared to

4.5 percent, which is the typical estimate for the 1950s and 1960s. Other estimates place the current natural rate much higher, some as high as 6.5 percent. This is not the place to go into the reasons for the increase except to note that some of them may be related to the persistence of high inflation in the 1970s. What is relevant for our purposes is that by the beginning of the 1970s the natural rate was higher than it had been prior to 1965. Consequently, the relatively high (by historical standards) unemployment rate in 1971 was misinterpreted as indicating considerable economic slack. The persistence of high inflation at the same time was viewed as merely an extrapolation of the Vietnam war period that was no longer appropriate. Wage demands, so the theory went, were based on past inflationary experience and were unrealistically high, given the current state of job markets. Once expectations adjusted to the new reality, wage increases—and hence price increases—would slow down. The game plan therefore was to short-circuit the feedback of wages onto prices by imposing price and wage controls while at the same time to use expansionary monetary and fiscal policy to take up the unemployment slack.

The plan backfired. The amount of slack in the economy was much less than thought, with the result that prices began to soar once controls were lifted. At the same time, inflationary expectations were not dampened because the episode only confirmed market beliefs that the authorities were predisposed to sacrifice price stability to keep unemployment down.

Ironically, the oil price shock of 1973–1974 on balance may have contributed to long-term price stability, although it clearly made short-term inflation worse. The jump in oil prices put the authorities in a cruel dilemma. To protect employment and output from the shock meant accommodating the price rise through easier monetary policy. But to do that would be interpreted by the market as yet another piece of confirming evidence that policy was not committed to containing inflation, a judgment that would make the task of doing so even harder. In the end, it appears that much of the oil price rise was not accommodated, a decision that was one of the causes of the severe 1973–1975 recession. Whatever potential gains in reducing the underlying inflation rate were made by this action, however, were frittered away by repeating the mistake of too stimulatory a policy in the expansion that followed.

CONTROLLING MONEY

It was noted at the beginning of this chapter that most of the U.S. experience with inflation is confined to wars and their aftermaths. A comparison of the inflations of the Civil War, World War I, and World War II reveals an interesting regularity. The prolonging of inflation past the cessation of hostilities progressively lengthens. In each case, this can be explained by the same cause—a change in institutional arrangements for supplying money, which means that the monetary authority temporarily lost a significant measure of control over money. Thus in the Civil War the inflation abated almost as soon as the government stopped printing money. After World War I, access to the Federal Reserve discount window allowed banks to prolong the period of high money growth past the end of the war. The same thing happened after World War II, when the continuation of the Federal Reserve's wartime commitment to keep interest rates low—which did not end until 1950—meant excessive money growth.

With this perspective, it is possible to argue that the inflation of the 1970s also represents the aftermath of war inflation—in this case, Vietnam war inflation. It is not difficult to identify what has hindered the Federal Reserve's control of the money stock in this case. At a technical level, at least, the cause was the reliance on a technique for controlling money which was highly unreliable in an environment of high inflation.

Until recently, money was controlled by targeting the federal funds rate. There was no reason, in principle, why this was less reliable than trying to control money by targeting bank reserves. However, the *manner* in which the Federal Reserve operated made it so. Specifically, the Federal Reserve tended to move its funds rate target cautiously, changing it relatively infrequently and typically by small amounts. This is to be expected, given the necessarily fragmentary information it worked with. The risk of aggressive action is high when information is incomplete, and it quite naturally creates a predisposition to prefer the status quo. Unfortunately, this is not an optimal response if the object is to control money. The reason has to do with the procyclical behavior of interest rates. Rates rise during an expansion and fall during a contraction. Cautious control of the funds rate therefore means that policy tries to hold down interest rates when business is expanding and tries to prop them up when business is contracting. Holding interest rates down means that money growth has to accelerate; holding them up, that it must decelerate. Hence the outcome is a procyclical monetary policy—one that tends to reinforce cyclical swings rather than moderate them.

This undesirable trait of a funds rate target is strengthened when inflation is significant because changes in inflation expectations also tend to be procyclical. The outcome in this case is potentially explosive. A rise in inflation, for example, first raises inflation expectations, which in turn push interest rates up. If the Federal Reserve initially attempts to resist higher interest rates, money accelerates, providing the fuel for a further increase in inflation. The stage is thereby set for another round of inflation and money acceleration.

It became increasingly clear as the 1970s drew to a close that the funds rate technique was not working. On 6 October 1979 the Federal Reserve announced that it was embarking on an experiment of placing greater reliance on the targeting of bank reserves as a way of controlling money. Given the predisposition to caution control, the switch to reserves is likely to provide much better control over money. Procyclical influences on the money stock will now be confined to the effect of rising interest rates on the money multiplier, an effect which most empirical evidence suggests will be small. Thus the potential now exists that monetary policy will be much less procyclical than it has been in the past.

CAN INFLATION BE REDUCED?

This reform in the Federal Reserve's technique for controlling the money supply is a heartening one. The admittedly limited evidence we have so far suggests that the change has in fact resulted in better control over money. Money growth has been significantly curbed since 6 October 1979; the aggregates have been kept within their longer-run targets; and the corrections to the monetary aggregates, when they stray from target, appear to be more prompt and vigorous. The 6 October reform thus appears to have allowed the Federal Reserve to regain control of the money stock in the same way that the end of the bond support program did after World War II. It was probably necessary if any successful sustained assault was to be made on inflation. But it is not sufficient. Sufficiency requires the political will to tolerate what are likely to be significant costs from reducing inflation.

Table 4 summarizes some econometric evidence of just how large these losses are likely to be. Recall that a percentage point rise in unemployment is equivalent to a loss in real GNP growth of approximately 3.0 percentage points. Recent estimates have suggested that this should be scaled down to the vicinity of 2.0 to 2.5 percent. Even so, the losses in terms of foregone output would be substantial. Keeping unemployment higher by 1.0 percentage point for three years would mean a cumulative loss in terms of 1979 GNP of nearly $178 billion. The most generous estimate of the gain that would be made on the inflation rate is Cagan's (1978)—3.0 percentage points—and all of the other estimates are much smaller. One wonders whether the political motivation exists to assume such burdens. In earlier episodes the authorities could appeal to their commitment under the gold standard to preserve the international value of the dollar. That formal commitment at least no longer exists, and it is not clear what new excuse can be put in its place. Policy was also aided in earlier times by prevailing expectations that price stability was the norm. That anchor is no longer there either, which makes the consequences of returning to price stability potentially enormous.

Table 4
Estimates of Reduction in Inflation from a Sustained 1-Percentage Point Unemployment Increase

Author	Short Run (1 year)	Long Run (3 years) *
Perry	0.30%	0.70%
Gordon**	0.70	0.85
Cagan	0.80	3.20
	0.37	1.70

*Cagan's estimate for a average business cycle.
**Calculated from the example in Gordon assuming that potential GNP grows at 3.6% per year, and that for each percentage point that actual GNP growth is below potential growth, unemployment increases by a third of a percent.

Of course, some observers have argued that if labor and business could be convinced that the authorities were determined to reduce inflation, inflation would be easier and less costly to reduce. The estimates in Table 4 are based on an historical record during a period in which such a commitment was largely lacking. Consequently, inflation stubbornly persisted when unemployment rose, because expectations were that policy would quickly turn stimulatory again—a perception that was confirmed time and again. If expectations had been that policy would remain restrictive until inflation had permanently fallen, expectations—and hence, inflation—might have subsided more quickly. The problem with such a scenario is that it rests mostly on faith; we have no modern experience to substantiate it.

Nevertheless, three things may ultimately stiffen the resolve to fight inflation this time, even if the costs are high. One is that the distortions caused by inflation have turned out to be much more severe than were imagined fifteen years ago. The second is that social tensions have clearly been increased because of inflation. The burdens of inflation are unequally distributed across groups (and perhaps more important, the incidence is *perceived* as uneven and unfair), with resulting damage to morale and social cohesion. Perhaps most important of all, however, is the growing awareness that it is not possible to stabilize inflation except at a zero rate. Once society comes to view 5 percent inflation as tolerable, a natural temptation arises to believe that 8 percent won't be so bad—and then that 10 percent won't hurt either. And so on. It makes sense to speak of a commitment to price stability; a commitment to, say, a 10 percent inflation rate is by comparison vacuous. Because of this, there is no such thing as a "little" inflation. We have proceeded for the past fifteen years as if there were and the disastrous consequences are all too visible today. Perhaps these reminders will embarrass us into mending our ways.

DISCUSSION

McKINNON: Solving inflation is a simple technical problem concerning the Federal Reserve Bank, which has had
much more independence from the government of the day
than central banks in almost any other country. While the
Fed did all right through the 1950s and early 1960s, in the
1970s it lost control over the money supply. The reasons are
fairly straightforward. For one thing, the Fed does not have
full jurisdiction over all agencies in the economy that issue
money. There are banks that are not members of the Federal
Reserve System and which are not subject to its reserve requirements. We have all seen the spreading of money-
market funds. I have a very nice checking account with Mer-
rill Lynch which pays 13 percent. I can write checks which
are just as good as money, but there were no reserves of any
sort which the government imposed on that checking account. Similarly, there exist credit unions, "now" accounts,
and a variety of financial institutions of this character that
issued money in a relatively uncontrolled way—at least until
14 March 1980, when the Fed greatly broadened its regulatory reach. As long as we are not on a commodity standard like
gold where each private institution has the obligation to convert its money into gold, then it is necessary for the central
bank to secure complete control over the money supply
system, and this is mainly a question of appropriate legislation.

BOSKIN: I had an interesting experience I want to share
with you on the uncertainty engendered by inflation. This
fact is being brought home to Congress itself in a very interesting way, as congressional committees are totally in-
capable of analyzing the budget any more. Every few weeks
they get different estimates of spending and revenues
because the inflation estimates keep changing. I find in talk-

ing to the people in Congress that this fact more than anything else is driving home to them what inflation really does in disrupting long-term views of planning of business or government spending and revenue.

McKINNON: On the neutrality problem, John mentioned that the revenue from anticipated inflation to the government is nontrivial, although not very large—on the order of 10 or 20 billion dollars. With new measures taken by the Federal Reserve Bank to spread noninterest-bearing reserve requirements to manage liabilities for the banks, "now" accounts, credit union money-market funds, and so forth, potential revenue to the government is greatly increased; and although I don't agree with each one of these measures, from the point of view of monetary control this spread of reserve requirements is necessary. But to preserve neutrality in financial markets and in the tax system, with the spread of reserve requirements the government should begin to pay interest on reserves held with it at a rate comparable, say, to the treasury bill rate. This should be an important part of the government's financial policy at the present time. That would dissipate the earnings of the Federal Reserve that are turned over to the U.S. Treasury.

OLSEN: On the relation between inflation rates and budget deficits, we did a study at Citibank which demonstrated with scatter diagrams and others that in fact deficits do not explain the acceleration of inflation over the last fifteen years. If you were to assume—and some more elegant studies do conclude—that there may have been reasons at times that increased deficits induced the Fed to become more expansionary in its monetary policy, that was only for a year or two. Our study showed that the Fed actually provided about three times as much money as the treasury ever needed to finance deficits. You can just take the last five years since the end of the recession in 1975, for example. Monetary policy, through money growth and velocity, enabled money GNP to grow at 11 to 12 percent annual rates in each of the last four years at the same time that the budget deficit, as a matter of fact, was coming down. And it was clear that the rate of inflation was going to accelerate once the economy reached its potential growth rate, beginning in 1978.

Looking ahead to the 1980s, we now are at a cyclical turning point in the economy, with the probability of a recession ahead and some cooling off in the inflation rate on a cyclical basis. Whether we are able to reduce the rate of inflation over the longer run through the 1980s is still problematical. I have not found anyone with any good ideas for reducing the inflation rate in any way other than to run the economy at the lowest potential growth rate for an indefinite period of time.

This requires, incidentally, remarkable political leadership and, of course, public support on the part of the electorate as well. It's possible that this episode we are going through right now, depending on how deep the recession is that follows this, may scare people enough to get the necessary support for anti-inflationary policies for more than just brief periods—instead, through the 1980s. We don't know whether that will be the case or not in the particular episode. If people are not particularly troubled by it to give that kind of support, we will get a cyclical rebound in the economy once again with an increase in money growth, and of course fiscal policy will make its contribution as well.

One other note about inflation: inflation is also known to have a deadening effect on capital investment because of the unwillingness to take risks. When you have sudden acceleration of inflation above expected trends that we have had, it tends to shorten further and further not only the commitments in the financial assets, but also the commitments in real assets that investors are willing to undertake. The shortfall in capital investment of course will have an increasing erosion on our standard of living. This is particularly deceptive, because people can't readily see such declines until some period of time has passed. For this reason you can't find anybody willing to take responsibility for it. Congress, for example, whose horizons at best are six to twelve months out (as far as the economy is concerned, even that long), simply cannot take responsibility for what they may perceive as a decline in the standard of living for one year in a business cycle. When this goes on over a protracted period, they do not seem to comprehend what it means for the standard of living at the end of a decade or the end of a fifteen- to twenty-year period. Moreover, the social strains inflicted in such a decline, unless something is done to correct it, will only make political management of the economy even more difficult.

Let me add one final thought to the argument that inflation is a social or political phenomenon, that it stems from greed or from the political mechanism that seeks to increase government spending and so forth. This argument that inflation may not be wholly a monetary phenomenon is somewhat like the local bartender who argues that the alcoholic who comes into his pub and gets intoxicated every day doesn't become drunk because of the alcoholic beverages served there, but because of social and emotional problems that he is trying to escape. And if you could just solve those social and emotional problems, the argument goes, he wouldn't drink so much and he wouldn't get drunk. The fact is that it still takes the alcohol to make him intoxicated, and there is no way that you can avoid that. Moreover, it is likely that his emotional and social problems have at least been compounded—if not created—by the fact that he drank excessively in the first place. So that I think a lot of the illnesses in our society that are used to explain why we have inflation are in fact *products* of inflation rather than the other way around.

4

JOHN H. PENCAVEL[1]

The Nature of the Contemporary Unemployment Problem

Attitudes toward unemployment and their influence on policy. Measuring employment and unemployment. Youth unemployment. The effects of government programs on employment rates. Chronic unemployment.

Because a long period of unemployment can impose considerable economic and emotional distress on an able-bodied worker in a modern industrial society, many people regard the nation's unemployment rate as the single most important index of hardship in the U.S. economy. The unemployment rate achieved this prominent place as a welfare indicator largely as a consequence of the nation's experiences in the 1930s, and much of our thinking on unemployment today is still conditioned by these events and by our interpretation of them. The attitude prevalent then—which lingers today—may be loosely described as a problem of "too few jobs" for the available workers. Stated thus, it is only a short step to prescribe for government an unemployment policy of increasing the number of "jobs" so that the excess of workers over "jobs" disappears. This notion of job creation and its role in relieving unemployment lie behind a whole series of legislative schemes from the Full Employment Act of 1946 to the recent Humphrey-Hawkins Bill. That such thinking has persisted for four decades indicates that, for some purposes, it has its uses: for instance, part of the movement in the nation's unemployment rate from year to year is clearly attributable to changes in the aggregate demand for labor (itself influenced by government economic policy) which gives rise to new job vacancies.

Nevertheless, it has become increasingly evident that, on balance, this way of thinking inhibits rather than enlightens sensible discussion of unemployment. It draws attention to the provision of jobs without concern for the terms and conditions attached to them. Its emphasis is upon one side of the market transaction, the demand for labor, and the supply of labor is treated mechanically. Above all, an approach to a problem that talks in terms of an "inadequacy of jobs" contradicts the reality, which is that there are *too many* competing tasks and jobs to perform, not too few.

A modern approach to understanding the problem of unemployment fully recognizes the hardships for a worker and his or her family associated with a long spell of unemployment, but it also avoids the sort of naive normative implications associated with the metaphor of "too few jobs." After all, both in terms of the loss in income and of the emotional distress, it is less the fact of being without a job that causes privation, but more the *length* of that unemployment: if 10 percent of the labor force were unemployed at all times but each person were unemployed for only one week at a time, this would surely cause us much less concern than a 5 percent unemployment rate when each person unemployed remained without a job for an entire year. Thus the problem for research is to delve beyond the unemployment rate to identify those groups in the population that experience frequent spells of unemployment and those groups whose duration of unemployment is unusually long. It is these groups, the chronically unemployed, for whom unemployment is a serious blight, and an appropriate government policy with respect to unemployment would be one that is designed to relieve the distress experienced by these particular groups in the population.

By contrast, a policy that concentrates on the aggregative unemployment rate and which tailors macroeconomic monetary and fiscal policy to minimize this aggregative rate is likely to provide no more than transitory assistance to the chronically unemployed. The assistance will be transitory because recent experience indicates that a stimulative macroeconomic policy directed to minimizing the aggregate unemployment rate sets in motion, not a constant rate of inflation (as is suggested by the now largely discredited notion of a stable unemployment/inflation trade-off, the so-called Phillips curve), but rather increases in prices and wages that tend to accelerate and which can only be corrected by abandoning the goal of unemployment rate minimization. Therefore, the issue is less whether a policy of minimizing the unemployment rate is *desirable*; the fact is that such a policy is not *sustainable*, and for this reason more selective measures to assist the chronically unemployed are necessary. The purpose of this chapter is to consider whether those groups in the population that constitute the chronically unemployed can be identified and then to explore measures for assisting them.

In particular, the next section provides some necessary information on the measurement and definition of unemployment in the U.S. economy while the third section attempts to determine for which groups in the population unemployment has become an increasing problem over the last twenty-five years. This disaggregated analysis of unemployment is relevant in part because the aggregate unemployment rate today describes a labor force whose composition is considerably different from what it was just after the second world war: whereas 46 percent of the labor force in 1947 were males aged 25 to 55 years (a group sometimes called "prime-aged males" whose attachment to the labor market seems to be less sensitive to differences in nonmarket opportunities), in 1979 this group constituted only 36 percent of the labor force. This disaggregated analysis indicates that the unemployment problem has become more serious for young black males, so an analysis follows of the teenage unemployment problem. The fourth section examines the role of unemployment insurance and of minimum wage legislation, followed by a section concerned with alternative policies that serve effectively to alleviate the plight of the chronically unemployed.

CONCEPTS AND DEFINITIONS

Measuring Employment and Unemployment

According to the household survey conducted each month by the Bureau of the Census for the Bureau of Labor Statistics, at any time the adult population is classified into one of three groups: those employed, those unemployed, and those not in the labor force. The labor force is defined as the sum of the employed and unemployed, while the unemployment rate expresses the ratio of the number unemployed to the number in the labor force. The unemployed are (i) those persons not having a job during the survey week but stating as having taken steps to look for one during the previous four weeks, and (ii) those persons not at work but awaiting recall to a job from which they have been laid off. The presence of this latter group (those temporarily laid off) among the unemployed implies that some of those classified as unemployed actually have a "job" to which they anticipate returning. It is the former group, those searching for a job, that fits the popular notion of what constitutes unemployment. However, since the respondent (or his spouse) is left to judge whether he has been looking for work, the distinction between the unemployed and those not in the labor force raises problems of interpretation. The numbers recorded as unemployed in this way thus exclude potentially employable individuals who have become discouraged in their search for employment and who have ceased looking for work. Conversely, some individuals will feign activity in job search to ensure their eligibility for welfare benefits or simply to avoid social disapproval. For these reasons, some economists find it more appropriate for their purposes to avoid the problems of demarcating between those who are unemployed and those who are not in the labor force and they analyze not the unemployment rate but the employment-to-population ratio, that is, the fraction of the population who are classified as employed.

The stylized facts on aggregate employment, unemployment, and the labor force for the U.S. economy during the period since the second world war are contained in Table 1. The most noticeable trends are the steeply rising labor force participation rate (L/P) of women and the mildly declining labor force participation rates of men. Since male unemployment rates (U/L) have tended to rise while male labor force participation rates have fallen, the percentage of all adult males not employed (100 − E/P) has fallen almost ten points from 80.4 percent in 1947 to 72.1 percent in 1979.

Percentage Labor Force Participation Rates, Employment-to-Population Rates, Unemployment Rates, and the Average Duration of Unemployment, 1974–1979

	Males and Females			Males			Females			All Workers' Mean Duration of Unemployment (weeks)	
	L/P	E/P	U/L	L/P	E/P	U/L	L/P	E/P	U/L	Incomplete Spells	Complete Spells
1947	58.9	55.2	3.9	86.8	80.4	4.0	31.8	30.6	3.7	—	—
1952	60.4	55.4	3.0	87.2	78.3	2.8	34.8	33.4	3.6	8.4	4.0
1957	60.6	55.7	4.3	85.5	77.3	4.1	36.9	35.1	4.7	10.5	5.7
1962	59.7	54.2	5.5	82.8	74.1	5.2	38.0	35.6	6.2	14.7	6.2
1967	60.6	55.8	3.8	81.5	73.8	3.1	41.2	39.0	5.2	8.8	5.0
1972	61.0	56.0	5.6	79.7	72.5	4.9	43.9	40.9	6.6	12.1	6.2
1977	62.8	57.1	7.0	78.3	70.9	6.2	48.5	44.4	8.2	14.3	7.2
1979	63.7	59.3	5.8	77.9	72.1	5.1	51.0	47.5	6.8	10.8	—

Note: These data describe individuals aged 16 years and over. P stands for the total noninstitutional population; L, for the labor force; E for employment; U, for unemployment. The sources for these data are U.S. Department of Labor (1979, Tables 1, 2 and 65), *Monthly Labor Review*, recent issues. The information on the duration of unemployment under "incomplete spells" is derived by asking unemployed individuals how long they have been unemployed. Since these individuals have not completed their spell of unemployment, these data measure the average duration of *incomplete* spells of unemployment. The series in the final column describes the mean duration of *completed* spells of unemployment and was estimated by a procedure developed by Kaitz (1970, pp. 11–20).

Turnover and Unemployment Duration

The unemployment rate is a stock concept measuring the fraction of the labor force classified as unemployed at a particular date. This unemployed stock is continually being depleted by individuals either moving into employment or out of the labor force, and it is continually supplemented by those leaving employment or joining the labor force. In a steady state with constant unemployment, the stock of unemployed workers (U) will equal the flow of workers into the unemployed pool (S) times the average amount of time spent in the unemployed pool (D): $U = S.D$. Thus S ("separations") consists of individuals whose separation from employment was ostensibly initiated by their employers ("discharges"), individuals whose entry into unemployment was self-initiated ("quits"), and individuals who are entering unemployment from outside the labor force. Hence, if L denotes the size of the labor force, movements in the unemployment rate (U/L) will tend to be associated with movements in the separations rate (S/L) and in the average duration of unemployment (D). Indeed, increases in the unemployment rate are associated both with greater average duration of unemployment and with a larger fraction of the unemployed poor entering by way of being discharged by their former employer.

This decomposition of the unemployment rate into the separations rate and the duration of unemployment is important because, if government undertakes major efforts to reduce unemployment, it becomes relevant to determine whether policy will be more effective in reducing the probability of entering the unemployed pool or in reducing the duration of unemployment conditional upon entering the pool. Thus the appropriate policies may well be different in Europe from those in the United States, since there is some evidence to the effect that European workers tend to experience unemployment less frequently than workers in the United States but, once unemployed, they remain in that state for a considerably longer period than their American counterparts.[2]   Or, since the probability of becoming unemployed falls sharply with years of schooling (at least until years of schooling equivalent to college attendance), while the duration of unemployment reveals only a weak association with schooling, the most effective policies to reduce unemployment among the unskilled are not likely to be the same as those designed to reduce the unemployment of skilled workers.[3]

THE PROBLEM OF YOUTH UNEMPLOYMENT

The Cyclical Vulnerability of Youths

To place the U.S. unemployment experience in an international perspective, Table 2 presents percentage unemployment rates for nine countries. It is clear from the table that, except for Sweden and Italy, unemployment rates have been higher in the second half of the 1970s than at almost any time since 1950. Moreover, the forecasts for the immediate future indicate that this unemployment is going to increase rather than to diminish.

One sometimes hears the proposition that this increase in the unemployment rate represents a statistical artefact. The argument here is that, since the aging of the post—World War II baby boom has increased the proportion of youths in the labor market and since the young tend to display higher unemployment rates than older people, a higher total unemployment rate today merely manifests demographic changes in the U.S. economy. In fact, the most careful analysis of this argument suggests that these demographic

Table 2

Percentage Unemployment Rates Adjusted to U.S. Concepts, 1950–1978

	United States	Australia	Canada	France	West Germany	Italy	Japan	Sweden	Great Britain
1950–1954	4.0	1.1	3.3	2.4	5.8	8.5	1.9	1.5	2.3
1955–1959	5.0	1.4	5.1	1.8	2.4	7.8	2.2	2.4	2.4
1960–1964	5.7	2.2	6.0	1.5	0.5	3.4	1.4	1.7	2.7
1965–1969	3.8	1.5	4.2	2.1	0.7	3.9	1.2	1.8	2.9
1970–1974	5.4	1.9	5.9	2.8	1.1	3.6	1.3	2.3	3.5
1975–1978	7.3	5.4	7.6	4.9	3.6	3.4	2.1	1.8	5.5

Note: Through 1974 these data are taken from Sorrentino (1975). Subsequent data are from Moy (1979, pp. 8-16).

changes would raise the U.S. unemployment rate only between 0.5 percent to 1.0 percent in 1976 compared with its
value twenty years earlier (see Antos, Mellow, and Triplett
1979, pp. 36–46). If so, then explanations for the rising
unemployment rate are not to be sought primarily in a "com-
positional" effect.

In examining the unemployment rates of particular groups
in the population, it is clear that the most noticeable increases have occurred among the young, especially among
black youths (see Table 3). Consequently, much of recent
research effort has been directed towards understanding
youth unemployment. It is an unusually awkward subject to
analyze, in part because the problems in measuring
unemployment for young blacks are particularly acute. It is
hard to read Malcom X's *Autobiography* or Elliot Liebow's
Tally's Corner without wondering how much of the high
recorded unemployment rates of black youths really indicates the comparative net returns in intermittent, sometimes illegal, activities that the prevailing norms of society
do not classify as "work."[4]   But presumably these difficulties
in defining unemployment in slum areas have always been
present and thus it is hard to find an explanation here for the
rising trend in youth unemployment.

One reason for the higher unemployment of black youths
in the 1970s is simply that they have always been the most
vulnerable to movements in the business cycle and that the
overall level of industrial production has been particularly
sluggish in recent years. This vulnerability results from their
lack of *specific* skills (that is, what skills they possess are
easily transferred across firms), which results in relatively
high layoff and voluntary quit rates. In a business downtown,
a firm is less willing to discharge workers whose skills are
specific to that firm and cannot be reproduced in a new
worker without costly training (Becker 1975, pp. 26–37).

The same sort of business cycle vulnerability is evident in
the unemployment rates of unskilled workers of all ages,

Table 3

Percentage Unemployment Rates for Selected Groups, 1948–1979

Year	All	Males 20 yrs +	Females 20 yrs +	Both Sexes 16–19 yrs	Aged 18–19 Years			
					White Males	Black Males	White Females	Black Females
1948	3.8	3.2	3.6	9.2	9.4	10.5	6.8	14.6
1950	5.3	4.7	5.1	12.2	11.7	17.7	9.4	14.1
1955	4.4	3.8	4.4	11.0	10.4	12.9	7.7	21.4
1960	5.5	4.7	5.1	14.7	13.5	25.1	11.5	24.5
1965	4.5	3.2	4.5	14.8	11.4	20.2	13.4	27.8
1970	4.9	3.5	4.8	15.2	12.0	23.1	11.9	32.9
1975	8.5	6.7	8.0	19.9	17.2	32.9	16.1	38.3
1977	7.0	5.2	7.0	17.7	13.0	36.1	14.2	37.4
1979	5.8	4.1	5.7	16.1	—	—	—	—

Note: In this table, "black" also includes other minority racial groups. Data are taken from U.S. Department of Labor (1979, Tables 56, 57, 60); also from recent issues of *Monthly Labor Review*.

although the importance of this was not fully appreciated during the so-called "structuralist" debate in the early 1960s. At that time, the unemployment rates of unskilled workers were high relative to their levels some ten or fifteen years earlier, and this induced some economists to claim that the labor market had altered fundamentally such that low unemployment rates for these groups could not be restored without extensive manpower training programs.[5] In fact, the higher level of aggregate economic activity in the late 1960s brought down all unemployment rates—the blue-collar worker unemployment rate fell from 9.2 percent in 1961 to 3.9 percent in 1969—with little contribution from government training programs or other special schemes. Similarly, there is a danger of misinterpreting the relatively high unemployment rates of youths in the 1970s and of not allowing due weight to the well-attested fact that youth unemployment always rises more steeply than that of others when the growth rate of the economy falters.

The question then arises of quantifying the vulnerability of the unemployment rates of youths to movements in the business cycle. A statistical analysis of this issue is contained in the appendix to this chapter. It suggests that when the unemployment rate of prime-age (that is, 35 to 45 year old) white males increases by 1 percentage point, the associated increase in the unemployment rates of teenagers is between 1.5 and 3.0 percentage points. In other words, the amplitude of movements in the unemployment rates of young workers is approximately two to three times that of prime-age white males. Nevertheless, even after accounting for these cyclical movements in the unemployment rates of young workers, there remains a sizable increase in the unemployment rates of young black workers over the past twenty-five years that requires some explanation. The analysis in the appendix indicates a similar set of inferences from an examination of movements in employment as well as of unemployment: the amplitude of swings in the employment rates of young workers is greater than that in those of prime-age white males, and the employment rates of young black workers display a noticeable downward trend.

Schooling

These results are consistent with the widely held belief that, in terms of employment opportunities, the labor market has become increasingly bleak for young black workers, especially for young black males. But this cheerless conclusion represents an incomplete picture, since it ignores the dramatic advances that young blacks have made in their years of schooling. Whereas some 21.6 percent of black males aged 18 to 19 years and 25.7 percent of black females aged 18 to 19 years were enrolled in school in 1954, the corresponding percentages in 1977 were 52.9 percent and 47.7 percent, respectively. In this respect, young blacks were becoming more like young whites, whose school enrollment rates were 47.7 percent and 43.4 percent for 18 to 19 year old males and females, respectively, in 1977. Moreover, these schooling trends of black youths may not be unrelated to their rising unemployment rates since, according to the Bureau of the Census's data collection methods, an individual may be categorized as unemployed and looking for work even though he may also be enrolled in school. Indeed, in October 1964 about 16 percent of unemployed white males aged 18 to 19 years and 17 percent of unemployed black males aged 18 to 19 years were enrolled in school. By October 1977 these percentages had risen to 24.0 percent for white youths and to 41.0 percent for black youths. That is, about two out of every five unemployed black males were also enrolled in school in 1977 and presumably they were looking for the sort of part-time employment that would provide financial support for them through school. The unemployment problem for these students is the search for jobs with flexible working schedules and casual employment practices that permit them to attend first to their schooling program. Regrettably, these are also the sort of jobs that have suffered from the extension of the coverage of federal minimum wage legislation.

Higher Unemployment Rates of Youths

It is important in examining youth unemployment in the United States to distinguish two dimensions. One is that the measured unemployment rates of young people are higher than those of older people, and the second is that the unemployment rates of black youths have been increasing. Explanations for the greater incidence of unemployment among youths are not difficult to find; by contrast, a satisfactory explanation for the rising trend in black teenage unemployment is really lacking. First, let us understand the meaning of the higher unemployment rates of young people.

Making use of the decomposition of the unemployment rate into the product of the probability of experiencing a spell of unemployment and the duration of unemployment, it appears that the higher unemployment rates of young people are explicable in terms of their much higher probabilities of entering (or leaving) the pool of unemployment and not to their duration of unemployment (see, for instance, Leighton and Mincer 1979). Indeed, there are indications that the duration of unemployment for unemployed younger workers is shorter than that for unemployed older workers. The greater probability of young people leaving employment and becoming unemployed at any time seems to hold whether the job separation is ostensibly initiated by the employer (a layoff) or by the worker (a quit). The reason for this is that younger workers have accumulated few skills that are specific to a single employer so that the value of the worker to one employer differs little from his value to another employer. This increases the worker's readiness to move between employers and also increases any single employer's readiness to lay off that worker permanently and replace him with an equally valuable substitute.

The decline in the quit rate and in the layoff rate with job tenure is marked so that, as the duration of a worker's employment in a firm increases and as the worker ages, so his probability of entering the unemployment pool falls. And it does appear to be tenure in a particular job rather than simply total labor market experience, spread perhaps over several jobs, that produces the large effects on the separations rate. The quit rate is especially responsive to the length of job tenure, which has raised the possibility that older workers are deterred from quitting their jobs by the fact that they are less likely to be offered a job at any given wage than a younger worker. This would also account for the fact that, once unemployed, the older worker typically experiences a longer period of unemployment.

The fear has been voiced that periods of long and/or frequent unemployment handicap a teenager for life. Indeed, research indicates that work experience early in an individual's career does make a difference subsequently to that individual's wages. On the other hand, time not at work early in a teenager's career appears to have little effect on the subsequent probability of that worker being employed several years hence, once due account is taken of factors such as years of schooling completed which affects the probability of unemployment at all ages. This should guard us against the popular idea that government-sponsored "job creation" programs for those who have just left high school will increase their probability of employment in future years.

Rising Unemployment of Black Youths

The second dimension of the teenage unemployment problem is that over the past twenty-five years black youth unemployment has grown relative to white youth unemployment, and employment-to-population ratios of black youths have fallen relative to those of white youths. The reasons for these racial differences are not fully understood, although it is becoming increasingly evident that some radical changes have occurred in youth employment over the last thirty years which to date have received only scant attention. In particular, in some unpublished research John Cogan (1980) has shown that the marked regional variations in the employment rates for each race (especially for nonwhites) in 1950 had virtually disappeared in 1970. Particularly pronounced in Table 4 is the halving of the employment ratio for nonwhites in the South between 1950 and 1970. As is well known, this period witnessed a substantial migration of labor (and especially of black labor) out of the South; indeed, as Table 4 shows, whereas 71.5 percent of all 16 to 19 year old nonwhite males lived in the South in 1950, twenty years later this percentage had fallen to 57.0. Cogan explains the decline in the nonwhite male youth employment ratio in the United States as a whole primarily in terms of the decline in this ratio in the South.

Within the South itself, the steep decline in agriculture as an employer of labor (and especially of nonwhite labor) has been dramatic: the change in the percentage of 16 to 19 year old male nonwhites employed in agriculture fell by over 40 percent between 1950 and 1970. Across regions of the United States between 1950 and 1970 changes in young male employment rates paralleled closely changes in the percentage of working teenagers employed in agriculture: where agricultural employment fell considerably (as in the South) the overall employment-to-population ratio also fell, and this association is stronger for nonwhites than it is for whites. Hence, between 1950 and 1970 mechanization in agriculture has produced a startling decline in agricultural employment throughout the United States, especially for nonwhite male teenagers in the South who (at least, up to 1970) have not been fully absorbed into employment in other sectors of the economy. The question follows why these individuals, who

Table 4

Employment-to-Population (E/P) Ratios and Regional Population Distribution for Males Aged 16–19 Years, White and Nonwhite (percentage)

| | E/P | | | | |
	Entire United States	North-east	North Central	South	West
Whites, 1950	40.2	33.2	46.7	42.5	33.8
Nonwhites, 1950	46.4	23.5	28.2	54.8	23.3
Whites, 1970	40.3	39.6	44.9	37.6	38.1
Nonwhites, 1970	26.2	26.0	27.7	27.5	22.2
Male teenage population:					
Whites, 1950	100.0	25.42	29.82	31.48	13.28
Nonwhites, 1950	100.0	10.89	11.91	71.50	5.71
Whites, 1970	100.0	23.22	29.27	28.71	18.88
Nonwhites, 1970	100.0	16.45	19.41	56.69	7.45

Note: Taken from information appearing in Cogan (1980), based on data from the 1950 and 1970 *Census of Population.*

two decades ago would have been employed in agriculture, are now not employed elsewhere.

Two popular responses to this question involve the policies of government. One concerns the growth of income transfer programs that allegedly have raised the relative returns to not working, and the other concerns the extension of the coverage of federal minimum wage legislation that has foreclosed job opportunities to low-wage labor. Let us consider each of these government policies in turn.

UNEMPLOYED INSURANCE AND MINIMUM WAGES

Income Transfer Programs

In searching for explanations for the falling employment rates and rising unemployment rates of nonwhite male teenagers, it is natural for economists to inquire whether the after-tax wage rate has fallen for these individuals relative to the rewards for not being employed. In fact, what evidence there is suggests that the (before-tax) wages of black youths have been rising relative to those of white youths, though it is uncertain whether this is attributable to a decline in black/white schooling differences or to the intended or unintended effects of government programs.

With respect to incomes received for not working, clearly over the last thirty years there has been a substantial increase in incomes transferred through welfare programs. Naturally, any income transferred to individuals to alleviate the economic hardship associated with not working will create corresponding incentives for individuals to acquire the characteristics that render them eligible for the receipt of such income. Hence, the growth in these income transfer programs is sometimes held to be responsible for the lower employment rates of certain groups in the 1970s. In particular, the implicit tax rates on these welfare programs (i.e., the rate at which payments fall with each dollar of labor income the individual earns) are widely believed to be so high as to constitute a serious disincentive to work. However, the major welfare programs—Aid to Families with Dependent Children, food stamps, and support for the disabled and aged— are likely to have had their greatest effect on groups in the population (on mothers, on the aged, and on the physically infirm) other than teenagers, although teenagers may well benefit from these payments to the extent that other members of the household receive these payments and to the extent that these incomes are pooled.

One income transfer program is, of course, specifically designed to cushion reductions in income associated with unemployment—namely, the unemployment insurance system. It has been argued, in fact, that both in its payment of benefits to unemployed individuals and in its system of payroll taxation, the current unemployment insurance system raises measured unemployment. By increasing the return to unemployment vis-à-vis work, unemployment compensation provides an incentive for the unemployed to extend their unemployment as compared with a situation of no unemployment benefits. By how much the duration of unemployment is increased will vary from individual to individual since unemployment benefits depend upon each individual's employment experiences. There are cases in which weekly unemployment benefits fall little short of an individual's after-tax earnings, and this observation has given rise to the proposal to treat unemployment compensation as taxable income. In examining twelve empirical studies of the effect of unemployment compensation on the duration of unemployment, Hamermesh (1977, p. 49) concluded that those receiving unemployment insurance benefits extended their unemployment about 2.5 weeks, which in turn raises

the measured aggregate unemployment rate by about 0.5
percentage points.

As far as the system of financing unemployment insurance is concerned, much has been made of the fact that
the payroll tax on firms is incompletely experience-rated:
each firm's payroll tax for unemployment compensation is
only loosely related to its past employment practices, so that
the benefits paid to the firm's former employees frequently
do not equal the taxes imposed on the firm. Consequently,
imperfectly experience-rated unemployment insurance
represents a payment valued by workers but whose full cost
is not borne by the relevant firm, implying that firms will
substitute toward compensating their employees with
unemployment benefits by making more frequent use of
temporary layoffs than would occur under a fully experience-
rated unemployment insurance system. Since temporary
layoffs constitute an important fraction of the unemployed,
one is led to conclude that the measured unemployment rate
is likely to fall if the unemployment insurance system were
more completely experience-rated.

However, relevant though they may be for other groups of
the population, these arguments concerning the system of
unemployment insurance are unlikely to contribute much
towards an explanation for the falling employment rates of
black teenagers. For these teenagers do not possess the
characteristics that would cause them to enjoy a high ratio of
unemployment benefits to net wages; in many cases, in fact,
teenagers will not have accumulated the required amount of
time on the job or will not have earned sufficient income to
make them eligible for the receipt of unemployment compensation. Moreover, the arguments with respect to the
unemployment insurance system's method of taxation increasing temporary layoffs are clearly more relevant to the
older population than to teenagers who are more likely to be
permanently laid off. In short, if it is an explanation for the
falling employment rates of black youths that we seek, then

the unemployment insurance system is not likely to provide much in the way of an explanation.

Minimum Wage Legislation

A more likely candidate as an explanation for the rising unemployment rates and falling employment rates of black youths is the extension of the coverage of federal minimum wage legislation. Because the minimum wage increases the cost to an employer of hiring relatively unskilled labor, such legislation is often purported to be the cause of the high teenage unemployment rates. Unfortuntely, the reasoning often provided to link the minimum wage to unemployment is poorly articulated; furthermore, the empirical evidence is by no means convincing. If individuals who cannot find employment because of the minimum wage floor leave the labor force, then they will not be counted as unemployed and it becomes pointless to look for an association between the minimum wage rate and unemployment. Until the 1970s, moreover, the statutory coverage of the minimum wage law left a sizable fraction of the labor force exempt so that, in principle, individuals could find low-paying jobs in the un-covered sector.

A more subtle argument is that, although the existence of a sector of the economy exempt from statutory minimum wage legislation implies that jobs are available for low-wage labor, identifying and locating these jobs takes time, so that the duration of unemployment is probably lengthened as a result. However, as is evident from Table 5, by the 1970s only a small fraction of nonsupervisory employees worked in jobs not covered by federal minimum wage legislation. But then the effective coverage of the law is the same as its statutory definition: penalties imposed on firms for violating the law are minor and few resources are allocated to enforcing compliance, so that one would expect a number of firms to be successfully evading the provisions of the law. Be that as it may, it is difficult to avoid the conclusion that the federal minimum wage reduces the employment rates of teenagers despite the absence of rigorous supporting evidence.

It should be pointed out that the existence of the federal minimum wage is likely to increase not only the "permanent" or "average" rate of unemployment, but also that unemployment which results from transitory movements in the economy over the business cycle. By preventing nominal wages from falling in a recession, the minimum wage obliges employers of low-skilled labor to economize on labor costs by reducing employment rather than by some mix of employment and wage reductions. Thus Kosters and Welch (1972, pp. 323–32) estimated that the federal minimum wage more than doubled the cyclical sensitivity of teenage employment.

In short, although the harmful effects of the minimum wage are sometimes exaggerated, it is very difficult to resist the conclusion that the youth employment problem would be helped somewhat by elimination of the statutory minimum wage or, as a second-best policy, by a lower minimum wage for teenagers. It is not merely a matter of promoting employment, but also of encouraging the development of those jobs with long-term prospects. Such jobs are characterized by new hires engaging in intensive on-the-job training which is financed in part in the form of a lower initial wage and then in capturing the returns to this investment in skills through a subsequent higher wage rate. A minimum wage floor prevents employees from paying for on-the-job training through a reduced initial wage rate and, by reducing the opportunities for individuals to accumulate specific job-related skills, it affects their incomes for many years ahead.

POLICY FOR THE CHRONICALLY UNEMPLOYED

Although most attention in recent discussions of unemploy-

Table 5

The Federal Basis Minimum Wage
and Aggregate Coverage,
1938–1981

	Basic Minimum		
Month and Year of Change	Amount Changed to	As % of Average (Straight-Time) Manufacturing Wage	% of Nonsupervisory Employees in Private, Nonagricultural Work
10/1938	$0.25	41.7	43.4
10/1939	0.30	49.5	47.1
10/1945	0.40	42.1	55.4
1/1950	0.75	54.0	53.4
3/1956	1.00	52.9	53.1
9/1961	1.15	51.2	62.1
9/1963	1.25	52.7	62.1
2/1967	1.40	51.5	75.3
2/1968	1.60	55.6	72.6
5/1974	2.00	47.2	83.7
1/1975	2.10	45.1	83.3
1/1976	2.30	46.0	83.0
1/1978	2.65	48.4	83.8
1/1979	2.90	49.7	83.8
1/1980	3.10	49.9	83.8
1/1981	3.35	51.9	83.8

Note: From Welch (1978, p. 3), based on data from Employment Standards Administration, U.S. Department of Labor.

Table 6

Incidence, Duration, and Costs, of Unemployment of Male Household Heads Aged 35 to 64 Years in 1976 for the Decade 1967–1976

Characteristics in 1976	Number in Survey	Incidence		Duration among Unemployed		Cost in 1976 Dollars		
		Number Unemployed	Percent Unemployed	Mean Number of Weeks	Percent of Labor Market Time Spent Unemployed	Mean Lost Earnings	Mean Lost Disposable Income	Mean Lost Income as a Percent of Expected After-Tax Income
Total	1,251	548	38.4	27.3	5.3	$7,360	$5,113	4.2
All whites	937	361	37.2	27.2	5.3	7,577	5,241	4.1
Whites aged 35-44	335	144	41.5	25.9	5.0	7,225	5,189	4.0
Whites aged 45-54	413	148	34.5	28.8	5.6	8,547	5,739	4.2
Whites aged 55-64	189	69	35.6	26.3	5.2	6,278	4,327	4.1

All blacks	314	187	53.6	28.9	5.6	5,448	3,987	4.5
Blacks aged 35-44	128	90	66.9	25.0	4.8	4,741	3,398	3.8
Blacks aged 45-54	113	61	44.7	32.5	6.2	6,417	4,870	5.3
Blacks aged 55-64	73	36	45.5	32.7	6.3	5,652	4,040	5.1
Blue-collar workers	709	428	58.5	29.8	5.9	7,606	5,170	4.5
White-collar workers	496	109	22.2	21.4	4.1	6,884	5,017	3.4
Farm workers	46	11	17.1	—	—	—	—	—
Less than high school education	545	317	53.9	34.8	6.9	8,555	5,879	5.4
High school education	361	156	42.4	22.6	4.3	6,379	4,468	3.3
More than high school education	345	75	21.6	19.6	3.7	6,514	4,603	2.9

Note: In the column "percent of labor market time spent unemployed," labor market time is defined as the sum of reported hours worked and reported hours unemployed over the ten years. "Lost earnings" is defined as the product of the average wage earned and the reported hours unemployed where the average wage is computed as the total labor income (in 1976 dollars) over the ten-year period divided by hours worked in that same period. "Lost disposable income" consists of lost earnings times one minus the average tax rate and then subtracting unemployment compensation received. In the final column, "expected after-tax income" is defined as sum of reported labor income and estimated lost earnings all multiplied by one minus the average tax rate. This table is taken from Hill and Concoran (1979, pp. 19-23).

ment has been devoted to the employment problems of
youths, unemployment is a recurring problem for other
groups in the population. This is evident from a recent in-
vestigation of the unemployment experiences of 1,251 prime-
age men (that is, those aged 35 to 64 years in 1976) who were
heads of households and labor market participants in each
year of a ten-year period from 1967 to 1976 (Hill and Corcoran 1979). In the national unemployment statistics, such
prime-age men reveal lower unemployment rates than young
people and women; yet they are important because they constitute such a large fraction of the total labor force and
because they are often the primary earners in their families,
so their unemployment imposes the greatest financial
strains on the family.

Over this decade, as shown in Table 6, 38.4 percent of
these men experienced at least one spell of unemployment,
with black workers, blue-collar workers, and less-educated
workers disproportionately represented in this group.
Unemployment was infrequent for most workers, and for
these it did not involve a large drop in income. For a smaller
group, however, unemployment was frequent and extensive,
with a marked drop in income. Thus, only 5.0 percent of the
sample accounted for almost half (46.6 percent) of all the
working hours "lost" by the entire group through unemployment over the decade. These men averaged almost two years
(ninety-six weeks) of unemployment. These chronically
unemployed men were more likely to be blue-collar or construction workers and were more likely to have no more than
a high school education. However, a considerable number of
other workers who did not have these characteristics were
also among the chronically unemployed, so we do not get very
far with an accurate profile of these unemployed by identifying them as blue-collar workers with little schooling. The
fact is that for a small group of prime-age males unemployment constitutes a recurring and serious blight in their lives,

and for them the unemployment insurance system is largely irrelevant to ameliorating their loss of incomes.

Therefore, while unemployment is an infrequent or short-lived affair for most Americans, it is a common and often financially tragic affair for a small group of people in the economy. Much popular discussion of unemployment unfortunately does not distinguish between these groups. Surely it is the situation of the chronically unemployed that deserves our special attention and, in essence, government policy has two strategies to assist these people. One strategy is through devices designed to promote patterns of stable employment for them. This is the reasoning behind government manpower training programs, but it appears as if they have not had much success in attracting the chronically unemployed; moreover, their effect in raising the earnings of trainees seems not to extend much beyond a short time after the training period.

A preferable policy would be one that actually provides employment subsidies to firms and, given the present structure of taxation on business, this could be achieved simply by reducing payroll taxes. There is evidence that tax incentives encouraging physical capital investment (such as accelerated depreciation allowances and investment tax credits) tend to benefit highly skilled workers more than low-skilled workers so that, partly to neutralize these regressive effects, various schemes have been advanced to provide subsidies to firms that *increase* their employment from some base level. Unless these employment subsidies were highly skewed towards low-wage workers, however, one suspects that the chronically unemployed would not benefit much from these policies. In short, there is good reason to question the efficacy of government policies to promote stable and continuous employment patterns of people who currently experience frequent and/or long spells of unemployment. This is a reflection of our current lack of understanding of the reasons for the recurrent unemployment of these people.

However, a second strategy for assisting chronically unemployed people is available to government. This consists simply of providing them and their families with the necessary income to meet their basic physiological requirements. Many of these people currently slip through the net provided by the unemployment insurance system; often they have not earned sufficient income while employed to render them eligible for unemployment compensation and, even if they do qualify for payments, their long spell of unemployment may well exceed the duration of their unemployment compensation. What is needed is to replace the present medley of welfare programs with a comprehensive income maintenance system that provides a guaranteed minimum income for all families, whether or not members of these families are at work in the labor market. Now there is a good deal of evidence to suggest that a long spell of unemployment also brings considerable emotional distress as well as financial hardship (see, for instance, Tiffany, Cowan, and Tiffany 1970), and a guaranteed minimum income may do little to address these very real emotional problems. Yet there seems no good reason why a wealthy society such as this cannot do better at providing at least a higher and more secure standard of living for the chronically unemployed. There is now a large number of studies that have computed the work incentive effects and that have measured the budgetary costs of such a program (for instance, Keeley et al, 1978, pp. 3–36) and, provided such a program substituted rather than augmented the present welfare system, these costs do not appear to be exhorbitant. In this event, the case for relieving the material distress of the chronically unemployed in this way seems difficult to resist.

APPENDIX

The purpose of this appendix is to report the results of a sim-

ple analysis designed to identify trends and cyclical movements in the unemployment and employment rates of
different groups in the population. Consider first the annual
movements of unemployment rates over the years from 1954
to 1977 (which is the period for which consistent data on
teenagers are available). The entries in Table 7 under the
headings "Trend" and "Cycle" are the ordinary least-squares
estimates of the α and β parameters, respectively, in the
following regression equation:

$$\Delta(U/L)_{it} = \alpha_i + \beta_i[\Delta(U/L)_t^r] + \epsilon_{it}$$

where $\Delta(U/L)_{it}$ is the year-to-year change in the employment rate of the i-th sex-age-race group and $\Delta(U/L)_t^r$ is the
year-to-year change in the unemployment rate of the
reference group, white males aged 35–44 years. The term ϵ_{it}
is a stochastic disturbance. Note that there is no measurable
trend in the reference group's unemployment rate:

$$\Delta(U/L)_t^r = -.019 \text{ or } \Delta(U/L)_t^r = -.213 + .015\, t$$
$$\quad (.185) \qquad\qquad (.413)\ (.028)$$

where the numbers in parentheses are estimated standard
errors.

The entry in Table 7 under "Trend" for white males aged
16 to 18 years means that, after accounting for cyclical
movements in unemployment, each year the unemployment
rate for this group has tended to rise by .191 points, or that
the trend in the unemployment rate for this group accounts
for a rise of 4.37 percent (that is, .191 × 23) in their
unemployment between 1954 and 1977. The entry under
"Cycle" for white males aged 16–18 years means that, after
removing the trend in their unemployment rate, an increase
of 1 percentage point in the prime-age white male unemployment rate is associated with a 1.6 percentage point increase
in the unemployment rate of white males aged 16–18 years.
(The asterisk attached to this estimate of 1.6 means that it
is, indeed, significantly different from unity, a one-for-one

Table 7

Estimated Trends and Cyclical Movements in Unemployment Rates

	White Workers			Black and Other Workers		
	Trend	Cycle	R^2	Trend	Cycle	R^2
Males aged 16-18	.191	1.600*	.63	1.148	3.177*	.41
Females aged 16-18	.300	1.483	.62	1.160	2.024*	.16
Males aged 18-20	.057	2.747*	.91	.954	2.080*	.28
Females aged 18-20	.236	1.520*	.63	.773	2.150*	.29
Males aged 20-25	.024	2.562*	.96	.281	3.174*	.78
Females aged 20-25	.148	1.190	.82	.500	2.288*	.57
Males aged 25-35	.059	1.281*	.96	.072	2.334*	.88
Females aged 25-35	.065	1.154	.85	.119	1.350	.52
Males aged 35-45	—	—	—	.087	1.944*	.87
Females aged 35-45	.034	1.007	.89	.078	1.461	.55
Males aged 45-55	−.017	.887*	.96	−.145	2.072*	.86
Females aged 45-55	.040	.907	.90	.009	.500*	.22
Males aged 55-65	−.031	.637*	.47	−.018	1.223	.42
Females aged 55-65	.009	.691*	.75	.018	.858	.45
Males aged 65+	.047	.750*	.75	.049	1.297	.26
Females aged 65+	.097	.367*	.23	−.051	1.252	.39

*Asterisk attached to cycle parameters indicates those estimates of β significantly different from unity at the 5 percent level of significance. None of the trend parameters α is significantly different from zero at the 5 percent level. The R^2 measures the fraction of the year-to-year movements in each sex-age-race group's unemployment rates accounted for by the movements in the reference group's unemployment rate.

correspondence by conventional criteria.) Examination of the results presented in Table 7 reveals that (1) among younger workers the positive trend in the unemployment rate for each group is invariably smaller for whites than for blacks and other workers although none of these trends would be judged as significantly different from zero by conventional criteria, (2) among younger workers the trend in the unemployment rate for each group tends to be larger for females than for males, and (3) the unemployment rates of younger workers and especially younger black workers are particularly sensitive to movements in business cycle conditions. None of these inferences is altered if quadratic (rather than linear) trends are fitted to the data.

Now consider an analysis of annual movements in employment-to-population ratios. The entries in Table 8 under the headings "Trend" and "Cycle" are the ordinary least-squares estimates of the γ and ∂ parameters, respectively, in the following regression equation:

$$\Delta(E/P)_{it} = \gamma_i + \partial_i[\Delta(E/P)^r_t] + \epsilon_{it}$$

where $\Delta(E/P)_{it}$ is the year-to-year change in the employment-to-population ratio of the i-th sex-age-race group and $\Delta(E/P)^r_t$ is the year-to-year change in the employment-to-population ratio of the reference group, white males aged 35–44 years. The term ϵ_{it} is a stochastic disturbance. Observe that there is no discernible trend in the reference group's employment-to-population ratio:

$$\Delta(E/P)^r_t = -.065 \text{ or } \Delta(E/P)^r_t = .195 - .020 \text{ t}$$
$$\quad\quad (.188) \quad\quad\quad\quad\quad (.419) \quad (.029)$$

where the numbers in parentheses are estimated standard errors.

The results are contained in Table 8 which correlated the de-trended movements in each sex-age-race group's employment-to-population ratio with the movements in the employment-to-population ratio of prime-age (35–45 year old) white

Table 8

Estimated Trends and Cyclical Movements in Employment-to-Population Ratios

	White Workers			Black and Other Workers		
	Trend	Cycle	R^2	Trend	Cycle	R^2
Males aged 16-18	.261	1.488	.45	− .807	1.952*	.45
Females aged 16-18	.587*	1.220	.43	− .295	.362	.04
Males aged 18-20	.327	2.478*	.82	−1.165*	1.873	.35
Females aged 18-20	.376	1.064	.39	− .001	1.222	.14
Males aged 20-25	.186	2.313*	.82	− .423	3.216*	.73
Females aged 20-25	.898*	.560	.20	.184	1.348	.28
Males aged 25-35	− .006	1.342*	.93	− .100	2.187*	.81
Females aged 25-35	1.060*	.398	.13	.648*	.933	.41
Males aged 35-45	—	—	—	.027	1.866*	.81
Females aged 35-45	.833*	.531*	.37	.245	.376	.11
Males aged 45-55	− .112*	.799*	.90	− .138	1.983*	.75
Females aged 45-55	.669*	.566*	.36	.219	.043	.01
Males aged 55-65	− .538*	.480*	.20	− .558	.781	.14
Females aged 55-65	.518*	.464*	.22	.133	1.168	.17
Males aged 65+	− .830*	.319*	.12	− .856*	.422	.06
Females aged 65+	− .049	.114*	.05	− .084	.029*	.01

*Asterisk attached to trend parameters identified estimates of γ significantly different from zero; asterisk attached to cycle parameters indicates those estimates of ∂ significantly different from unity. The criterion here is the 5 percent significance level applying a standard t-test. The R^2 measures the fraction of the year-to-year movements in each sex-age-race group's employment-to-population ratio accounted for by the movements in the reference group's employment-to-population ratio.

males over the period from 1954 to 1977. Again to illustrate with white males aged 16–18 years, the entry under "Trend" means that, after accounting for cyclical movements in employment, each year the employment ratio for this group accounts for a rise of 6.0 percent (that is, .261 × 23) in their employment-to-population ratio between 1954 and 1977. The entry under "Cycle" for white males 'aged 16–18 years means that, after removing the trend in their employment-to-population ratio, a decrease of 1 percentage point in the prime-age white male employment ratio is associated with a 1.49 percentage point decrease in the employment ratio of white males aged 16–18 years. In other words, the fact that the estimates under the heading "Cycle" tend to exceed unity for young workers confirms the results with respect to the unemployment rate in Table 7, namely, that the employment experiences of young people (and of males in particular) tend to be especially sensitive to the state of the business cycle. As far as the estimates concerning trends in employment, it is evident from Table 8 that white women have displayed strongly rising trends while young black males and older men of all races have shown markedly falling trends in their employment-to-population ratios. As with the analysis of unemployment rates, adding a trend term to the above regression equation (that is, permitting a quadratic time trend in measuring employment rates) leaves the basic inferences from Table 8 unaltered.

IV

Regulation

5

DAVID J. TEECE[1]

The New Social Regulation: Implications and Alternatives

Federal v. state control of social programs. The price of social investment. Impact on technological innovation. The strength of the marketplace. The environment. Occupational safety and health. Cost-benefit analyses of regulation. Regulatory reform.

Social regulation is a recently popularized term employed to represent the set of regulatory programs directed at various social goals such as improved health, safety, and the environmental conditions. While this genre of regulation is by no means new—a Federal Food and Drug Act was passed in 1906—its intensity increased markedly in the 1960s and 1970s, especially at the federal level. Hence, the term "new social regulation." The new social regulation is quite different from the more familiar or "older" regulation which focuses on various economic targets such as prices, returns, and entry conditions for particular industries.

The accomplishments of the new social regulation during the past decade have been discouragingly modest, while the costs appear to have been high. In certain areas social deregulation may be appropriate, but in general what is needed are more efficient and more effective regulatory approaches. This can be accomplished by harnessing rather than subjugating private interests. When markets do not work well, one approach is to adjust the incentives facing consumers and producers so that producer and consumer behavior is consonant with important social goals. Regulatory strategies employing incentives and related measures have either been ignored or too readily dismissed in the past. Instead, there has been an overwhelming reliance on "command-and-control" type regulations. Alternative approaches warrant serious consideration by the Congress and the regulatory agencies.

This paper is a short introduction and analysis of the implications and alternatives to social regulation. The terrain occupied by social regulation is so immense that the treatment here must of necessity be modest and selective. The objective is to put the issues in perspective and to suggest the efficacy of alternative approaches. While environmental and health and safety regulation are given a more extended treatment than the many other areas of social regulation, the emphasis is for illustrative purposes only.

The current malaise of the American economy is cause for considerable alarm. Social regulation has been a contributing factor. The objectives of this chapter will have been substantially fulfilled if readers can comprehend that much social regulation has been noble in spirit but wrong-headed in application. Fortunately, there are often better ways of confronting social problems. The 1980s can accordingly be a decade of considerable economic and social accomplishment if the political system can accommodate these alternative regulatory approaches.

THE NEW REGULATION AND THE OLD

Since the late 1960s there has been a marked increase in federal regulation of the U.S. economy, its objective to promote such social goals as assuring the safety and performance of consumer products, protecting the environment, and assuring worker health and safety. While state and local governments have been administering social regulation programs—occupational licensing, business and trade practices, restaurant sanitation, housing conditions—for decades, a distinctive feature of the new social regulation is its sponsorship by the federal government. A multiplicity of new federal agencies has been established to help fulfill this promise, including the Environmental Protection Agency (EPA) in 1970, the Occupational Safety and Health Administration (OSHA) in 1971, and the Consumer Product Safety Commission (CPSC) in 1972. Between 1970 and 1977 the number of major federal social regulatory agencies rose from twelve to seventeen, total budgeted expenditures increased fivefold, and the number of pages printed annually in the *Federal Register* more than tripled (Miller and Yandle 1979, p.1).

Whereas the "old" regulation has focused on prices, entry, and the service quality of specific firms and industries (e.g., airlines, natural gas, trucking, broadcasting, telecommunications), the "new social regulation" is not industry specific and involves a much deeper penetration of the federal government into the nation's institutions and economic activity. The older regulatory agencies—such as the Interstate Commerce Commission (ICC), the Civil Aeronautics Board (CAB), and the Federal Communications Commission (FCC)—were organized on an industry basis and were mandated to protect as well as to regulate industry. Indeed, it is often alleged that these agencies were "captured" by the firms they were supposed to regulate. The new regulatory agencies, however, have no specific mandate to promote the industries they regulate or to assure their continued existence. The new agencies have been deliberately organized along functional lines; their jurisdictions therefore cut across industry boundaries, each agency being interested in only specialized segments of a firm's operation. For instance, the EPA deals with pollution problems common to all industries, and OSHA's regulations similarly know no industry boundaries. This feature makes it more difficult for these agencies to be co-opted by the firms they regulate.

Another hallmark of the new social regulation is its reliance on an enforcement approach involving standard setting, the mobilization of a force of inspectors, and the imposition of penalties for violation. For example, the new regulation dictates the contents of labels attached to consumer products, prescribes in minute detail a multitude of work practices, mandates specific processes for the treatment of industrial wastes, and establishes uniform designs for products as simple as book matches or as complex as automobiles.

Paradoxically, the new social regulation addresses problems which are very old. Environmental degradation, workplace injuries, and unsafe products have been present since the industrial revolution and before. What is new is the priority which these problems now command. An important reason for the new emphasis is that rising income levels have freed society from concern over basic necessities, permitting greater attention to the quality of life. The United States has been, until very recently, enjoying a period of unprecedented prosperity and economic growth. The engine of capitalism, which economists as diverse as Marx, Schumpeter, and Friedman have so eloquently extolled, has been producing goods and services in incredible quantities and thrusting prosperity upon its participants. Reform in the environmental and social area has accordingly appeared both affordable and desirable. Few could disagree, and both the Johnson and Nixon administrations witnessed a number of successful legislative initiatives. But while Congress had a clear notion of what it wanted in the abstract (such as a cleaner environment, improved health, safer products and workplace environments), it was not so clear on the specifics and had little idea of how to get from here to there. Furthermore, much of the legislation enacted fashioned extremely blunt instruments to repair the identified problems. The results have been disappointing.

REGULATORY COSTS AND BENEFITS

Costs

Because of the many subtle impacts on society and the economy—such as the impact on technological innovation and entrepreneurship—only an omniscient being could accurately document all of the costs of the new social regulation. The only estimates generated have focused just on static economic costs; although they differ markedly, they have one feature in common—they are almost all extremely large.

Perhaps the most widely cited estimate of regulatory cost is that constructed by the Center for the Study of American Business at Washington University in St. Louis.[2] According

Table 1

Estimated Cost of Federal Regulation of Business
(fiscal years; in billions of dollars)

	1976	1977	1978	1979
Administrative costs	$ 3.2	$ 3.7	$ 4.5	$ 4.8
Compliance costs	62.9	75.4	92.2	97.9
Total	$66.1	$79.1	$96.7	$102.7

Source: Center for the Study of American Business.

to these estimates (see Table 1), each dollar that Congress appropriates for regulation imposes an additional $20 of costs on the private sector. Total regulatory costs in 1979 are estimated at $102.7 billion. This figure was approximately 2.5 times the rate of real net investment in private plant and equipment in the United States in the same year.[3] It translates into per capita costs of approximately $500.

Edward Denison (1979) has estimated that compliance with environmental constraints introduced since 1967 diverted nearly 1 percent of 1975 nonresidential business resources away from final output, with another 0.42 percent diverted by regulations to improve worker health and safety. Denison estimates that by 1975 this reduction was equivalent to knocking half of 1 percentage point off the economy's annual growth rate—which, in turn, represents fully a 25 percent reduction in the economy's long-term rate of improvement in output per unit of input. Moreover, Denison reports that the share of resources being diverted has been steadily rising.

Regulation has undoubtedly contributed to the slower rate of productivity growth documented in Table 2.[4] Table 3 sum-

Table 2

Growth in U.S. Labor Productivity, 1948–1979[a]

	1948/ 1955	1955/ 1965	1965/ 1973	1973/ 1978	1978 IV/ 1979 IV & I
Private business sector	2.5	2.4	1.6	0.8	−2.0
Nonfarm	2.4	2.5	1.6	0.9	−2.2
Manufacturing	3.2	2.8	2.4	1.5	(b)
Nonmanufacturing	2.1	2.2	1.2	0.5	(c)

Source: *Economic Report of the President 1980*, p. 85.

[a]Data relate to the annual percentage change in output per hour for all employees.

[b]Preliminary.

[c]Not available.

marizes other studies which have attempted to estimate regulatory costs for particular industries. The level of methodological and statistical sophistication varies widely, but all cost estimates are substantial.

Benefits

Whatever the costs, it is not possible to assess whether they are warranted without measuring benefits—which is an even more difficult task, both methodologically and statistically. It is true that the gross national product (GNP) accounts often do not capture the benefits from environmental improvement; in fact, they may do just the opposite. As Mancur Olsen (1969) has pointed out, "when a smoke-spewing factory is constructed near a residential area, the expenditures on that factory add to the national income, but so do the expenses of additional housepainting and cleaning forced on the nearby householders by soot from the factory." Accordingly, it is not necessary that the benefits of environmental cleanup be unambiguously reflected in the GNP.

Table 3

Impact of Multiple Regulations on a Specific Group or Industry

Source	Group or Industry	Year
Arthur D. Little, Inc., *Economic Impact of Environmental Regulations on the U.S. Copper Industry*	Copper Industry	1978–1987 and 1974–1987
Russell G. Thompson, James A. Calloway and Lillicen A. Nawalanic, *The Cost of Electricity: Cheap Power vs. a Clean Environment*	Electrical utilities	1975–1985
Joan Norris Booth, *Cleaning Up: The Cost of Refinery Pollution Control*	Petroleum refinery industry	1973–1974
Temple, Barker, and Sloan, Inc., *Economic and Financial Impacts of Federal Air and Water Pollution Controls on the Electric Utility Industry: Executive Summary* (EPA)	Petroleum industry	Base year 1985
URS Research Company, *The Economic Impacts on the American Paper Industry of Pollution Control Costs*	Paper industry	1969–1974
Arthur D. Little, Inc. *Steel and the Environment: A Cost Impact Analysis: Report to the American Iron and Steel Institute*	Steel industry	1978–1985

Regulations Included	Total Costs
Clean Air Act as amended (1979 and 1977); Federal Water Pollution Control Act as amended (1972)	1974–1987: $2,771.9/$2,987.3 million (1974 dollars); 1978–1987: $1,861.9/$2,067.7 million (1974 dollars)
Air and water pollution	Investment (1973 dollars): $40.09/$68.25 billion (range due to five sets of assumptions regarding pollution control levels)
Air and water pollution	Investment (1974 dollars): $3,350 million; added product costs (1974 dollars): $5,042/$6,408 million
Control of air, water, and noise pollution	$10.3/$17 billion (1974 dollars)
Air and water pollution	$1.2 billion for pollution abatement project
Environmental control	Zero growth: $4.9 billion; 2 percent growth: $8.0 billion (1978 dollars)

While it is inevitable that the price system will fail to some extent in measuring the benefits derived from social investment, the price system does have an important role in estimating benefits. Kenneth Arrow (1965) has remarked that "there really is no benefit calculation possible that is not based on a set of at least hypothetical prices." This is because, without market prices, it is necessary to impute values or shadow prices to the benefits and, lacking a market to reveal them, shadow prices are extremely difficult to measure. Though the problem will sometimes yield to sophisticated analysis, comprehensive application of these techniques would not be feasible except at an inordinate cost. It is not, therefore, surprising that no one has attempted to quantify the benefits of social regulation for the economy as a whole. However, one economist has concluded that the United States has obtained "little if anything in return" for the enormous costs of regulation (MacAvoy 1979, p. 127).

Barring comprehensive assessment, one can examine individual regulations or sets of regulations and evaluate their impacts. Unfortunately, the findings are not especially encouraging. While there are indications of benefits in some areas—air quality may be one—in others there are indications that regulation has had a neutral or even negative impact as, for example, in occupational safety. If costs are large and benefits are problematic, the desirability of regulation into present form must seriously be questioned.

Implications for Technological Innovation

If social regulation were purely a matter of resource costs and static inefficiencies, there would be limited cause for concern. The American economy represents the most productive assemblage of men and machines that civilization has ever created, and allocating several hundred billions of dollars of output to social investment is affordable—though unfortunate if the costs exceed the benefits. If productivity grows at a modest pace, in several years that increased output could cover the cost of social programs. To quote Scherer (1980, p. 407):

An output handicap amounting to 10 percent of GNP owing to static inefficiency is surmounted in just 5 years if the output growth rate can be raised through more rapid technical progress from 3 to 5 percent per annum, or in 20 years if the growth rate can be increased from 3 to 3.5 percent.

The price of social investment can be readily absorbed so long as the economy yields improvements in per capita income. However, if regulation has a deleterious impact on innovation, then a danger exists that the social fabric will be torn as groups and individuals clamor for a larger portion of a stagnant national output. There is also a danger that political support for the market system may be mistakenly destroyed. A related danger concerns the shift in decision-making from private institutions (business firms, nonprofit hospitals and universities, etc.) to the federal government. The upshot here may be the destruction of the administrative efficiency and adaptive flexibility of the economy. While these contentions are speculative, they are consistent with much evidence that the rate of innovation and productivity improvement (Table 2) in the American economy is falling.

Consider, then, the impact of social regulation on technological innovation. Social regulation is likely to alter the pace and direction of technological advance in unpredictable ways, some of which may be beneficial. For instance, in the context of environmental regulation Kneese and Schultz (1975) argue that

Over the long haul, perhaps the most important single criterion on which to judge environmental policies is the extent to which they spur new technology toward the efficient conservation of environmental quality.

Unfortunately, there have been very few theoretical or empirical studies of the relationship between social regulation and innovation. The analysis here is therefore rather speculative. Discussion is facilitated, however, if a distinction is made between "private," "social," and "public" innovation. Private innovations are defined here as the class of innovations which are privately profitable but socially undesirable because of negative externalities. A pesticide which wreaks environmental havoc but yields profit to farmer and manufacturer is a good example. Social innovations are both privately and socially profitable, and they include many innovations yielded by unassisted market processes. An example is a new engine lubricant which generates large profits to both innovator and user and doesn't generate pollution in its production and use. One of the few studies of private and social return to innovation showed that for a small sample of privately funded innovations the social returns were typically much greater than the private returns (Mansfield et al. 1977).[5]

However, sometimes an innovation might yield positive social returns but zero profits for the innovator. For obvious reasons, private markets do not generally provide such innovations. To the extent that the absence of incentives can be traded to the "public good" [6] characteristics of the innovation, this class of innovation can be referred to as public innovations. A new, completely nonpolluting, automobile engine might fall into this category if more polluting engines met emissions standards and had similar performance characteristics but were cheaper to produce.

Figure 1 summarizes the definitions which have been developed. Note that since the market will support both social and private innovations—although it will underprovide the former—both classes can be considered market innovations. Unassisted markets, however, will not provide innovations falling into quadrants three and four. In any case, innovations in quadrant four would be socially undesirable.

Regulation is beneficial to the extent it suppresses private innovations and promotes both social and public innovations. Unfortunately, it may be that regulation is suppressing social innovation. While as an empirical matter this is difficult to verify, several factors suggest this may be the case. To the extent that compliance costs are higher for new products and processes than for existing products and processes, then regulation will bias production in favor of the older technologies. Regulation may cause delay in ascertaining and meeting regulatory requirements. This postpones and therefore reduces the return from investment in inventive activities. Regulation may also create uncertainty with respect to anticipated returns from investment in research and development (R&D), sometimes eliminating returns altogether by the unexpected imposition of debilitating constraints.

Regulatory decisions are typically more capricious and unpredictable than the marketplace. Furthermore, sanctions are typically applied after development and commercialization costs have been incurred. This kind of uncertainty translates into lower returns. Regulation may also politicize the research process. If scientists are dragged into advocacy proceedings, the dispassionate character of successful research may be jeopardized. Regulation may also divert research funds into sterile compliance activities. While the terminology may be a little misleading, regulation may channel resources from "productive" R&D to "defensive" R&D. For instance, if the safety and performance of the firm's product are at issue, then extensive testing and research may be needed to support corporate advertising claims, to display adherence to government standards, or to persuade regulatory agencies to accept one set of standards rather than another. These activities typically add to the cost of R&D associated with introducing new products. Whether

Figure 1

Classification of Innovations Based on
Internal Rates of Return*

		Social returns	
		(+)	(—)
Private returns	(+)	1 "Social"	2 "Private"
	(—)	3 "Public"	4 ϕ**

* The internal private (social) return is the discount rate that makes the present value of the net private (social) benefits equal to zero. In other words, it is the discount rate r that results in the following equality:

$$B(t) \;+\; \frac{B(t+1)}{1+r} \quad \frac{B(t+2)}{(1+r)^2} \;+\; \cdots \;+\; \frac{B(t+n)}{(1+r)^n} \;=\; 0$$

where $B(t)$ is the net private (social) benefit in year t, t is the first year in which the net benefit is nonzero, and $(t+n)$ is the last year in which the net benefit is nonzero.

** ϕ signifies an empty quadrant.

there is a net gain or a net loss to societal welfare will depend on the value of the information thereby generated and the opportunity cost of providing it.

These considerations highlight the need for new approaches to regulation. What is needed is a tilt in regulatory practices to permit firms maximum technological flexibility in meeting regulatory objectives. Regulations must also avoid placing disproportionate compliance costs on new and existing products and processes, and regulatory decision-making needs to minimize associated uncertainties.

The impact of regulation on private innovations is of interest since these new products and processes are ostensibly the culprits in the degradation of human life addressed by social regulation. The regulatory strategy adopted across a wide range of industries involves eliminating or banning continued sale in the market of chemicals, drugs, and other undesirable products that fail to meet screening criteria. The difficulty with this approach is that the regulators may not be able to discriminate adequately between private innovations and social and public innovations. Some socially desirable innovations may be suppressed, while undesirable innovations may be licensed.

With respect to public innovations, the approaches adopted in the United States have been extremely blunt. Rather than providing incentives to encourage their production, there has been a proclivity to engage in "technology forcing" strategies. For automobile emissions and safety, for instance, Congress and the regulatory agencies have imposed essentially arbitrary timetables for achievement of specified performance improvements beyond that achieved for existing vehicles. While effective in forcing rapid commercialization and diffusion of essentially state-of-the-art technology, these policies have done very little to facilitate fundamental innovation in engine technology and automobile design.

Regulation also affects innovation in the way that it deflects the attention of managers from market to regulatory considerations. What happens in Washington often has more impact on the firms' profits than what happens in the market. Regulations on microwave ovens, for example, may favor one producer's product over another since it is never entirely clear exactly how strict the regulations will be and what dimensions of safety they will stress. Whatever standards are selected will impact a firm's marketplace position. It is conceivable, for instance, that a firm in anticipation of safety regulation might engineer "too much" safety relative to the selected standards and the market. It would then be disadvantaged in having a very safe yet high-cost product. The point here is not that standards are always undesirable, but that regulatory decisions of federal agencies are typically more capricious than those of the consumer. Consumer choices rarely dichotomize the market into acceptable and unacceptable products. In the new regulatory environment, firms able to predict regulatory decisions therefore have a competitive advantage. To the extent this detracts from the ability to respond quickly to changing consumer tastes and requirements, regulation may obstruct the responsiveness of the economic system to consumer tastes—thereby eroding an important attribute of a market economy.

The pervasiveness of regulation is now legend. Line-of-business decisions, product development decisions, plant location decisions, marketing and pricing decisions are influenced enormously by federal regulations. Accordingly, it is reasonable to posit that in some industries the most successful business graduates from Stanford, Harvard, Wharton, and Chicago will be those who can outsmart the regulators. A second degree in law rather than in engineering is likely to provide the best preparation for today's business milieu. The implications for productivity growth and income distribution are not encouraging. An improved regulatory regime is clearly needed.

Towards an Incentive Approach to Regulation

As public awareness that social regulations have significant costs and sometimes unintended indirect effects on the economy increases, pressure to eliminate or modify regulation is likely to mount. Alternatives are needed to the command and control approach which uses detailed regulations to specify permissible behavior. The political appeal of this type of regulation is understandable. Open and visible regulations offer important political advantages to major political interest groups. Two major classes of adverse consequences result, however, when the government attempts to mandate private behavior. First, the outcomes are likely to be inefficient in the sense that goals are unlikely to be achieved in the least-cost fashion. Second, individual freedom of action is restricted, carrying with it the possible challenge to other liberties. Fortunately, these adverse consequences can be relieved in many important circumstances if the government employs incentives that attempt to influence individual actions rather than directives which specify them.

The principle behind government incentives mechanisms is as follows. Certain classes of private actions convey social benefits or impose social costs. Individuals and firms, in the processes of self-interest seeking, do not take account of these ramifications. In short, these are externalities.[7] An incentive to correct such a situation takes the form of a payment to an individual if he creates a positive externality or a charge imposed if a detrimental externality is generated.

While the principle is straightforward, application of the approach requires creative financial engineering. The gross simplicity of "thou shalt not" dicta associated with command and control type regulation is absent. But the incentives approach has appeal on grounds of both efficacy and efficiency. It is elaborated below in the context of environmental and occupational safety regulation. The treatment is illustrative of the direction in which regulatory reform might proceed.

ENVIRONMENTAL REGULATION

Benefits

The United States has now experienced over a decade of fairly severe and costly environmental regulation which began with the signing on 1 January 1970 of the National Environmental Policy Act. The first Earth Day in April 1970 displayed the nation's environmental awareness. Congress and the executive branch have passed more than two dozen additional pieces of environmental legislation since then. The Council on Environmental Quality (1979) identified the following consequences for air and water quality:

1. Overall, the nation's air quality is improving. Combined data from 25 major metropolitan areas show that the number of unhealthy days declined by 15% between 1974 and 1977, while the number of very unhealthy days declined 32% (p. ix).

2. The available evidence, based on analysis of USGS [U.S. Geological Survey] data, suggests that water quality in the United States, while not showing vast improvements since the early 70's, is at least not getting worse (p. x).

These are modest claims, but the measurement problem is difficult. Environmental quality can be measured along many dimensions and, lacking a meaningful index of quality, statements about its changes are likely to be hazardous. An examination of available evidence led Baumol and Oates (1979, p. 9) to conclude that trends in environmental deterioration are varied and uneven. Environmental programs, for example, have apparently produced improvements in the purity of some of the Great Lakes. Air quality has improved in a number of major U.S. cities; the sulfur dioxide content in the atmosphere has declined in New York, Chicago, Boston, and St. Louis, and air quality has also improved in the San Francisco Bay Area. It is by no means clear, however, what credit if any should be attributed to regulation. For instance, the substitution of oil and natural gas for coal, first in home heating and later in industrial and electric power generation, undoubtedly was a contributing factor. And while particulates in the air over New York have declined markedly in recent years, they have increased over Denver.

It is hard to avoid the conclusion that the improvements caused by regulation have been both disappointing and far below expectations. Since tremendous costs have been incurred in order to improve environmental quality, it behooves all concerned about environmental quality to examine regulatory procedures for suggestions on how to achieve greater cost effectiveness.

Existing Regulatory Approaches to Environmental Policy

The basic policy strategy adopted in the United States to improve the environment has been a miscellany of direct control programs mandating reduction in air and water pollution. At the federal, state, and local levels, environmental officials have sought to control the behavior of pollutants by issuing individual permits for waste discharge and by specifying detailed standards for the construction and operation of industrial plants and for household heating and waste disposal systems. Similarly, to combat the environmental side effects of the automobile, policymakers have relied primarily upon setting emission standards for new models. To enforce these standards, environmental agencies invoke penalties and often turn to the courts for validation of their decisions. The EPA has thus been attempting, through a system of permits and other specified instructions concerning treatment procedures, to regulate the activities of each polluter in the economy directly.

Both theory and practice strongly suggest that this is the wrong course. The existing strategy involves administrative complexity and economic inefficiency; it is inefficient because pollution abatement is not being achieved at minimum cost. A serious commitment to reducing pollution will be signaled only when the current rigid commitments to direct control are abandoned in favor of reliance on incentives. Direct controls, involving agency specifications or mandatory processes or equipment or agency regulation limiting the permissible level of discharge, tend to be rigid and inflexible. With direct controls, efficient standards require more information than a regulatory agency can typically acquire. The pricing approach is an attractive alternative.

The Pricing Approach:
Taxes, Subsidies, and Permits

The basis of the pollution problem is that production and consumption processes discharge wastes and that some environmental resources are not priced and therefore are available to individuals and firms free to charge. One regulatory response is to charge a price for these resources (or equivalently, a tax on effluents) which reflect their social cost. The tax will provide a direct and clear signal that the resource is scarce and should be conserved. This tax is deliberately designed to encourage the use of its glaring loophole—the polluter can reduce taxes by decreasing emissions. As firms and individuals respond to the tax, the environmental abuse will be corrected.

The tax approach is likely to be more efficient than direct controls since those firms which can reduce pollution cheaply will have the incentive to take advantage of the potential for savings. The tax approach, therefore, assigns the abatement problem to those firms which can do it most efficiently. If there are differences in abatement costs amongst firms, it is clearly inefficient to use mandatory controls requiring that all firms within a broad class reduce pollution by an equivalent amount. Furthermore, direct controls rely on the enforcement machinery of the criminal justice system. If a firm violates the rules, the violation must first be discovered and then documented. A court case must then be brought. Only a successful case will result in a penalty, and the penalty must be large enough to deter future noncompliance. The process is cumbersome and unpredictable. In contrast, taxes are automatic and certain.

The pricing approach also encourages innovation. Polluters can choose amongst existing pollution control technologies (rather than adopting the mandated technology), and they are free to investigate the feasibility of redesign of the polluting process (or product) to reduce pollution in innovative ways. In contrast, direct controls provide no such incentives; they may actually encourage producers to suppress less/polluting—though more/costly—technologies for fear that the regulatory agency might impose the more/costly (though cleaner) technology. In short, the pricing approach permits each polluter to use the least-cost method of compliance. This minimizes not only interferences with private decisions, but also the informational demands on the regulatory agency—demands which are likely to be extremely high if the direct control approach is to function efficiently.[8]

One reason why pricing has been spurned is that standards superficially appear to be more equitable. Somehow it is supposed to be fair if each polluter cuts back by the same percentage, with each appearing to shoulder the burden equally. But there is no equality if cutting back equally involves different costs to different polluters. Another criticism of pricing is that it is a license to pollute—which some see as immoral. However, the standards approach also gives a license to pollute in permitting pollution amounts below the standards. Since total pollution permitted may be the same, there is no moral difference between the two basic approaches.

Perhaps the chief difficulty of pricing, a difficulty which is shared with some forms of direct control, is that to levy taxes or fees the enforcement agency must monitor and measure discharges—which may not be a simple, accurate, or costless matter. However, except where emissions are minor, measurement problems are often tractable.

Besides effluent taxes, the pricing approach encompasses subsidies and the auctioning of pollution permits. Subsidies to induce cutbacks in emissions are essentially alternatives to effluent fees. Whereas with an effluent fee a polluting firm must pay $X per unit of effluent discharge, with a subsidy the environmental authority pays $X for each per unit reduction in effluent—in which case the firm which continues to pollute foregoes a subsidy. While the short-run effects on pollution may not be very different, it is possible that subsidies may keep alive a polluting enterprise and may in fact attract new entry—leaving total industry emissions unchanged or even increased. Subsidies are also faulted on other grounds because the environmental authority must determine as a point of reference some hypothetical "normal" level of emissions for each polluter. The incentives for opportunistic behavior on the part of the polluter are clearly apparent. Effluent charges avoid these problems since they discourage rather than encourage the flow of resources into polluting industries by making them less rather than more profitable; in addition, there is no need to determine a benchmark pollution level.

Whereas unit subsidies have some virtues in common with effluent fees, it goes without saying that lump sum subsidies or grants offer few redeeming features. Yet, in practice, a major component of federal environmental expenditure has been assistance for the construction of municipal waste treatment plants running into many billions of dollars. As Baumol and Oates (1979, p. 148) point out:

This type of subsidy program suffers from a number of shortcomings. First, it reduces the firm's freedom of choice in the means it uses to decrease its damage to the environment. Investment in purification equipment is not always the most effective way to combat pollution. Yet this form of subsidy makes it relatively disadvantageous financially for the firm to use any other technique. Most notably, it provides no encouragement for the firm to decrease its output of goods that generate pollution.... The biggest problem besetting this sort of subsidy is that it rewards the wrong thing. Not a demonstrated reduction in emissions, but something loosely connected with it, such as the purchase of control equipment.

The one redeeming feature of subsidies may be that they can spread costs more equitably and thereby increase the political acceptability of environmental programs.

A third method of using pricing incentives involves establishing and selling pollution permits. Rather than levying charges on pollution activities, this technique involves issuing a prescribed number of pollution permits, each authorizing the purchaser to expel a specified quantity of discharges. The environmental authority determines the aggregate level of waste emissions consistent with environmental objectives and then simply auctions off the rights to this limited quantity of emissions. The firms willing to pay for the permits would be those whose production necessitates a certain amount of pollution which is just too expensive to eliminate. Only those holding permits for pollutants (SO_2, NO_x, etc.) would be allowed to discharge them. Because pollution rights would be expensive, firms would have an incentive to search for less-polluting methods of production.

In principle, both effluent charges and the sale of pollution permits lead to the same outcome. With effluent charges, the regulatory agency raises the fee until the target level of emissions is achieved, while under the pollution permit scheme it offers for sale emission rights equal in total to the target amount. Moreover, permits have essentially all the ad-

vantages of effluent fees and they also minimize uncertainty
about the resulting emissions levels, which are determined
by the agency and do not depend upon response of polluters
to a fee. As with fees, however, the validity of the procedure
depends on the regulators' ability to identify pollution
sources and to monitor emission levels.

By way of summary, it appears that pricing will be superior
where (1) treatment costs vary greatly among polluters,
(2) effluent fees that will induce target levels of pollution can
be easily determined, (3) effluents can be easily monitored at
their source, and (4) a system can be developed to prevent
permits from being purchased for the purpose of excluding
rivals.

Experience with Price Incentives

The Congress and the regulatory agencies too often have re-
jected price incentives on many grounds, one of which is
practicality. However, there has been sufficient experimentation to demonstrate the feasibility and desirability of the
incentives approach. Ironically, much of this experience has
come from Western Europe, where the socialist democracies
have been willing to experiment with market-type solutions
to environmental problems.

The Ruhr river-basin water control management is a
classic case in point. Since before World War II the Ruhr district has had eight management authorities that have controlled the construction and operation of all waste treatment
plants, dams, and pump stations. These authorities also impose effluent charges which vary according to both the
quality and the quantity of emissions, thereby providing
direct incentives to industry to reduce waste discharges. The
results are impressive. Despite the great concentration of
population and industrial production in the area, the quality
of the water is high enough not only to sustain fish life, but
also to permit fishing and other recreational use. France has

also moved to embrace the effluent fee approach after disappointment in the 1960s with direct controls. In the 1970s river basin agencies have begun to assess and collect charges on polluters and to disburse these funds for pollution control, with impressive results (see Johnson and Brown 1976). In the United States the limited experimentation which has taken place with effluent charges—or more specifically, sewer charges to effect water quality improvement—has also been very successful.

With respect to air pollution, the evidence is more limited. A simulation study by James Griffin (1974) of sulfur emissions in the electric utility industry indicates that emissions would be extremely responsive to effluent charges. More importantly, EPA's "bubble concept" is a modest attempt to incorporate incentives in regulation of air pollution. Under this policy, EPA has encouraged states to allow increases in air pollution from one or more sources at a single plant as long as equivalent reductions in emissions are accomplished at other sources in the same plant—as if a bubble covered the entire plant from which pollution emanated at but a single point. As long as the total emissions escaping the bubble remain constant, emissions can be controlled at those points where control can be done most cheaply. The bubble concept simulates a marketplace permit system in which one source in a plant "purchases" a right to increase emissions by securing an offsetting reduction elsewhere in the plant. Among the implementation requirements is the rule that reductions in one class of pollutants cannot be "swapped" for increases in another class, especially toxic pollutants. The bubble concept is currently being applied, and preliminary findings are encouraging.

The EPA's "offset policy" represents an additional flirtation with the economic incentives approach, and it has met with considerable success. Under the Clean Air Act, new growth in geographical areas already violating the primary air quality standards appeared to be prohibited. To circumvent this problem, the EPA proposed that new plants seeking to locate in nonattainment areas, or existing sources wishing to expand, be allowed to do so provided they obtained offsetting reductions in air pollution from existing sources. This means a new plant that would be a source of SO_2 could move into an area currently violating the SO_2 ambient air quality standard if it could induce existing SO_2 sources in that area to undertake equivalent or greater reductions. Similarly, an existing plant could add new sources of pollution as long as it reduced its own pollution elsewhere or induced some other polluter to cut back. The offset policy has met with considerable success and does offer some of the advantages of a full-fledged, marketable-permit approach. As of 1 March 1979 there had been 115 transactions between institutions seeking offsets and other institutions willing to offer reductions (Council on Environmental Quality 1980, p. 680). One has to conclude, in the face of persuasive theoretical arguments and empirical evidence, that the time for a more comprehensive but careful adoption of the incentives approach has arrived.

Role for Direct Controls

While regulatory policy has placed far too much emphasis on direct controls, there is still a limited role for direct controls—in three circumstances: (a) where the metering of emissions is prohibitively costly, (b) in cases of rapidly changing environmental conditions that may threaten real catastrophe, and (c) in situations involving extremely hazardous pollutants.

The metering problem is obvious. However, it is difficult to generalize on the feasibility of monitoring effluents, for the method of measurement varies with different pollutants. Furthermore, the cost of metering can vary widely from one case to another. For example, the source of noise pollution in urban areas is very difficult to ascertain. A second role for direct controls lies in the inherent uncertainty of future environmental conditions. The damage to the environment depends not only on the quantity of the pollutant, but also on the capacity of the waters or the atmosphere which may vary from period to period. Auto emissions thus have graver consequences when there is an atmospheric inversion, and effluent discharge into a river may be more serious in a period of drought. Accordingly, if the level of permissible emissions is to vary with environmental conditions, then either a sliding scale of effluent fees must be designed or the fee must be high enough to deal with unfavorable circumstances. The latter approach is costly in terms of the abatement expenses it will engender, and the former may be cumbersome to administer and the short-run response may not be certain. Direct controls have clear advantages in such circumstances, as the most expedient course may simply be to prohibit temporarily certain polluting activities when environmental conditions begin to deteriorate.[9] Pricing solutions can best be employed as longer-run measures to bring basic pollution-abatement procedures into line with normal environmental conditions.

A third use for direct controls is in regulating emissions of particularly hazardous pollutants. Where there is reason to believe that the discharge of even small quantities of a certain substance can have very serious consequences on human health, environmental officials should be able to prohibit them altogether. In such circumstances, the risks to life may indicate that it is hazardous to rely on a polluter's response to fees.

OCCUPATIONAL SAFETY AND HEALTH REGULATION

In 1970 Congress created the Occupational Safety and Health Administration for a noble purpose—namely, to provide safer and healthier working conditions. Yet, as so often is the case, the noblest intentions were confounded by an insufficient attention to economic issues. The need for reform of OSHA's regulations, and perhaps their abolition, is compelling. Indeed, the agency has managed to alienate almost everyone. Employers find its regulations confusing and ambiguous and their connections to occupational safety and health often tenuous. The unions, disturbed that occupational disease and injury have not declined, fault the agency for not promulgating tighter standards. Members of Congress report more complaints about OSHA than about any other agency. OSHA regularly provides cartoonists with an endless source of stories about bureaucratic nonsense and well-intentional regulation gone amuck. "OSHA . . . has become a prominent symbol of misguided Federal regulation. It accomplishes little for occupational safety and health, yet imposes significant economic cost" (Nichols and Zeckhauser 1977, p. 30).

But the problems with OSHA are not unique to the agency. Some of its shortcomings are attributable to the fact that no one analyzed the problem the agency was supposed to address in terms of likely causes, cures, and costs. As a result, no alternatives to direct regulation was considered. OSHA's fetish for standards has condemned it to failure.

Origins

The reported injury rate of American workers climbed sharply in the 1960s, making it evident to many that the state safety programs, based on consultation and voluntary compliance with existing standards, were not working well. Trade unions and activists such as Ralph Nader were instrumental in the passage of the Occupational Safety and Health Act in 1970. OSHA's problems began in large measure with that act, which instructed OSHA to "establish as rapidly as possible national occupational safety and health standards."

OSHA thus spent its earliest days searching for standards, making hasty determinations as to whether the standards would increase safety in the workplace, and then editing them into regulatory language. Within six months OSHA occupied an entire volume in the *Code of Federal Regulations*. But according to the Bureau of Labor Statistics, days lost due to work-related injuries have been rising ever since OSHA started (Weidenbaum 1979).

If elementary economic analysis had preceded establishment of OSHA, sensible policies might have evolved, yielding acceptable results at modest cost. To understand the essential problem, one must begin by recognizing that workplace health and safety are determined by decisions and actions of both workers and employers. Accidents and illnesses impose economic costs on workers (lost wages, medical care costs, pain and suffering) as well as on employers (wage premiums for hazardous work, downtime caused by accidents, loss of skilled employees due to injury or death). However, injury costs to the employer can be reduced if accident prevention expenditures are incurred. The firm therefore confronts a trade-off between accident prevention costs and the disruption and other costs which accidents impose on the firm. It is in the self-interest of firms to minimize the sum of their accident prevention costs and the portion of accident costs which they bear, hence they have some incentives to provide safety. However, several factors prevent the labor market from fully achieving efficient outcomes—interpreted as the minimization of the sum of society's accident costs and accident prevention costs. A case for intervention exists to the extent that intervention can produce better outcomes.

Inefficient outcomes can be expected because of imperfect information and externalities. If workers are not well informed on occupational health and safety risks, their employment decisions may be subject to error. Unfortunately, the data relating occupational conditions to health and safety is very poor. Even if available, it is not clear that it would affect decisions in completely rational ways. Experimental and empirical evidence suggests that individuals have considerable difficulty processing information about small probabilities (Kunreuther and Slovic 1978) which are characteristic of many health and safety risks. Furthermore, health risks may be considerably more difficult for an individual to estimate than risks of an accident, since health losses may not show up for many years.

Unassisted markets will also fail to yield efficient results if externalities exist—that is, if the welfare of others is affected by the health and safety provided. But there are externalities because society cares for and compensates individuals who are sick or injured. Life insurance benefits, health care costs, and the expense of supporting a family whose wage earner is ill or deceased are borne only in small part by the workers whose health is impaired or by his employer. Government-provided insurance, including social security and welfare payments, is not experience-rated. That is, employers who impose higher costs on the insurance fund by taking inadequate precautions to alleviate unhealthy working conditions are charged nothing extra for their negligence, nor are workers who take risky jobs or those who are careless on the job. Workmen's compensation was conceived in part as a way of giving employers incentives to provide greater safety, but only the largest firms are experienced-rated and the limits on liability are far too modest. Because of these externalities, individual workers and firms are not bearing the full cost of accidents and illnesses. Accordingly, it can be expected that occupational health and safety will be underprovided. This is probably more true for health than for safety, in that the health effects of noise, dust, and toxic substances may not manifest themselves for many years—perhaps not until retirement—so that the entire cost may be shifted to the employee.

Equity considerations also need to be injected into the analysis to the extent that those exposed to the highest risks are disproportionately the poor. Indeed, the legislature history of the Occupational Safety and Health Act shows quite clearly that equity arguments were politically effective in securing federal intervention.

The Standards Approach

In writing the Occupational Safety and Health Act, Congress unfortunately selected the time-honored approach to regulation—namely, the implementation of standards. Congress chose to override market processes and force delinquent firms to adjust their behavior. Nichols and Zeckhauser (1977, p. 47) observe:

Within one month of its creation, OSHA had adopted 4400 "interim" standards from preexisting federal regulations and from voluntary codes written by organizations such as the American National Standards Institute. Virtually all these standards were safety related; adopted en masse under great pressure to do something quickly, without any kind of sensible review.

OSHA's use of standards has been widely criticized as misguided because its inevitable emphasis on capital equipment conflicts with evidence suggesting that it is the worker's own behavior rather than his environment which is the principal cause of accidents. What is known about the causes of accidents is sketchy, but "it seems clear that inexperienced workers have high accident rates. The same applies to tired workers on long or varying shifts" (Weidenbaum 1979). If this diagnosis is correct, training would appear to be the needed cornerstone of a program to reduce the risks of occupational injury. In this regard, OSHA may have made matters worse. As Weidenbaum points out:

Many companies had professional safety departments long before the Occupational Safety and Health Act was enacted in 1970. In practice, OSHA may have diverted much of the focus of these safety units from their traditional task of training workers in safer procedures—studying the regulations, filling out the forms, meeting with inspectors, responding to their charges, and so forth.

The current strategy, relying as it does on standards and their enforcement, is not working and cannot be expected to work. Because of the cognitive limits on man's ability to gather and process information, it is naive to expect that regulators sitting in Washington can possibly devise standards which will make sense for the million of disparate workplaces across the nation. OSHA is responsible, either directly or through its supervision of state programs, for the health and safety of about 60 million workers employed in roughly five million workplaces. Even if full compliance were to be achieved, large numbers of job-related accidents are still to be expected. A number of state-level studies show that most accidents on the job do not involve violating standards, which suggests that the solution will not be found in more careful fashioning of standards. Rather, the emphasis in OSHA regulation should be shifted to performance. Management ought to be given discretion with respect to how to engineer a safer and healthier work environment, and sanctions for failure to achieve these objectives must be levied against those responsible, be it employer or employee.

OSHA Reform

If standards are to be used, then performance standards need to be engineered. A performance standard, for example, would set maximum noise limits but allow each firm to achieve those levels in the least costly manner. If there is considerable firm-to-firm variation, then performance standards will be more efficient than equipment standards. Admittedly, monitoring becomes more difficult.

Tort law reform may also be needed. The legal system would certainly produce more efficient outcomes if employers' limited liability on accident compensation were to be raised or removed.[10] Workers compensation insurance also should be provided on an experience-rated basis.

Incentive mechanisms hold particular promise for occupational safety. In place of its standard-setting activities, OSHA could place a tax on employers for each injury sustained by its employees. This would involve fining employers for those violations that cause injuries—the fine increasing with the magnitude of the accident costs. This approach would enable OSHA to do away with routine inspections and standard-setting procedures. An "injury" tax would give firms generalized incentives to improve safety education and stimulate them to control the factors that contribute to accidents. The mix of safety and health related measures taken would vary according to management's knowledge and judgment of its own environment. The incentive approach holds great promise for lowering the cost of any given level of safety. Unfortunately, it is likely to be politically unpopular. Mendeloff (1980) has explained that the legislators most deeply involved in OSHA affairs derive influence from the opportunities for intervention that a standards enforcement system provides as disgruntled employers and unions seek their help; and because inspections impose costs on firms, a union threat to request an inspection carries weight and increases bargaining power with management. These features would be lost if safety standards were replaced by an injury tax (Mendeloff 1980).

Incentive approaches may not be as tractable for occupational health, basically because it is difficult to distinguish most cases of occupational illness from illness caused by other factors. Even if an illness can be identified as occupational in origin, it may be unclear which employer should be taxed if the worker has held similar jobs with different employers. Given the difficulties of establishing cause and effect, the incentive approach to health would involve levying a tax on workers' exposure—an approach analogous to effluent fees discussed above. Of course, this would also require the monitoring of exposure levels.

There may also be a role for provision of information. Laboratory experimentation, epidemiological studies, and technical and economic analysis should be conducted and the results widely distributed. Workers need to be informed on health hazards and safety risks; the government has an important role to play in this activity. This point is taken up again below.

COST-BENEFIT AND RISK-BENEFIT ANALYSES

For many regulatory issues, especially when pricing is not feasible, cost-benefit analyses of regulation are critical. Unfortunately, application of cost-benefit techniques is seldom straightforward. Its viability depends on the availability of data. It may be that firms to be regulated are the sole possessors of pertinent information and that their incentives are strong for selective or opportunistic disclosure. Furthermore, measuring benefits may be difficult if not impossible, as it is with certain toxic substances. While the task is difficult, it is often tractable, and measurement problems do not provide an excuse for ignoring the costs which may be involved.

The problem of measuring benefits often stems from difficulties determining the value of goods and services not directly traded in markets.[11] For instance, although consumers are thought to place a high value on the environment, no directly observable market prices exist to show what consumers would be willing to pay for environmental attributes. But it is possible to approach this problem indirectly. Health studies have been undertaken, for instance, which seek to assess the relationship between human health and improvements in the environment and then to place a dollar value on the improvements;[12] cost studies have also sought to judge the extra costs created by environmental problems such as the physical damage to buildings caused by air pollution (see, for example, Salmon 1970); wage rate studies have tried to evaluate wage differentials necessary to compensate labor for urban disamenities. There have also been property value studies which seek to quantify the relationship between property values and environmental amenities in order to predict changes in those values (interpreted as willingness to pay) resulting from an environmental improvement.[13]

These studies indicate that it is possible to measure benefits through the use of sophisticated analysis. Regulatory policy also is often assisted, even if upper and lower bounds on costs and benefits can be derived. Certainly the absence of benefit data does not absolve regulators from considering costs. Cost estimates, after all, give some idea of how large benefits must be before implementation of a regulation is warranted. Nor does the fact that a savings in human lives is involved vitiate the cost-benefit approach. Individuals and regulations implicitly make assumptions about these values every day and act accordingly. Lives could surely be saved, for example, if automobile speed limits were reduced from 55 to 45 miles per hour. That this is not done reflects the fact that society has implicitly determined that the costs exceed the expected benefits from reduced mortality. It is not callous to require explicit treatment of costs. Indeed, it may be callous to deny such measurements and thereby waste resources which could be used for other purposes, including activities which save lives—e.g., highway safety expenditures. Admittedly, the abuses in cost-benefit analysis are legend. It is true that cost-benefit estimates are sometimes open to manipulation. And the fact that technicians have to be employed to advise on the appropriateness of methodology and estimates compromises the role of the decision-maker.

What is referred to as risk-benefit assessment occasionally responds to some of these concerns, at least in the area of toxic substance and drug regulation. Risk assessment is a two-state analysis followed by judgment of trade-offs between health hazards and health benefits which can be expressed in terms such as a "quality adjusted life year" (Zeckhauser 1973), avoiding the need to monetize health aspects. All other economic consequences are assessed in the second stage, avoiding all attempts to aggregate stages one and two. The results from both parts are then reported to the decision-maker who considers the trade-offs and makes a decision. Accordingly, risk-benefit assessment is a decision aid which is economical in the use of data and often has appeal when cost-benefit analysis is not tractable.

OTHER APPROACHES TO REGULATORY REFORM

Information Dissemination and Disclosure

While this paper has focused on tax, subsidy, and related incentives which coalesce private and social costs, these approaches do not work well in some cases. Alternative approaches involving minimal direct regulation can often achieve improved results. For instance, where consumer or employee ignorance is part of the problem, mandatory disclosure of information (such as labeling requirements and dissemination of safety information) can alleviate the problem at low cost. The disclosure or "information" approach often has appeal when compared against the alternatives. Before embracing regulation via disclosure, however, it is important to analyze private incentives to provide accurate information.

With most commodities, consumption by one person prevents consumption by others; but this often is not so when the commodity is information. For instance, the value of information on how to use chain saws safely or how to install wood-burning stoves safely can be absorbed and utilized by many different consumers without impairing the informational value of the data. Thus, information has some characteristics of a "public good," and unassisted markets tend to underprovide commodities with public goods characteristics.

Another problem may be externalities in the production and disclosure of information — i.e., information about one product or brand by inference or innuendo gives information about other products or brands. Data showing that passengers in one make of automobile had relatively lower fatalities for particular kinds of accidents might communicate something about competing makes. In a competitive economy these kinds of characteristics will enhance both the value of information and private incentives to produce it. The existence of market failure resulting from such "spillover" phenomena is not apparent.

An important externality may emerge from standardizing information, however. The value of product quality information for comparing brands will decline if it is not standardized, and collective action by private groups such as trade associations or professional societies may be necessary to realize these economies. In the absence of a private response, mandatory standards may be justified.

A related concern is whether producers of dangerous or unsafe products have incentives to suppress information. Although consumers may be generally aware of this problem, they may not know the specific nature and significance of the concealment and therefore may be unable to distinguish "quality" differences which they could distinguish with fuller disclosure. This, in turn, can lead to overprovision of low quality or unsafe products, to the extent they are cheaper to produce. Since producers of higher quality products, however, have an incentive to advertise the superiority of their products, if producers of inferior products withhold information their silence will itself communicate something important—something implying the low quality or danger of their products. Despite this countervailing possibility, the problem may remain because of the non-routine (one-shot) nature of many transactions (and related difficulties involved in developing an experience rating on producers), because of problems associated with contract execution and enforcement, and because of fraud. Markets do not work well if fraud is hard to detect. Nonfraudulent producers have incentives to signal the truthfulness of their pronouncements and may hire auditors and provide guarantees, warrantees, etc., to back up their claims. Such measures can be expected to be effective in the long run, but temporary advantages may nevertheless go to opportunistic suppliers while reputations are being built and destroyed. Criminal law against fraud and related antisocial behavior undoubtedly discourages flagrant abuses but may be ineffectual against subtle abuse and against "fly by night" promoters. Clearly, the government has important obligations in the contract and criminal law enforcement area.

Although mandatory disclosure policies may not apply to most social problems, they are likely to be relevant to an important subset of problems, especially in the product safety area. In cases where disclosure has advantages, the government might usefully provide information itself, subsidize others to produce and disseminate it, or require firms and other organizations to supply it to their customers. Education is one form of information disclosure, and agencies like the Occupational Safety and Health Administration and the Consumer Product Safety Commission could facilitate this process for the problems within their purview. The Food and Drug Administration could also use this approach with profit where a product involves beneficial effects as well as some modest side effects. Allowing consumers a choice is consistent with notions of individual freedom and will often enhance consumer welfare. There may be limits to the amount of information one can expect consumers to comprehend, however, and so wholesale adoption of the disclosure approach might encounter diminishing returns.

CONCLUSION

The command and control approach to regulation has yielded a modest list of accomplishments with a colossal price tag. The decade of the 1980s therefore presents a tremendous opportunity to restructure the regulatory system so that more can be accomplished with less. The selective and careful introduction of marketlike instruments can proceed immediately, with one success building on another.

There is good reason to believe that this will happen. The shortcomings and costs of direct regulation are now becoming common knowledge. The 1980s can be a decade for redesigning regulation and for taking a more modest view of what government and the regulatory system can accomplish. If the lessons of the 1970s are appreciated, the 1980s can be transformed into a decade of considerable economic and social accomplishment.

DISCUSSION

ROWEN: One basic point that really needs treatment is under the heading of market failures—why it really is necessary, or certainly it has been successful, in getting the government to intervene in many of these cases. Why—with regard, for example, to many health and safety questions—why hasn't the market been able to internalize many of these problems? When one examines the private regulations that emerged during the nineteenth century on into the twentieth century, quite a lot was done. That is, organizations were set up in the private sector, for example, to check on the safety of steam boilers. The market rewarded those having safer steam boilers. That experience seems to have been brushed aside. The notion emerged that the government had to act. Maybe it does in some cases, but it is obvious that the market can do a lot more than it has done—or been permitted to do.

CHICKERING: The problem of measuring benefits of social regulation has serious distributive implications. For instance, what happens when you overcorrect for market failure and force automobile manufacturers to install more safety equipment than consumers want? Who would win and who would lose if we mandated that all cars be as safe and high quality as Audis, BMWs, and Volvos? The *poor* would be very much the losers if they were forced to buy cars desired by upper-income reformers.

On environmental laws and regulations, it is clear that different income and social classes place far higher relative value on environmental qualities than do lower-income groups. Social regulations, of course, must be established for all citizens, but it is a serious question how and to what extent the relatively high-income groups who form the leadership class in all societies (and their lobbyists) can and do represent the values and preferences of ordinary citizens— particularly those of low-income people.

OLSEN: On regulation, I am fascinated by the proposal that industry, where feasible, be permitted to transfer back to the regulatory agency the cost of a regulation. I say where feasible, because one problem with regulation, which Mike alluded to on the pollution control devices on automobiles, is the agencies treat regulation as a free good. And thus they never assign a cost-benefit test to it. Indeed, one anecdote recalls when the Council on Prices and Wages got into quite a debate with the Environmental Protection Agency because they were imposing costs on industry which simply passed them through into higher price increases without consideration of costs and benefits.

V

The International Economy

6

JOHN T. CUDDINGTON

RONALD I. McKINNON

The United States and the World Economy

Postwar growth of international economy. Reciprocal Trade Agreements Act and GATT. Protectionism v. liberalization in U.S. policy. The Kennedy Round and the Tokyo Round. The safeguards issue. Export-import banks and credit subsidies. Bretton Woods and the IMF. U.S. monetary policy today.

For more than two decades following the second world war, the international economy experienced unprecedented growth. The volume of world production, which had increased at an average annual rate of about 2 percent from

1913 to 1948, grew at an average rate of 5 percent from 1948 to 1973. During the same periods the volume of world trade increased from an average annual rate of .5 percent to a rate of approximately 7 percent, respectively (Blackhurst et al. 1977, pp. 7–8). This increasing importance of international trade, and the mutual dependence among national economies, was due to several factors.

First, the spurt of growth in world output itself tended to promote trade among nations. Rapid technological innovation, particularly in the areas of transportation and communication, facilitated greater international specialization. Access to inexpensive raw materials and energy resources also contributed to the growth of output and trade.

Second, international trade was fostered by the restoration in 1958 of currency convertibility among industrial countries. The postwar system of exchange controls by European countries and Japan was largely dismantled with the encouragement of the United States, including financial assurance under the Marshall Plan. The subsequent integration of world financial and capital markets based on the convertible currencies of Western industrial countries has been remarkable—particularly the burgeoning growth of the Eurocurrency market. By 1980 the enormous expansion of the private financial sector has, to a large extent, displaced national governments in financing trade and foreign investment. Even communist countries and less-developed countries (LDCs), whose own currencies are inconvertible, use Western monies and Western banks for international commerce. The International Monetary Fund (IMF), which was of fundamental importance in monitoring exchange-rate practices and financing balance of payments disequilibria after the war, has become correspondingly less significant. But the American dollar continues to play a key central role within a world monetary system based on the exchange of convertible currencies.

Third, in the field of commercial policy the ongoing efforts at trade liberalization among the industrial nations under the auspices of the General Agreement on Tariffs and Trade (GATT) were highly successful. Tariff and quota restrictions on industrial products were greatly reduced from the late 1940s to the early 1970s. The growth of trade in manufactures, much of it the exchange of similar products from any given industry such as automobiles, has proceeded even faster than growth in trade of war materials. In contrast, with a few notable exceptions, LDCs did not reduce their tariff and nontariff barriers. Largely due to special waivers for LDCs from various articles of the GATT, most LDCs became increasingly protectionist in the 1950s and 1960s. This prevented them from reaping the huge dividends from trade-related growth experienced by the developed nations. Despite this lapse, LDCs continued to receive most-favored-nation treatment for most manufactured and many raw material exports to noncommunist industrial countries.

The 1970s, in contrast to the 1950s and 1960s, can hardly be characterized as a period of growth or stability. Twenty-five years of sustained output growth in both developed and developing economies ended in 1973 as the major economies of the world simultaneously entered what was to be the most severe and prolonged economic downturn since the Great Depression. Trade expansion slowed but did not stop, in spite of the resurgence of protectionism in many industrial countries in the 1970s. Although strained, the essentials of the liberal world trading order were maintained in this period of slower growth in the gross national product (GNP).

Professional economists have, almost without exception, defended the need for liberal international commercial policy where nations are mutually restrained in the use of tariffs, quotas, and other trade barriers. Somewhat surprisingly, however, there has been no professional consensus regarding the need for mutual restraint and international harmonization of macroeconomic policies in general or of monetary policies in particular. National autonomy rather than international coordination has been the hallmark of both Keynesians, such as James Meade, and monetarists, such as Milton Friedman. In this chapter we take a different tack: that monetary cooperation and coordination is a necessary complement to securing a liberal world trading order free from tariffs, quotas, or other trade restrictions. Moreover, such mutual action may be necessary to restore financial stability in the United States itself as well as in other Western economies.

U.S. TRADE POLICY: LIBERALIZATION VERSUS PROTECTIONISM[1]

The folly of isolationism and protectionist trade policy became abundantly clear to American policymakers in the 1930s. Repeated attempts to increase domestic employment by restricting the inflow of foreign goods only invited retaliation by trading partners. International trade was stifled, thereby exacerbating the worldwide economic recession. By 1934 the futility of such beggar-thy-neighbor policies led the U.S. Congress to pass the Reciprocal Trade Agreements (RTA) Act under which tariff reductions of up to 50 percent could be negotiated with foreign countries on a bilateral basis. As Franklin Root (1978, p. 169) points out:

Each agreement was to contain an *unconditional most-favored-nation* clause so that all concessions made by either party to third countries would freely and automatically apply to the trade of the other party to an agreement. Thus, the United States would always receive most-favored-nation treatment of its exports from every agreement country.

Although the RTA Act represented a definite shift toward economic liberalism in U.S. commercial policy, it had little impact until after World War II. In 1947 when the General Agreement on Tariffs and Trade was established, however, it largely reflected the "free trade" philosophy of the United States. The agreement presupposed that trade relations would involve primarily market-based, free enterprise economies with minimal government regulation or interference in both international and domestic commerce.

In cases where government intervention in the international economy was deemed necessary or unavoidable, the GATT expressed a strong preference·for tariffs instead of nontariff barriers (such as quantitative restrictions, export subsidies, concessional trade financing, etc.). Melvyn Krauss (1978, pp. 35–36) puts it thus:

The GATT vision is that of an international system which consists of free enterprise market economies, based on the price system, linked to one another by unrestricted international economic exchange, whose governments seldom intervene in the private economy except when protectionist pressure becomes irresistible, in which case protection would be rendered by an instrument compatible with the workings of the market economy—namely, the nondiscriminatory tariff. The GATT vision never came to pass in its entirety. But it did have a profound effect in guiding the dismantling of the manifold controls that hampered international trade during the post–World War II period.

An important aspect of the GATT is the high degree of uniformity in commercial regulations that it has striven to attain. In contrast to the bilateral nature of trade negotiations conceived by the United States under the RTA Act in the 1930s, the negotiations under GATT were to be multilateral. Through its principle of nondiscrimination and the unconditional most-favored-nation clause, considerable progress has been made in harmonizing and unifying tariffs as well as other national controls and regulations affecting foreign trade. Such harmonization encourages more efficient allocation of the world's productive resources by minimizing differential regulation across national boundaries. Sustained output growth and general economic prosperity are thereby promoted.

Under the GATT quantitative restrictions were allowed under limited circumstances, most importantly (1) to help alleviate balance-of-payments difficulties and (2) to facilitate economic development objectives. Both of these justifications for quotas were frequently resorted to by LDCs which had elaborate restrictions on trade as part of comprehensive import substitution policies. Ultimately, such policies were far less successful in attaining rapid economic growth than the export-promotion strategies more common among developed nations.

Since the initial agreement, the periodic renewals of the U.S. Reciprocal Trade Agreements Act have reflected growing concern about possible harmful effects on domestic industries of further trade liberalization. This concern was evident in the implementation of the "peril point" provision, escape clauses, and national security arguments for limiting foreign competition.

Under the peril-point provision, the U.S. Tariff Commission [later called the International Trade Commission] was required to determine *before* negotiations the level to which the tariff rate on each product could be lowered before causing serious injury to any domestic industry. Our delegation is not allowed to offer concessions that would reduce rates below this level. (Kreinin 1979, p. 316)

Once tariff reductions had been negotiated, a domestic industry that was injured as a direct result of a previous tariff concession could apply for reversal of the concession under the "escape clause" provision of the RTA Act.

U.S. commercial policy in the 1960s and 1970s has been characterized by an intensifying conflict between increased efforts to protect U.S. industry from "ruinous" foreign competition and the desire for trade liberalization with the increased efficiency of resource allocation it bestows on the international economy. Of course, protectionist measures are inconsistent with the need to adjust to changing economic conditions emphasized by the proponents of commercial liberalism. Although the domestic industry in question may gain from government protection, the fact that domestic consumers are worse off is seldom given much heed.

The high-water mark for trade liberalization in the United States probably occurred with the passage of the Trade Expansion Act of 1962.

It was under the authority of this legislation that the United States participated in the Kennedy Round of the GATT negotiations. What finally emerged from the five years of laborious bargaining was an average reduction of 35 percent on industrial tariff rates. These reductions took effect gradually over the 1967–1972 period. (Kreinin 1979, p. 319)

The 35 percent tariff cuts achieved during the Kennedy Round far surpassed the 4 and 5 percent average tariff reductions agreed upon at the two previous GATT conferences: the Geneva conference of 1956 and the Dillon Round in 1962.

The 1962 Trade Expansion Act was notable not only for the huge tariff cuts it authorized. The way it dealt with the perpetual conflict between the economic efficiency gains of liberalized trade and the possibility of injury to domestic industry was also innovative. Although it retained the escape clause provision which could be used to shelter uncompetitive domestic industries, the act also established a program of adjustment assistance to help workers and firms adversely affected by an earlier tariff concession.

Under this program, workers made unemployed because of tariff concessions can obtain 65 percent of their weekly wage for 52 weeks plus an additional 26 weeks of pay if they enrolled in a training program. Eligible firms can obtain technical and managerial assistance to help find new market outlets or develop new products, long-term, low-interest loans, and some minor tax relief. (Kreinin 1979, p. 319)

The possibility of awarding adjustment assistance gave the U.S. International Trade Commission considerably more leeway in resolving cases where domestic industries claimed injury from foreign competition. Whereas the escape clause was necessarily protectionist, adjustment assistance encouraged trade liberalization by facilitating efficient reallocation of productive resources.

Although the provisions concerning adjustment assistance were broadened and extended in the Trade Reform Act of 1974, it is probably fair to say that in practice greater emphasis has been placed on protective tariffs or import quotas than on adjustment assistance in cases where U.S. firms have complained of injurious foreign competition. Greater use and expansion of adjustment assistance programs would be useful steps in reducing resistance to further trade liberalization.

Besides introducing adjustment assistance, the Kennedy Round also broke new ground by opening discussion on agricultural trade restrictions as well as on nontariff barriers to trade. These proved to be particularly sensitive areas for negotiation.

Since 1962 the European Economic Community (EEC) has had a complicated price support program which maintains its members' agricultural commodity prices at a uniform level, generally above those prevailing outside the community. The objective is to raise European farm income and to encourage self-sufficiency in the agriculture sector. Such a policy is hardly conducive to free trade. The EEC sees its common agricultural policy (CAP) as a unifying political force that strengthens ties within the community; hence it has been unwilling to reduce the external tariffs which ensure that the CAP is not undermined by low-cost imports.

European wishes prevailed during the Kennedy Round. Later negotiations under the Tokyo Round were also unsuccessful in securing trade concessions in agriculture. Consequently, agriculture remains one of the most troublesome omissions from the GATT. The political obstacles to significant trade liberalization in this area, due to the powerful national farm interests within the EEC as well as in the United States, are immense.

While nontariff barriers were first considered during the Kennedy Round, it was in the Tokyo Round (1973–1979) that they came to the forefront. Nontariff barriers to trade include quantitative import restrictions (quotas); overly complicated customs classification and valuation procedures; antidumping regulations; production and export subsidies; government procurement policies favoring domestically produced goods; and technical, health, and environmental regulations. These nontariff barriers have proliferated as governments have taken increasingly active, interventionist roles in both the domestic and international aspects of their economies. Governmental infringements in their respective national marketplaces, allegedly to improve upon the resource allocation and income distribution which would otherwise be dictated by the competitive market mechanism, has important implications for international trade patterns and trade policy. Governments that exert control in the marketplace are hardly likely to stand by while their influence and control is eroded by unregulated (or differentially regulated) behavior of foreign firms and consumers. The EEC's commitment to its common agricultural policy and its refusal to consider trade liberalization in the agricultural sector provide an obvious example of this conflict between growing government controls and the liberal trade ideals espoused by the GATT.

Melvyn Krauss (1978) emphasizes in his recent book on the "welfare state" and international trade that government policies can greatly alter the apparent costs of various goods produced domestically and abroad. Trade patterns based on distorted costs and prices may bear little relation to true comparative advantage. To give a recent example (*Business Week*, 25 February 1980, p. 66), synthetic fiber producers in the European Economic Community are seeking protection from U.S. firms that have grabbed 25.0 percent of both the British and Italian markets in recent months compared to 7.1 and 2.0 percent, respectively, in 1978. The Europeans claim that the United States has an unfair trade advantage due to its artificially low energy and petrochemical feedstock prices. If the Europeans are allowed under new (but untested) GATT rules to impose countervailing duties in this situation, a wide variety of U.S. goods may face import restrictions due to their "cheap energy" content. Again we see the unavoidable implications of ostensibly domestic policies—in this case, the subsidization of U.S. energy users—for international trade relations.

Unquestionably, the conduct of trade among "welfare states," as Krauss calls them, imposes obstacles for trade liberalization that are immense compared to those that faced the founders of GATT in 1947. The growing importance of centrally planned economies and regulation-ridden LDCs further complicates the task of determining the efficient allocation of world production as well as socially beneficial patterns of trade. The potential for protectionist legislation grows with the increasing complexity of national economies and the pro-interventionist tendencies of welfare capitalism. In the perhaps mistaken belief that the resource allocation and income distribution outcomes of the competitive market can be improved upon, governments are willing to consider the possible benefits of their increased involvement in the marketplace. Special interest groups quickly capitalize on the activist tendencies of legislators. The latter, of course, are anxious to associate themselves with supposedly "worthy causes," thereby increasing their own public exposure and, hopefully, political longevity. In contrast, those espousing the virtues of doing nothing, in the belief that any social damage attributable to unregulated markets is minor relative to the costs of unrestrained and pervasive government, are seldom heard.

Even as the unprecedented, liberalizing Kennedy Round negotiations were reaching completion in June 1967, protectionism began gaining new strength and respectability in the United States and abroad. Root (1978, p. 183) points out that "scores of bills were introduced in the U.S. Congress calling for the imposition of quotas on imports of steel, textiles, shoes, watches, meats, dairy products, lead, zinc, and a host of other products." The rapid deterioration in the U.S. current account in the last half of the 1960s, and particularly the growing bilateral deficits with Germany and Japan, contributed to protectionist sentiment.

The Nixon administration became particularly sympathetic to the pleas of domestic industries suffering from continually evolving competitive conditions and shifts in comparative advantage. Demands for quantitative restrictions snowballed as the House of Representatives began hearings on the Nixon trade proposals. Attempts to pacify one group with protectionist measures inevitably led to more strident claims by others convinced that their cases were equally deserving. Congress, bogged down by intense logrolling and lobbying efforts, failed to complete trade legislation in 1970. Protectionists regrouped the following year to put forth the Foreign Trade and Investment Act of 1972, the most protectionist piece of trade legislation since the debilitating Hawley-Smoot tariffs of 1934. As Root (1978, p. 184) observes, the bill, inspired by the lobbying efforts of organized labor (AFL–CIO), "was intended to bring about a fundamental reorientation of U.S. policies in international trade and investment." According to most economists, the effect of the Burke-Hartke bill (as it was commonly called) on international trade would have been devastating:

It would be difficult to imagine a more protectionist piece of legislation than that embodied in the Burke-Hartke Bill. Its application would freeze the 1965–1969 ratio of imported goods to the production of "similar" domestic goods for the indefinite future. Moreover, it would freeze the geographical pattern of each import goods category. The adoption of such legislation would reverse nearly 40 years of liberal trade policies; and by provoking massive retaliation by the EEC, Japan, and other countries, it would probably fragment the world economy into mutually hostile trade blocs. It would signal a withdrawal of the United States into economic isolationism with manifold political as well as economic consequences. (Root 1978, p. 185)

In addition to the *trade* restrictions of the Burke-Hartke bill, it also proposed restrictions on direct foreign investment and international technology transfer by U.S.-based multinational corporations—supposedly to prevent the export of American jobs. Although empirical research inspired by the bill indicates that restricting foreign investment by U.S. firms would *not* increase U.S. employment and indeed might decrease it (as discussed in Root [1978, pp. 547−49]), it would undoubtedly help to preserve union bargaining power by preventing disgruntled multinationals from relocating their production facilities overseas. In any event, the Burke-Hartke bill represents a sharp reversal of the AFL−CIO's previous "free trade" position.

THE TRADE REFORM ACT OF 1974: IMPLICIT PROTECTIONISM?

Due to the severity of the measures embodied in the Burke-Hartke bill, it failed to obtain congressional approval. In 1974 a compromise bill, the Trade Reform Act, was passed. This act cautiously approved further trade liberalization through the renewed authority it granted the president, allowing the administration to participate in the Tokyo Round of GATT (which began in late 1973). On the other hand, the bill also contained quite a number of potentially restrictive provisions. Thus the future course of American trade policy was left largely to the administration's discretion, depending on the force with which industrial lobbyists advocating protection could make their case. The interests of consumers were conspicuously unrepresented, as has been the case in previous U.S. trade legislation.

The Trade Reform Act of 1974 eased considerably the conditions under which domestic industries could obtain protection from import competition. Unlike the requirements in earlier legislation, it was no longer necessary to demonstrate that a previous tariff concession was the cause of increased imports or that the imports were the *major* cause of injury. "The 1974 Act eliminates the causal link between increased imports and concessions and requires that imports be only a 'substantial' cause (not less than any other cause) of injury or threat of injury" (Root 1978, p. 187).

Once the legitimacy of a domestic industry's claim of injury from foreign competition is established, the president may opt for protection (in the form of tariffs, quotas, or obtaining "voluntary" export limitations by foreign suppliers) and/or adjustment assistance may be recommended. Such "safeguard" provisions protecting the interests of domestic industries have become an integral part of U.S. trade legislation. Kreinin (1979, p. 315) emphasizes that the "no-injury" philosophy pervading the legislation—whereby trade liberalization was to be accomplished while safeguarding the interests of domestic industry—is clearly inconsistent with the general spirit of the reciprocal trade acts:

They regard tariff reduction first and foremost as a means to improve economic efficiency through increased international specialization. A larger volume of trade is expected to drive domestic resources away from relatively inefficient import-competing industries into industries that have competitive advantage. A similar process would take place abroad with the obvious result of increased efficiency all around. The safeguard provisions constitute a mechanism for preventing such shifts of resources. By protecting industries from import competition, they perpetuate allocative inefficiency and are therefore in direct conflict with what the act first set out to accomplish.

The safeguard provisions of various nations, like those condoned by the U.S. Trade Reform Act, were a major point of contention during the Tokyo Round of the GATT. Some negotiators maintained that even the threat of countervailing duties or quotas, which might be levied retroactively after long drawn-out investigative procedures, acted as a significant barrier to trade. In situations where it was agreed that safeguards were justified, countries disagreed as to whether safeguard measures ought to be levied in a non-discriminatory fashion against all foreign exporters of the product in question or whether they could be directed at specific countries or suppliers. More generally it was argued that the liberal world trading system would be enhanced if reasonable bounds could be placed on governments' willingness to capitulate to the demands of domestic pressure groups impacted by increased trade. As governments play an increasingly active role in allocating resources rather than adhering strictly to the dictates of the marketplace, they are likely to become more reluctant to allow external factors to have prolonged negative influences on domestic industries. An increased desire for national autonomy has accompanied the rise of the welfare state. While domestic policymakers acknowledge the possibility (but not the certainty) of gains from trade liberalization, they have been meticulous in retaining a way out should the costs in terms of domestic employment and structural adjustment seem prohibitive.

The safeguards issue proved to be particularly intractable during the Tokyo Round. After protracted negotiation, this issue had to be held back when the remainder of the Tokyo trade agreement was approved by the nations' negotiating committees.

The conflict over national safeguard provisions is important in that it exemplifies the type of problem that is likely to arise repeatedly in future trade negotiations: how to make the proliferation of extensive government controls, regulations, and intervention in the private economy consistent with the objective of further trade liberalization.

To return to the no-injury philosophy of American trade legislation, great care is taken to prevent domestic *producers* from being injured by import competition resulting from trade liberalization. The need to protect domestic *consumers* from "injury" attributable to policies protecting domestic industry is consistently ignored. It is urgent that the general public, consumer interest groups, and legislators be educated about the gains from international exchange. The total costs of protectionist measures—not just the benefits to specific domestic industries—must be made explicit. U.S. trade legislation has espoused the need to consider the detrimental effects of trade on domestic industry. Yet the desirability of assessing the losses to domestic consumers from greater protection is never mentioned in trade legislation or given much emphasis in public policy discussions.

The recent attempts of the United Automobile Workers (UAW) and the automobile industry to limit Japanese imports, which recently captured about 20 percent of the U.S. market, provide a typical example. Newspaper articles rail about the 210,000 U.S. auto workers who have been laid off, the huge losses incurred by Chrysler and the U.S. operations of Ford last year, and the ever-increasing market share of foreign imports, particularly those from Japan. UAW president Douglas Fraser has recently returned from Japan where he threatened Japanese automobile producers with severe U.S. import restrictions unless they "voluntarily" limit their exports to the United States, increase the U.S. content of their U.S. sales, and initiate plans to establish U.S. production facilities. The goal is obviously to increase his members' employment in the ailing domestic auto industry.

Unfortunately, this goal would be accomplished at the expense not only of the Japanese producers but also of American consumers. Import restrictions would slow the transition to smaller, fuel-efficient cars because of limited U.S. capacity to produce compact cars at a time when consumers are suffering from skyrocketing energy costs. Higher automobile prices would also be inflicted upon consumers, thereby contributing to already rampant U.S. inflation. Indeed, the costs to the American consumer of subsidizing the domestic automobile industry, which is in desperate straits largely because of its refusal to adapt to changing consumer preferences, are tremendous. These costs must be detailed and quantified when evaluating the benefits of further direct and indirect government subsidization of the U.S. automobile industry.

A more subtle point is that restrictions on imports coming into the American economy effectively reduce exports flowing out of it. Once import restrictions are in place—say, tariffs from the trigger price mechanism protecting the steel industries—American machinery exporters, who must buy the higher-priced domestic steel and face a less favorable exchange rate, are disadvantaged. Similarly, foreigners will restrict the access of American exports—say, jet aircraft or computers—to their home markets. Because American export activities are very productive and, on average, pay workers wages higher than those elsewhere in the economy, a reduction in exports will reduce average U.S. wages. Protectionism therefore militates against the welfare of workers in general, even though it may temporarily preserve old patterns of employment and leave trade union hierarchies intact.

EXPORT CREDIT SUBSIDIES AND THE U.S. EXPORT-IMPORT BANK

Government participation in the financing of international trade played a vital role in restoring economic prosperity after World War II. The growth of trade would have been seriously hampered if merchants had had to rely on the fragmented money and capital markets then existing rather than on official financing. Government trade credit programs filled an important gap in the international economy.

Today the world financial markets are efficient and relatively well integrated—at least, among industrial nations. Consequently they are ideally suited to the job of matching borrowers and lenders anywhere in the world in order to satisfy short-run and intermediate-run trade financing needs or to facilitate long-run foreign investment. In this environment, government involvement in the allocation of credit is redundant. Furthermore, it could actually reduce national welfare if interest rates on official export credits are kept below market levels. Most countries nevertheless have growing government-backed programs to make credit available to domestic exporters or to the foreign purchasers of their products. In addition to providing heavily subsidized credit, official agencies typically insure export credits against political risks and, to a lesser extent, against the commercial risks inherent in international trade. These programs are common for heavy industrial exports and overseas construction projects because of their large financing requirements. For mercantilist reasons, each national government wishes to promote its country's exports over those of its rivals abroad. The result is that many overseas investment projects of dubious commercial validity, particularly in LDCs, receive undue financial support from industrial countries.

In recent years such government-sponsored export financing institutions as the U.S. Export-Import (ex-im) Bank have taken increasingly active roles in export promotion. Competition among ex-im banks in different countries has been fierce as nations attempted to spur domestic growth and employment, particularly in manufacturing. Interest rates and repayment schedules offered by ex-im banks have been considerably more favorable than those available from commercial banks. Loan rates of ex-im banks have been lowered repeatedly, in spite of the increased inflation premiums being reflected in private market rates, as governments attempt to assist their exporters in outbidding foreign competitors. Many official financing agencies, furthermore, offer *fixed* interest rates well below market rates for the duration of the loan, thereby giving their producers a cost advantage over competitors who may have to resort to commercial loans where floating interest rates are typical. (The uncertainty associated with the latter type of financing has increased greatly with the rise in national inflation rates and uncertainty about them.) For example, in early 1980 the U.S. Export-Import Bank was offering insured credits of five years or more duration at 8.0 to 8.5 percent to finance the export of jet aircraft and similar large items. The equivalent uninsured market rate was closer to 15.0 percent. Export credit agencies in Europe and Japan often are even more generous.

Government involvement in export financing may seem benign at first glance, perhaps even beneficial, in that it encourages more international trade than would otherwise occur. Such an assessment, however, is incorrect. The U.S. Ex-Im Bank and its foreign counterparts in fact encourage trade which ultimately reduces the efficiency of world resource allocation. The interest rate subsidies and credit guarantees which are central to the ex-im banks' programs lead to misallocation of credit within and among countries. Businessmen are induced to go ahead with production for export when, in the absence of subsidized credit, they might have found it more profitable to sell their output domestically or to reduce production levels. Because the ex-im programs subsidize production for export but not for domestic consumption, they may lead to excessive interpenetration of national markets. That is, foreign goods are imported because of subsidized financing provided by a foreign government, even though domestically produced goods may actually be cheaper in terms of true resource cost. Similarly, domestic producers may export their output due to the subsidized credit available, when efficient allocation of world output would have dictated domestic use.

These undesirable resource allocation effects of export credit subsidization also occur if exports are subsidized directly. Fortunately, *direct* export subsidies, like many other trade distortions, are illegal under the GATT. The GATT does allow *production* subsidies, which may encourage expansion in a particular industry to achieve some political, social, or economic objective. However, it prohibits cash or other grants explicitly for exporting which distort firms' decisions about whether to sell their output at home or abroad. The objective is to prevent any one country from taking an unfair mercantilistic advantage in world markets. Retaliatory actions by foreign governments and the concomitant contraction in world trade are thereby prevented.

Given the judicious stance of the GATT in disallowing direct export subsidies, it is unfortunate that its rules have not been extended to cover indirect subsidies in the form of cheap export credits. To be consistent with the current distinction between direct production and export subsidies, the GATT should prohibit governments from subsidizing credit solely for financing exports. No attempt should be made, however, to prevent nations from using general credit subsidies that do not discriminate between domestic and foreign transactions. National governments can scarcely be expected to approve a sweeping policy that denies them the right from time to time to provide cheap finance to ailing domestic firms, such as a Chrysler or a British Leyland. The most that GATT can do is to ensure that such policies do not provide unnecessary biases either in favor of foreign trade or against it.

Two observations about official export credit financing remain. The first involves current agreements to prevent excessively low interest rate quotations by official institutions. The second involves the ex-im bank's role of insuring domestic exporters against political and commercial risk.

On the first point, the United States and twenty-one other nations recently entered a new International Arrangement on Export Credits. According to the 1978 *Annual Report* of the U.S. Export-Import Bank (p. 2):

This arrangement codified and clarified minimum credit terms. . . . It also created procedures designed to enable participating export credit agencies to operate with more accurate knowledge of the credit offers of competitor agencies.

Limiting competitive interest rate cuts by setting minimum .1ominal interest rates, however, is hardly sufficient to prevent gross misallocation of credit, domestically and internationally. Particularly in times of high and variable inflation rates that differ from country to country, *market* interest rates will not be equal across national money markets. Inflation premiums, with nominal rates of interest incorporating expected rates of currency depreciation, will be reflected in international interest differentials. These discrepancies among national interest rates are quite consistent with the efficient functioning of worldwide, integrated financial markets. An official arrangement to equalize the *nominal* (submarket) rates of interest charged by export-financing agencies does not equalize *real* credit costs across countries.

For example, because market rates of interest in Deutsch marks (DM) are below those in American dollars at the present time, an agreement prohibiting subsidized interest rates below 8 percent provides a greater subsidy to American as compared to German exporters. In spite of the evolution of distortionary official financing policies, one might be encouraged by the U.S. Export-Import Bank's intelligent perspective on these developments (*Annual Report* 1978, p. 2):

We continue to believe that it is in the interest of our trading partners to concur in the premise that financing on commercially unsound terms is an unwarranted intervention in normal trade. Our position has been that purchasing decisions should be based primarily on price, quality, service and performance, and not on government-subsidized finance.

The area of export credit subsidization is undoubtedly one where the GATT regulations could potentially reduce conflicting objectives of national governments and the disruptive effects they have on international trade.

Finally, it should be pointed out that in addition to providing cheap export credits, the U.S. Export-Import Bank and its foreign counterparts have programs to insure domestic exporters against political risk and certain types of commercial risk. To the extent that such programs are operated on a self-sustaining actuarial basis, they perform a function that could potentially be performed by private insurance firms or commercial banks. In many instances, however, the fees charged by ex-im banks to insure exporters and overseas contractors against losses due to currency inconvertibility, war, confiscation of assets, etc., are very low. Needless to say, government programs absolving exporters of much of the risk of international transactions can significantly increase the volume of international trade.

As in the case of export subsidies, however, these programs encourage too much trade from a social welfare standpoint. Particularly at a time when governments are becoming increasingly aware of the costs of extreme interdependence of national economies, it is inadvisable for exporters to underestimate or undervalue the losses they may experience in international dealings. Well-designed government programs may be able to help exporters pool their risks, thereby providing mutual insurance. On the other hand, government *subsidization* of such programs, which amounts to a bearing of the risks of international transactions by the general public, is certainly without merit and should be discouraged. Insuring U.S. direct investment in foreign economies, as is currently done by the Overseas Private Investment Corporation of the United States government, is similarly unwarranted.

In conclusion, inappropriate government policies may either increase the levels of exports and imports above the socially desirable level or decrease them below the social optimum. The composition of total exports and total imports may also be dramatically altered. Such policies inevitably have profound effects on the allocation of productive resources as well as on the distribution of income within and among countries. Multilateral negotiations under the auspices of GATT can play a valuable role in bringing them under control, to the mutual advantage of all trading nations.

U.S. MONETARY POLICY AND EXTERNAL BALANCE: LESSONS FROM THE BRETTON WOODS ERA[2]

The United States was the dominant force in the international economy in the years following the second world war. In addition to spearheading liberalization in the world trading system through the General Agreement on Tariffs and Trade, the United States played a central role in the international monetary system. When the International Monetary Fund was established at Bretton Woods, New Hampshire, in 1944, the major industrial nations agreed to maintain fixed *par values* for their currencies vis-à-vis the American dollar. The value of the dollar, in turn, was pegged to gold at a ratio of $35 per ounce. Thus the dollar in effect became the *numéraire*—or standard of value—in the international monetary system. Furthermore, the commitment by other nations to maintain fixed exchange rates in terms of the dollar (as specified in Article IV of the IMF Articles of Agreement) meant that they had to intervene periodically in the foreign exchange markets, buying or selling their respective currencies in exchange for dollars. In so doing they were to prevent exchange rate movements in excess of 1 percent on either side of their par values. Central banks therefore found it necessary to hold official reserves of dollars—and, to a lesser extent, of gold—to ensure that the required foreign exchange market intervention could be effected.

In the immediate postwar reconstruction period the dollar was in great demand not only as a reserve currency for central banks but also as a medium of exchange in commercial transactions because it was the only major currency widely accepted by foreigners. Due to the severe shortage of dollars in war-torn belligerent countries needing American-produced goods, central banks were unwilling to give up dollars to buy back their own currencies at the official exchange rates. Consequently, exporters would not accept payment in foreign currencies other than the dollar because of their uncertain purchasing power. In effect, the currencies of other industrial countries were "inconvertible," or not usable in international commerce. Hence, Western European and Japanese trade was severely restricted in the late 1940s.

The critical importance of exchange rate convertibility for promoting international trade and investment was recognized when the Bretton Woods system was established. Article VIII of the IMF Articles of Agreement obligates its members to maintain the convertibility of foreign-held balances of domestic money acquired as a result of *current account* transactions. The IMF, however, realized that severe adjustment problems following World War II would prevent most countries from immediately achieving convertibility as required by Article VIII. Hence Article XIV specified that members who had restrictions on current account transactions when they joined the fund could maintain these restrictions. As Root (1978, p. 364) points out:

The decision to abandon exchange restrictions permitted under Article XIV was left to the member country, but it was supposed to occur when such restrictions were no longer necessary to settle the balance of payments without undue dependence on the Fund's resources. Once a member abolished its exchange control over current payments and accepted the obligations of Article VIII, it could not reimpose similar restrictions without the approval of the Fund.

By 1959 the Western industrial countries' currencies had again become convertible, as they had been prior to the currency upheavals of the 1930s.

Capital account transactions, which were not included in the convertibility obligation of Article VIII, remained under stricter control throughout the 1960s, varying from year to year and country to country. In Japan they were quite strict and in Germany rather relaxed. As international capital flows became increasingly sensitive to interest rate differentials and anticipated exchange rate realignments, policymakers often turned to capital controls to reduce the massive amounts of foreign exchange market intervention which would otherwise be required to maintain official rates. Throughout most of the postwar period, however, the American capital market remained relatively open to foreigners. The fairly weak temporary restraints imposed by presidents Kennedy and Johnson—the interest equalization tax and the "voluntary" restrictions on commercial bank lending abroad—were abolished in January 1974.

What are the essential elements in American financial policy for the 1980s that will allow world trade to continue to be monetized, thereby minimizing the need for barter transactions?

Throughout the 1980s foreign central banks will continue to hold reserves in the form of U.S. Treasury bills and bonds, and nonofficial foreigners will hold working balances of U.S. dollars. Thus an essential aspect of the postwar monetary system is that the U.S. capital market—and its Eurodollar extension—remains open to foreigners. Other industrial countries, such as Britain or Japan, can impose quite strict and comprehensive controls on capital moving in or out of their economies. But this option is not open to the United States without severely impairing the world's payments mechanism and stock of international liquidity. It is also important that foreigners be able to borrow freely (at equilibrium rates of interest) in either the New York or London dollar-based capital markets. If the American government ever contemplated imposing comprehensive restrictions on interest rates or on the flow of credit in the economy (perhaps as part of a package of wage/price controls), the international consequences would be disastrous.

Under the Bretton Woods system, the United States had an implicit commitment to refrain from direct intervention in the foreign exchange markets. Given that all other nations were to intervene in terms of dollars to establish the foreign exchange value of their currencies, unilateral action by the U.S. Federal Reserve Board would at best be unnecessary and could potentially create destructive internal inconsistencies in the fixed rate system. The Federal Reserve thus was to follow a policy of "benign neglect," as it has been called. Even under the current floating exchange rate regime, where official parities no longer exist, foreign central banks have continued to intervene heavily in dollars. Thus it remains essential that the American central bank either remain passive or coordinate its exchange market intervention with that of foreign central banks to achieve mutually acceptable exchange rate adjustment.

A further largely implicit American responsibility under the old Bretton Woods system was to maintain a stable-valued money, as it did in the 1950s and early 1960s. It was not, as many people thought, to avoid "deficits"—however measured—in the American balance of payments. As the world economy grew, foreigners inevitably would build up their international reserves and working balances of short-term dollar-denominated bank accounts or of treasury bills and bonds. Because these dollar assets were also the liquid liabilities of the United States, deficits in American foreign payments—in a narrow accounting sense—were inevitable and, in fact, desirable. What was essential was that the United States maintain the real purchasing power of the dollar claims owned by foreigners and by U.S. citizens. They would not then be frightened into suddenly selling off their dollar assets in order to acquire other, more stable, currencies, thereby destabilizing the foreign exchange markets. Hence, the restoration of monetary stability in the United States for the 1980s is of paramount importance for the world economy.

Unfortunately, the Federal Reserve lost monetary control in the late 1960s—in part because of pressure from the U.S. government to finance Great Society social programs without sharp increases in interest rates. The inflationary pressure in the United States at first was mitigated by importing more goods from abroad and by increased holdings of dollars by foreign central banks (to ensure that the then-fixed exchange rates were maintained). The European nations and Japan found the previously stabilizing system of fixed exchange rates leading to an unduly rapid expansion in their domestic money supplies. A series of foreign exchange crises from 1969 to 1973, including the American suspension of gold convertibility, ensued. Finally the major convertible currency countries abrogated their commitment under IMF Article IV to fixed exchange rates.

In spite of the suspension of gold convertibility and fixed exchange rate obligation, the international monetary system did not collapse as it had in the Great Depression of the 1930s. It continued to function effectively, largely due to the fact that countries did not renege on their commitments under Article VIII to maintain convertibility of foreigners' holdings of domestic currencies into domestic goods or into the foreigners' own currencies. This prevented international trade from reverting to barter, with the dramatic contraction in trade and world output that this would have entailed. Thus the events of the early 1970s indicate that the key aspect of the Bretton Woods accord was not the commitment to fixed exchange rates, as is widely presumed, but the commitment to convertibility for current account transactions. In this sense the Bretton Woods system did not "collapse" with the closing of the U.S. gold window in the fall of 1971. Had currency convertibility (as opposed to gold convertibility of the U.S. dollar) been suspended, the tumultuous events of the mid-1970s, including the quadrupling of oil prices in 1973–1974, would have been devastating for the international economy.

Since 1973 the world has been on a "weak" dollar standard where exchange rates are no longer fixed among industrial countries; the dollar remains the principal vehicle currency and official reserve asset in international trade. By floating their exchange rates, Europe and Japan have severed the previously strong link between their own domestic money supplies and that of the United States. International differences in monetary policy are now possible, and probably are responsible for the surprisingly wide swings in foreign exchange rates—10 to 20 percent in the course of a year—that we have observed in the 1970s. This monetary instability—and movement away from a regime of "one money"—has probably lessened the efficiency of international (and domestic) trade and contributed to the recent decline in the rate of productivity growth in the United States and abroad. Nevertheless, under the weak dollar standard, international trade has grown faster than national output in each of the industrial countries.

INTERNATIONALIZING AMERICAN MONETARY POLICY IN THE 1980s

What steps should be taken in the 1980s to strengthen the world dollar standard and the commitment to currency convertibility on the part of the Western industrial countries? At present there are no tractable alternatives for organizing the world's money machine.

Under the fixed exchange rates of the 1950s and 1960s the money supplies of industrial economies other than that of the United States were largely determined by the balance of payments. Hence, in order to avoid indeterminacy in the world's money stock and price level, it was appropriate for the U.S. Federal Reserve to control autonomously the domestic supply of base money in dollars without reference to the U.S. balance of payments. This policy basis of the strong dollar standard had two important facets:

(i)   The effect on the American monetary base of frequently building up or drawing down dollar reserves by foreign central banks was completely sterilized; only outstanding U.S. Treasury bonds and bills, but not depository claims on the Federal Reserve Bank itself, were affected.

(ii)   The U.S. government had a strong commitment, and sufficient financial control, to independently stabilize the dollar's purchasing power over internationally tradable goods and services.

True, automatic sterilization under (i) greatly accentuated the multiplier effect of any increase in the U.S. monetary base on the world's stock of money aggregated over all currencies. But the inherited stability in price-level expectations, coupled with a fixed exchange rate, served to stabilize the demand for base money (and for M_1) in dollars. Thus, under the strong dollar standard, American monetary authorities could tailor the supply of *domestic* base money to the demand for it.

Under the present weak dollar standard, what modifications in those Federal Reserve operating procedures are called for?

Unstable price inflation in the 1970s and fluctuations among convertible currencies have led to extrapolative expectations about further changes in exchange rates. These in turn can destabilize the demand for noninterest-bearing dollar balances—including the derived demand for base money. During the prolonged fall of the dollar through 1977 to 1 November 1978, a remarkable switching out of dollars into Deutsch marks, yen, Swiss francs, and so on occurred. The demand for U.S. monetary aggregates grew at a slower rate, substantially below the rate of growth in nominal American GNP. Due to violent shifts of funds among alternative, potential reserve currencies, the once-useful strategy of operating

American monetary policy independently of foreign exchange considerations has become obsolete.

How then does one substitute "benign attention" for "benign neglect"? First, a credible commitment to stabilize the purchasing power of the dollar is very important. The Federal Reserve's draconian measures to slow growth in the American money supply, implemented on 6 October 1979 and reinforced on 14 March 1980, are certainly steps in the right direction. Second, the United States should provide an exchange rate guarantee to foreign official holders of dollar balances by taking a full equity position in the new Special Drawing Rights Substitution Account proposed by the International Monetary Fund. Because the international value of the U.S. dollar has been so unstable in the 1970s, an exchange rate guarantee to induce foreign governments not to diversify out of their U.S. Treasury securities is now warranted; it is described in more technical detail by McKinnon (1980).

Third, the mechanics of short-run control over the American money supply should be reorganized. The recent abandonment of an official interest rate target on federal funds was long overdue. When dominated by expected changes in prices or exchange rates, nominal rates of interest are worse than useless targets or indicators for monetary policy; they led the Federal Reserve badly astray during the 1977–1978 fall of the dollar. While appropriate in the long run, a simple Friedman rule of smooth growth in the American monetary base may not by itself be adequate in the short run. Instability in money demand is now rife because monetary policy credibility is lacking. International currency substitution has become commonplace, and fringe banks and money-market funds are offering competing forms of money. An additional governor on the short-run rate of base money creation in the United States therefore would seem warranted.

Whether the dollar is strong or weak in the foreign exchanges is one immediate and potentially reliable source of information for the Federal Reserve to judge the tightness of the American money market. On 1 November 1978 the American government finally recognized the importance of the foreign exchanges by intervening massively to halt the dollar's twenty-month slide and by allowing the American monetary base to contract commensurately with this intervention. The postwar policy of benign neglect was abruptly terminated. But how should the Federal Reserve process foreign-exchange information, including the size of dollar transactions by foreign central banks, on a regular noncrisis basis?

Suppose the United States focuses on adjusting its monetary policy to its two largest and most financially stable trading partners: Germany and Japan. Let the German and Japanese governments continue daily or weekly interventions to prevent excessive volatility in the DM/dollar and yen/dollar rates and to maintain a rough purchasing power parity. Then let the Federal Reserve Bank, the Bundesbank, and the Bank of Japan mutually adjust their domestic money supplies by the amount of these official interventions (McKinnon 1974). For example, if the dollar is sufficiently weak against the DM to warrant dollar purchases by the Bundesbank, the market is signaling that private demand for dollars has fallen and for DM has risen. Hence the authorities should reduce the supply of base money in dollars and, symmetrically, increase the German money supply. In the short run, all three governments could better tailor their money supplies to shifting cross-currency demands, thus enhancing domestic financial stability in each country. Moreover, the possibility of a foreign exchange crisis would be drastically reduced.

To better manage this monetary accommodation on the American side, Germany and Japan could keep working dollar reserves directly in interest-bearing deposits with the Federal Reserve Bank of New York. (Other countries would continue to hold their main reserves only in nonmonetary

U.S. Treasury bonds and bills with automatic sterilization of any impact on the American monetary base.) Hence, an intervention by, say, the Bank of Japan to buy yen and sell dollars would increase the American monetary base—as dollars are switched out of the Federal Reserve into American commercial banks—paralleling a contraction in the Japanese monetary base. Full sterilization—automatic or discretionary—of these foreign exchange transactions would contravene the agreement.

Over longer periods of time, the success of this tripartite agreement requires that each of the three central banks maintain a relatively constant rate of *domestic* credit expansion. The long-run growth rate of nominal gross national product in Japan would seem higher than that of the United States if both countries strove for stability in the yen/dollar prices of a broad basket of internationally tradable goods. Hence, domestic credit expansion by the Bank of Japan, through open-market operations or lending to commercial banks, would exhibit higher growth—say, 9 percent per year against 5 percent for the United States, with Germany somewhere in between. Long-run monetary growth of the triumvirate would then be anchored, but short-run changes in national money supplies would be dominated by the foreign exchanges. Once the foreign exchange market perceived that the triumvirate's domestic money supplies were adjusting appropriately to shifting international demands, the need for official stabilizing intervention would diminish.

CONCLUDING NOTE

In the postwar period, industrial economies (but not most LDCs) have become more open, both in terms of the ratio to GNP of exports and imports and of the degree of international integration of dollar-based money and capital markets. Due to this increased interdependence, government

policies often have significant effects on international economic relationships even when not specifically directed at
the foreign sector. The General Agreement on Tariffs and
Trade is meeting this challenge by extending its purview
from tariff reduction and harmonization to a wide range of
other tax, welfare, and government procurement policies
which influence international trade. Nevertheless, to prevent burgeoning statism from misallocating world resources
and thereby reducing American as well as foreign standards
of living, a concerted effort to strengthen the GATT is
necessary. For example, the proclivity of governments to give
credit subsidies to exporters—through a variety of national
agencies similar to the U.S. Export-Import Bank—has a distortionary effect on world trade patterns and should be
reduced.

In light of the ongoing efforts of the GATT to achieve
policy coordination and harmonization in the area of international trade, it is somewhat surprising that analogous
efforts at policy harmonization in the monetary sphere
under the jurisdiction of the IMF have been less evident.
Granted, the important commitment to currency convertibility among the major industrial countries has endured
their transition to flexible exchange rates. Nevertheless,
greater harmonization of national monetary policies is essential if excessive turbulence in the foreign exchange
markets is to be eliminated. Unless the oscillations between
overvaluation and undervaluation of major trading currencies are damped, governments may feel compelled to restrict
international capital flows as well as exports and imports.

In this chapter it has been suggested that American monetary policy be revamped. By focusing on the value of dollar in
the foreign exchange markets and paying less attention to
domestic interest rates, the Federal Reserve can improve
short-run control over the money supply. It is explained that
if Federal Reserve intervention in the foreign exchange
markets is accompanied by mutually reenforcing interven-

tion by the German and Japanese central banks, the possibility of foreign exchange crises can be greatly reduced. In addition to lessening exchange market instability in the short run, the specified coordination of the monetary policies of the United States, Germany, and Japan would contribute importantly to the long-run problem of reducing the currently high worldwide inflation rates.

DISCUSSION

WEINBERGER: I was interested in the arguments about statism and the suggestions that were reported that other countries—Japan and others—take an active role in helping their export industries. I am interested in the reverse side of that coin—not that we want the U.S. government to do likewise, but that it would be extremely useful if the U.S. government would refrain from putting active barriers in the way of U.S. corporations doing business abroad. We have a saying in San Francisco and in the concern with which I am connected that our biggest competitor overseas is the U.S. government. And in many ways the barriers that are put up do substantially restrict the ability, not just of one company but of a number of American companies, to do business or to improve the balance of trade and balance of payments because they put us in a very noncompetitive position with other governments and companies from other governments.

One of the first ways in which this was seen was, of course, in taxation. We are one of two countries in the world that taxes foreign-earned income by our nationals; the other is the Philippine Islands. We therefore are in a substantially noncompetitive position when we have companies which are bidding on jobs where the wage rate of the Americans employed on that job has to be reimbursed with funds which have to be secured from the foreign client. And whereas other countries do not have to add any kind of tax payment to that, American companies do. And so this means that we go in with a competitive disadvantage pretty much from the beginning.

Moreover, we have a number of problems not caused by American statutes, such as taxation, but by American government practice. I don't know how many people realize it, but there is now a policy, for example, on projects financed by the Export-Import Bank whereby the Export-Import Bank will consult with the foreign government that is doing the job which is being partially financed by the Export-Import Bank to persuade theose governments that they are not making sufficiently strong contracts, from the point of view of the foreign governmemt, with American contractors. Thus they will require that before the Export-Import Bank financing goes to a country such as Egypt or Algeria or Indonesia, those countries must revise contracts already entered into with American builders and contractors, making them much more stringent and much more expensive for the American contractors to fulfill. This in turn often requires revision of bid, again making American contractors somewhat noncompetitive.

There is also a group from the Department of Commerce that actively advises lesser developed countries on how they should contract, and frequently those countries retain a New York law firm. You therefore have not only an unequal—but a very difficult—negotiation to get a contract that can be performed within a competitive range. If the lesser-developed country has not retained the New York law firm, the U.S. Department of Commerce will assist it by providing counsel and advice, which again makes it much more expensive and much more difficult for an American company to carry out the contract.

And we have a couple of other statutes. We have the so-called Foreign Corrupt Practices Act. If you attack this, the implication is immediately that you are in favor of bribing foreign officials to get jobs. While this is an unfair implication, that act has a perfectly good motive and is designed to prevent practices which have been far too frequent to get foreign contracts. But often—because of the way it is administered, because of its wording—it so puts off or irritates some foreign governments that American companies cannot get contracts. At other times, the interpretations of that act are so extreme that it seems better for many foreign countries or foreign clients (and they are usually identical) to deal with contractors of other countries. Not all payments, for example, are banned under that act. Those payments inelegantly referred to as "grease payments" are specifically authorized, and the question of whether or not you have a grease payment or an illegal bribe is a very narrow one. But it causes all kinds of problems.

I don't think we have paid nearly enough attention to laws that can encourage and increase our foreign trade—not to subsidize it, but to remove hurdles and barriers.

VI

The Role of Government in the Economy

7

JOHN B. SHOVEN

Federal Government Taxes and Tax Reform

Tax and nontax sources of revenue. The economic inefficiency of heavy taxation. The negative income tax. Income tax indexation or integration. The consumption tax.

The United States enters the 1980s with a growing dissatisfaction over the equity and efficiency consequences of its tax system. We are in the midst of a "tax revolt" with calls for major across-the-board rate reductions, complete revamping of the basis of tax computation, and broader appeals for controls on the size of government. Clearly, the rapid and accelerating inflation the country has experienced in the past decade has prompted much of the furor regarding taxes, as has the decline in the rate of growth of real income. This chapter will examine trends in the relative importance of various federal tax instruments, will discuss their economic impacts, and will address several major tax reform alternatives.

HISTORICAL TRENDS IN SOURCES
OF GOVERNMENT REVENUE

While it is natural to concentrate attention on the personal income tax, the fact is that this source provides only 45 percent of federal government revenue. This fraction has been relatively constant, as shown in Figure 1, yet there have been major shifts in the relative importance of the other revenue sources. Social security's "contributions" have risen dramatically; in 1953 these collections were one-fourth as large as the personal income tax, while today they are nearly three-fourths as big. The corporation income tax, on the other hand, has been steadily declining in importance, as shown in the figure. In the early 1950s it brought in over two and one-half times what social security did; by 1980 the social security system collected more than twice as much as the corporation income tax. Finally, indirect business taxes and nontax accruals (excise taxes, franchise fees, tariffs, deposits of earnings of the Federal Reserve System, etc.) have also significantly declined in relative importance. Given these trends, it seems appropriate that the social insurance system be given intensive examination, as is done in Chapter 10 of this book. I will concentrate here on the personal income tax and the corporation income tax. The latter, despite its declining relative importance, still generates

Figure 1

Trends in Sources of Federal Government Revenue

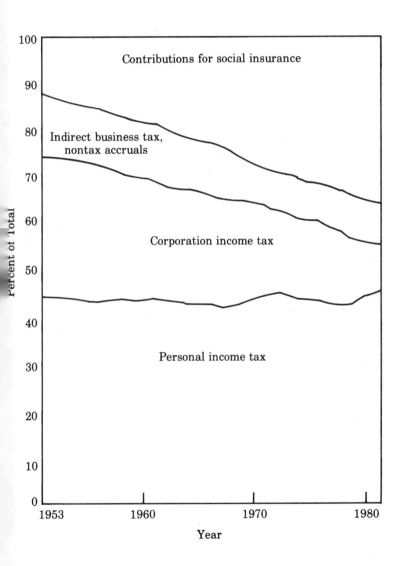

Contributions for social insurance

Indirect business tax, nontax accruals

Corporation income tax

Personal income tax

Percent of Total

Year

Source: *Economic Report of the President, 1980,* Table B-73, p. 289.

almost $80 billion. Yet it is the least widely understood of our major taxes; there is significant confusion about who bears its burden.

In the short run, the federal government can finance its activities with nontax sources, primarily with the issuance of money or bonds. In the long run, however, the service costs on the debt must be borne, presumably through taxation. So financing government expenditure with bonds simply postpones the tax burden rather than eliminating it. Further, money creation fuels inflation and creates a hidden "inflation tax." This results because interest is not paid on the money stock. The higher the inflation rate and nominal interest rates, the more the foregone interest (i.e., the "tax") of those who hold money. Households lose wealth because of the decline in the value of their money holdings, while the government gains as the real value of its money debt is reduced. The real transfer is thus from the household sector to the government, just as with explicit taxes. Having said that even nontax financing methods are implicitly equivalent to taxes, I will now discuss only explicit tax programs.

THE ECONOMIC EFFECTS OF TAXES

Clearly, the primary effect of taxes on the economy is a transfer of control of economic power from individuals to the collective society or government. It is not the purpose of this chapter to determine whether or not the government is of the proper size, but rather whether this transfer is being made in a reasonably and efficient manner.

Economists are concerned with the fact that taxes distort individuals' behavior. People naturally try to maximize their economic welfare, which involves doing as well as possible after taxes. They certainly value some of the government's activities, but logically reason that their personal taxes have only a negligible effect on the government's resources. If some private activities are taxed more than others, the rational consumer will reallocate his behavior away from the more heavily taxed items. This reallocation typically causes *economic inefficiency* because taxes drive a wedge between the interests of the individual and those of society.[1]   In the absence of externalities and market imperfections, private and social interests align without taxes; each individual's decisions are therefore both personally and socially optimal, given resource constraints. Taxes cause people to deviate from this pleasant circumstance of compatible interests. The biggest of these effects is probably the reallocation from market to nonmarket activities. Only market (i.e., dollar) transactions are subject to taxation, and people therefore engage in less activity within the market. Not only is leisure time untaxed, but so is economic activity and production within the household. The fact that labor income is taxed distorts labor supply. The general empirical evidence is that taxes do not affect adult male labor supply greatly (although recent estimates by Hausman [1979] are larger than previous ones). The labor supply of women, teenagers, and elderly workers is, however, quite sensitive to the *after-tax* wage rate offered. The same incentives which cause individuals to reallocate time and effort away from market activities and the labor force also are largely responsible for the much-heralded "underground" economy. There is some evidence and widespread feeling that high tax rates have led to a rapid growth in this untaxed "off-the-record" sector of our economy.

Another distortion which receives and deserves a lot of attention is the tax system's effect on saving and investment. An income tax taxes saving twice. First, the money which is earned and set aside for saving is taxed and, second, the earnings or return on that saving are also taxed. The income tax system favors consumption over saving. Another way to look at this same phenomenon is that savers are not offered the total return on their savings (the social return possible on investment [postponed consumption]), but only the after-tax return on those investments. Recent evidence (Boskin 1978) indicates that total saving is sensitive to the after-tax real rate of return. If these estimates are correct, then this heavy taxation of saving reduces total saving and capital formation in the economy; this is particularly unfortunate in the country which has the lowest saving propensity among the world's leading economies and which is dissatisfied with the pace of economic growth. This policy of taxing the return to saving causes economic inefficiency. The incentives given to taxpayers (present consumption is made cheaper than providing for future consumption by saving) are not equal to the social trade-off between provisions for the present and the future. The income tax works against efficient allocation of resources as well.

Of course, the United States does not have a straightforward income tax anyhow. Calling it an "income tax" is a misnomer. Some types of investment income are taxed very heavily (corporate equity income is taxed both at the corporate and personal levels), whereas other types of capital income—particularly the imputed rental income on owner-occupied housing—is taxed lightly. The result is that the allocation of investment across industries and economic sectors is distorted. Capital is not located where it has the highest social value but rather where it earns the highest after-tax rate of return for its owners. This misallocation across sectors is as costly for the economy as the misallocation between aggregate consumption and saving. So we have a situation where the aggregate quantity of saving is depressed and, in addition, its investment allocation across industries is distorted.

So far I have been emphasizing economic efficiency and taking the position that the government should raise its required revenue with as few distortions as possible. (A complete, distortion-free, tax system is not feasible.) But people are also interested, of course, in the equity of the tax system. Who bears the tax burden in the United States and who should bear it? Further, can one pursue a tax policy designed to promote economic equality without seriously damaging the aforementioned economic efficiency?

The present tax system is ostensibly directed at achieving equality, but it is only mildly progressive. The rich face somewhat higher average tax rates than the poor, but the difference is not as great as the rate structure would indicate because there are large numbers of partial tax shelters available to those in high marginal tax brackets (e.g., capital gains treatment, tax-free municipal bonds, maximum 50 percent rate on personal service income). The difference between the distribution of before-tax and after-tax income is rather small. This is not a good measure of the impact of the tax system on the overall distribution of income, though, because the before-tax behavior of households is itself a function of the tax system. How much you work (and therefore your labor income) and how much you invest (both in financial assets and in yourself through education) depends upon your expectations about the taxes those earnings will face. A frequent mistake made in the press and in Washington is the assumption that before-tax behavior is unaffected by the design of the tax system.

The economic literature which has examined both equity and efficiency issues simultaneously generally concludes that steeply increasing marginal rates would cause significant efficiency losses for the economy. This may mean that relief for the rich from the present rate structure is appropriate, although it would be better accomplished by tax rate reductions than by the array of shelters and escapes now offered. Further, while there is a trade-off between equity and efficiency, the present tax/transfer treatment of the poor is so badly designed that we could improve both equity and efficiency by rationalizing the design of the system.

The significant government impact on the distribution of income is achieved not through the tax system anyway, but through transfer programs such as Aid to Families with Dependent Children (AFDC), welfare, food stamps, public housing, and to some extent, the payout of social security benefits (see Chapter 10). These programs, many of them the result of the Great Society of the 1960s, have succeeded in raising the real incomes of the poor and reducing the numbers of households in extreme poverty. They have, however, also introduced very large inefficiencies in the economy, much larger than necessitated by their redistributive function.

The present set of U.S. transfer programs involves a number of inefficiencies, including family desertion (in many states only single-parent families are eligible), uneconomic migration due to the wide variance in welfare generosity across states, and excessive surveillance of the expenditure patterns of the poor. An additional distortion stems from their implicit or hidden marginal tax rates, which are the highest in the economy. While attention has been focused on the high marginal tax rates faced by the rich and by those owning capital—and they are high—those faced by welfare recipients are even greater. The implicit tax is due to the fact that the government aid is reduced as the welfare recipient earns more money. For example, a household's AFDC payments are lowered by roughly 50 cents for each additional dollar of earnings. The actual law puts the figure at 67 cents, but liberal interpretation of the rules by social workers lowers the figure somewhat. Nonetheless, AFDC households face an implicit marginal tax rate equal to the maximum rate on personal service income. And that is not all. The eligibility rules for AFDC and for food stamps are almost identical, and the net subsidy involved in food stamps also diminishes as earnings increase. Add to this the 25 percent marginal tax involved with most subsidized housing programs and you can easily get a combined effective tax rate of

85 to 90 percent on earnings for those on transfer programs. This leaves precious little incentive for the poor to work.

Economists have been concerned about income distribution and incentives for a long time and would, in general, assess the current array of "means tested" welfare programs as poor social engineering. To be sure, it is difficult to be generous and to preserve incentives at the same time, but the current multiprogram mess can be improved. The most satisfactory alternative would be to introduce a general, national, negative income tax (NIT) system which would guarantee a certain level of income to households and then tax this grant away at the modest (compared to current programs) rate of 40 percent.

Several defects of the present system and of previously proposed NIT programs could be alleviated. Many systems (including our present one, by a large margin) are less than twice as generous for families of four than they are for the family split into two units of one and three or two and two. While this may make sense—in that there may be some economies to larger family units—it creates very undesirable incentives for family separation. However, a welfare system which granted a constant amount per person (like McGovern's ill-fated $1,000 Demogrant program) would favor large units too much. The answer is to base the income guarantee on individuals, but have the amount depend on age. Children would get less than adults, young children possibly less than older ones. Since age is immutable (except through the passage of time), the total grant of a family would not depend on its structure. The government would discontinue the present incentives for family repackaging.

The negative income tax could be structured as a system of income-contingent loans if desired. That is, the tax authorities could keep track of the aid a household has received and could demand repayment in the event the family's economic fortunes improve dramatically. This might remove much of the "welfare stigma" attached to the present program, but the recapture tax would create its own incentive problems. It is an idea which needs careful consideration before implementation.

INCOME TAX REFORM AGENDA

The three major reforms of the U.S. federal income tax systems discussed below are not new ideas, having been advocated by some economists for the past twenty-five years or so. But they are more needed in the 1980s than ever, so a reexamination of the country's unfinished (or stillborn) tax reforms seems valuable.[2]

Indexing the Tax Systems for Inflation

The United States does not really have income tax systems because it does not base taxes on real incomes. Investors have become painfully aware in recent years that a bond's 14 percent interest rate translates into a 1 percent real return when accompanied by 13 percent inflation. The tax code does not recognize this, however, and bases taxes on the full 14 percent. Similarly, nominal capital gains are taxed, even if they translate into real capital losses because of inflation during the holding period. For corporations and the corporation income tax there are analogous problems. They are only allowed to base depreciation deductions on the original purchase price of assets (instead of on their current replacement value) and under some accounting schemes record the nominal appreciation of inventoried stock as income. These two accounting treatments mean that higher inflation will lead to (more) exaggerated profits and to higher corporation income taxes.

The current tax system permits inflation to distort the base of the corporation income tax in other ways as well, some of which tend to lower taxes. For instance, all interest payments are deductible for the corporation (the full 14 percent for the bond mentioned above) rather than only allowing deduction of real interest charges. Despite the fact that the distortions go in both directions, it would take an unjustified leap of faith to assume that they approximately offset each other. The fact is that the government has failed to grant tax relief to those whom inflation has hurt (i.e., savers), even though doing so would not necessarily open new concessions for these people; it would simply reestablish real income as the tax base.

I have concentrated on the importance of establishing real income as the basis of taxation for both the corporation and personal income tax systems. I would also advocate indexing the tax codes themselves. This would involve multiplying the many dollar numbers in the tax computation by a factor reflecting inflation. For example, if there had been 12 percent inflation in the year, the $1,000 personal exemption of last year would be raised to $1,120. The $2,300 standard deduction for single returns would be increased to $2,576 while the $28,800 to $34,100 income range subject to the 44 percent marginal tax rate would be lifted to $32,256 and $38,192, respectively. If the tax base were computed as real income and all numbers in the code were multiplied by a factor of one plus the inflation rate (1.12 in this example), then those with constant real income would pay constant real taxes. Presently we find that taxes go up 50 percent faster than nominal income, allowing inflation to raise taxes silently. The periodic tax "cuts" Congress passes are actually just rebates of some of the extra money taken in this way.

An inflation-indexed tax system would be much fairer than our present one and would likely increase investment demand and economic activity. It is time the government dropped the false assumption on which it bases its current tax program—that a dollar is a dollar regardless of the date of reference—and admit that a 1970 dollar is more like a

1980 British pound than a 1980 dollar. The numbers should be adjusted to take into account the erosion of the dollar's purchasing power.

Integrating the Corporate and Personal Tax Systems

The corporation income tax is relatively hidden from public awareness and is widely misunderstood. Hardly a week goes by in which a politician does not talk about the taxes corporations pay. But who really pays a corporation's taxes? Ultimately, only people can pay taxes. In the case of the corporation income tax is it their stockholders, their workers, their customers?[3]   It would be far more direct to tax people (however we desire to do so) instead of taxing an intermediary like the corporation.

The mystery of the ultimate incidence of the corporation income tax is not its greatest problem. As stated earlier, the tax distorts the industrial allocation of capital because it applies only to corporations. The cost to the economy of having capital in less than its most productive locale because of the tax differentials has been estimated to be roughly (in 1980 dollars) $300 billion (Fullerton et al. 1979). The corporation income tax may also depress aggregate saving. Since it applies only to the earnings of equity holders, it creates a bias in favor of debt financing. Finally, it is undesirable because it cannot discriminate among individuals. Rich stockholders, poor widows, and tax-exempt nonprofit institutions all face a 46 percent marginal rate on their equity earnings. Since the tax is collected from the corporation, it does not permit exceptions for disability or special circumstances as does a direct personal tax.

At least two proposals for integrating the personal and corporation income tax systems merit consideration. The first is termed the "partnership method" and would tax stockholders on the entire earnings of their shares according to their personal income tax rates. The corporation income tax would be effectively eliminated, although it could remain as a withholding mechanism. The capital gains tax would be modified such that the basis from which capital gains are computed is increased by the cumulated retained earnings during the holding period.

The partnership method would tax all corporate earnings once—at the personal tax rates of the holder. Capital gains would be taxed only to the extent they exceeded retained earnings. This system has many advantages over the present corporate and personal tax arrangement, but it does have one serious shortcoming: it relies on the reported earnings of the corporation, and thus the tax base is subject to a myriad of accounting problems. When a company reports $8 per share earnings, pays a $3 dividend, and the shares do not change in value during the year, who got the $8 per share? The answer is, no one. It is imply the number the accountant deemed appropriate.

The other method of integrating the two tax systems can be termed the "accrual method." It would simply tax stockholders at the present level on dividends and real capital gains as they accrue. The corporation income tax would be removed as a separate revenue source. The existing $100 dividend exclusion and the special treatment of long-term capital gains would also be eliminated. The advantage of this integration plan is that it relies on the market for tax base determination rather than the figures generated by accountants. A separate treatment (perhaps the partnership method) would be required for assets which are not valued in a public market.

Either of these plans would improve economic efficiency and rationalize the overall U.S. tax system. Corporate equity income would be put on a par with other types of income in terms of taxation. Investment in corporations would be relatively more attractive, which would likely lead to more capital in these industries and to a higher level of productivity.

An Expenditure Tax

To this point, we have discussed establishing real income as the tax base and unifying the two separate income tax systems now in existence. A growing majority of economists are questioning whether income is the best base for taxation. The alternative they suggest is to tax consumption or expenditure. Since consumption is equal to income less saving, one way to arrive at consumption as a tax base is to first ask taxpayers to record income and then allow deductions for all saving. The general nature of the current filing system could be retained and the rate structure could be made as progressive as desired.

The idea of taxing consumption rather than income has a long history and is frequently credited initially to John Stuart Mill. In more recent times Irving Fisher (1942) and Nicholas Kaldor (1957) have been strong advocates. The arguments in favor of a consumption tax can be separated into the three broad categories of equity, economic efficiency, and administrative efficiency.

On equity grounds there is the philosophical position that it is more reasonable to base relative tax burdens on withdrawals from the economic system rather than on additions to it. Clearly a household's consumption reflects its take from the collective output of society, while (under competition) its income reflects the value of the inputs it offers to the production process. The idea of basing taxes on social burden rather than on contribution is appealing; however, it is difficult to assess in economic terms. Fortunately, there are other arguments for a consumption tax.

The economic efficiency case has previously been mentioned. An income tax distorts intertemporal consumption choice because savings must be made out of net of tax income and the earnings of investments are further taxed before future consumption can occur. The consumption tax, on the other hand, would be neutral towards the timing of consumption. Thus, relative to an income tax, it would encourage provision for future consumption (i.e., saving) and result in more capital formation.

Finally, the administrative efficiency argument is that many of the present deficiencies of the income and other related taxes could be removed with the adoption of a consumption tax. With such a system, the difficult task of defining real income by making the appropriate inflation adjustments can be avoided. Further, the existing weak logic for a separate corporation income tax and special capital gains treatment would be eliminated. The direct consumption tax offers the promise of a simple unified system of tax collection, which is far more efficient than the current array of taxes.

It is important to note that the consumption tax being proposed here is not similar to the value-added tax or any other tax based on the direct purchases by individuals. It is not another type of sales tax, but rather a personal tax where the base is income less savings. So-called "qualifying accounts" would be established and all deposits into such accounts would be tax deductible. The funds could be invested in savings accounts, bonds, stocks, mutual funds, and a wide array of financial instruments. The earnings of the assets of the account would not be taxed unless they were withdrawn and spent. Assets within the account could be sold and reinvested in other securities without taxation. These funds would be subject to taxation only when withdrawn, or possibly when transferred by gift or bequest.

Some saving and investment in the United States is already taxed in a manner consistent with a consumption tax. For instance, all consumer durables and owner-occupied housing are purchased with after-tax dollars but the imputed return on these items remains untaxed. Thus they are not subject to the "double taxation" implied by an income tax.

Most proposals for a consumption tax would not change the tax treatment of these items. They are very important in that roughly 20 percent of the country's net savings are made in the form of net accumulation of new owner-occupied housing alone. Further, there is also a significant amount of retirement savings which flows through private, state, local or federal government pension plans (excluding social security), and through cash value life insurance policies. These are either taxed on a deferral basis (where both the initial contribution and the return are sheltered from taxation but the payouts are taxable) or on a prepayment basis (where the initial contribution is subject to tax but both the return and payout are tax free). The two methods are identical except that the tax rate at the time of withdrawal may be different from that at the time of contribution. Both methods are similar to the treatment under a consumption tax, the deferral method being identical. In recent years roughly 30 percent of the net savings of the United States flow through these vehicles.

In aggregate, then, around 50 percent of savings currently enjoys taxation consistent with the consumption tax concept. We have already moved halfway towards a consumption tax. Unfortunately, we have gained none of its economic efficiency benefits. The reason is that the other half of savings is not only taxed heavily by the personal income tax, but much of it is further subject to the corporation income tax. When tax concessions are given to only particular forms of saving for particular purposes, the distortions created (the reallocation of savings and investment toward these favored forms and away from those which remain heavily taxed) offset the gain caused by the increased amount of total saving and capital formation.

In a recent study with Don Fullerton of Princeton and John Whalley of the University of Western Ontario (Fullerton, Shoven, and Whalley 1979), I examined the efficiency benefits that a consumption tax offers the economy. We found that making all savings deductible (and maintaining government revenue by raising the basic rate structure) would offer efficiency gains whose total present value is between $80 and $130 billion (1980 dollars). The benefits of doing this and also integrating the corporation income tax could total as high as half a trillion dollars. We found that in many ways the position we have assumed halfway between an income and consumption tax is worse than either extreme. A pure income tax (which would double-tax all saving regardless of source) combined with corporation income tax integration would also be more efficient than the present system. The gain would total around $300 billion, or 60 percent as much as moving to a consumption tax. The inference is that removing the uneven treatment of savings is extremely important and would be beneficial even if it was accomplished by taxing all savings heavily.

The consumption tax is attractive in many respects and need not be more regressive than the current tax system. Nothing prevents establishing any rate schedule desired—it can be as progressive as one likes. The implementation of a consumption tax could be quite simple. The method that Michael Boskin and I have advocated elsewhere (Boskin and Shoven 1980, pp. 164–70) would involve extreme liberalization of Keogh and Individual Retirement Account (IRA) pension-savings vehicles. If the limits on these were raised, if the assets which could be held were very inclusive, and if the taxable withdrawal could be made at any time, then these existing institutions could effectively institute a consumption or expenditure tax.

THREE VIEWS OF TAX POLICY

The three broad reforms just discussed are not mutually exclusive. Integrating the corporation income tax with the personal tax system is desirable under either an inflation-indexed income tax or a consumption tax. The indexation issue would be less pressing, however, should savings be made fully deductible in that many of the inflation problems deal with the taxation of capital income.

This chapter has emphasized long-run structural improvements in tax policy by concentrating on the issues of efficiency and equity. Fortunately, these considerations seem to be getting increased political attention today, but much of the discussion regarding tax policy centers around other aspects of the policies. Taxes are a major Keynesian tool in stabilizing the level of economic activity. Therefore, much of the debate concerning appropriate tax policy concerns the short-run situation of the business cycle. Surtaxes are proposed to slow inflation, or rebate programs are advocated as stimulative measure. These tax adjustments typically are aimed at affecting aggregate demand, both consumption and investment. Examples of policies aimed at investment and capital formation are the investment tax credit (which has often been adjusted according to the stage in the business cycle) and the acceleration of depreciation deductions. While it is my opinion that taxes can be a constructive tool in stabilizing the economy, I believe that attention to this matter has diverted too much attention from the effects of taxes on the long-run structure of the economy.

Recently there has been a great deal of interest at both the state and federal levels in regulating taxes and spending by constitutional amendment or federal legislation. This movement has been fueled by the observation that governments spent as much money as is generated by their tax sources, and the funds from these sources have been growing very rapidly due to inflation. The feeling seems to be that the only way to check government spending is to institutionalize an overall control either on tax collections or on spending. There is some validity to this line of argument, although more so at the state and local levels than at the federal. Federal tax rates have been periodically lowered, roughly counteracting the continual increases due to inflation. The limitation measures are not good substitutes for fundamental reforms of the type which have been advocated here. They fail to address most of the inefficiencies and inequities of the current tax system and they sacrifice a valuable degree of flexibility. A firm effective tax limitation would not allow adjustments to changes in the state of the economy or such policy shocks as were created by the formation of the Organization of Petroleum Exporting Countries in 1974. A far more sound approach would be to establish real income as a tax base through indexation and remove the redundant corporation income tax. An attractive alternative is to establish consumption as the basis for taxation in this country. Either program of reform would generate substantial efficiency gains for the economy and would attack the problems we have in the design of our tax system more fundamentally than merely putting a cap on total collections.

Economists have long advocated the tax reforms discussed in this chapter and are in substantial agreement regarding their attractiveness. Nonetheless, very little progress has been made in implementing them. The three proposals I have examined are sweeping in scope and would involve a thorough revamping of the federal tax system. It may be politically naive to think that such large changes can be accomplished in a single step. A more reasonable hope may be for a sequence of partial reforms which would ultimately result in the revised tax program. Some of the steps might involve indexing capital gains taxation, gradually liberalizing individual retirement accounts, and offering some relief for individuals from their current double taxation.

While I would support a planned phase-in of the three major reform proposals of this chapter, I caution that halfway towards the goal of an efficient and rational tax policy is not necessarily a desirable location for our tax system; it may not even be an improvement from the present situation. The current U.S. system suffers greatly from its failure to implement a consistent philosophy of taxation. For example, while roughly half of savings is taxed on a basis consistent with an expenditure tax, none of the efficiency benefits of this system are enjoyed. Today the problems of inflation, capital formation, and the inequities of the existing system of tax collection have become so severe as to demand attention. These policies could alleviate the perceived tax crisis and aid in reestablishing a pattern of real economic growth. It is time to think in terms of fundamental tax revision rather than to continue with the policy of incremental modification followed for so long. Today we have a tax program which is unsatisfactory from almost every perspective.

DISCUSSION

BREAK: I think continuing high rates of inflation pose a very serious threat to the income tax. The income tax, as you well know, is the major source of revenue for the federal government, so I suppose that if inflation poses a serious threat to the income tax, it also poses a very serious threat to the federal government unless the federal government does something to change the nature of its tax system. The reason for this threat is that inflation makes that tax one of the worst taxes that we have—not only because the rate structure is not adjusted for inflation, which means that many people get pushed up into higher brackets each year, but also because income is very badly mismeasured in an inflationary economy.

Property income is simply not measured accurately at all. It is measured in nominal terms, and it ought to be adjusted for inflation and measured in real terms. For example, tax-exempt municipal bonds are now being overtaxed. Just think about that for a minute. The reason they are is that the nominal interest rate on tax-exempt municipals is, say, 8.5

percent to 9.0 percent, while the rate of inflation is substantially bigger than that number. Therefore, the real rate of return to the investor is negative and should be entered into his tax base as a negative number. This means that such income is now being overtaxed, even though it is not taxed at all. The fact is that you get into some very strange situations when you have a high rate of inflation and are using as your major source of federal revenue a tax which measures the base very badly indeed.

Let me add to Sweeney's law that "regulation begets regulations," Break's law that "tax inequity begets other tax inequities." The failure to index the income tax base makes it difficult if not impossible to treat capital gains and losses equitably. I think we are likely to get various kinds of ad hoc schemes for treating savings, either exempting small amounts—I believe there is a bill in Sacramento right now that would allow young people to put money into a special account, exempt from state income tax, to save up to buy a house. If we don't index the income tax base for inflation, we are going to get a lot of those ad hoc reforms, which would make for a very bad tax system.

I would expect one of two lines of development during the 1980s if we don't succeed in dealing with inflation. Either the role of the income tax in the federal system will be greatly reduced and we will go to a value-added tax, retail sales tax, expenditure tax, or something of that sort, or there will be very serious opposition to continued high levels of spending on the part of the federal government because it is financing itself from a very bad tax.

I hope very much that none of these extreme moves are necessary and that the inflation rate can be brought down. Yet if it isn't, we should either move away from heavy reliance on the income tax or give very serious thought to indexing its base. That is *very* difficult to do, unfortunately. It is complex, but essential if we are going to continue to rely as heavily as we have on the income tax.

KOTLIKOFF: In terms of equity and efficiency, I think it would be worthwhile for policymakers to take a more lifetime prospective in terms of redistribution. The profession in general has moved in this direction with the advent of the life-cycle model and the permanent income hypothesis to a view of people as living more in their average income year than in any one specific year. The interesting question is not redistribution within a year, but over a lifetime. I also agree that one has to look at the entire tax transfer system to understand how our redistribution is really working. For example, in the social security sphere we engage in a gigantic program to try and redistribute funds to the elderly on the one hand, while on the other the reality since the 1940s is that the relative income position of the elderly has not changed. Part of the reason is the tax on earnings after retirement has greatly reduced their work effort. On the one hand, we make these transfers; on the other, we set up an implicit tax system which encourages them to reduce their work, thereby reducing their income—we hand it here, and we take it away there. Our great problem is to develop policies which are consistent, so that one is not undoing another.

Going to a consumption tax as opposed to an income tax will almost immediately increase savings. However, I would be somewhat concerned about the distribution of wealth that might ensue, and distribution of wealth as a value might compete with capital accumulation to determine on a national level whether we want to go to a consumption tax.

BOSKIN: I would like to return to the question of the equity of the tax transfer system as a whole. It would be useful to distinguish people's views about the progressivity or regressivity of a *particular* tax device and the very modest changes that they may achieve relative to some neutral tax, given the amount of tax revenue raised, on the distribution of income. Given the enormous changes the *transfer* payment system has created in the overall after-tax and transfer distribution of income, the gain from trying to play around with the rest of the distribution is perhaps not worth the large cost.

Another important issue is the unit of account. We have a lot of transfer payments that are paid to individuals, a lot paid to families, some taxes collected from individuals, others from families. Many other economies, many other tax systems in other economies, have been moving toward the individual as the most appropriate taxable unit. This is particularly important—and perhaps understandable, since the demographic and household structure of the population is changing so much, with increasing numbers of single-headed households for people who are in different states at different times.

SHOVEN: On the distributional consequences of taxes on oil companies, Ron McKinnon made an observation a long time ago that to a large extent the big oil companies are owned by pension funds and small investors. There are no richer people in the economy than the owners of the independent oil companies, so in some sense the independents, who still have a depletion allowance and so forth, continue to ask for special favors, while Exxon and other large companies, on which your retirement depends, continue to get taxed more and more heavily.

OLSEN: A lot of tax accountants have said for years that whenever you try to make substantial and wholesale changes that are called tax reform, you are amazed at the number of vested interests opposed to them. In fact, it was very difficult to develop a proposal that satisfies all corporations on the issue of integrating the corporate and personal income taxes because many people tend to maximize the advantages of the existing tax structure, whatever it is. Since many of them are taking full advantage of the existing credits and would derive no benefits from the integration of the tax structure, they opposed integration.

8

GEORGE F. BREAK

State and Local
Finance in the 1980s

The taxpayer's view of government spending. California's Proposition 13. The role of income and sales taxes. Local financing of needed services. The value-added tax. Intergovernmental grants. Revenue sharing. The current challenge to state and local administrations.

Trying to describe the condition of state and local finance as it is likely to develop during the decade of the 1980s is like reporting on the probable future of a young person in the throes of adolescence. Rapid changes, forced by a complex admixture of economic necessity and volatile political climate, eliminate almost all certainty except that of change itself. Local governments throughout the country, staggered by the damaging conjunction of inflation and slow economic growth and beset by an aroused populace that either has put or threatens to put rigorous limits on their powers to tax, look to their state capitals and to Washington for help. Where public expenditure needs are most pressing, tax resources are becoming harder to come by. As a result, the fiscal structure of our federal system is undergoing a process of alteration almost as sweeping as the one which in recent years has transformed our city skylines.

The multistate movement to limit government's ability to tax and spend is particularly significant because it has very largely, as in California, come about through ballot box legislation. This populist wave has obviously formed because the process of representative democracy has not proven effective as a means of reining the growth of the public sector. Yet it is elected officials, with the help of their civil service staffs, who have to implement these often crudely drafted expressions of public will. The partnership this creates is reminiscent of a shotgun wedding, with a reluctant groom made to profess his commitment to marriage under the determined gaze of an aroused and fully assembled clan. Two questions emerge from the paradoxical picture of an impatient public tired of promises—promises from representatives who seem unable to use their own legislative powers to respond to the increasingly strident demands of their constituents for slowing the momentum of big government. Why didn't they do it on their own? And can they do it now?

Perhaps the key to the first question is that a whole combination of circumstances—including inflation, a changing population age structure, and the deeply entrenched assumption that when there is a problem government should deal with it—finally reached a point of impasse. Between 1955 and 1975 state and local government expenditures outpaced the economy's growth, rising from $33 billion, or 8 percent of the gross national product (GNP), to $231 billion, or 15 percent of GNP. While this increase has slowed down in relative terms, state and local budgets still absorb nearly 14 percent of GNP. Rapid rises in the cost of welfare services, unemployment insurance, and other benefits for labor have been particularly heavy contributors to the pressure. As postwar babies grew older, increased costs of higher education offset what modest declines occurred in public school spending. A major drop in expenditures has come in the transportation area as the interstate highway system nears completion, yet future needs for public transport may reverse that trend.

Ironically, even as public expenditures surged upward, the average citizen's perception was that service levels were declining. Schools were a case in point. Increasing disillusionment with educational quality coincided with escalating costs, which were slow to fall even when enrollments began to drop sharply. School boards seemed helpless in the face of these developments—unable either to improve educational standards or to scale down their oversize establishments. They tended to avoid the painful difficulties of making strategic, policy-oriented cuts in staff by leaving matters to fate. Reducing staff by attrition obviates political confrontation but takes its toll of program; if several English teachers happen to leave or retire, people trained in mathematics or physical education may have to be pushed into those slots. Like salary freezes, such methods often drive out the best teachers by lowering morale and inducing those with the most attractive alternatives to move elsewhere. Such institutional rigidities as State Educational Code restrictions, union regulations, and political alignments turn budget reductions into nightmares. All this comes across to the public as a clear indication that their interests are subordinate to those of the system.

Disillusioned with government's obvious lack of success in solving such problems and pressured by rapidly rising, inflation-fed tax burdens, people in increasing numbers seem suddenly to have decided that they want to get off this merry-go-round. Unable to face the complex reasons for it or their own share of the responsibility for producing it, they focus on the theme of waste in government, insisting that the public sector is too big and that it must somehow be made to work more efficiently.

EFFICIENCY, EQUITY, OR WHAT?

That there is an extraordinary irony in this demand seems to have escaped many voters. What they are now asking is that an economic criterion of efficiency be imposed on a political system dedicated to many worthy goals but certainly not to efficiency. Democracy is inherently inefficient, and the more protective it becomes of each and every individual, the less efficiently it deals with the problems of the society as a whole. It must answer to such a wide range of tastes and needs that it necessarily operates on the basis of compromise or of stalemated nonaction, adopting not first but second, third, or fourth best answers when weighed on the scale of efficiency. Politicians know individually that they win few friends by making hard decisions, as those only polarize antagonism. In fiscal matters, they win supporters by authorizing spending, for which they get direct credit. Cutting taxes simply allows people to keep what is already theirs, and politicians get little credit for that. The political system, in other words, responds more readily to pinpointed, limited interests than to general ones. In time, however, broadly based antagonisms gradually build up into ground swells like the one in California which swept Proposition 13 into law. In the general *mêlée*, agile politicians who have passively waited for the wave to grow, doing nothing on their own to calm its force, can pick up friends by riding it along. Only those bold enough to stand in the way of history are likely to suffer.

So neither efficiency nor difficult decisions are anything that politicians are particularly interested in advancing or talented at achieving. But can they, under duress, respond to a tough-minded economy imperative from the public? That essentially remains to be seen as state and local officials in a number of states wrestle with the task that their electorates have laid on them. While California is only one of these states, it provides an excellent example for other states, with somewhat less fully aroused electorates, to observe.

That the belt-tightening job is a thankless one is obvious. Politicians know that Mussolini made the trains run on time and that efficiency comes at a price which people in the United States really do not want to pay. So what does the taxpayer rebellion really mean? Two years after Proposition 13 California officials are still trying to figure that out, responding more to necessity than to calculated policy but meanwhile making adjustments that may not be far off the mark. The direct message of Proposition 13 was clear enough — people want less reliance on the property tax. Whether they also want less government spending was not an explicit part of that message, as the presence of a multi-billion-dollar state surplus, fed by inflated receipts from the income and sales taxes, obscured that issue. Proposition 4, passed in 1979, did place limits on the growth of state and local spending, but their effectiveness remains to be seen. Proposition 13 may well prove to be the greater spending constraint in the long run.

Since the tax cut imposed by Proposition 13 was at the local level and the surplus was at the state level, this adjustment could not even be begun without a remarkable degree of cooperation between the two levels of government. The first reaction was semi-panic. While local officials reeled under the impact of losing more than half the revenue from the principal tax source, the governor sent a similar shock wave through the ranks of state government by imposing a hiring and salary freeze there, despite the burgeoning state coffers. Local officials busily authorized such new nonproperty taxes as they could before the Proposition 13 deadline on such authorizations took effect; some also quickly imposed a number of user charges that were not forbidden by the Proposition 13 ukase. Meanwhile Sacramento began working out the means of implementing the clumsily written initiative and slowly started to disgorge the vast store of surplus state revenue, doling out measured amounts of temporary "bail-out" funds to local governments. Sacramento's largesse did not extend to all of the special districts dependent on property tax support, so the proffered relief by no means filled all the depleted porridge bowls. Some of these deficiencies have resulted in sharp drops in service levels; others have been at least partially made up by increased user charges.

Amid all this backing, shuffling, and filling, one major fact stands out. This drastic cut in the importance of the property tax as a local revenue source, combined with a filling-in of some of the void—but not all of it—by state revenue, has produced a pronounced change in the profile of the California tax system. How much further surgery on this profile will be approved by the voters as new initiatives are presented to them remains to be seen. In the short run, the significant reshuffling that has occurred since the passage of Proposition 13 has produced an effect that many liberal tax reformers should applaud, as it has shifted the weight of local government financing away from the property tax and toward the income and sales taxes.

WHAT ABOUT THE PROPERTY TAX?

While economists can easily adduce evidence to show that the property tax is not the regressive horror it is widely believed to be, there are certainly many reasons why it should not be relied upon as heavily as California was doing. A family's housing expenditures may, over an extended period of time, be an excellent index of their "normal" or average long-term ability to pay; yet a tax imposed on a capital asset that yields income in kind but not in cash still exacts regular cash payments, and these impose hardships on taxpayers whose income flow is not evenly stretched out over the long period. Typically the liquidity pinch has been hardest for young people with housing needs larger than their current incomes and old people living on reduced, often fixed levels of income in houses they acquired and paid for during their working years.

These problems are greatly exacerbated during periods of rapid inflation, when housing purchased for modest amounts is suddenly assessed at values far exceeding the owner's current ability to pay taxes. It is not only having to pay tax on rapidly rising unrealized gains, but the frightening uncertainty of what the liability will be from year to year that makes this levy so vexatious. And added to these distressing features are the uncertainties inherent in the assessment process. It is very hard to attach accurate values to property that has not changed hands for long periods of time—or even short periods in times of rapid inflation. These assessment difficulties produce obvious inequities that lower public confidence in the tax. All these elements make the property tax an unattractive one to rely on heavily.

Unfortunately for California, the particular formula by which Proposition 13 performs its surgery on this hated tax will have the effect of increasing its inequity rather than improving it. This comes from the fact that the measure decrees the use of a double standard for assessment: property remaining in the same hands since 1975 must be assessed on the basis of its value then, plus an increase of no more than 2 percent per year, while property constructed, sold, or transferred after that time is assessed at its actual market value, with the 2 percent annual increase thereafter computed from that base. Given the almost astronomical rise in housing prices since 1975, this process generates remarkable

assessment differentials which can be expected before long
to elicit demands for reform from new purchasers who find
their effective tax rates considerably higher than those of
their neighbors who have moved in less recently.

A further effect of this inequitable assessment basis is
that business property, which tends to change hands less frequently than residential property, will soon be carrying a
substantially diminished portion of the total property tax
load. This may well have the effect of pushing "reform" in
the questionable direction of demands for a split roll or
classified property tax, with business property taxed at a
higher rate than residential property. In other states such as
Minnesota and Ohio, where this has been tried, it has
resulted in a hodge-podge multiplication of classes based
more on political maneuvering than on economic equity. In
most opinions the net result of classified property taxes has
been a general decrease in the respectability of the levy.

A possible alternative to the classified tax might be the old
land-only tax or a modern variation of it known as the
"graded" tax which assesses land at a higher ratio to market
value than the buildings on it. Though passionately advocated by land-tax proponents who seem driven by an almost
religious fervor, this approach to reform, too, has serious
drawbacks. The pure land tax may be administrable in newly
developing areas where many parcels of vacant land provide
a basis of comparison for the valuation of built-upon land;
but in highly developed cities with few vacant lots, the land
underlying buildings can only be assessed by estimating the
value of the structures and abstracting that from the potential sales price of the package. Even the graded tax is sufficiently difficult to administer that the Department of Taxation of the State of Hawaii, where it has been in effect, has
recommended abolishing it. Its avowed object, of course, is to
encourage intensive land use; the effects on Waikiki, for example, where the phalanx of high-rise structures has become

all but impenetrable, has given a number of former admirers second thoughts about the advisability of the policy.

Aside from the administrative problems inherent in the land or graded tax and the high-density consequence of it, which would appear to be sharply at variance with the current enthusiasm for preserving and rehabilitating old houses and neighborhoods, changes in the property tax base cannot be made without producing serious equity effects. Since expected property tax burdens become capitalized in property values, changes in the way these burdens are apportioned produce immediate windfall gains for those whose burdens are lightened and windfall losses for those who lose in the exchange. These immediate inequities could, of course, be overbalanced by long-run gains from the tax change, but that case remains to be made.

One way in which a low-rate property tax of the kind California has opted for could be rehabilitated and given new respectability would be to give it a new and unashamed image as a benefits tax, a means of paying for property-related services. Some plastic surgery on the clumsily slimmed-down profile of the California tax would be necessary to diminish the inequities arising from the lack of a unified assessment standard. With that gap bridged sufficiently to guarantee a reasonably fair distribution of burdens, a carefully contained property tax with rates adjusted downward when assessments rose disproportionately could quite equitably be used to finance the wide range of protective, maintenance, and civic-enhancement services that directly relate to property values. Determining the extent of the services to be financed wholly or largely from property tax revenue would be one of the key functions of local lawmakers. Competition with neighboring jurisdictions would be confined to the quite rational game of providing a satisfactorily high level of services at a satisfactorily low price. Comparative property values would be the measure of success. Unless a higher effective property tax brought better services, property values would decline in relation to those elsewhere; residents would in effect be getting what they paid for. In the case of business property, a property tax based on current market value would, just as in the case of residential property, provide a means of paying for the local services from which it benefited.

Assuming that in the wake of Proposition 13 and its counterparts elsewhere the property tax could be streamlined in something of this fashion, the question next arises as to where the rest of the money required by local governments to finance their many and increasingly expensive needs can be expected to come from. The ad hoc arrangements made in California in response to voter action on the property tax indicate one of the directions that may be followed. That is greater assumption by the state of fiscal responsibility for many services and facilities that in most states have weighed heavily on local governments. How feasible, over the long period, will prove to be any major shift in this direction will depend to a large extent on the tolerance of the public to the two mainstays of state revenue—the income and sales taxes. If California is again a bellwether, 1980 may be a decisive year in determining how the present rather hectic reshuffling of the state/local tax load will be resolved.

WILL THE INCOME TAX BE NEXT?

California's decision to dismantle its property tax might have been seen, in light of the state surplus, as a clear vote of confidence in the income tax which supplies much of that surplus revenue. It has become a major tax source for forty-three states. Many people, in fact, have long looked upon the income tax as the very model of a modern ability-to-pay levy and have advocated its widespread use at the local as well as the state and federal levels. It is predictable, familiar, and (given withholding) convenient to pay. Yet it too has an uncertain future.

Pressure has grown on the income tax as more and more states have intensified their reliance on it, partly as a way of increasing the progressivity of their tax systems. Commendable as that aim may be, the effect has been to turn the levy into a considerable irritant. Part of the difficulty comes from inflation, which pushes taxpayers into ever higher tax brackets even though in constant-dollar terms they are not earning more. This problem can be easily solved by "indexing" the tax structure—i.e., adjusting it for inflation. California's failure to do this before the passage of Proposition 13 was a primary reason for the huge surplus in state tax revenue that made that initiative possible.

Ironically, a year after it was passed the legislature did enact an indexing provision, a move probably taken in the hope of forestalling the second Jarvis proposal that would not only mandate indexing but cut income tax rates in half (1980's Proposition 9). The legislature's temporary indexing plan, which doubtless will be made permanent if the initiative fails, greatly improves the equity of the tax by recognizing that the paper gains created by inflation do not indicate real increases in ability to pay. Even more important than this kind of structural indexation, but more difficult to implement, would be indexation of the income tax base. Inflation distorts the measurement of all kinds of property income, and unless the necessary adjustments are made in such items as depreciation allowances, inventory accounting, and capital gains and losses, the equity of the income tax will be seriously undermined.

Even indexed for inflation, however, the income tax may be in some jeopardy as a primary source of state revenue because of the intensive use being made of it at the federal level where it supplies the lion's share of tax revenue. Current income is certainly one important measure of ability to pay, but it is by no means the only one, particularly as it is defined for income tax purposes. Tax laws necessarily make some rather arbitrary distinctions in defining a tax base, and the income tax is no exception. Tax literature and newspapers alike abound with discussions of the nontaxed and lightly taxed kinds of income—ranging from three-martini business lunches to interest from municipal bonds to social security benefits. The problems arise not only from the difficulty of drawing a line between personal income and necessary business expenses, but also from differing opinions as to what kinds of income and uses of income should be exempt from tax.

If contributions to educational and charitable causes, for example, were not deductible for tax purposes, many useful institutions now supported by private donations would go out of business. Unless the government stepped in to support them directly, instead of indirectly through "tax expenditures," society would lose their benefits. Special rates for capital gains draw much criticism, but taxing them fully would seriously affect the economy by drying up investment capital and the net tax gain would be very little. Employee fringe benefits provide income in kind, but suggestions to tax them bring down storms of protest.

Few people would agree that the federal income tax law defines these matters to their perfect satisfaction, but such things are a matter of compromise, political expediency, and administrative feasibility. So they live with the law and work periodically to make changes in it. As more and more states, however, adopt the federal income tax base with few modifications, all the inequities and imperfections that are built into it become magnified. The magnification process grows as state (and even local) income taxes added onto this base become more and more important sources of revenue. The problems then become acute.

One time-honored rule of public finance is that the more diversified a tax system is, the more bearable the imperfections of any one levy. The possibility that our tax system as a whole is leaning too much toward the income tax has worrisome implications. Such concentrated pressure leads people to find ways of avoiding or even evading the tax. The much-touted exploitation of tax loopholes is probably the most innocent form of this, since upon close inspection the loopholes nearly always turn out to be valid and necessary aspects of income definition. Yet they do present a danger, for when tax law provisions cause people to change their normal working, spending, or investing patterns in order to take advantage of tax breaks, that tax begins to violate the cardinal rule of neutrality. And when heavy income tax burdens cause people to take the illegal route of evading the tax by not reporting income, the situation turns even uglier. The average wage and salary earner, who cannot and probably would not take this course, winds up carrying more than his or her share of the burden because others are not carrying theirs.

This situation is made possible by the fact that some types of income (tips and other types of gratuities are obvious examples, though by no means the only ones) are not matters of record and can therefore be reported pretty much at the discretion of the taxpayer. The "subterranean economy," as it is often called, has under the pressure of a growing income tax shown signs of reaching monumental proportions. Aside from outright concealment of income, padding of expense accounts, and the like, many noncash transactions, involving such things as exchanges of services instead of money, contribute to the underground economy. The net result is that the income tax is fast losing its reputation as a paragon of equity.

HOW ABOUT THE SALES TAX?

With the property tax on the ropes and the income tax in doubt, most states—including California—are left with the sales tax. This has been a traditional bête noire of tax reformers, who often have accused it of regressiveness; but the time may have come to take a new look at it. Paradoxically, while inflation has made both the property tax and the income tax harder to justify, it has made the sales tax somewhat easier. Whereas rapidly rising housing prices push the property tax beyond the current ability to pay of many taxpayers and inflation of incomes produces serious equity problems in an unindexed and overburdened income tax, the sales tax can, as long as it provides some buffering mechanism for the poor, maintain a relatively defensible position in times of inflation. First, however, its regressive impact on the poor must be moderated.

There is more than one way of doing this. Many states exempt food, prescription drugs, and selected other basic necessities, as well as the sale of some services. A number of states, however, have adopted a more comprehensive approach to sales taxation which many economists find more equitable than the exemption device. This is to make all sales subject to tax (the wider base allowing a lower tax rate to produce the same revenue) and then to return to low-income families the amount of money they could be expected to spend on tax payments for a basic subsistence budget. The return is paid in the form either of cash rebates to families not subject to income tax or of income tax credits for those who are. This tax equivalent reimbursement allows people complete freedom of choice; it comes to them even if they grow their own food instead of buying it and spend their cash rebate on other things that in states using exemptions might well be taxed. It has the further equity advantage of not subsidizing the relatively lavish food budgets of the more affluent. Exempting all food purchases, in other words, means subsidizing the rich more than the poor, since the rich buy far more food. With a credit arrangement it is possible not only to relieve the sales tax of its regressive impact at the bottom of the income scale but to make it, to a limited degree, positively progressive by phasing out the credit for wealthier people.

The kinds of distortions and perverse effects that inflation-driven income taxes inflict on the economy are less likely to be created by the sales tax. Although the recent proliferation of flea markets and garage sales indicates an increasing tendency to conduct sales outside the normal channels, the great preponderance of purchases unquestionably is made in the form of recorded sales. The amount of money people spend on consumer goods (and services) is certainly one important measure of their ability to pay taxes. And, in contrast to the income tax, which makes no distinction between what is spent for consumption and what is invested or saved, the sales tax does. To the extent, therefore, that inflation is fed by an excess of consumption at the expense of saving and investment, the sales tax should help by making consumption more expensive relative to the other uses. The fact that the Consumer Price Index includes it in its measurement of price increases gives it an inflation-push effect that it should not have, in the opinion of many economists. If it were properly treated as a tax, they argue, rather than as a part of the price, it would be excluded from the complex network of elements that feed on each other and fuel the inflationary spiral. Particularly in view of the uncertain future of the property and income taxes and the distinct probability that sales taxes will become increasingly important components of state tax systems, it would be wise to eliminate this misinterpretation. Removed from its role as one of the agents that push wage rates higher, the sales tax could better serve as a restraint on consumption.

WHERE ARE LOCAL GOVERNMENTS TO TURN?

All these factors—the strengths, weaknesses, and revenue

limitations—of the tax sources traditionally used by state
and local governments must be carefully weighed when considering how the void left by voter-mandated tax limits is to
be filled. While the specific circumstances differ from state to
state, depending on the extent and nature of the limitations
enacted, California's immediate response to Proposition 13
was to accomplish quickly two long-sought reforms. One was
to do what many thought should have been done much
earlier in response to the *Serrano* decision—i.e., to make
school financing largely a state responsibility. Another was
to take a heavy and misplaced load off county budgets by
having the state assume most of their welfare costs.
Although there is no guarantee that the State of California
will continue to shoulder these burdens after the surplus is
exhausted, especially if its own taxing capacity is severely
limited by voter action, there is much to be said for the logic
of financing education and welfare from broadly based state
taxes rather than from local sources. Increased tax limitations at the state level could even contribute to pressure to
move the financing of these services up to the federal level,
though such a shift could pose a serious threat to local control. How much real local policy control actually remains,
given current federal and state regulations, is a moot question, but it is a concept that is still much prized, particularly
with respect to schools.

In the event that the California pattern of trimming the
property tax, long the mainstay of local finance, becomes a
general trend, there can be little doubt that there will be important shifts of fiscal responsibility for many basic services
to higher levels of government. Another likelihood, as the
Proposition 13 experience illustrates, is that local governments will have to turn to user charges as a means of financing some public goods. Many California cities, for example,
discovered that they had been heavily subsidizing the construction industry by supporting planning, engineering, and
inspection agencies largely at public expense. Their imposi-

tion of sharply increased fees produced some cries of woe and some hikes in construction costs, but the logic of charging those who benefited was, under the circumstances, hard to refute. Another common practice in the wake of Proposition 13 was to place higher charges on the use of leisure-time facilities, like libraries and swimming pools, that had been available for little or no cost to the user.

This new dependence on user charges is a combination of necessity and reaction to the standard practice in pre-Proposition 13 days of adding the costs of local services rather indiscriminately to the property tax load. The property tax was so available and assessments were rising so abundantly that the revenue from it seemed like manna from heaven. It was hard to resist simply paying for everything out of that money fount, and local officials were unfortunately slow to respond to the pain of taxpayers who assumed that mushrooming assessments would result in substantially lowered tax rates. The state even made an attempt to put ceilings on school, municipal, and county property taxes, but these did not make enough difference soon enough to head off the Proposition 13 meat axe. One defusing mechanism that few jurisdictions seemed to think of was to charge, on a marginal cost basis, for some services specifically benefiting identifiable users. Obviously, services going primarily to the poor could not be funded in this manner, but those provided for contractors, homeowners, and other individuals quite capable of paying their fair share of the costs could have been priced this way and need not have been so heavily subsidized by the general taxpayer.

One factor which has discouraged intensive use of user charges and taxes clearly based on the benefits-received principle is the apparently common assumption that virtually all levies should be tied to the ability-to-pay standard of equity. With more and more money coming to local governments in the form of grants from the federal and state levels where broad-based ability taxes dominate, it becomes increasingly tantalizing to suggest that local jurisdictions might well reacquaint themselves with the merits of the benefits-received standard.

As suggested earlier, the stripped-down property tax lends itself readily to the benefits concept; but it is by no means alone, for the principle can easily be extended to a good many parts of the local finance scene. When, for example, the heavy costs inflicted on cities by automobile traffic are considered, the motorcar seems to be a very much undertaxed commodity. Why automobile owners should use the streets for storing their vehicles is one question. Long-term day and night parking of large numbers of vehicles on the public streets impedes access by maintenance crews to utility lines, by customers to places of business, and by citizens to public facilities. Car owners who provide their own off-street parking pay a price for it in the form of parking fees or added property taxes or rents. There seems no reason why those who use the streets for this purpose should not pay a user charge. Traffic law violators, too, could be made to pay a much higher proportion of the costs of traffic law enforcement than they customarily do.

Although many people would be opposed to attaching charges to such public "merit goods" as libraries and parks, it makes sense to ask why heavy users should not, if able, contribute to the support of these facilities by paying for library cards and for admission to tennis courts and swimming pools, just as golfers have long been accustomed to paying greens fees. To lay the cost of such facilities entirely on the general citizenry, many of whom (poor as well as rich) do not use them, can be questioned on grounds of equity. Those concerned about the regressiveness of marginal-cost user charges would do well to consider the equity aspects of charging all these facilities to the general taxpayer when their benefits largely accrue to the able-bodied and relatively affluent. Free tickets could easily be made available to anyone really unable to pay. Relieving the poor of the onus of subsidizing the recreational habits of the more affluent would reduce the regressive impact of local tax policies. This kind of pricing system should apply only, of course, to nonessential services such as leisure-time facilities. It would not be at all appropriate for needed services that benefit the entire community—such as police and fire protection, street maintenance, and the like. Those are required for the safety and well-being of the populace as a whole and should be supported by general revenue.

One reason why user charges have tended to be underutilized in the past is that they are not deductible from federal income taxes while state and local taxes are. Tax-supported facilities have therefore been subsidized by the federal government for the rich but not for the poor. Shifting to a user-charge basis would eliminate this inequity and have the further advantage of subjecting public services to the market test. Insufficient demand would show that people did not find them worth paying for. Such a finding would enhance the efficiency of government.

Local taxation of business has long been a sensitive issue; with a sharply curtailed property tax it becomes even more so. Localities have traditionally tended to compete for new business by offering temporary tax abatements or other inducements, on the obvious assumption that in the long run the business will supply more tax revenue than the city will spend to service the enterprise. In recent years ecological considerations have caused this assumption to be questioned, particularly in the case of firms with a high pollution potential. As this concern grows, penalty charges may well become more common than tax abatements.

In general, the prospect of limited property tax revenue and a business share that will gradually decline in relative importance is causing local governments in California to cast about for new ways of taxing business. Many cities are trying to increase business license taxes, but rising pressure focuses more attention on the controversial question of what these fees are based on. Since California, for reasons of its own, does not sanction local use of a net profits tax, most cities have imposed a flat fee or else a tax based either on gross receipts or on the average number of employees. The wide range of profit margins for different kinds of enterprises and the fact that both gross receipts and the number of employees are more functions of the kind of activity engaged in than of a firm's profitability give any of these levies low ratings on ability-to-pay grounds. When judged by the benefits-received standard, the average number of employees measure makes only a little more sense than the others; gross receipts (and even net profits) do not necessarily tell anything about a firm's utilization of local services or the extent of its business activity carried out in the taking jurisdiction.

One possibility worth considering as a substitute for these levies is a business tax based on value added (VAT). In California this would require approval by the voters, but it offers considerable advantages in both equity and neutrality. Measuring the amount of value added by a firm's operations within a given jurisdiction would involve some separation of accounting records for firms doing business in other places as well, but some method of allocation could be worked out. The result would register the amount of productive activity carried out at the taxed location and therefore would serve as a reasonable measure of the benefits received there. The value added tax has the further advantage of treating all factors of production—labor, land, and capital—equally.

Local governments concerned with rationalizing their tax systems by giving them a firm and consistent basis in the benefits-received principle would do well to give serious consideration to a value added tax for local business. If the administrative difficulties of implementing it were considered too great, a do-it-yourself substitute could rather easily be devised by combining the regular business property tax with a payroll tax. The combination would provide a far more equitable measure of the local benefits accruing to a business than would property alone or payroll alone. The rates of the property and payroll taxes would be coordinated so as to simulate a value added tax; the procedure for effecting this would not be particularly complex nor prove unduly burdensome for local tax authorities. In comparison with a multiclass gross receipts tax (such as Los Angeles uses, for example), the simulated VAT would be a model of simplicity, equity, and efficiency.

WHAT PROSPECTS FOR INTERGOVERNMENTAL GRANTS?

The most radically changed and changing aspect of local finance in recent years has been its increasing dependence on higher levels of government. The presence of an extensive network of federal and state grants-in-aid, supplying more than half the revenue for many city budgets and averaging over 40 percent for all local governments, probably helps to account for some of the antitax vehemence. Taxpayers have become extremely aware of this new element in local finance and may well attribute to it some of the government "waste" that has become such an irritant. Whether or not these funds contribute to waste, they have certainly expanded the scope of local government activity and, in the process, increased pressure on the local tax base. This pressure comes from several directions—fund-matching requirements, added administrative expenses, operational costs of capital projects built but not run with grant funds. An unintended effect of this intergovernmental largesse (particularly that of the federal government, since state grants tend to be directed into the standard government services) may be to reinforce the conviction that there is plenty of money around to take up the slack left by cuts in taxes nearer home.

That impression, however, may be an exaggerated one. Although federal grants-in-aid to state and local governments rose rapidly between 1958 and 1978, at an average pace of nearly 15.0 percent per year, that climb has abruptly leveled off. From a 1978 total of $77.9 billion, federal grants went up only about 6.0 percent to $82.9 billion in 1979, and are estimated at $88.9 billion (a 7.0 percent increase) for 1980. These increases lag behind both inflation and state and local government spending. Federal aid, for example, fell from 26.4 percent of state/local expenditures in 1978 to 25.6 percent in 1979 and is expected to be even lower in 1980 and 1981 (*Special Analyses: Budget of the U.S. Government, Fiscal Year 1981*, p. 254).

With the slowdown in federal grant funds, local officials are likely to find the outlook for new money somewhat bleak, even in that usually bright direction. For the past twenty years they have tended to find Washington a ready source of funds when new capital projects were needed or budgetary pressures tightened. Mayors, school superintendents, and other local officials in many communities have built careers on their skills at grantsmanship. Many have become adept at picking their way through the maze of nearly five hundred kinds of federal grants, most of them of the categorical variety. Categorical (including project) grants account for over three-quarters of the more than $80 billion total. They are aimed at specified objectives and often require recipient jurisdictions to put up funds of their own. The matching requirements are variable and may or may not produce more in efficiency gains than they add to the costs of administration.

Recognizing the costly administrative complexities, overlapping, and operational inefficiencies and inadequacies of the categorical approach, the federal government in recent years has designed its newer programs along broader lines, giving more discretion to state and local officials. One form is that of block grants aimed at broadly defined program areas such as employment training, health, and community development. The most unrestricted form of all is general revenue sharing which states and localities can spend in any way they choose so long as they adhere to the regulatory standards laid down by the federal government for all grant monies. Since these standards are numerous and far-reaching, aimed at assuring compliance with a host of national policy objectives such as nondiscrimination in hiring and fund use, wage rate minimums, environmental protection, public participation in planning, relocation assistance, etc., they introduce both administrative complexities and vulnerability to noncompliance suits which can prove burdensome and costly.

While Washington has loosened its programmatic strings on its grant outlays, it has tightened these regulatory requirements. Local officials complain that they often prove to be irrelevant distractions from the real purposes that unrestricted grants should serve. The question is reminiscent of the perpetual argument over the importance of the compulsory figures exercises in figure skating competitions: are they necessary preconditions to any appropriate public undertaking or nitpicking prescripts that decrease the flexibility needed for effective performance? If the fungibility of federal grant funds should become a legal issue in noncompliance suits, it could make virtually all the expenditures of recipient governments subject to the regulations.

Such questions are certain to figure importantly in the debate over whether the general revenue sharing program should be renewed or allowed to expire on 1 October 1980. Both Congress and the administration have been guarded in their enthusiasm about the program, but once again (as in 1972 and 1976) it comes up for reconsideration in the heat of a presidential election campaign. State and local officials have expressed a distinct preference for it over more restricted forms of federal aid, and the Davis-Bacon prevailing wage rate requirements have reduced the opposition of organized labor. Yet aside from the complex allocation for-

mulas and regulatory standards, Congress leaves few of its
fingerprints on the money, and the personal stake of its
members in the program seems correspondingly tenuous.
While its importance to hard-pressed local governments in
an election year makes it a hard horse not to back, the
amount Congress puts up may not be very generous.

Throughout its short life, which has already included two
incarnations, general revenue sharing has probably been the
most carefully monitored program in history. The Brookings
Institution, for one, has maintained a systematic watch on
its uses and effects and has traced some interesting changes.
Its overall impact has been expansionary, with four-fifths of
the money during the first five years going into new capital
outlay or enlarged programs and only one-fifth into taxpayer
relief, through tax reduction or avoidance of tax increases.
Where fiscal pressures have been most severe (as in many of
the larger jurisdictions), more of the shared revenue has
gone into program maintenance; smaller and less pressured
governments were, particularly at first, more likely to opt for
new capital projects and expanded current operations. With
the passage of time, however, these differences have become
less marked, and most jurisdictions have been using more of
the funds to maintain current spending levels and stabilize
taxes. Studies of specific uses of shared revenue show that
local governments have tended to reinforce their public
safety, transportation, and recreation programs, while state
governments have increased their funding of education.

The state/local differences in the use of revenue sharing
are particularly significant in view of the apparently growing
sentiment in Congress in favor of eliminating or greatly
reducing the distributions to state governments. Their
reasoning is that state governments in general are relatively
affluent, while cities (and especially some of the largest ones)
are hovering on the brink of insolvency and while the hard-
pressed federal government is desperately trying to bring inflation (and its own budget) under control.

The plausibility of this argument is a matter of concern to many observers, including the Advisory Commission on Intergovernmental Relations, whose job it is to study the operations of the federal system. These observers contend that the comparative affluence of some state governments is not shared by all and obscures more important factors which argue strongly for continuing and even strengthening the role of the states as intermediaries in revenue sharing. During 1979, they point out, the combined operating budgets of state and local governments moved from a substantial surplus to a deficit. The much-publicized state surpluses were mostly owned by California, Alaska, and Texas, and in general were due to inflated receipts from unindexed personal income taxes which (as in California) were drawing increasing fire from taxpayers. Not only could this affluence be wiped out by a recession, but it is already on the wane as states give more help to their less fortunate local units.

These intrastate problems might be expected to leave Washington somewhat unmoved, since states have considerable freedom to adjust their tax systems to changing needs. On the other hand, there are certain incontrovertible facts which give great strength to the case for continuing to use the states as active partners in the revenue sharing program. In purely fiscal terms, the states are of central importance to any equitable sharing of revenue because they determine how fiscal responsibilities within their boundaries are divided up. No two states are identical in this respect. Some, like Hawaii, are highly centralized, with the state assuming full or nearly full responsibility for some services (such as education) that other states delegate at least partially to local jurisdictions. The mix is extremely complicated, as illustrated by a study done of the division of responsibilities within states in 1972. When both revenue-raising and expenditure responsibilities were built into a composite index, Hawaii with a split of 80 percent state and 20 percent local was at one end of the spectrum, and New York with 38 percent state and 62 percent local was at the other. The national average was 53 percent state and 47 percent local.

The general tendency is for small states to be more centralized and large states more decentralized, but what seems particularly significant is the average, which leads to the conclusion that the present revenue sharing allocation of one-third to state governments and two-thirds to localities greatly underestimates the role of the states. This fact, plus the lack of uniformity, strongly argues for giving the states a large measure of responsibility for assessing the needs and distributing the funds accordingly. Elimination of the states would not only require an almost prohibitively complex reworking of the local allocation formulas to avoid serious inequities, but would probably mean rethinking the exclusion of special districts, and especially school districts, which currently receive no shared revenue directly but depend on the states to pass along what they can. It would be ironic to cut off this form of assistance to states just when they are increasing their own aid programs to local governments. This total rose from $13 billion, or 43 percent of local general revenue from own sources in fiscal 1964, to $61 billion, or 60 percent, in 1977. Much of the state aid increase, furthermore, is directed toward helping distressed communities, both urban and rural, and would therefore appear to reinforce the aims of revenue sharing. To cut them off just as their own interjurisdictional channels are becoming more effective conduits for serving needs could be counterproductive.

The fiscal reasons for retaining the states as partners in revenue sharing may have more immediate cogency than the structural ones, but these too have great long-range significance. One of the great advantages of the federal system of government, as it has developed in the United States, is the diversity that it permits. The fact that the federal government is the creature of the states, not vice versa, may lack the significance it once had, now that the residual powers have been greatly reduced by a combination of Supreme Court decisions and constitutional amendments. Nevertheless, one freedom prized by many people is that of "voting with their feet"—moving out of jurisdictions whose policies they do not approve of to those they find more congenial. Interstate differences in laws and the distribution of powers are keys to this diversity. Whether the pasteurizing, homogenizing effects of federal bureaucratic requirements could seriously erode these distinctive patterns may be open to question, but grant allocation rules that ignored the differences would certainly provide another push in the direction of uniformity. Again efficiency would appear to be at odds with some of the less tangible and more fundamental democratic values.

It remains to be seen whether these questions about revenue sharing are important or are much ado about little. Possibly the most that can be hoped for from Washington is a continuation of the present fixed level of funding, the value of which has been steadily decreased by inflation since it was established in 1976. Renewal of the program without change would therefore intensify the pressure on the states, which face not only angry taxpayers but still another possible threat from Washington if some congressional leaders have their way. That threat could come from the enactment of a national value added tax as a means of taking pressure off the income and social security payroll taxes. This could be a blow to state hopes of getting more revenue out of their sales taxes, as it could overload consumption levies and turn the taxpayer rebellion in that direction.

WHAT DOES THE FUTURE HOLD?

As the lines tighten, it seems clear that all three levels of government are going to have to make more efficient use of the revenue sources they have. There seems little doubt that the high administrative costs and lack of coordination among categorical grant programs should call for further reforms in that area. Unfortunately, political factors give the categorical approach particular appeal for Congress. Its members' fingerprints are very visible on this kind of aid; they can please special interests and claim credit for identifiable programs on the home scene. Their fingerprints become fainter as the aid becomes less targeted and more fungible.

Quite understandably, local and state officials prefer the broader scope of block grants and especially revenue sharing. This does not mean, however, that they are in any way reluctant to take federal aid in whatever form it is offered. Even though they believe that it tends to skew their budgets and induce them to spend money in ways they would not otherwise choose, they reach for whatever grants they can get, just as riders on a merry-go-round reach for the rings. With basic expenses for standard services eating up most of the revenue they can raise at home, local leaders look to grant funds to give them some political leverage. Their effectiveness at bringing in outside money is likely to give them whatever scope they have to improve their communities and win friends for their administrations. The pickings are becoming extremely slim.

The outlook for state and local government in the 1980s can be seen either as grim or as excitingly challenging. In a dark period nearly half a century ago a newly elected president raised hope and courage by assuring people that the only thing they had to fear was fear itself. His administration inaugurated a long era of accelerating inflation, increasing government activity, and assured economic growth. This trend has now reached a dangerous parting of the ways, with inflation running amok and economic growth slowing to a crawl. The appetite for goods and comforts and unlimited independence of movement has for the first time made us dependent on foreign energy sources and posed an economic threat from outside. Affluence has raised skepticism about the virtues of work, risk-taking, and sacrifice, and has intensified demands for security—assurances of safety, certainty, and long life. Economic enterprise, once taken for granted as the means to the good life, is viewed with ambivalence. While jobs are sought by a larger segment of the population than ever before, industry has come under increasing fire for the hazards it poses for personal and environmental health and safety.

Government, too, is both needed and distrusted as never before. Only a decade ago it was expected to solve all problems; embarking on a massive new wave of spending, it blew its own size out of proportion, assumed vastly increased responsibilities for regulating private industry, and somehow lost control of the mechanisms it had seemed to perfect for keeping the economy on a stable and advancing course. Its mass and momentum have made it an object of aversion to many, but bringing it under control will be a difficult task indeed. That is the challenge for the 1980s. The taxpayer rebellion can certainly be seen as a call for responsible gearing down. Priorities, self-discipline, and scaled-down expectations would seem to be the order of the day. Banishing fear was the best recipe for a nation facing starvation; reestablishing enough fear to pull an affluent society together and redirect its efforts toward common purposes may be more to the point today.

DISCUSSION

BREAK: Whether the tax and expenditure limitation movement is alive and well or not is debatable, but it clearly creates an uncertainty that state and local governments are going to have to live with. That uncertainty has already had some interesting effects. I mentioned one such effect of Proposition 13 relating to differential assessments on property—and the resulting violation of horizontal equity, taxing similar pieces of property very differently.

Another important effect recalled Adam Smith's maxim of certainty—that people must be certain about what their tax bills are going to be. And the success of Proposition 13 says to me that people voted for certainty over equity and raises an interesting question as to whether that kind of choice might carry over to other taxes at other levels of government. It may well. I think the certainty canon has been neglected in our professional discussions of tax reform and ought to come back into focus. Proposition 13 may have put it on center stage.

SHOVEN: I was going to say one thing about your certainty principle which is that it's a certain nominal obligation comprising 2 percent a year, but not a certain real obligation, and I don't know whether I would feel more certain about that contract or if somebody told me that I was going to get a half percent of the real value of my house about twenty years from now because of the underlying uncertainty about where the price level would be in the future.

If the federal government at the same time cuts grants towards the states, as it appears it is trying to do, the result is a rather large centralization of tax revenue. I am not sure this is a particularly good thing. Many of the benefit-related taxes may not be deductible—the entrance fees at parks, library fees, etc. So it is really quite funny that we are doing this to ourselves—substituting nondeductible for deductible taxes.

CHICKERING: On the politics, one problem in preferring an indexed tax system over tax or expenditure limitation concerns the difficulties that tax indexation seems to have generating political coalitions willing to support it. The problem gets back essentially to trying to find mechanisms to appeal to the general taxpayer's interest. So far, tax and expenditure limitations seem to have done a better job of getting coalitions to support them than indexation has.

SHOVEN: Right. I guess this is post-Proposition 13, but California seems to be ahead of the federal government on indexing its tax code.

ROWEN: It seems to me that—given the experience of New York City, New York State, and Massachusetts, the question of the level of taxes—the impact of the level of taxes on competitiveness and economic attractiveness of the particular regions or states really is much debated.

McKINNON: What I missed was a discussion of the classical Hamiltonian notion of fiscal federalism and how we assign taxes to various levels of government commensurate with their expenditures. It seems to me that we have mixed up all three levels and have experimented with assigning any tax to any level of government. For example, in Proposition 13 this division of labor has been upset, particularly when we think of the property tax as being a very natural local tax and the sales tax as being a state tax naturally. Now, because of the arbitrary cutbacks on 13 and the unfairness of the assessment procedure, we have sort of thrown all the revenue from the property tax to the state, which then redistributes back to the locality. One way to put state/local finance on a better basis, given the calamity that occurred with Proposition 13, is to recapture the Hamiltonian ideal. Suppose localities keep a high fraction of any new houses or industrial complexes in their property tax base, even though tax revenue raised from all of the old buildings goes to the state. The localities would have considerable incentive to try to attract industry into their area because they or their school districts would in fact share some of the revenues.

This business of not dividing up revenues properly also goes to the heart of the federal revenue sharing problem, something both Michael and George mentioned. Although revenue sharing has been declining, in a classic Hamiltonian system it shouldn't exist at all. Instead, we should assign the states certain tax bases which the federal government then does not invade. But the tax base should be adequate to handle the expenditure needs of the states. Here the sales tax is naturally the most lucrative tax that one could assign to the states. Some people have suggested the possibility of a federal value added tax and in a shortened form that could be called a national sales tax. I would oppose this very much, because I think that this is the natural tax domain of the states. It makes sense to let the states have the sales tax, but to get rid of revenue sharing altogether. That could, in one fell swoop, simplify much of our fiscal policy.

9

MICHAEL J. BOSKIN

Federal Government Spending and Budget Policy

Causes of government intervention. Public sector growth. Cost-benefit analysis of spending programs. Budgetary policy. The current budgetary mess. Reform proposals.

The large and growing role of government in economic activity is one of the most remarkable features of the advanced economies of the world. It is also becoming the single most controversial aspect of public policy in the United States. In the last several years, attempts by voters to limit state and local government spending and/or taxes have proliferated, and many such attempts have been successful. Many voters feel the same about federal government spending. Well-developed efforts are now underway either to limit government spending as a fraction of gross national product (GNP) or to require a balanced federal budget. It is clear that many more such bills, initiatives, referenda, and constitutional amendments are planned for the near future.

While discontent with the growth of government has always been expressed in some quarters, it now appears to have spread to the general public. This chapter will examine federal government spending and budget policy, giving special attention to the role of government in the economy. In the process I will expose several popular myths concerning that role, evaluate some recent reform proposals, and offer suggestions to reform the budget process and an overall framework within which to evaluate government spending. The discussion should reveal some interesting things about why people have suddenly become so upset with government spending and about whether this discontent, which caught opinion-makers by surprise, is likely to fade away, as many insist. The central question is whether there are fundamental economic causes of this discontent which are likely to keep tax and spending limit movements flourishing.

In addressing these questions, I will begin with brief discussions of the basic reasons for governmental intervention in the economy and then review briefly the history of the growth of government spending in the United States. We will then consider the details of the U.S. federal budgetary process and the basic elements of cost-benefit analysis—the principal means for evaluating particular spending programs. Following will be a look at the current budgetary mess—especially as related to the apparent inability of Congress to control spending. I will conclude with consideration of several major proposals for solving the problem and set forth an alternative proposal.

RATIONALE FOR GOVERNMENT ECONOMIC ACTIVITY

In all market economies, a basic presumption exists in favor of private decision-making. There are two principal reasons: first, because decentralized, competitive decision-making maximizes economic efficiency, and second, because free individual choice is considered an important element of a free political society. Despite the advantages of private competition, the conditions under which ideal outcomes result are not always satisfied in the real world. Hence the need for government intervention.

Governments generally intervene to protect competition or something similar to it. Most countries thus regulate natural monopolies (such as public utilities) which result when minimum production costs occur at so large a scale of activity as to exclude competition. When private monopolies arise, a case may exist for government intervention to increase competition (through antitrust law).

Two basic resource allocation problems may require intervention. The first involves external or third-party effects ("externalities") which occur when the behavior of one person or firm directly affects the opportunities available to others. Environmental problems often involve this problem—a smokestack, for example, which pollutes others. The problem occurs because there are no enforceable property rights in clean air, and a significant gap may therefore exist between private and social costs of running the smokestack. When few people are involved, private action may solve the problem; but when the numbers become large, governments increasingly step in to "internalize" the externality—by rules, regulations, prohibitions, fines, and so on. The important point is that government intervention is only justified when the benefits of intervention exceed the costs—which is not always the case (see Chapter 5).

The second major problem involves public goods, those which can be provided to one person only with simultaneous provision to others. Others, who don't have to pay, become "free riders." Classic cases are national defense and clean air. Since the market will underproduce public goods, governments frequently step in and either provide them directly or buy them from private firms (most military procurement is done this way). Either way, payment is made from tax revenues. But again, the case for government action only exists when benefits outweigh costs.

Governments are also concerned with income distribution—increasingly so in recent years, as evidenced by the increasing attempts to reduce inequality by transfer payments and progressive tax structures.

The final major reason for government intervention is to attempt to increase economic stability and growth. This role is an historically recent one for governments, but it has been very prominent in most Western countries since the Great Depression. Unfortunately, for reasons discussed elsewhere in this book, intervening to promote growth and stability has not had a particularly happy history in recent years. The reasons include lack of knowledge about how to do it, and political interference. Another problem involves the frequent necessity to trade off among different policy goals, such as redistributing income versus economic growth, and unintended outcomes may result whereby government's attempts to stabilize the economy actually destabilize it.

In all of these areas it is important to remember that the case for government intervention exists only when it actually improves the outcomes generated by the market. This often may not be the case—even when the abstract case exists to intervene; the gap between government's potential and actual performance is often very great.

HISTORIC TRENDS IN PUBLIC SECTOR GROWTH

Table 1 shows the growths of total government expenditure in current dollars, in constant 1958 dollars per person, and as a percentage of GNP. Even a casual glance at this table reveals a startling growth rate. Just before the outbreak of World War I in 1913, the government was spending less than $100 per capita (in 1958 dollars), and this amounted to less than 8 percent of the GNP. Today, in 1958 dollars, the corresponding figures are over $1,300 per person and over one-third of GNP.

Table 1

Growth of Government Expenditure in the United States

	Expenditures		
	Total Government ($ billions)	**Per Capita (1958 dollars)**	**Percent of GNP**
1890	0.8	45	6.5
1902	1.5	58	7.3
1913	3.2	89	7.8
1922	9.3	163	12.6
1929	10.3	143	10.0
1940	18.4	288	18.4
1950	61.0	484	21.3
1960	136.4	740	27.0
1970	311.9	1,138	31.8
1980	839.0	1,332	34.0

Source: 1890–1922: Musgrave and Musgrave 1973; 1929–1979: *Economic Report of the President, 1980.*

In fact, these figures actually understate this growth. For in addition to direct spending, the government levies a large number of what might be called quasi-taxes as substitutes for direct spending. When the government mandates certain safety devices on automobile manufacturers, they are not recorded as the equivalent of taxes but rather as an increase in that component of GNP relating to automobile sales. However—to pick one example—there is very little difference between the government's requiring installation of an air bag costing $500 and its imposing a tax of $500 which is then used to install the same air bag. Clearly, the growth of such rules and regulations for both consumers and producers has greatly increased this quasi-spending. Further, the national income accounts include only the net deficits of government agencies which sell part of their output; including all their spending would add several percentage points to the figure. Further, off-budget spending and tax and loan subsidies would further swell the total.

In any event, the total take of the public sector as a percentage of all economic activity has increased by a factor of five since the turn of the century. While it is instructive to examine the growth of aggregate government expenditures at all levels, adjusting for inflation and population growth, the aggregate data also hide a startling change in the composition of government spending by function and dramatic changes in the levels of government doing the spending.

For selected years from 1929 through 1980, Table 2 presents figures on total government spending, federal government spending, and federal government spending as a proportion of the total. As noted in the table, as late as 1929 only one dollar in four of government spending was done at the federal level. On the eve of World War II the corresponding figure was one dollar in two, and today it exceeds two out of three dollars. While state and local government expenditures have grown very rapidly relative to the GNP, as a proportion of total government spending they have declined substan-

Table 2
Changing Composition of Government Spending by Level of Government

	Total	Federal	Federal as Percent of Total
1929	10.3	2.6	25.2
1940	18.4	10.0	54.4
1950	61.0	40.8	66.9
1960	136.4	93.1	68.3
1970	311.9	204.2	65.5
1980	839.0	564.0	67.2

Source: *Economic Report of the President, 1980.*

Table 3
Changing Composition of Federal Expenditures, Selected Years 1952–1978
($ billions)

	Purchases of Goods and Services	Transfer Payments to Persons	Transfers as Percent of Transfers plus Purchases
1952	47.2	8.5	15.3
1960	52.9	20.6	28.0
1965	64.6	28.4	30.5
1970	97.0	55.0	36.2
1975	117.9	131.1	52.7
1980	186.0	231.0	55.0

Source: *Economic Report of the President, 1980.*

tially. The growth of state and local government spending, and of tax systems and intergovernmental fiscal relations relating to state and local governments, are discussed elsewhere in this volume (see Chapter 8).

In examining the composition of federal spending, it is instructive to note the relationship between government spending for goods and services (mostly public or quasi-public goods) and government spending on transfer payments. In 1952 transfer payments amounted to only $8.5 billion, compared to the almost $50 billion spent on direct purchases of goods and services. Since then transfers increased markedly as a proportion of total spending; by the early 1970s, for the first time in U.S. history, the federal government was spending more on transfer payments than on direct purchases of goods and services.

Short-Run Changes

With these broad historical trends in mind, let's look at projected short-run changes in federal government receipts and outlays. Estimates of these changes (as made by the administration and the Congressional Budget Office [CBO] for the next several years) are very sensitive to changes in economic assumptions—for example, those concerning future rates of unemployment and inflation. Table 4 highlights the fact that revenues are scheduled to grow enormously over the next several years, several hundred billion dollars more than necessary to fund current programs, even after adjusting for inflation. Further, the sharp increases projected in current outlays over the next five years occur almost entirely in benefit payments for individuals, such as social security, Medicare, and Medicaid. Clearly, there will be ample room in the next several years for phased-in tax cuts, even with projected increases in real defense spending, so long as major new spending programs are not enacted—so long as some control remains over these transfer payments.[1]   These tax

Table 4
Short-Run Projected Growth in
Federal Spending and Revenues
($ billions)

	1982	1983	1984	1985
Estimated outlays	686.3	774.3	838.9	902.6
Estimated revenues	691.1	798.8	920.5	1,061.2
Estimated surplus	4.8	24.5	81.6	158.6

Source: *Economic Report of the President, 1980;* Congressional Budget Office estimates are similar.

cuts should be made so as to maximize their favorable impact on saving and investment (see Chapters 2 and 7) and should only occur in the context of overall budget balance or modest surpluses in order to facilitate the Federal Reserve's fight against inflation.[2]

In brief summary, not only has the government grown extensively as a provider of goods and services and as a transferor of income in our society, but it has shifted from the former to the latter, it has become increasingly centralized at the federal level, and over the next several years a major battle will be fought over the potential continued rapid growth of its spending and its composition.

The Budget Process

The U.S. government budgetary process relates primarily to the timing and character of budget recommendations, authorizations, appropriations, and spending. In November of the year preceding each fiscal year, the Office of Management and Budget (OMB) prepares a current services budget forecast for the coming year. Under assumed economic forecast for the following year, this budget estimates spending necessary to maintain current services in the ensuing year. In January, still nine months before the start of the fiscal year, the president proposes his budget and presents it to Congress which, throughout the spring and summer, analyzes, debates, and approves concurrent resolutions on the budget through its appropriations, tax, and budget committees. As the budget is finally approved, agencies are authorized to spend appropriated funds. An audit determines exact spending and revenue amounts following the end of the fiscal year.

In reviewing this process, it is important to understand the difficulty in forecasting actual outlays and revenues up to a year or more in advance. First of all, the government does not *directly* control outlays and revenues. This may seem surprising, but a variety of aspects of tax laws and entitlement programs make actual revenues and outlays depend on economic conditions. For example, a higher than forecast inflation rate will drive people into higher tax brackets and raise tax revenues; a larger than anticipated influx of new retirees into social security will increase outlays above projected levels; and so on. If we divide the postwar period at 1968, around the time of the sharp acceleration of inflation in the United States, we note that the difference between projected and actual outlays in revenues was as likely to be positive as negative; in the last ten years, however, actual outlays have exceeded projected outlays nine times, although actual percentage deviations have averaged only 3 to 4 percent in the last ten years.

Despite these difficulties in making budget revenue and outlay forecasts, budgetary forecasts in the United States are heavily weighted toward countercyclical fiscal policy. The creation of the new budget committees pursuant to the 1974 Budget Control Act was widely heralded as a major vehicle for tying aggregate spending and aggregate taxation together. In principle, the budget committees were supposed to set spending limits and revenue minima within which the separate appropriations and tax committees would work. The overall level of the budget deficit was to be used in part to attempt to influence the aggregate performance of the economy.

In practice, it is unclear that much spending discipline has percolated down from the budget committees to the appropriations committees. Indeed, a cynic might well argue that the spending limits are merely the aggregate amounts of the separate appropriations recommendations. While the truth undoubtedly lies somewhere in between, it is clear that the current budgetary process is far from perfect as a mechanism either for controlling spending, promoting cost effectiveness, requiring explicit trade-offs among competing spending programs, or returning revenues to the general public. The problem of developing a sound overall budget process depends on the criteria one uses to evaluate both particular spending programs and the overall efficacy of budget policy.

EVALUATING PARTICULAR SPENDING PROGRAMS: COST-BENEFIT ANALYSIS

In recent decades, substantial improvements have been made in the criteria for evaluating spending programs. Social cost-benefit analysis is not dissimilar to decisions private firms make in considering alternative investment decisions. These analyses are important because analyses of individual programs should conceptually form the basis for setting the aggregate level of the budget under normal economic conditions. We can highlight some of the major issues in cost-benefit analysis with a particular example.

A Specific Example

Consider the possibility of the government building a dam over a particular river. The first item to consider is what are the potential benefits of goods and services from the project—including flood control, hydroelectric generating capacity, irrigation, and even recreational facilities. Estimating the value of these outputs is enormously difficult, since we must estimate for each year into the future both the amount that will be produced and consumed and the value to consumers of each output. In estimating demand, we must take account of future population growth, income growth, changes in prices of competing commodities, etc. In some instances we will have an approximate guide to the value to consumers because the outputs are bought and sold on private markets. Often, however, they are not, and no market information will help. Further, the actual benefits will depend on such things as scale (here, the size of the dam), timing of construction, and the potential prices charged (if any) for the services.

Cost estimates must consider initial costs of construction and future maintenance and operation expenses. In an economy operating close to full employment, resources for building the dam must be diverted from other uses, whether public or private. Since many costs, typically, occur at the outset or construction phase of the program and many of the benefits accrue further in the future, some consistent procedure must be used to discount costs and benefits to the present in order to compare them. The presence of taxes which distort investment and saving decisions make evaluation of an appropriate discount rate or opportunity cost of the funds quite difficult. Diverting funds from private to governmental use involves reducing private consumption and investment. Thus the costs of the dam or other government program must be estimated as foregone current consumption plus investment opportunities of the private sector. While there are technical disputes among economists about how to do this, all agree that some account must be made for the distortionary taxes in the social cost-benefit analysis.[3]

Having estimated costs and benefits and discounted them to the present, criteria may be employed to evaluate government projects which are very similar to the efficiency criteria economists use to analyze allocation efficiencies in the private sector.[4]

Although these criteria make systematic evaluations possible, substantial problems of measurement and interpretation remain, however. For example, many projects may have so-called spillover, secondary, or intangible benefits. These might include such things as allowing a related activity (such as retailing in the area) to operate at a larger and more efficient scale of operation; increasing the productivity of immobile resources; or providing increased diversity and pluralism. It may be even harder to quantify such benefits than to quantify the direct ones. Conceptually, by reducing the outcomes of government spending programs to a single substantive measure, it is easier to make comparisons and decisions (hopefully) improve.

A thorny problem for social cost-benefit analysis, and one of increasing practical importance because of the enormous expansion of transfer payment programs and other government subsidies, concerns whether benefits and costs should carry distributional weights with them. Should the government be blind to whom benefits or costs accrue? Or should it weight more heavily benefits accruing to some members of the population (e.g., income groups) than others? In large measure, the practical answer depends on how much concerns about inequality and poverty are taken care of elsewhere in the budget, and how much spending programs directly affect the overall well-being of different groups of the population differently.[5]

Were it possible to estimate the benefits and costs of each

program precisely, cost-benefit analysis would give us an exact guide for budgetary policy in normal times: individual programs should be undertaken and/or expanded exactly to the point where benefits exceed costs (foregone private sector opportunities). The total budget would then add the sum total of expenditures on all such programs. The problem here is less with the conceptual apparatus, however, than with its implementation by fallible human beings with particular personal and bureaucratic incentives. An arms-length cost-benefit analysis done outside of agencies with particular responsibility for specific programs—for example, in OMB as opposed to the departments of agriculture or transportation or energy—is a useful way to monitor cost-benefit analyses prepared for Congress and the administration in the individual agencies.

EVALUATING OVERALL BUDGETARY POLICY

Even if individual analyses were done properly, it would still be necessary to place overall budget policy in a broader context.[6] Since the impact on private incentives of the overall budget is obviously much greater than that of any individual program, in evaluating the desirability of specific programs it is impossible to estimate the opportunity costs of diverting funds from the private sector to the government without knowing the total size of the budget. We would expect that the larger the spending package, tax rates would increase and hence the greater would be the disincentives to the private economy to work, save, invest, and innovate.

This is one extremely important type of overall budget policy concern. Another—and one that frequently dominates short-run spending and tax decisions—concerns the likely effect of the budget on economic stability. That is, budget policy often is devoted to attempted countercyclical fiscal activity at the expense of explicit cost-effective and target-effective spending evaluation.

Many economists used to believe that increases in government spending on purchases of goods and services, when financed by deficits, could substantially increase GNP. Operating in the familiar "multiplier" fashion of Keynesian economics, the increased government spending would increase GNP by a multiple of the original spending increase. In such a climate, when it was presumed that the economy was well below full employment, spending programs were presumed to generate extra income and hence little pressure was felt for careful cost-benefit analyses.

Economists now question the extent to which changes in government spending can influence GNP, how rapidly they can do so, and whether the attempt to "fine tune" the economy by variations in spending levels makes much sense. Some of the reasons are lags in the economy and the implementation of budget policy, difficulties in forecasting, and longer-term considerations concerning the ultimate need to pay future taxes to finance the interest payments on any debt issue (see Chapters 4 and 7).

Considering also that federal spending on transfer payments now exceeds spending on goods and services, it is highly misleading to think that the budget deficit can be a measure of the stimulative or contractionary effect of the government's operations on the economy. The issue is further clouded by an attempt to use a so-called "high employment" or "full employment" estimated budget surplus or deficit—one which adjusts actual or estimated spending and revenues, and hence deficit or surplus, to estimated levels at high or full employment. Unfortunately, economists are far from agreed about the natural unemployment rate. Most of us would now put it at 6.0 percent or more. The administration currently is using 4.9 percent. The Humphrey-Hawkins Act uses 4.0 percent. Yet the sensitivity of both

budget revenues and spending to changes in the unemployment rate can be substantial. Disagreements over the full
employment level therefore can produce substantial
differences in estimations of surpluses or deficits at full
employment. Policymakers have often used the high employment estimates to justify increased spending to reach the
alleged high employment level.[7]

Thus, recent increases or decreases in spending (or rather,
its growth rate) have probably had little impact on overall
real GNP, as they have been mostly transfer payments.
Some economists believe that the impact of fiscal policy is
likely to be more generally and/or strongly felt through
changes in taxes when the economy is below full employment. While the countercyclical aims of fiscal policy may at
times be legitimate, they should not be allowed to dominate
cost and target effectiveness in the budgetary process.

From a longer-term perspective, our greatest need may
well be to leave a greater share of society's resources in private hands to promote saving, investment, and innovation in
the years ahead. Rather than thinking of increased spending
as a means of stimulating short-term growth, at times increased spending may well inhibit growth by transferring
resources from these vital activities to transfer payments. A
more cost-effective and target-effective implementation of
cost-benefit analysis for specific programs should provide opportunities to free resources for increased incentives to save,
work, and invest and for increased defense spending.

A CLOSER LOOK AT THE CURRENT
BUDGETARY MESS

As noted above, the notion is spreading rapidly through the
general population that government, especially the federal
government, has become "too large." Discontent with aggregate spending, taxation, and deficits, together with con-

cern over the changing composition of that spending, probably stem largely from the rapid slowdown in the rate of economic progress noted in Chapter 1. Workers and taxpayers simply are not content with no gain in their living standards while our modest income growth is funneled through the government into transfer payments. Concern is also spreading about the process by which federal budgetary decisions are made and the ability of Congress and the executive branch to slow the growth of government spending and/or to prevent continuing large budget deficits.

A closer look at the current budgetary scenario reveals that the official budget of the U.S. government accounts for only part of total government spending and deficits. Additional government spending or "quasi-government" spending occurs off the books in federally sponsored agencies, in mandated private activity, in tax "expenditures," and in running down the government's capital stock. Further, there is an enormous implicit debt in the long-term obligation of the social insurance fund. And the share of government spending considered "uncontrollable" has grown rapidly and is approaching four-fifths of the entire direct budget.

Table 5 presents estimates of an expanded definition of federal government spending and deficits for fiscal 1980. In addition to the $564 billion of direct outlays and the estimated $40 billion deficit, there is an estimated almost $400 billion of additional outlays and more than $60 billion of additional debt.[8]

Some of these augmented figures are extremely rough estimates. The net outlays and deficits of off-budget federal government entities, primarily the federal financing bank, are estimated quite precisely and add about $17 billion to total outlays and to the deficit. There is also about $25 billion in federally sponsored agencies such as the intermediate credit banks for agriculture and the student loan program. While these activities incur substantial direct net spending and deficits currently, some also have offsetting future

Table 5

Expanded Federal Government Spending and Deficit Fiscal 1980[a]

	Outlays		Deficit	
Direct budget		564		40
+ Off-budget	(17)	581	(17)	57
+ Federally sponsored	(25)	606	(25)	82
+ Net disinvestment[b]	(25)	631	(25)	107
+ Mandated private[c]	(102)[d]	733[d]	—	107[d]
+ "Tax expenditures"[e]	(124)[d]	857[d]	—	107[d]
Percent GNP		34		

[a]The state and local government sector is running a modest *surplus* with spending of over $300 billion.

[b]Author's estimate.

[c]Estimate from Chapter 5,

[d]Estimates are very rough and should be interpreted only as representing very approximate orders of magnitude.

[e]Congressional Budget Office estimate.

assets. For example, the student loan program spends more than it takes in but may recoup some of that difference in the future. The student loan program provides loans at well below market interest rates (in one case, 3 percent on a deferred basis), although the treasury must borrow in the private market to fund the program. Further, the default rate for such programs is extremely high. So it is unclear exactly how much of the $25 billion deficit currently being run in these programs will be recouped in the future, if any. Adding this total brings total outlays to $606 billion and the total deficit to $81 billion.

Adding to this total the net outlays and deficit from running down the capital stock—which I estimate to approximate $25 billion in fiscal year 1980—produces net spending of $631 billion and a deficit of $106 billion, two and a half times the officially recorded deficit. If we added to this total quasi-government spending in the form of mandated private activity and tax expenditures, total spending would swell to $857 billion, or 34 percent of GNP (half again the officially recorded figure).

These numbers—especially from mandated private activity and tax expenditures—should be interpreted cautiously; these estimates are subject to substantial inaccuracy. But the augmented figures do provide an insight into a fuller array of government spending and quasi-spending practices, and they provide some insight into the possibilities of circumvention in implementing any specific spending limit proposals.

Many government spending programs are considered "uncontrollable" because they are open-ended entitlement programs. For example, we do not know in advance how many people will retire and become eligible for social security benefits; current law only specifies a formula by which their benefits will be calculated if and when they retire. If more or fewer people retire than anticipated, spending will change accordingly. Table 6 presents an estimate of the percentage of outlays considered "relatively uncontrollable" by the Congressional Budget Office and the administration. In the last decade this fraction of a now much larger absolute and relative government budget has crept up from two-thirds to well

Table 6
Portion of Federal Budget Considered "Relatively Uncontrollable"

Year	Percentage
1971	66
1978	74
1981 (est.)	77

Source: Congressional Budget Office.

over three-quarters. This obviously substantially reduces the short-run flexibility that Congress and the administration have in controlling spending. But today's relatively uncontrollable outlays were yesterday's pilot programs, and one of the major problems in the budget process is the failure to account for the long-run cost implications of new spending initiatives. More on this below.

Another interesting and perplexing item concerns the method by which we finance our social insurance programs. They are financed on a pay-as-you-go basis, whereby the taxes paid by current workers finance the benefits received by current retirees, the disabled, survivors, and hospital patients covered by the program. Unfortunately, even with the enormous tax increases voted in 1977 due to take effect throughout the 1980s and 1990, the social security system has an immense long-term deficit which occurs primarily because of the changing age structure in the population—especially the impending dramatic increase in the ratio of retirees to workers as the baby boom generation begins to retire early in the next century. My own estimate of this long-term deficit for the old-age part of the system alone amounts to $630 billion adjusted for inflation and discounted to the present—almost as large as the privately held national debt. But these obligations are implicit, not explicit. While it would be undesirable—almost immoral—to reduce dramatically the benefits received by current retirees or those soon to retire, the same is not necessarily true for persons due to retire in the distant future. Therefore, some combination of reduced benefits and increased taxes is possible as a substitute for enormous tax increases—on the order of 8 percentage points of payroll above those already legislated—early in the next century. A number of methods for controlling this explosion in expenditures are possible, perhaps the most important being a gradual increase in the retirement age.

The long-term deficit in social security should be discussed and debated publicly far more than it has been; but it should not be included on the same basis as regular national debt in the accounting process of the federal budget. For this, in essence, would enshrine pay-as-you-go finance and the currently promised benefits in the budget and would make it more difficult to rationalize future benefit payments.

Because the budget process covers a period of many months, estimated spending and revenue totals must be made conditional on economic assumptions concerning real GNP, the unemployment rate, inflation, interest rates, etc. We have noted the difficulties in making these estimates; these difficulties are compounded by an obvious incentive to shade assumptions in a manner that sheds favorable light on the spending, revenue, and deficit totals. The Humphrey-Hawkins Act requires forecasts over a five-year period to assume that the economy is making steady progress toward achieving the act's inflation and unemployment goals. I know of no economist who believes those goals are attainable over this period.

The administration and the CBO, however, do make longer-term budget projections, assuming current law revenues, discretionary inflation offsets, and fiscal policy changes. Despite improvements, these methods are still subject to much debate and contention.[9]

Of potentially much greater importance is the difficulty in estimating long-run implications of new spending initiatives. Not only is this conceptually difficult—for example, involving estimates of potential beneficiaries for a new entitlement program—but the current budget process explicitly shies away from doing this, thus missing an important opportunity to expose the long-run spending implications of new programs. Instead, the process focuses on spending implications for the next fiscal year. Indeed, new programs often start late in the fiscal year, thereby running a very small fraction of regular spending in the first year in order to stay within spending limits. Outlays can also be a small fraction of budget authorization for future spending. A good example in the 1981 budget is a new subsidized housing program for which only $100 million of outlays are estimated but which carries budget authorization of almost $3 billion. Since our large spending programs started at a much smaller level earlier, it is of paramount importance to develop procedures for forecasting such growth in any new initiatives or existing programs.

In brief summary, to get a substantially accurate estimate of net government spending, revenues, deficits, and their course through time requires much more than a cursory glance at the estimated outlays and revenues—and hence, deficit—in the current year budget. It requires us to take a somewhat broader conceptual view of the budgetary process and of government spending itself, and to delve into difficult problems of measurement and forecasting. There simply is no alternative to doing so if we wish to provide accurate information from which to make spending decisions.

PROPOSALS FOR REFORM

The discussion above serves as an excellent introduction for analyzing and understanding problems related to the two general proposals for changing the process by which spending and tax decisions are made: a constitutional amendment (whether initiated through Congress or through a constitutional convention) to require a balanced federal government budget, or a limit on federal government spending as a proportion of GNP.

The growth of government spending and taxes, combined with increased regulation, has seriously impeded private incentives to work, save, and invest. These adverse incentives are perhaps the most important reasons to attempt to slow the growth of public spending; but the principal proposals advanced for this purpose have significant conceptual and practical problems in implementation, the broadest of which relate to the discussion above—defining spending and taxes, and therefore deficits. As we have noted, in the official accounts of the United States not all government spending is included, not all taxes are included, no separation is made between a capital account and a current account. These and many other problems greatly complicate the problem of defining basic terms.

The Balanced Budget Proposal

Proponents of the balanced budget amendment claim that a balanced budget amendment would provide greater long-run flexibility than a spending limit in allowing changes in government spending in relation to GNP. Such flexibility could be important to accommodate such things as changes in demography which put particular pressures on, say, educational spending for young children or social security payments for the elderly. The basic argument is that although Congress does not feel constrained by tax revenues because it can run deficits, forcing legislators to vote higher taxes in order to spend will put a break on spending. Unfortunately, in an inflationary economy with an unindexed tax system, tax revenues accrue much more rapidly than do automatic increases in government spending. Indeed, when nominal income increases by 10 percent, federal government tax revenues increase by about 15 percent—thereby allowing substantial increases in government spending without legislative action. The balanced budget proposal therefore does not strongly restrict federal spending as a percentage of GNP through time, without an indexed tax system or elimination of inflation. Most of us would prefer a public sector of current size with a modest deficit to a much larger public sector with a balanced budget.

Once it is decided to balance the budget annually, the questions remain as to what should be included on each side of the budget. We have mentioned off-budget federal items, such as the Federal Financing Bank, which are excluded at the moment from the federal government budget and which now amount to well over 2 percent of unified budget amounts and will probably rise substantially if a balanced budget proposal or a spending limit proposal passes. The most important of these revolve around federal government lending. Also excluded from the budget are rents and royalties on the outer continental shelf, which amounted to about $3 billion in 1978. This $3 billion is counted as a negative outlay rather than as a receipt.

Finally is the question of whether to include social insurance programs in government spending and taxes as in the unified budget. The biggest item here, which we have already discussed, is social security, with its large long-term deficit.

A next set of questions involves the timing of implementation of a balanced budget proposal. If we take an *annually* balanced budget, we face the following scenario: OMB by law must prepare a current services budget by 15 November preceding the beginning of the fiscal year. This budget must estimate what would happen to the federal budget assuming current policies are unchanged. The president submits his budget message in January, nine months before the start of the fiscal year, and later that spring Congress passes a series of concurrent resolutions. All of these refer to the budget— taxes, spending, and implied borrowing—for the year beginning the following October and lasting through the twelve-month period ending in September of the following calendar year. The budget cycle thus begins about twenty-three months prior to the end of the fiscal year to which it applies; projecting tax revenues and budget outlays is therefore an important problem. As we noted, however, both tax revenues and budget outlays are affected substantially by the course of the economy. Although government policies can influence the course of the economy to some extent, many of these are only imperfectly contrólled by the federal government.

The question for the balanced budget proposal is: are we going to require an *ex post* balanced budget? Since we cannot even know if the budget was balanced until the audit years after the president's original budget message, we must be discussing proposals for an *ex ante* planned or forecast balanced budget. This obviously creates political incentives to shade forecasts of receipts and outlays—i.e., assumptions about the future course of the economy and the revenues and outlays they will generate and require, respectively. While such incentives certainly exist currently, and certainly have been used in the past, the incentive to do this would be strongly increased. The problem is particularly interesting at the present moment, when considerable skepticism exists about President Carter's forecast of a balanced budget for next fiscal year; I expect a large deficit.

Another problem is whether or not there should be a separate capital account analogous to the separate accounting procedures adopted by most private firms and by a large number of state and local governments. If we maintained a separate and conceptually correct current and capital account system, the deficit on current account would be the true deficit, although the government could change asset purchases and sales to change the net (current) surplus.[10]

Yet another issue with respect to a separate capital budget is whether only federally owned assets should be included, or whether assets financed by the federal government but owned by others (e.g., the interstate highway system) should be included.

Finally, by far the most important consideration concerns another aspect of timing and the overall economic effects of requiring an annually balanced budget. The cyclical fluctuation of the economy is partly ameliorated by what are called automatic stabilizers, the propensity of revenues to rise and expenditures to fall countercyclically. When a deep recession hits, incomes fall via our progressive tax system, revenues fall more than proportionally to income, and unemployment insurance payments go up, thereby cushioning the fall in total spending power. That is, receipts and expenditures automatically vary as the economy fluctuates. To give another example, as the inflation rate increases and people are driven into higher and higher tax brackets with our unindexed tax system, tax revenues accrue more than proportionately to income gains, thereby slowing the growth of private demand for goods and services. Many opponents of balanced budget proposals fear that an annually balanced budget will severely restrict the desirable feature of the automatic stabilization of the economy. Suppose we are running a balanced budget for a few years and the economy suddenly careens into a deep recession; receipts fall off sharply. Will we then be required to quickly lower government spending? Raise taxes? In either of these cases the general feeling of economists is that the already untoward economic fluctuation might be accentuated. This fact explains why most economists oppose an *annually* balanced budget, fearing that it would substantially impede the self-correcting tendency of the economy to deal with cyclical fluctuations. It would certainly require changes in government spending and taxes in a direction opposite to that usually proposed in such situations.

Many economists, however, would favor balancing the budget over a longer period. Conceptually, many would like to balance the budget over the course of the business cycle, but the duration, severity, and predictability of business cycles are extremely difficult to forecast.

Each of these proposals, and many proposals we still hear, unfortunately assume that the government can rely virtually exclusively on fiscal policy—changes in taxes and spending—to restore full employment or to control inflation. This appears to be overly optimistic. Indeed, it appears not only that fiscal policy, as currently used, is insufficient, but that monetary policy is at least equally important, particularly in dealing with inflation. To be effective, therefore, any proposed budget balancing would require assumptions about future Federal Reserve Board activity; it might even result in pressures for direct supervision of the Federal Reserve to meet particular guidelines, thereby impairing its independence. In any event, it is clear that any particular federal policy to raise or lower taxes can be offset in part by changes in monetary policy.

Finally, it should be mentioned that much of the impetus for a balanced budget comes from the perceived correlation between deficit spending and inflation. While deficits often start—and certainly may accentuate—an inflation, they are not the major cause of our current inflation. A balanced budget next year would reduce the inflation rate only slightly, not nearly so much or so predictably as a sustained moderate growth of the money supply by the Federal Reserve (see Chapter 3).

In brief summary, some of these problems could be overcome by focusing on a balanced budget over a longer period rather than annually; by including, rather than a unified budget for capital and current accounts, a separate capital account; and by indexing the tax system, which would force politicians actually to vote tax increases when they wanted to spend more, rather than allowing them to rely on inflation with a balanced budget to generate increases in tax revenues exceeding income growth.

The Spending Limit Proposal

The spending limit proposal would provide more short-run flexibility for fiscal policy but much less long-run spending flexibility. It should require substantial foresight and revision in response to changes in the economy and in the population which might make increases or decreases in the spending limits desirable. For example, as the baby boom

generation approaches retirement shortly after the turn of
the next century, it may be desirable social policy to have
total social security benefits as a proportion of GNP rise
somewhat; therefore, we may not want all of this increase to
come out of other government spending programs but may
be willing to vote some extra taxes to increase the total share
of spending in GNP.

If the spending limit is binding, it will combine with our
unindexed tax system to reduce quickly the current budget
deficit. Indeed, at current rates of growth of nominal income,
a surplus would begin to accrue after about two years. This
would leave us with the choice of indexing the tax system,
periodic discretionary tax cuts, accumulating surpluses, or
creating an automatic triggering mechanism to require tax
cuts when the surplus reached certain levels (or proportions).

The spending limit proposals also suffer from many of the
same problems as the balanced budget proposals—what to do
about off-budget items, problems of timing, predictability *ex
ante* and *ex post* forecasts and realizations, and other issues.
First, GNP is not necessarily a very good measure of total
economic activity. Indeed, when wide swings and fluctuations exist in the ratio of work in the market to work in the
home, by including only work in the market for pay GNP can
reflect total economic activity more or less accurately. Since
the labor force and employment have grown at unprecedented rates for peacetime activity, GNP has become a somewhat larger fraction of total economic activity than it was,
say, ten years ago. Comparisons of federal spending to GNP
can therefore be misleading unless we account, for example,
for the decline in the percentage of women working in the
home versus the market.

Second, not only must we decide what to include in the
budget, we must also deal with the fact that many government enterprises have gross outlays, but that they sell some
of their services and hence have gross receipts. In some cases

only net outlays are included as outlays in the current budget. Should we include gross outlays in spending and the gross receipts as revenues, or should we only continue to include as government expenditure net outlays for market-oriented government enterprises? Further, should we have a separate capital budget, as discussed above?

Most important is the potential ambiguity in spending limitation proposals about the definition of spending. We have discussed the problem of government regulations (mandating pollution and safety equipment on automobiles, for instance) which turn what amount to government spending and taxes into private spending in lieu of taxes. Yet these expenditures show up in our accounts as private sales, not as government spending and taxes. These quasi-tax and expenditure cum regulation programs have proliferated greatly in the last ten or fifteen years, and a spending limit proposal would provide additional incentives to shift from direct spending programs into such mandated private activity.

Worse yet, the federal government can change an expenditure item into a negative tax, thereby maintaining expenditures below or at the spending limit. Expenditures on housing and education, for example, can be transformed from direct expenditures into tax credits or other tax devices. With a balanced budget proposal, the decline in direct outlays would be matched by roughly equal declines in tax revenues. But with a purely spending limit proposal, we have to decide what to include in spending and what negative taxes count as government outlays. We have already confronted such a problem in our current tax system. For example, we have a refundable tax credit. The refund is treated as a budget outlay, but the part of the tax credit which results in a decreased tax liability for people who pay positive tax is treated as a decrease in receipts, not as an outlay. If we eventually move to a comprehensive negative income tax ‚and follow the same general procedure, billions of dollars would be counted as decreases in receipts rather than as direct budgetary expenditures.

This general problem is sometimes labeled the problem of "tax expenditures," i.e., the financing by special provisions of the tax laws of a variety of programs is considered similar to direct federal expenditures. Good examples are the tax credit for child care for working parents, the differential tax treatment of capital gains, the treatment of state and local government bond interest, and the deductibility of mortgage interest. Tax expenditures are now listed in each budget. Their total for fiscal 1978 amounted to $124 billion, and the CBO now projects them for five years. While I do not in general approve of how the tax expenditure budget is either estimated or used, since the estimates of foregone revenue fail to include the induced behavioral responses of individuals and firms to the tax changes and hence drastically overstate the alleged subsidies involved, those who hope that spending limitations would seriously impede automatic or continual growth of government spending must take seriously the fact that at present the government can change a direct spending item into a negative tax and hence circumvent spending limitations.

STRUCTURAL REFORM IN THE CURRENT SYSTEM

As an alternative to spending limits or balanced budget requirements, structural reform in the budget process, following on the 1974 Budget Reform Act, could be tried as a means to get all spending into the open, to demand explicit trade-offs, to identify impending growth of "uncontrollables," and so on. Such a process would encompass several features: more explicit accounting of off-budget activity and deficits; attempts to cost out federally mandated activity (though I would keep these numbers separate from direct spending figures since they are subject to much greater inaccuracy); direct measures of government investment, depreciation, and the obsolescence of government capital stock, etc.[11]

With the information improvement must come some reforms of decision-making authority. Three proposals worthy of consideration are the extension of the authority of congressional budget committees to establish separate spending ceilings on each appropriations bill rather than on just their total; requirement of a two- or three-year budget growth forecast for all items in the budget;[12] and establishment of more specific, perhaps even line item, veto power for the president. Each of these proposals would provide an additional "screening" of all spending and could aid substantially in promoting the cost-effectiveness and target-effectiveness of government spending.

There are those who believe the Congress is not capable of serious attempts to curtail spending growth. It is too easy, the argument goes, to say yes to the specific constituencies demanding spending programs and therefore no to the much more diffuse taxpayer pressure. If the budget reforms outlined above are tried and found to be inadequate, and if problems with the level and growth of government spending continue, we may ultimately have to turn to a constitutional amendment which forces Congress to limit spending. Let us hope our representative democracy can indeed be exactly that, and bring government spending decisions closer to the wishes of the public.

THE POLITICS OF THE PROBLEM: TOWARD A BUDGET CONTROL ACT

It is clear that government spending and the process by which it is generated is deeply rooted in a series of complicated political interactions. The competing claims for

resources among different constituent groups in our population, most importantly between the tax-paying part of the
population and those receiving income through transfer payments from the government; the internal power structure of
the Congress and the Congress versus the administration in
setting spending priorities and developing specific proposals
and programs; a variety of other important political dimensions—all of these make control of the budgetary process
and of spending growth extremely difficult. Obviously, legislators whose primary decision-making responsibility
revolves around the budget might be expected to oppose any
restrictions on their responsibility, despite any general sym-
pathy with those who wish to impose restrictions. Therefore,
gaining control over the budget will not be an easy task. The
goal for the short run should be to improve the flow of information concerning direct and indirect government spending
and the longer-term implications of new initiatives, and to
reform the structural budget process so that the fraction of
the budget deemed uncontrollable can be gradually reduced
and also to provide a better screening process for government spending programs.

In the previous section we discussed the possibility of a
Budget Accountability and Control Act which followed up on
the Budget Reform Act of 1974. It would go far toward providing vehicles and information for better budgetary responsibility, but it will not force the political will to implement
such responsibility. That can only come from our elected
representatives' political will and power to do so. Can we do
so? Will we? The answer depends upon a variety of factors
outside the province of economists to judge. My own view is
that there is a substantial and genuine growth of concern
about budget controllability in both houses of Congress. But
even this, backed by a growing perception of the demands of
the voters and taxpayers to get the federal government's financial house in order, may not be sufficient to do so. Only
time will tell. If moderate proposals for reform are not

enacted over the next several years, the inevitable result will be more explicit restrictions on the authority of the Congress and the administration on government spending. Despite all the difficulties such limitations and restrictions would create, the overriding point is that some action is inevitable if we are to control government taxing and spending and to recover the healthy noninflationary growing economy that is essential to economic progress and to social stability. This, above all, will lend to federal government budgetary policy over the next decade a sense of urgency and importance it has not achieved in many decades.

DISCUSSION

McKINNON: Now let me mention the transfer payments and the untouchable programs that are 77 percent of the expenditures and which are growing in an apparently uncontrollable way. My own feeling is that these must be dealt with collectively to get them under control. You can't take away disability benefits, unemployment insurance, food stamps, etc., one at a time. What we need is a standard cash floor under everybody that will relieve distress. Then you can think of those other programs as making contributions to that cash floor. So people lose the cash floor insofar as they are participating in other programs on a dollar-for-dollar basis. But those that are left out of the other transfer payments would in fact get cash support.

Once we get that cash floor in place, we could phase out in a very general way all of the other transfer payment programs that we have—unemployment benefits, public housing, food stamps, welfare relief, and so forth.

Finally a comment on Michael's need for distinguishing between the capital account and the current account in the federal budget. In principle, this is correct. We should make this distinction in order to understand better the federal government's contribution to real capital formation. In practice, though, this is one distinction that works terribly in most countries I have looked at. Because once you make the distinction in a bookkeeping way, and you may also pass an amendment to your constitution that says the current account must always be balanced, the way governments get around it is to throw all expenditures into the capital account. This has happened in Germany; it happened in Latin America; it happens everywhere. New York City! So, though in principle it is a good idea, in practice it is not. And as long at the U.S. government is not heavily involved in capital accumulation because it is not yet a socialist economy, it might be better to leave the two together and try to impose a restriction of budget balance.

ROWEN: I really like this question about budget as a conceptual document. I would like to say that Michael pointed out that there may be some items that are not in the budget that we could conceptually think of as being in the budget. There are also items in the budget that we can think of conceptually as being out of the budget. Take a world in which all income was taxed in lump-sum fashion and immediately transferred back, so that expenditure would equal taxes and it would be very big—it would be very big as measured by total government spending. If that really was not doing anything it probably wouldn't be very interesting to talk about the size of government. I would like to encourage Michael to target in on the levels of government consumption, the levels of government capital formation, and then maybe to take his other programs—the transfer programs—and ask, "What is their net impact in changing relative prices and redistributing across generations?"

CHICKERING: In analyzing our current economic problems, I think it is important that we remember that they are not *only* economic problems. They are also political problems, reflecting underlying political and social realities. To pick the broadest possible example—what to do about inflation and growth—by and large economists seem to agree on what is necessary. The trouble is, there seems to be no way to address either problem successfully without asking people to defer gratification—without asking them to make sacrifices now on behalf of progress later. Unfortunately, as we all know, that is not something politicians are especially good at encouraging people to do. For most politicians the longest time frame of interest is the next election, which may be less than two years away. On the other hand, of course, very few people live entirely in the present; many, perhaps most, take account of the future in their judgments about the present. Therefore, since most people have a stake in the long-term health of the economy, the educational challenge is to encourage them to understand both the nature of that stake and what must be done to improve the future. That, of course, is a burden of this project and this book—to encourage citizens to understand the issues. If any substantial number do, politicians will also get the message.

That is a broad problem. If you look at the growth of government spending from the individual voter's standpoint, the overall problem is the same but the issue changes somewhat. The fact is, voters have a special problem on the issue of government spending, and that problem is reflected in the enormous voter frustration and volatility expressed in opinion polls. Wild fluctuations in recent polls suggest, I think, just how volatile the situation is.

The biggest problem for voters is that they wear two hats at once. On the one hand, they have a general taxpayer/citizen interest in reduced spending, reduced inflation, and increased growth. That general taxpayer interest focuses on the size of the overall, aggregate budget. Although this general taxpayer interest is strong, it must compete with another interest which finds each individual voter and citizen as a member of one or another of the special interest groups which have highly concentrated stakes in particular spending programs. Each person has a very intense stake in those *particular* benefits. This is true of business and labor, incidentally, every bit as much as it is for individuals. And therein lies the problem and the source of conflict: how to reconcile and resolve these two positions which go in absolutely opposite directions. The central difficulty, of course, is that everybody likes benefits and nobody likes costs.

These two conflicting interests may explain the apparent inconsistency of much voting. Voting for Congress, for instance, which finds individual representatives closest to the particular interests they represent, provides the principal means to vote one's special interest in favor of selective spending—which perhaps explains why Congress often seems to push for more spending than the White House wants, no matter who occupies it. Elections for the presidency, on the other hand, seem to offer greater opportunities to vote one's general citizen/taxpayer interest. Tax and expenditure limitation initiatives and constitutional amendments clearly appeal to voters in their general interest.

These factors are important in considering political strategies to encourage more sensible policies. It may often be the case that second-best strategies from an economic standpoint may have far greater political appeal—and therefore far greater chances of passage—than approaches which economists would support in an ideal world. The problem is particularly critical for the overall objective of limiting government spending and freeing increased resources for the private sector.

VII

Potential Policy Problems
of the 1980s

10

LAURENCE J. KOTLIKOFF

Social Security and Welfare: What We Have, Want, and Can Afford[1]

The U.S. income transfer system. Shortcomings in equitable distribution. Intergenerational transfers. The social security earnings test. Poverty perpetuated. Redesigning the social security system. Six proposed reforms. The Unified Welfare Tax System.

The dismal economic performance of the U.S. economy in the 1970s and the prospects for continued stagflation in the 1980s have created a climate of adversity and accusation. Consumers increasingly question the integrity of big business, business protests "excessive" environmental and consumer protection, workers accuse welfare recipients of fraud and indolence, the young are alarmed by their increasing social security tax payments to the old, and everyone is pointing his finger at the government. The general growth of government and the intrusion of government in the day-to-day workings of the private economy highlight the chorus of concerns. Welfare and social security systems are particular objects of intense public criticism.

The fact is that in the past twenty years government has grown relative to the size of the economy, but that growth has been primarily in the area of transfer programs. In 1960 total federal, state, and local government budgets represented 27 percent of the gross national product (GNP); today the figure is 32 percent.[2] This 18 percent growth in government expenditures relative to GNP in the last two decades does not, however, reflect an increase in the purchase of goods and services by governments. Indeed, the ratio to GNP of real government purchases of goods and services was 20 percent in 1960 and is still 20 percent today. The ratio of government transfer payments to GNP has, in contrast, doubled since 1920 from 5 to 10 percent (*Economic Report of the President, 1980*, pp. 203, 289, 290). Twenty cents of every dollar spent by governments in 1960 was a transfer payment; today 32 cents of every dollar of government expenditure represents a transfer payment. Government is not consuming a bigger chunk of the collective pie; rather, it is increasingly engaged in a process of collecting and redistributing the pie.

Virtually every American will be directly affected by the income transfer system during his lifetime. In 1979 over a third of the population directly received an income transfer from the federal government, whether in the form of social security benefits, Medicare, welfare benefits, food stamps, Medicaid, general assistance, unemployment insurance, veterans benefits, or disability benefits. The large and growing income transfer expenditures have necessitated substantial tax increases in the past twenty years. The social security tax in particular has emerged as the major source of federal revenue after the federal income tax. Over half of the nation's income recipients now pay more social security taxes than income taxes, and social security taxes are still on the rise (Campbell 1977, p. xiii). Between 1978 and 1982 the real value of these taxes paid by middle-income Americans will rise by 50 percent (Kotlikoff 1978, p. 127), as much as $1,200 in 1979 dollars. Even these impressive tax increases are insufficient to finance the program through the first half of the twenty-first century. Because of dramatic changes in demographics, tax rates may have to increase by an additional 8 percent by the year 2025 to meet currently legislated benefits (Robertson 1978).

The enormous growth of income transfers has greatly alleviated poverty, but it has by no means eliminated poverty. Since 1960 the number of persons remaining in poverty after cash and in-kind transfers has been reduced by almost 11 million (U.S. Department of Health, Education, and Welfare 1980, p. 3). Yet 20 million Americans, roughly one in every ten, still live below the official poverty line. As with the welfare system, some but not all of the goals of the social security system have been met. Despite massive efforts to redistribute to the elderly through social security, the relative income position of the elderly is lower today than it was thirty years ago (Kotlikoff 1978, p. 139).

This chapter will provide an overview of the social security and welfare systems, indicate their accomplishments, point out serious problems in their structuring and financing, and suggest ideas for reform. The response to mounting pressure to reduce the size of government, or at least to retard its growth, need not mean abandonment of the reasonable humanitarian goals of these programs. Both the welfare and social security systems can and should be more efficiently designed. The welfare system is a bureaucratic nightmare.

The social security system is much more efficiently organized, but is still engaged in activities that are both costly and have nothing to do with its reasonable purpose.

The chapter proceeds with a discussion of the general objectives of the income transfer system as well as of the problems inherent in meeting those objectives. Any cogent analysis of what we have and what we need must be predicated on a clear view of what we want. The social security system in particular has expanded enormously, partly because its goals have never been clearly articulated.

The following section turns to the issue of equity, to the long-standing and serious inequities in welfare and social security that need to be addressed. Some of these problems are well known; others are apparent only after a close examination of the complex provisions in the enabling legislation.

Labor supply is the next topic. Both the welfare and social security systems contain major work disincentives that reduce the nation's supply of labor and thus total national output.

The final two sections focus in more detail on specific problems and reform ideas for social security and welfare. A number of different methods for resolving the long-term funding problems of social security are considered, as is also an alternative to our current welfare system, which I describe as the Unified Welfare Tax System, that incorporates many features of our current system as well as the negative income tax.

GENERAL OBJECTIVES OF THE INCOME TRANSFER SYSTEM

Income redistribution, paternalistic control of the economic choices of individuals, and the provision of insurance appear to be the major objectives of our income transfer system. The desire to redistribute income presumably arises from a sense that income inequality is largely capricious, beyond the control of individuals, arising from differences in native ability and in financial and nonfinancial inheritances. While society wishes to redistribute resources to those truly in need, the practical problem is to distinguish those who are truly unable to earn a decent living because of inherent low ability from those who are able.

The inability to distinguish target recipients from a larger pool means that a second-best redistribution mechanism must be applied that redistributes on the basis of characteristics that are closely, but not perfectly, correlated with true inability to earn a decent living. These characteristics include earnings and assets as well as more immutable features such as an individual's state of health, age, sex, and the presence of small children. Viewed in this light, it is hardly surprising that our current welfare system is characterized by earnings and asset tests as well as by categorical coverage. These are clearly imperfect sorting mechanisms, but they are the best one can do, given incomplete information.

The decision to use a particular sorting criterion must balance the gains from better identification of the true target recipient group with the costs arising from the incentive of individuals to alter their behavior to meet the criterion. The welfare system, for instance, redistributes substantially more to "single mothers with children" than to poor married couples with children. "Single mothers with children" are truly needier than others, given male/female earnings differentials and the time required at home to raise children. But using this criterion has the effect of encouraging single females with children to remain single, and of encouraging married females with children to become single to increase their transfer incomes.

On these terms, some criteria will be judged too costly to

justify their use. One essential question is whether to use any criterion other than income. The negative income tax differs from the existing welfare system in its reliance on income as the sole sorting criterion. Under a negative income tax, each individual receives a lump sum payment independent of health, sex, age, marital status, etc.; this payment (plus other income) is then subject to tax—perhaps at graduated rates, but at rates that are uniform for all individuals. The negative income tax has not been adopted, presumably because most Americans judge that the benefits from using additional sorting criteria exceed the costs. Realistic welfare reform proposals must then accept categorical coverage as a political reality.

Paternalism is a second motivation underlying the U.S. income transfer system. In the case of social security, the government is, in part, attempting to force individuals to save for their old age. In the welfare area, the government supervises the goods consumers purchase with food stamps, Medicaid, and subsidized housing. In-kind transfers force the recipient to consume in a manner pleasing to the donor; they also serve as a sorting device, aiding the most those individuals with preferences similar to the donor's.

Paternalistic in-kind transfers may be undermined by private behavior. Either food stamps themselves or food purchased with food stamps can be sold to permit the purchase of other commodities. Individuals may be able to consume at "excessive" levels when young by borrowing against future social security benefits, thus to arrive at retirement with the same level of resources as they would have had without social security. But government attempts to regulate individual decisions appear to be effective. Kotlikoff, Spivak, and Summers (1979, p. 27) concluded that "without social security and private pensions, consumption in old age relative to lifetime consumption would be about 40 percent lower for the average person." This finding suggests that, because of either capital market constraints or myopia, social security significantly raises the level of retirement consumption.

I have also made use of the 1972–1973 *Consumer Expenditure Survey* to examine the effectiveness of the food stamp program. I find that families with food stamps allocate a significantly larger fraction of their total budgets to food. For low-income (less than $6,000), young and middle-aged (18–45), single-headed households with children, the budget fraction spent on food is 34.4 percent for those on food stamps and 25.9 percent for those not on food stamps. In addition, 37 percent of households without food stamps, but only 16 percent of households with food stamps, spend less than 20.0 percent of their budget on food.[3]

A third objective of our income transfer system is simply the provision of insurance against risks that are not insurable at reasonable rates in private markets. The provision of insurance, while conceptually distinct from the other objectives, often involves paternalistic supervision of individual choices and income redistribution. Government provision of insurance forces individuals, in effect, to buy insurance, and represents as such an in-kind transfer. Redistribution is also involved, because the premia for government insurance correspond to taxes levied on the more affluent members of society. The real distinction between the insurance objective and these other objectives is that the government is actually setting up the insurance market rather than simply paying the poor to purchase insurance privately.

Examples of government provision of insurance through the income transfer system are disability insurance, unemployment insurance, and insurance against abject poverty due to family dissolution, unintended pregnancies, macroeconomic fluctuations, etc. The problem of "moral hazard" is the principle reason that private insurance markets do not handle these risks very well. "Moral hazard" refers to the fact that the availability of insurance may, itself, influence the likelihood that an uncertain event will occur. Consider unemployment insurance as one example: given this insurance, an employed worker has less of an incentive to try to keep his job and an unemployed worker has less of an incentive to find a new job. Unemployment benefits both increase the probability that a worker becomes unemployed and reduce the probability of reemployment once he becomes unemployed. As the probability of the insured event increases, the premium that the insurance company must charge to break even rises as well. At some point the premium may be too high to justify the market. Again, the problem is fundamentally one of lack of information. Neither the insurance company nor the government can observe how hard the worker is trying to keep his job or to find a new one.

Both private insurance markets and the government try to combat the moral hazard problem through the use of deductibles, coinsurance rates, and experience rating. Unemployed workers, for example, generally receive less than their previous earnings in the form of unemployment benefits, and they must work for an extended period after becoming unemployed before they can requalify for benefits. The deductible here is the difference between previous earnings and unemployment benefits, while the inability to become reinsurable for a period of time reflects implicit experience rating.

Given the government's imperfect information on the one hand and, on the other, its policy objectives of redistribution to the genuinely poor, paternalistic supervision of individual decisions, and provision of insurance, the optimal design of an income transfer system will most certainly involve categorical provision of benefits, in-kind transfers, work tests, and special work incentives to offset the moral hazard problem associated with transfers based on the extent of earned income. There is no simplistic design of the income transfer system that will satisfy all social objectives. However, more simple designs can eliminate the gross inequities, administrative overlap, excessive work disincentives, and incredibly complex benefit provisions that characterize current programs.

ISSUES OF EQUITY

Equity requires equal treatment of equals; it also requires, in the absence of persuasive ethical arguments to the contrary, equal treatment of unequals. Income transfers should be fair; they should not be capricious. The U.S. income transfer system is a long way from satisfying either of these principles. Still, it appears to be moving—albeit slowly—in the right direction. The 1977 Social Security Amendments earn points for preserving and strengthening the link between an individual's tax contributions and retirement benefits. This relationship should be strengthened even further. Indeed, the Social Security Administration should be required to report to taxpayers on an annual basis their accumulated amount of taxes paid into the system and their level of expected retirement benefits based on those tax contributions. These social security tax account statements will permit each individual to more clearly understand from whom and to whom redistribution is occurring under social security.

The need for greater equity has also been addressed in past and current welfare reform proposals. The relative growth of the food stamp programs, and the introduction of Supplemental Security Income for the Aged, Blind, and Disabled (SSI) in 1972 and Earned Income Tax Credit (EITC) in 1975, reflect the need to standardize benefits across all states in the country. President Carter's 1980 welfare reform proposal calls for a national minimum welfare benefit level as well as uniform welfare eligibility rules.

The distance between the current system and a system that could be described as equitable is very great indeed. The social security system, in particular, redistributes resources across and within generations in a manner that is in part unreasonable and in part outrageous. The redistribution of resources across generations represents the most problematic feature of the system; it is responsible for the current massive tax increases, it imperils the long-run financial integrity of the program, and it may be significantly reducing national savings. This intergenerational redistribution is the counterpart of the fact that social security is financed on a "pay as you go" or unfunded basis. Rather than accumulate each worker's social security contributions in a trust fund to be paid out when the worker retires, taxes paid by young workers have, since 1939, been immediately paid out as current social security benefits. Over the last forty years social security beneficiaries have enjoyed enormous windfalls from the program, in part because they have spent few years of their lives paying in taxes (social security taxation started in 1939), in part because tax rates until the 1970s have been low, but primarily because benefit levels, the tax contributions of younger generations, have been high.

A recent study by Boskin, Arvin, and Cone (1980, p. 30) indicates that current retirees are receiving benefits that average six times the amount of taxes paid in plus interest; the average net intergenerational transfer to current retirees amounts to $42,000 in present value computed at a 3 percent rate of return. These large intergenerational transfers are not, however, an enduring feature of the system. Current and scheduled tax increases imply that young workers will barely break even from the system. But the taxes now mandated are clearly insufficient to provide retirement benefits in the twenty-first century for the baby boom generation which has, itself, produced a baby bust. The projected social security deficit is roughly $600 billion (Boskin, Arvin, and Cone 1980, p. 18). If taxes are raised to eliminate this deficit, the net intergenerational transfer to current young workers will be large and negative.

It is important to understand that these social security intergenerational transfers which, on a yearly basis, are comparable in magnitude to the total of all other government
public assistance programs, are not a case of the rich paying
the poor (Parsons and Munro 1977, pp. 65—86). What we
have is rich young people, middle-class young people, and
poor young people transferring large sums of money to rich
old people, middle-class old people, and poor old people. It is
true that poor old people fare better under the program than
rich old people, but extremely rich as well as extremely poor
old people are currently receiving an enormous windfall from
social security. There is simply no sensible argument for this
massive transfer from one generation to another, but this
has been and is today the major activity of social security. It
is this capricious activity that threatens social security's survival.

Social security has other redistributive features that, quite
simply, have little to do with its reasonable purpose. The
system extracts 33 percent lower taxes from doctors, law-
yers, and accountants while providing these and other high
income self-employed individuals with the same retirement
benefits as wage and salaried workers. The tax break to the
self-employed is based on the mistaken view that taxes
levied on employers have different economic consequences
than taxes levied on employees. Intuitively, who mails the
tax check to the government can be of no economic significance, but misunderstanding of this simple point has led to
an unwarranted and large tax break for the self-employed.
The system pays housewives and househusbands who
haven't worked a day in their lives the same benefits as
many working people who annually contribute 12 percent of
their labor earnings to social security. These dependent and
survivor benefits that pay respectively 50 and 100 percent of
the principle earner's benefits were instituted in 1939 at a
time when the labor market experience of married females
was fairly limited. Annual work experience rates of middle·

aged females now exceed 60 percent; times have changed, and so must the outdated free provision of dependent benefits.

It is unfair and unreasonable to pay social security benefits only in the form of an annual annuity, given that males die earlier than females and that nonwhites die earlier than whites. Current life expectancy for 20-year-old black males is age 67; for white females, it is age 79 (U.S. Department of Commerce 1979, p. 71). These figures are averages and do not adjust for income differences; they still suggest that a white female performing exactly the same job as a black male and paying exactly the same social security taxes will, on average, receive twelve years more social security benefits than a black male. Note that the current average annual social security benefit for retired workers is $3,168 a year, and that twelve years times $3,168 a year is $38,016— certainly not peanuts. The $38,016 is only one estimate of the potential unequal lifetime treatment of black males and white females measured as of age 20. It corresponds to treating dollars received in the future as equivalent to dollars received today. Treating dollars received in the future as less valuable than dollars received today would significantly lower this figure.

To those who are currently aged, the most upsetting aspect of the system may well be the social security earnings test. Between the ages of 65 and 72 (70 after 1981), the social security earnings test reduces or eliminates benefits for many of the working aged;[4] many elderly people who have paid social security taxes for years receive little or no benefits between 65 and 72 simply because they desire to work and to continue to contribute to the productivity of the nation.[5] The earnings test considers only labor income; hence, a retired millionaire in 1980 with hundreds of thousands of dollars of interest and dividend income will receive full benefits, while a 65-year-old working full time at the minimum wage will lose as much as $774 in retirement benefits.

The welfare system presents equally appalling cases of unequal treatment of equals. A nonworking single mother with three children living in New York City can currently collect monthly AFDC (Aid to Families with Dependent Children) benefits plus food stamps totaling $565. The same mother living in Indiana would receive $424 a month, while she would receive only $316 a month in Mississippi (U.S. Department of Health, Education, and Welfare 1980, p. 16). Is a poor mother with children 34 percent less deserving of assistance because she lives in Mississippi rather than in Indiana? Is she 80 percent less deserving than a mother in New York City?[6] Welfare coverage as well as benefit levels vary greatly from state to state. In twenty-six states impoverished married couples with unemployed husbands can collect AFDC benefits; the other twenty-four states provide no benefits at all for this recipient category.

Within states, there is egregious unequal treatment of identically situated families. Welfare caseworkers have considerable latitude in determining work-related expenses that may be deducted from earnings in the welfare benefit calculation. Caseworkers can manipulate these expenses for nonprofessional as well as professional reasons to raise or lower benefits by as much as 30 percent (Heffernan 1973, p. 65). Even when the law is uniformly administered, two equally situated poor families may receive very different levels of support because there is a rationing of some welfare benefits. Although most poor families are eligible for housing assistance, less than a third of AFDC recipients receive housing assistance (U.S. Department of Health, Education, and Welfare 1978, p. 278). There are long waiting lists—over two years in many cases—for receipt of housing assistance. In 1980 projected housing assistance averages $138 a month for those families actually receiving benefits (U.S. Department of Health Education, and Welfare 1978, p. 43). Within the same state, two equally poor families with identical characteristics may end up with total income differentials of more than 30 percent due solely to housing assistance.

There is also disturbing and unfair treatment of similar but not identical families. Two-parent, two-child families in which the father earns the minimum wage have less income in many states than an AFDC family consisting of a mother with three children (U.S. Department of Health, Education, and Welfare 1979a, p. 333). Certainly the income needs of these two families are quite similar, but the working family may end up with 15 percent less income than the nonworking AFDC family. In about half of the states, a poor elderly couple on SSI receives a larger welfare benefit than does a non-aged AFDC mother with three children. Apart from outright fraud, there are cases of legitimate welfare payments to individuals with incomes well over the poverty level. These cases, relatively few in number, arise in food stamps and housing assistance programs, both of which have liberal eligibility rules and liberal deduction allowances.

SOCIAL SECURITY AND WELFARE/WORK DISINCENTIVES

It is ironic that the social security and welfare programs may, themselves, be largely responsible for the perpetuation of poverty and the relatively low income level of the elderly. Social security and welfare recipients are probably the highest taxed individuals in society. The system provides virtually no incentive to work; not surprisingly, few recipients work, and those who do work very little. While many taxpayers have a penchant for accusing welfare recipients of being "lazy" and "unmotivated," one wonders how many nonwelfare recipients would be willing to work in 1980 for as little as 31 cents per hour, which is the net wage a welfare recipient earning the minimum wage would receive in many states for marginal hours of work if he or she worked full time. The difference between the gross wage of $3.10 per hour and the net wage of 31 cents corresponds to explicit and implicit taxation of labor earnings at a 90 percent rate. "Explicit" taxation occurs from federal, state, and local income taxes as well as from social security payroll taxes. "Implicit" taxation refers to the loss of welfare or social security benefits when gross earnings rise. Both programs have work tests that reduce benefits at specified rates for each additional dollar of earned income. Explicit and implicit tax rates of 50 to 90 percent are assessed on the labor earnings of the majority of the poor and elderly over a wide range of potential working hours.

There is mounting evidence that the social security earnings test is a chief cause of the dramatic increase in early retirement. In 1950 the labor force participation rate of males 65 and over was 46 percent; today it is only 20 percent. Not only are there fewer elderly men working on any given day during the year, but there are fewer elderly men who work at any time during the year. The fraction of men 65 to 69 who are completely retired during the year has risen from 40 percent to 60 percent since 1960. For males 60 to 64, the retirement rate is now 30 percent, double the 1960 figure of 15 percent (U.S. Department of Labor 1979*a*, p. 314). Those elderly males who do choose to work are working fewer hours during the year. Since 1967 the fraction of working males 65 and over who work part time has increased from one-third to almost one-half (U.S. Department of Labor 1979*a*, pp. 282, 283).

The social security earnings test currently reduces benefits 50 cents for every dollar of earnings beyond $5,000 and represents a 50 percent implicit tax for workers age 65 to 72;[7] in combination with the federal income tax, state income taxes, and the social security tax, this 50 percent tax on earnings penalizes the work effort of the elderly at rates that can easily exceed 80 and even 90 percent. Reasonable people are simply not going to work for unreasonable levels of compensation. Data from the *Current Population Survey* for the years 1967 to 1974 bear this out. In 1967 the exempt amount of earnings, the amount before which no benefits were lost, was $1,500. Of those males 65 to 71 who worked in 1967, 11.5 percent arranged their labor supply to earn $1,400 to $1,600. In vivid contrast, only 1.9 percent earned $1,600 to $1,800. As the exempt amount increases over time, the proportion of both male and female elderly workers earning just under the exempt amount increases as well (Kotlikoff 1978, p. 141).

Eliminating the earnings test would unquestionably increase the incomes of the elderly as well as generate tax revenues that would offset a large proportion of the costs of doing so. Because of impending changes in the demographic structure of the population, the need to reverse the trend towards early retirement is greater today than at any time in this century. By the year 2025 the proportion of the population age 62 and over will rise from 13.6 percent to 24.5 percent (U.S. Department of Commerce 1977, pp. 39, 71). The ratio of workers paying social security taxes to retired beneficiaries will fall from a current level of 3.2 to about 2. Unless the elderly are permitted to remain employed, U.S. per capita income will decline and social security taxes will rise as the ratio of dependent to nondependent persons in the economy increases.

Welfare recipients do not face a single and easily understood tax schedule relating their gross labor earnings to their net disposable income; rather, they are confronted with eight different and highly complicated implicit and explicit tax schedules. These correspond to the work and income tests of AFDC, food stamps, housing assistance, SSI, Medicaid, the Earned Income Tax Credit, the federal income tax, and the state income tax. Each of the above has its own eligibility requirements, its own definition of testable income, its own set of deductions and exclusions, and its own tax rates. Not only do these explicit and implicit tax systems differ across programs, but their structures differ markedly across states.

Even within a state, tax schedules will vary depending on both the characteristics of the recipient and the discretion of the social worker. The result of all this is a horribly complex set of uncoordinated rules and regulations that bewilder trained academics and surely leave welfare recipients confused and dismayed. As a substitute for fundamental reform, recent "reform" of the system has simply added more and more programs to the system with little concern with how the work disincentives of the new program would interact with those of the old programs.

The Earned Income Tax Credit introduced in 1975 is a case in point. The EITC subsidizes labor supply at a 10.0 percent rate up to $5,000 of earnings, and it taxes labor supply at a 12.5 percent rate for earnings between $6,000 and $10,000. While the 10.0 percent subsidy below $5,000 has probably increased the incomes and the labor supply of those workers initially earning less than $5,000 a year, the 12.5 percent additional tax on earnings from $6,000 to $10,000 induces many poor earners initially in this range to reduce their labor supply; while the incomes of some impoverished families are certainly increased, the EITC may, in effect, be impoverishing other low-income families.

The efficacy of any particular income transfer program cannot be determined in isolation from the rest of the system. Figure 1 presents my best estimate of the work and income choices of a single California mother with three children who is eligible to receive AFDC, food stamps, Medicaid, housing assistance, and the EITC but who faces federal and state income as well as social security taxes. Two monthly budget frontiers are drawn for the cases of a mother earning gross wages of $3.10 per hour and $8.00 per hour. The vertical segment of the frontier at zero hours per month gives the combined average benefit level for a nonworking AFDC mother of three with food stamps, Medicaid, and housing assistance. The numbers along the frontier indicate the total marginal tax rates applying to additional hours of work,

Figure 1

Budget Constraints Showing Effective Marginal Tax Rates:
Working Mother Earning $3.10/hour

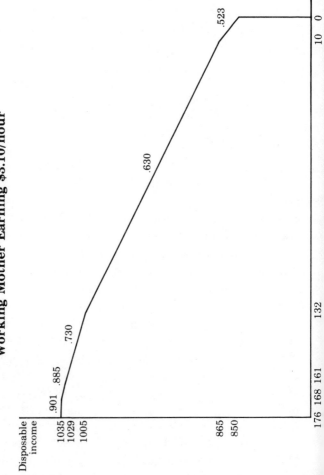

Working Mother Earning $8.00/hour

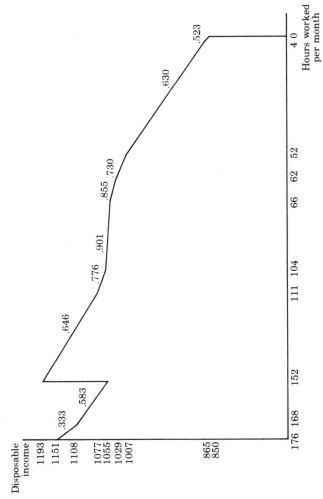

Disposable income

Hours worked per month

taking all the eligibility and earnings test provisions of different programs into account. Take the 85.5 percent marginal tax rate segment on the $8.00 per hour budget frontier as an example. A welfare mother earning another dollar in this range will lose $0.40 of AFDC benefits, $0.15 of housing assistance, $0.14 of food stamps, and $0.125 of her earned income tax credit.[8] In addition, she will pay 12.23 percent in social security taxes, but since these taxes are deductible from countable income in AFDC, the social security tax adds only an additional 4.0 percent to the total marginal tax.

The rates change along the frontier, in part because EITC and AFDC implicit tax rates are based on the level of earnings, in part because the implicit food stamps and AFDC taxes fall to zero when all food stamps and AFDC benefits are "taxed" away, and in part because the federal income tax does not come into effect until earnings exceed federal income tax deductions and exemption levels. The implicit tax rate of any one program along the frontier depends on the provision of benefits of other programs along the frontier. The housing tax rate thus rises from 15 percent to 25 percent at the point where all AFDC benefits have been taxed away; the loss of AFDC benefits can be deducted from the implicit housing tax, hence when AFDC benefits run out so does this deduction. An abrupt change in the shape of the $8.00 frontier occurs at 152 hours of work. At this point the welfare mother earns enough income to lose all her AFDC benefits. But since her eligibility for Medicaid is predicated on receipt of AFDC benefits, complete loss of AFDC will mean complete loss of Medicaid benefits. The loss of Medicaid does not occur gradually, and this fact means that a small increase in work effort at 152 hours will precipitate a sharp reduction in total income. The marginal tax at this point exceeds 100 percent.

As strange as it may seem, some—but not many—AFDC recipients work despite these oppressive tax rates. In 1975, of the 3.4 million AFDC families, 80 percent were headed by women. Sixteen percent of these were employed, the majority (64 percent) at full-time jobs.[9] Hausman (1979) finds that the labor supply of female heads is fairly responsive to their level of net compensation. His findings suggest that tax rates above 66 percent are inefficient; rates above 66 percent will reduce the labor supply of female heads so much that total tax revenues will fall, leaving both the government and welfare recipients with lower incomes.[10] But current revenue should not be the sole consideration in setting tax rates. Lowering tax rates significantly below 66 percent may cost a bit more in the short run, but will save money in the long run. As welfare recipients acquire training and skills in the labor market, more of these people will be able to permanently escape from the welfare rolls. Almost half of current AFDC recipients have been on public assistance for over three years (U.S. Department of Health, Education, and Welfare 1977, p. 297).

These high marginal tax rates are not confined simply to AFDC recipients. A full-time minimum wage earner with a nonworking spouse and two children whose only form of assistance is food stamps is taxed at a combined 55 percent marginal rate on additional hours at full-time work. The 55 percent rate reflects implicit food stamp and EITC taxation and explicit social security taxation.

Significantly lower tax rates are worth a try. Other approaches, including the Work Incentive Program (WIN), have had only a marginal impact, if any, on the employment of welfare recipients (U.S. Department of Health, Education, and Welfare 1979*a*, p. 328). Indeed, job programs such as WIN and that of the Comprehensive Employment and Training Act (CETA) will be much more effective if tax rates on the poor are lowered to sensible levels.

REDESIGNING SOCIAL SECURITY FOR THE 1980s AND BEYOND

The social security system is in financial crisis. Projected deficits on the order of half a trillion dollars require either lowering benefits or raising taxes. The longer we wait to make these adjustments, the more painful these adjustments will be. Proposals to finance social security benefits through other tax vehicles, including the income tax and even a gasoline tax, do not resolve the basic problem that promised benefit levels are very high relative to the projected tax base.

The prospects of lowering benefits are not good. The political environment is adverse to even public discussion of reductions in benefits. The political reality is that a sizable fraction of the population, namely, current retirees, have a direct stake in insuring high benefits. Middle-aged workers, many of whom have paid social security taxes for years, also desire to keep benefits high since they soon will be receiving their own. If any group is going to oppose increases in benefits and tax rates, it will have to be young.

The young do have a direct stake in lowering benefits and their taxes, but they may not realize it. One way a young person might judge the value of contributing more money into social security is to compare the expected rate of return on social security tax contributions with the rate of return on private investments such as savings accounts, stocks, bonds, or real estate. The problem is that both these numbers are highly uncertain. An attempt to figure out the implicit rate of return on social security contributions with any degree of accuracy, based on the current exceedingly complex provisions, requires skills in mathematics, accounting, and economics. Furthermore, judging any "expert's appraisal" requires these same skills. Unfortunately in this case (although fortunately for our collective sanity), very few young people are accountants or economists. Indeed, even highly trained economists may differ as to what constitutes a reasonable calculation. Even if the young people perceived that they were getting a bad deal from social security, the possibility always exists that once the young become old they, together with the middle-aged workers, could legislate higher benefits for themselves.

The real losers from the expansion of unfunded social security are, for the most part, not yet born. The long-term costs of unfunded social security are difficult to see at the personal level; they take the form of reduced levels of national savings, which translate into a lower rate of capital formation. Further generations will have less capital to work with and will, as a consequence, earn lower wages throughout their lives. The extent to which social security's intergenerational "windfalls" are increasing consumption and therefore reducing savings is a subject of hot debate among economists. Estimates range from a 40 percent savings reduction to no reduction at all (Feldstein 1974; Barro 1974, 1978). Although there is no hard evidence that social security has reduced the nation's savings, there is also no hard evidence that it hasn't. Hence, a real possibility exists that social security's current massive intergenerational transfers are significantly reducing savings and the future standard of living of the nation.

It is time to stop mortgaging the welfare of our children and to design a social security system that pays benefits if, and only if, those benefits are related to its reasonable purpose. Social security should be in the business of requiring individuals to save an adequate amount for their retirement; it should also be in the business of redistributing resources from well-off members of an age cohort to disadvantaged numbers of that cohort. Social security should not be in the business of redistributing resources from the well-off young to the well-off old, from wage earners to the self-employed, from males to females, from blacks to whites, from single people to married couples, from workers to househusbands and housewives, and from the employed elderly to the non-employed elderly. Social security should be structured as an earned entitlements program—benefits paid out should correspond to a *reasonable* return on each individual's lifetime tax contributions. The rate of return should be higher for the lifetime poor than for the lifetime rich. This lifetime progressivity of the social security system is a feature of our current system that should be maintained. Any other benefit payments that do not correspond to a reasonable but progressive rate of return on an individual's own tax contributions are unwarranted. Indigent elderly people who do not, for some reason, qualify for social security benefits or who qualify for very small levels of benefits are provided assistance through Supplemental Security Income; hence the social security system per se should not be structured to provide welfare to the impoverished elderly.

To increase equity and insure social security's financial integrity, the following steps should be taken:

(1) *Gradually eliminate positive intergenerational transfers to workers who have not yet retired.* Rather than paying workers who retire in the next twenty years two or three times what they contributed to social security, promised benefits to these near-term retirees should be lowered so their benefits more closely reflect their contributions. This benefit reduction can be done on a progressive basis, so the lifetime poor of these cohorts are not significantly affected.

(2) *Eliminate the tax break to the self-employed.* Raise the self-employment tax to the sum of the employer's and employee's contribution to Old Age, Survivors, Disability, and Hospital Insurance (OASDHI).

(3) *Pay social security benefits partly in a lump sum at retirement.* Even at age 60, a black male's life expectancy is six years less than that of a white female.

(4) *Require tax contributions on behalf of dependents.* In situations where one spouse does not work, contributions of the working spouse should either be divided and counted as separate contributions by each spouse, or additional tax contributions should be required to pay for the future dependent and survivor benefits available to the nonworking spouse.

(5) *Eliminate the social security earnings test.* The earnings test represents a major obstacle to the employment of the aged. It is serving no useful purpose; on the contrary, it is immiserating the aged.

(6) *Require annual reporting of accumulated social security contributions and projected benefits.*

These six reforms can easily be incorporated within the existing tax and benefit structure of social security. Their adoption will restore social security to financial balance. They will obviate future tax increases and other draconian measures such as raising the social security retirement age. These reforms are politically feasible, because they do not involve across-the-board increases in taxes or reductions in benefits; rather, they simply make the system fair, and that is something the majority of Americans will support. These reforms will require new legislation, but our current legislation will have to be altered anyway since it is locking us into an untenable deficit.

The link between lifetime taxes paid and lifetime benefits received, the earned entitlements feature of social security, will be greatly tightened. Tightening this link rather than loosening it through general revenue funding is the direction in which to move. If the payroll tax were replaced by higher income taxes and benefits received were not tied to taxes paid in, then payments to social security would be perceived as taxes rather than as a form of savings. Since the progressive income tax system and welfare system already generate major work disincentives, every attempt should be made to convince workers that on the margin the 12.23 cents of every earned dollar they pay to social security represents approximately 12.23 cents that they will eventually receive back.

The establishment of social security as an earned entitlements program, and only an earned entitlements program, will clarify the inappropriateness of certain other "reform" proposals such as taxing social security benefits under the income tax. Since individuals will have earned their social security benefits through their own social security payroll tax contributions, income taxation of these earned benefits could not be justified.

FUNDAMENTAL WELFARE REFORM—THE UNIFIED WELFARE TAX SYSTEM

There are straightforward ways to save money and improve the lot of the disadvantaged in this country, but the approach cannot be piecemeal. The major problem with the existing welfare system is that there are too many uncoordinated agencies working at cross-purposes and duplicating efforts. In AFDC alone there are fifty-four state and local agencies administering the provision of benefits. Administrative expenses in these programs are quite high; for every 90 cents paid out in AFDC benefits, 10 cents is spent on administration. The food stamps breakdown is even worse; here, 15 to 20 cents of every dollar is used to run the program. Despite these large expenditures, error rates in welfare programs are very high. Errors have been found in roughly one-quarter of AFDC and food stamp cases and in 10 percent of SSI cases (U.S. Department of Health, Education, and Welfare 1979a, p. 15). There is such a jumble of federal and state programs that more agencies and bureaucracies are being proposed to coordinate the existing agencies and bureaucracies (U.S. Department of Health, Education, and Welfare 1979b, p. 50).

Inevitably, agencies to coordinate the coordinating agencies will be established unless a fundamental overhaul of the system is undertaken.

The following is a proposal for the creation of a single federal agency that would administer a single national welfare program that I will refer to as the Unified Welfare Tax System (UWTS). The UWTS would have the following features:

(1) *A national system with uniform federal benefits* for each recipient category across all states, but adjusted for state costs of living; state and local administration of federal welfare would be eliminated. UWTS does not completely eliminate state discretion in setting welfare benefits. Under UWTS, each state is still free to mandate additional welfare benefits, but UWTS benefits will be sufficiently large that few states would probably exercise that option. UWTS will, therefore, discourage poor states from exporting their poverty to rich states by setting welfare benefits so low that their poor are induced to migrate to higher-benefit paying states.

(2) *Universal eligibility.* Like the negative income tax, all individuals would be enrolled in UWTS, thus eliminating the stigma of "being on welfare."

(3) *Categorical coverage.* UWTS would establish a short list of family recipient categories, and each household head would be enrolled in UWTS under the appropriate category.

(4) *A basic benefit amount for each recipient category.* This amount would be provided if the recipient had no income.

(5) *A single definition of taxable income.* Such a definition would include earnings, interest income, and social security benefits.

(6) *A single, simple, and reasonable tax schedule for each recipient category.* These tax schedules will differ, depending on the type of recipient in question, and will merge with the federal income tax as earnings increase.

(7) *Provision of in-kind as well as cash benefits.* The net of tax benefit will be paid partly in cash and partly in food, housing, and health stamps; the ratio of cash to in-kind transfers will depend on the recipient category. The food stamps administration and housing assistance administration would be eliminated. The number of health stamps a recipient receives will determine the coinsurance rate the recipient must pay for health expenses. The coinsurance rate will vary from zero to unity as the number of health stamps rises from the maximum to zero. Hence, health benefits can be taxed away gradually—indeed, at the same rate as cash payments and in-kind food and housing payments.

UWTS represents a conservative as well as a radical approach to straightening out the welfare system. UWTS is conservative in that it maintains the categorical coverage and in-kind transfer features of the existing system. UWTS is radical because it eliminates state administration of welfare and also eliminates the food stamp, housing, and SSI bureaucracies. In contrast with the current system, UWTS is both equitable and efficient. Benefits will be uniform across the country. We will no longer pay benefits to recipients with income above a reasonable level, and we will automatically pay benefits to all recipients with incomes below a reasonable level. All families of a particular type will be treated uniformly; case worker discretion will be eliminated. The potential welfare fraud under UWTS is greatly reduced because UWTS can easily compare recipients' income declarations with IRS employee W−2 forms.

A panel of experts will set basic (zero income) benefits and will design a single and easily understood tax schedule for each type of recipient with significantly lower marginal tax rates than exist now, so that labor supply will be encouraged rather than discouraged. The experts will set tax schedules, using the best available information concerning the labor responses of different types of recipients. Tax rates will, at a minimum, be efficient; i.e., they will never be set so high that both recipients and the government lose money. These experts will clearly have to grapple with the basic dilemma that high benefits require high taxes and reduce work incentives. But even if basic benefits under UWTS remain at roughly their current levels, the efficient tax schedules under UWTS will greatly reduce the costs of providing those benefits.

For some recipient categories, such as unemployed fathers, the optimal tax and benefit schedule may involve sharp subsidies (negative taxes) at low levels of earnings to induce these recipients to become employed. If the UWTS' basic (zero income) benefits were set to zero, then substantial subsidies at low levels of earnings would constitute, in effect, a work test, since benefits (the subsidy) are received only if the individual works. Enrollment in CETA and WIN could be treated as equivalent to a certain level of earnings. An individual would be permitted to remain enrolled in CETA or WIN provided he (she) accepted CETA and WIN employment offers.

CONCLUSION

This chapter has attempted in a brief space to indicate the reasonable goals of our income transfer system and to contrast these goals with the performance of the actual system. The comparison of what we have with what we want led quite naturally to the proposals for reform of the social security and welfare systems. The proposals reflect simple commonsense approaches to the problems. Unfortunately, common sense and the U.S. political process are often at odds with one another. Implementation of these proposals will require bold and effective political leadership that can overcome narrow sectarian interests by appealing directly to the common sense and good judgment of the American people.

DISCUSSION

BOSKIN: When you think about where we are going to get resources for defense and industrial expansion in the future, the greates potential exists in reducing the growth of transfer payments. The sums involved are enormous, and with the stakes so high great political battles can be expected to rage over them in the next couple of decades. When you think that current expenditures for these programs plus the various assumptions different people make about the implicit promises of future payments, especially in social security, there are literally trillions of dollars at stake. In the old-age part of the social security system alone, the long-run deficit is about three-quarters of a trillion dollars; in hospital insurance, disability, substantial additional sums are involved. It is true that these deficits are not caused by legal obligations to pay future benefits, only implicit obligations. But expectations are only partly altered by this fact, and the political trauma in dealing with the problem almost certainly will be considerable.

I am concerned about a slightly longer-run issue—not just the current benefits that are being paid and the tax burden they impose, although those are obviously very important. Although it is difficult to quantify, I think a much deeper social and economic issue is what happens when you have different portions of the population—or larger or smaller portions of the population—relatively heavily dependent upon transfer payments for their income over long periods of time. When that gets repeated over several generations, are we permanently disenfranchising some significant fraction of our population from the mainstream of our society by condemning them to permanently being on the "dole"? And also, are we condemning *ourselves* to permanently be paying taxes to finance them? Is there that kind of cycle across generations? If so, is there a way to break it?

OLSEN: One other thing about the transfer payment and the social security system: you may be aware of the fact that people who operate the country's private pension fund structure have in recent years become terribly intimidated by what is in effect an attack on the private pension fund system—intimidated in the sense that there is concern that in fact the private pension system may be either phased out or replaced by something, and they are very much on the defensive right now. And why this is so important is because the private pension fund system in the United States, which you might say complements the social security system or vice versa, is also a very important source of savings—or private savings—and more importantly, I would stress privately managed savings; whereas the social security system is not a funded system at all. So that there is no implicit savings there whatsoever. Whereas in the private pension fund there is, and it is privately managed and it is important to capital formation.

I mention this because in discussing the whole social security system a lot of people seem to think that there is no alternative, in a sense, or that private pension systems are poor secondary sources of retirement benefits. But if anything, the private systems should receive additional encouragement.

CHICKERING: My own feeling about welfare reform is that people tend to be too hopeful about what reform might accomplish, not taking sufficient account of its inherent limitations. In a critical sense, there can *be* no good welfare system; there are intrinsic problems that prevent satisfactory solutions. The essential problem is that "good" welfare systems are supposed to do mutually exclusive things: on the one hand, they are supposed to provide relatively high minimum benefits to the genuinely needy—to those who cannot provide for themselves. On the other hand, they are supposed to preserve incentives for people to work their way off welfare, which can be done only by establishing marginal tax rates that are not prohibitive.

The fact is, it is impossible to do both of these things without expanding welfare to the point where it would break the society economically. You would have to include too many people. You can only accomplish these results if you establish draconian regulations and screening devices to try and determine who is "genuinely needy." It is not clear that would not be worse than the disease.

Society has made its decision about how to trade off these two values: it has chosen a relatively high minimum payment combined with confiscatory tax rates as people come off relief. Perhaps as a society we have weighed these two values improperly. But the first principle of any serious discussion of welfare reform must acknowledge the inherent problems restricting reform.

11

HENRY S. ROWEN

Defense Spending and the Uncertain Future

Current Soviet strategy and the U.S. defense posture. The loss of overseas facilities. The reluctant allies. Persian Gulf oil. Pay erosion and the all-volunteer force. Seven military categories needing attention.

A paramount issue facing the United States is the meaning for our security of the steadily growing military power of the Soviet Union and the increasing use of that power beyond its borders. Neither the increase in Soviet forces nor their exercise abroad are new phenomena. However, the invasion of Afghanistan has been so visible and dramatic as to compel attention by those in government who should have been keenly aware of the threat much earlier and have acted more vigorously to counter it.

For many years the Soviet Union has been steadily building its capabilities in virtually all categories of military power. In 1979, using the measure of dollars, the Soviet Union is estimated to have spent 50 percent more on its military forces than we did. In some force categories the difference is very much larger; for example, in what is called "strategic" nuclear forces the difference is estimated at 3:1; in general purpose forces, 1.7:1. Other comparisons can be made which put U.S. allies and Soviet allies in the balance (as well as China); cost comparisons can be made in rubles as well as dollars; the qualitative differences in the forces on both sides can be assessed. There is something resembling a consensus on trends in the balance, although strong divergences exist on interpretation of these trends. The view expressed here is that an increase in forces by an adversary may be grounds for concern but might not, by itself, set off alarm bells unless there were other grounds for concern. These are now clearly present.

SOVIET EXERCISES IN THE PROJECTION OF POWER

For the past decade, to go back no further, the Soviet Union has been pursuing a strategy to extend its military power beyond its borders. For instance, in 1970 it had around 15,000 combat troops in Egypt which were removed after Egypt broke with the Soviet Union (a move which did not prevent Soviet assistance to Egypt during the 1973 war). In 1971 it apparently provided operational combat support to India in its war with Pakistan. Another early move in the exercise of power projection was the establishment of a base in Somalia in 1974. In 1975 the Soviets intervened in Angola, in cooperation with Cuban troops as the principal presence on the ground. This was a bold move in a far-distant region and could have been easily blocked by the United States. It was not, and that failure may have been decisive in persuading the Soviet leadership that it faced a series of heretofore unmatched opportunities. Our failure to act was also viewed by many people in the world as having important and ominous implications for their own security. There followed in rapid succession Soviet and Soviet-supported coups, attempted coups, assassinations, and interventions in Ethiopia, the Yemens, Afghanistan, and perhaps Iraq. This pattern provides ample support for the Chinese description of the Soviet leadership as being engaged in a frenzy of aggression.

Although there occur, inevitably, important questions concerning Soviet strategy and how it might be implemented in the years ahead, there should be little doubt that from its standpoint what has been called détente in the West has been on the Soviet side principally a tactic directed at gaining advantage and not an instrument for making underlying mutual interests operational. Which is not to assert that the Soviets do not perceive some mutual interests; these simply have to be reconciled with—or subordinated to—the higher objective of extending its power in the world.

U.S. DEFENSE DOCTRINES

For President Carter, "The implications of the Soviet invasion of Afghanistan could pose the most serious threat to the peace since the second world war" (Carter 1980, p. 196)— although it has not yet led him to make any changes in the defense budget formulated *before* this event. In fact, this Soviet pattern raises most serious issues for our defense policy. Until very recently, this policy had progressively narrowed in scope. During the early 1960s the stated goal of strategy was to be able to deal with 2.5 contingencies at one time: a major one in Europe, one in northeast Asia, and a minor one somewhere else—say, the Caribbean. The diversion of defense resources to the Vietnam war drained our capabilities and will, and our strategy followed suit. By the early 1970s the basic plan had shrunk to coping with 1.5 wars: one major conflict and a minor one. Europe has always been seen as the most important and threatened theater, so this strategy required that there not be a major conflict in northeast Asia—or at least not one at the same time as one in Europe. During this period, and much later, the Persian Gulf did not feature as an important theater; when our behavior is examined closely, we did not see it as worth even half a war. The Guam Doctrine of President Nixon announced to the American people and the world that other nations were going to bear more of the burden of their defense; although we would continue to support them, we would do so—in Asia—principally with air and naval forces and not with ground forces.

President Carter came into office with a commitment to cut defense. This policy concentrated American efforts further by focusing almost exclusively on Europe. And not all of Europe at that; this strategy, especially in the first two years, paid little attention to the southern flank including, in particular, Turkey, a pivotal country and one that had become increasingly alienated from the United States and, to a lesser extent, from Western Europe. In east Asia President Carter sought to remove American ground forces from Korea, an attempt which caused alarm in Korea and hardly less concern in Japan (but political constraints caused Japanese concern to be expressed in muted tones). There was little emphasis in this strategy for the defense of American interests in the Middle East, Africa, or elsewhere—other than Europe.

On nuclear forces, the Carter administration also chose to minimize the significance of the growing vulnerability of our

Minuteman intercontinental ballistic missile (ICBM) force, to cancel the B−1 bomber, to slow down our cruise missile programs, to suspend the neutron bomb program (doing so in a way which shook the confidence of many Europeans in the quality of American leadership), and to move slowly on making decisions on a new, post-Minuteman ICBM. Only after a lag did it move ahead with the modernization of nuclear delivery systems in Europe, an enterprise in which European political constraints have grown to substantial proportions. Only after extensive negotiations was agreement reached in December 1979 to proceed, but implementation remains uncertain. And the decision was also made to build the M−X ICBM, but on a timetable which hardly matches the rate at which the Minuteman ICBM is becoming vulnerable.

THE MISPLACED EMPHASIS ON ARMS CONTROL

The Carter administration clearly attaches greater importance to achieving additional arms control agreements with the Soviets, continuing the Strategic Arms Limitation process (SALT) pursued by the Nixon and Ford administrations. However, by the late 1970s a good deal was known, by members of Congress among others, about the extent to which the Soviet leadership shared American views on the use of so-called strategic nuclear arms. We had reached a peak in real expenditure on long-range nuclear delivery and continental defense systems in the late 1950s. In the early 1960s we made a decision to reduce future investments in this category, and our real expenditures on these forces dropped sharply through the 1960s and 1970s. For example, in 1980 dollars we spent $28 billion on long-range (strategic) forces in 1962; in 1980 the level of expenditure is approximately $8 billion.

It was against this background of declining expenditure

that the SALT negotiations began in 1969 and the Interim Accord and Antiballistic Missile (ABM) Treaty were signed in 1972. Throughout this process the American expectation has been that the Soviet leadership would come to share with us the conclusion that spending more money on these forces simply meant adding nuclear "overkill." By 1977, however, it should have been clear to all that this expectation was much too optimistic. Whereas ten years earlier the Soviets were spending almost twice as much as we were on these forces (estimated in dollars), by 1977 they were spending almost three times as much. And we had few new systems, missile or aircraft, in development while the Soviets had many (including four new types of ICBMs versus our one). Nevertheless, the president decided to make achieving a SALT II agreement one of his highest priorities. In 1977 he killed the B–1 bomber program, a move which hardly strengthened our negotiating posture.

The conceptual basis for the decline in U.S. spending on these forces and on active defenses, as well as the basis for the SALT process, is that of mutual assured destruction. This doctrine holds that it is mutually beneficial for the two great powers to be able to destroy each other's civilian societies and that it is bad for them to possess the capability to attack effectively each other's military forces or to have a doctrine for doing so. This amounts to a reversal of the ancient concept of sparing civilians and limiting war to the battlefield. Mutual destruction has been held to be desirable because it promises to restrain incentives of the adversaries to spend resources on these categories of weapons (i.e., the nuclear "arms race") and to reduce the incentives for preemptive attack in a crisis (i.e., reduce "first strike" instability).

Perhaps the most important among the several defects of this doctrine are, first, that the Soviet Union's leadership obviously doesn't believe in it. It continues to increase its investments in nuclear delivery systems, it has been pursuing a large civil defense program, and the doctrine instilled in its military professionals gives great (although not exclusive) weight to the use of nuclear weapons. Second, the United States' major alliances have, from the beginning, rested on the threat that if the allies are attacked our nuclear weapons would be used, if necessary, in their defense. This component of our policy has been deemed necessary because of the superiority of Soviet conventional forces in Europe (a superiority which results principally from the higher spending on these forces by the Soviet Union than by the North Atlantic Treaty Organization [NATO], not from some inherent superiority). It has also been deemed necessary by the fact that the Soviet Union could launch nuclear weapons only against our allies. Deterring that threat even more clearly requires an American nuclear response; without it there could hardly be an alliance. In short, several administrations, Republican and Democratic, have pursued an arms control policy which is inconsistent with a basic requirement of our alliance system.[1]

In 1979 the SALT II agreement was signed, but by then the cumulative impact of Soviet moves in Africa and elsewhere, together with the continued Soviet military buildup, including nuclear forces, had aroused opposition to SALT among a sizable fraction of the members of Congress. Even before the Soviet invasion of Afghanistan it was clear that the Senate would not ratify the treaty.

THE SOVIET FLANKING STRATEGY

In the past several years, while the United States concentrated on strengthening Central Europe, the Soviets pursued what can reasonably be labeled a flanking strategy. For many years it had been steadily improving its capacity to project its military power at a distance, a process which entailed converting its navy from a largely coastal defense organization to one with "blue water" capabilities able to operate globally. It began to acquire seaborne aviation capabilities useful in antisubmarine warfare, but with some surface ship and level attack capability. It invested in much improved amphibious ships (although its naval infantry remains much smaller than the U.S. Marine Corps). It steadily added to its long-range, strategic airlift and it has seven combat-ready airborne divisions (versus one in the United States) for its strategic airlift to carry. And during the 1970s it created a worldwide surveillance and command and control system.

Meanwhile, our power projection capabilities have been allowed to deteriorate. Much of this deterioration has taken place through the cutting back of investments in ships and in naval aviation. The number of ships in the U.S. Navy has fallen by about one-half over the past decade to 398 in the active fleet. Of course, more powerful ships have replaced less powerful ones, but the net effect, together with Soviet power projection increases, is to leave it much less able to cover the wide range of contingencies that now looms. There has also been a major cutback in planned ship and aircraft acquisitions in the past several years. We have also lagged in other dimensions of power projection, including long-range and tactical airlift and procurement of U.S. Air Force tactical aircraft.

At least as important has been the withering of our once extensive system of overseas bases, an invaluable — indeed, for many purposes, essential—asset in being able to operate effectively in remote areas. The consequences of this erosion were dramatically revealed during the 1973 Arab-Israeli war. We found, in trying to send supplies to Israel, that we could not use the bases of our southern European allies and, of course, we had lost the bases we had once had in Morocco and Libya. In that crisis, only the Azores were available (our aerial tankers were also allowed, tacitly, to operate out of Spanish bases). Today the most urgent power projections need that we face is being able to reach the Persian Gulf. Ten years ago the British still had a presence east of Suez, including a major base at Aden. Now the British are gone and the Soviets use Aden. We no longer have any facilities in Iran, Pakistan, or Ethiopia. The alienation of Turkey from the United States and its precarious domestic and international position make our use of Turkish bases unlikely in Persian Gulf contingencies. We have a facility in the middle of the Indian Ocean, however, at Diego Garcia, but it is 2,500 miles from the Strait of Hormuz and we are now seeking some facilities in Oman, Somalia, and Kenya.

The abandonment of overseas bases was in part a consequence of the belief, given great impetus by the Vietnam war, that we had no important interests in the world that supported a need for such bases, with the principal exceptions of Europe and Japan. This trend was strengthened by the view that foreign military establishments were becoming increasingly unpopular in many countries. From a domestic U.S. standpoint, the charge was leveled that these facilities put us in the position of supporting authoritarian governments; also, that these bases made it more likely that we would get sucked into local conflicts. This shedding process also stemmed in part from a failure to understand the Soviet Union strategy for extending its influence. That strategy has been aimed most immediately at regions in which the United States—and earlier, Britain and France—had reduced apparent interest and capabilities. (A longer-term aim of Soviet strategy is to divide and weaken the Western alliance system and dominate its former members.)

The upshot of these trends is that our capability and that of our allies to project power into the Middle East, the source of 40 percent of the noncommunist world's oil, is grossly inferior to that of the Soviet Union. For instance, consider our respective strategic airlift capabilities. Out to a distance of about 1,000 miles from respective starting points, the Soviet military airlift fleet has slightly greater lift capability than the United States; beyond 2,500 miles, the U.S. capability clearly dominates. But the northern end of the Persian Gulf is 500 miles from the Transcaucasus Military District and Soviet air units now in Afghanistan are about a similar distance from the Strait of Hormuz. Many important Soviet bases are about 1,000 miles away. Our principal air transportable forces, in contrast, are about 7,000 miles away. The Soviets could get in on the ground "fastest with the mostest."

We are now undertaking to reverse some of these policies which have brought us close to the brink. During the critical period in Iran in which the outcome was unclear, we deliberately refrained even from sending forces anywhere near the region (a decision which may have had a decisive effect on internal developments in Iran). We have now deployed two carrier battle groups to the Indian Ocean and are creating a rapid deployment force, consisting of mobile ground and air forces, for the most part located in the United States, but also having as a component cargo ships filled with heavy equipment to be stationed in the Indian Ocean. The concept is that U.S. Marines flown from the United States will meet with this equipment and go off to deal with adversaries. It has the great merit of stationing near this vital region equipment that is too heavy to be moved by air. It is also evident that such a force, useful as it promises to be, will not be a sufficient answer to the present military imbalance in the region. The other principal relevant initiative that has been announced is the development of a new cargo aircraft, the C–X, but this is a long-term prospect—one that cannot affect our airlift capacity until the late 1980s. Given the present imbalance in power projection capacities to this region, much more needs to be done than has been announced so far.

In effect, the Middle East has become a third major theater of the East-West contest, in addition to Europe and northeast Asia. It is a region both of high importance to the West because of its oil, and of great vulnerability because of the instabilities of its societies. By the year 2000, given present trends and current policies, the rest of the world may have found substitutes for the oil of this region, but this will take a major effort. (If necessary, this vulnerable dependency could be reduced more rapidly, but it would require a major and very costly effort for which the political will is not yet evident.)

It is at present by no means clear that a successful strategy for assuring the continued flow of oil, not subject to Soviet control, will be devised and implemented. A major obstacle is the fact that most of the countries of the region are internally as well as externally vulnerable to varying degrees. This makes many of them reluctant to have U.S. facilities and a U.S. presence within their territory. (Israel is an exception, and if we continue to improve our relations with Turkey, that country may prove to be another.) The power of the Soviet Union, unfriendly as it appears to many in the region, looks more impressive than ours. There is a natural tendency to trim policies so as not to antagonize the stronger party.

At this stage it is not clear exactly what military capabilities will be needed by the West to cope with this danger, and which ones will be feasible. It is clear, however, that the needs are substantial. Given the political obstacles to extensive land facilities, naval forces are especially important, but these will not be sufficient. Land-based air and a mobile ground force presence rapidly deployable to Saudi Arabia or elsewhere in the Persian Gulf area need to be stationed nearby. The candidate areas for such forces are Turkey, Israel, Egypt—with the former Israeli bases in the Sinai as an important possibility—and Oman. Also, additional airlift is needed, and quickly.

Moreover, at a time when we are attempting to reverse the process of abandoning overseas facilities and are trying to bolster threatened countries or those whose assistance we seek, such as Turkey, Egypt, and Pakistan, it is instructive to examine the budget for military assistance (a category which

includes grant aid and subsidies for foreign military sales).
Proposed fiscal year (FY) 1981 budget authority is $594
million. In contrast, in 1965—excluding Vietnam costs—the
total for this category was $1,229 million. In 1980 dollars, the
proposed FY 1981 level is only 20 percent of the 1965 level. It
appears that large increases are needed here (and in related
economic assistance).

ACTIONS BY U.S. ALLIES

Alliances have a "free rider" problem. The collective nature
of the security provided for all means that there is an incentive to shirk. During most of the period in which the United
States has played the role of leader of the Western alliance
system, it has usually found itself in the position of spending
a larger share of gross national product (GNP) on defense
than its allies, and it has tried, with varying degrees of success, to urge them to do more.

We are still urging them to do more, but our own spending
as a share of GNP on defense has fallen to within the range
of our principal allies. Britain is spending about the same
share as we are. In contrast, Japan is spending very much
less (in terms of Japanese national accounts, about 0.9 percent of GNP; on the NATO definition, about 1.5 percent). We
have been urging that the allies make a real increase in
defense spending of 3 percent annually. This has not
occurred generally within the alliance—partly because of
the under-estimation of inflation that has occurred, but
mostly because the political will has been lacking.

However, there is a growing perception of the interactions
among subregions and among regions as they impinge on the
security of our allies. Within Europe, the security of the
northern flank is very dependent on what happens in the
center region and vice versa. There is also a connection be-

tween Sino-Soviet interactions and Soviet-NATO ones; the Chinese have been articulate on the common interests between themselves and the Europeans. But this perception of interconnections also serves as a rationalization for not doing more; e.g., one might assume that having the Chinese on their eastern flank will deter the Soviets from moving in Europe even if the defenses there are weak.

The relative decline in U.S. strength—and the decline in confidence in our leadership which, viewed in perspective, goes back to the late 1960s—create two opposing incentives among our allies. On the one hand, there is a tendency to despair, on the grounds that there is little that they can do to arrest the decline of the West; on the other hand, the view that they need not do too much, because the United States will take care of things, is undermined. At this stage it is not clear which tendency will predominate.

Of course, the resources available to the West are far greater than those at the disposal of the Soviet Union and its allies. The West, including Japan, has an aggregate GNP of around $7 trillion versus about $2.5 trillion for the Warsaw Pact. But although these numbers are not irrelevant, they are very misleading if interpreted as bearing directly on conflict with the Soviet Union. Japan, for example, defines its security interests very narrowly. Its defense relation with the United States is one-sided, and Japan has no obligation to help the United States or anyone else; nor does it have the capability today to do so. Within Europe there are also sharp differences—for example, those between Greece and Turkey. In short, the will to devote the large resources of the West to a *common* cause does not exist—and the efficiency with which resources are used for security purposes is often low. Only the United States (and to a considerable extent, China—and, of course, the Soviet Union) takes an overall view of these matters.

The threat to Persian Gulf oil poses a new set of problems for our set of alliances. The oil resource which is in jeopardy is a common resource to all of the importing nations (70 percent of Persian Gulf oil is shipped to the United States and its allies). Who, then, should pay for its protection? The Japanese self-defense orientation has precluded them from any but the narrowest interpretation of the defense of Japan from direct attack, an improbable contingency. The Europeans are exposed to a direct threat from the Soviet Union and are largely inwardly focused. Britain, which played a big role in providing stability in the gulf, pulled out a decade ago. However, France has continued a more activist role in francophone Africa and has a substantial naval presence in the Indian Ocean, and Germany, which is the most exposed of the major European powers, has adopted a leading role in helping Turkey, a country of great strategic importance in the Middle East and Mediterranean regions.

Right now, the United States is taking actions with some help, largely symbolic, from the Europeans—although symbolic help has its utility. The most obvious role for the Japanese and Europeans is to replace the American forces that have to be moved to the Middle East or held in readiness for that region. The possibility of more than one major contingency occurring simultaneously is a serious one, e.g., in some combination of Europe, northeast Asia, and the Persian Gulf. But even with such gap-filling actions by our allies, there is a strong case for significant expansion of our forces and budget.

THE U.S. DEFENSE PROGRAMS AND BUDGET IN PERSPECTIVE

The defense budget proposed by President Carter for FY 1981 calls for $162 billion in budget authority and $146 billion in outlays. To put this budget in perspective, it is useful to examine trends over time as shown in Table 1.

Table 1

U.S. Defense Expenditures over Time

	1950	1952	1964	1968	1981*
Outlays (in billions of 1981 dollars)	55	157	150	200	146
Share of federal expenditures (%)	28.0	56.0	39.0	40.0	24.0
Share of GNP (%)	4.9	13.2	7.7	8.9	5.1

Source: *Budget of the United States Government.* FY 1981; *Economic Report of the President*, 1980.
*Proposed.

Table 2

Shares of Selected Government Sectors

	1956	1965	1969	1973	1978
Purchases of goods and services (% of GNP)					
Defense	9.6	7.2	8.1	5.6	4.7
State and local	8.0	10.4	11.8	12.8	13.3
Transfers to persons (% of GNP)					
All governments	4.1	5.5	6.7	8.7	10.2

Source: Tobin (1980).

This record shows the variations over time in American defense expenditures, especially the large fluctuations of the defense sector as a share of the federal budget and GNP, and the large decline in defense as a share of federal expenditures and of GNP in the past decade. The American style has been to devote a modest share of the GNP to defense until a crisis occurs and then to increase sharply. (The pattern of Soviet defense expenditures is very different; it shows a steady increase in expenditures.) In real terms, the proposed FY 1981 budget is at about the level of actual FY 1964 expenditures.

In order to gain perspective on trends in defense spending, it is helpful to examine other components of GNP. Table 2 shows some of the major shifts that have taken place over time. Between 1956 and 1978 defense purchases of goods and services fell by 5 percent of the GNP while state and local purchases increased by over 5 percent of the GNP. Transfer payments also increased by about 6 percent of the GNP. In short, there has been a large shift in the share of resources from defense and from private expenditures to government transfer payments and state and local expenditures. Pressures are now mounting to reverse this shift.

COMPARISON OF SOVIET AND U.S. DEFENSE EXPENDITURES

Just enumerating the principal items of Soviet growth and modernization of its military forces and contrasting them with our own programs makes for a long list. It includes the addition of 500,000 men to its armed forces in the past decade, whereas we cut back 1.5 million men and now have forces at below our pre-Vietnam level; the Soviet production in the past five years of 3,000 tactical aircraft versus our 1,400; 50 submarines to our 12; 1,000 new ICBMs to our 280;

the appearance of the first Soviet aircraft carriers while our carrier force declines—and on and on.

In addition to knowing about particular weapons, it is important to know how much the Soviets are spending. There are two reasons for this. One is to assess the burden on that society of its great military apparatus. This tells us a good deal about Russian priorities; it also informs us about how much scope there is for further increases. The Central Intelligence Agency (CIA) estimates of Soviet ruble spending do this. The second reason is to obtain a better measure of the relative size—and by inference, strength—of the two military establishments.

The CIA says that the defense spending has taken 11 to 12 percent of the Soviet gross national product for the past decade. Other sources, including the Defense Intelligence Agency and some independent analysts, have consistently made higher estimates, putting it at 14 to 18 percent of GNP. In contrast, we now spend less than 5 percent of GNP on defense. The credibility of the CIA's costing procedures received a jolt in 1975 when the agency abruptly increased its estimate of this burden from 6 to 8 percent of GNP to 11 to 13 percent. Of particular note was a 200 percent increase in its estimate of the cost of weapons and construction. Adjustment was apparently occasioned largely by the agency getting data on actual Soviet defense spending. In effect, the CIA change reflected not more weapons, but the conclusion that the Soviets were much less efficient in making them and therefore that the appropriate prices were higher. In short, the military was a much larger burden than had been assumed. This interpretation has been questioned by outside analysts; for example, Steven Rosefielde of the University of North Carolina suggests that the CIA might have been missing some weapons in its count or underestimating qualitative improvements in them.

There is also an issue about the growth rate of the Soviet military sector. The CIA estimates its real growth at between

4 and 5 percent annually, a rate somewhat larger than the growth rate of the economy as a whole. (Again, some outside analysts, including notably William Lee, put it much higher, around 9 percent.) In contrast, the U.S. defense budget in real terms declined from 1968 to the early 1970s as Vietnam wound down, and it has been pretty much on a plateau since. Our real level of defense expenditures is still below that in 1964, the last year before our Vietnam increases. The presidential promise to allies of a 3 percent real increase in defense has shrunk under pressure from the Office of Management and Budget, and has been largely negated anyway by unexpectedly high inflation.

The Soviet weapon investment account has been the source of particular concern and controversy. We observe enormous numbers of weapons coming out of Soviet factories. (Remember when Detroit was regarded as the arsenal of democracy without peer?) Unfortunately, the Russians don't publish price lists. Our analysts have to go through a complex process to arrive at the ruble cost of these weapons. The CIA comes up with a growth rate in the Soviet weapons investment account in the 1970s of 4 to 5 percent. The critics assert that this is a gross underestimate and that the true growth in this category has been much larger—perhaps 10 percent annually or more.

Making budget comparisons in assessing the size of the two military establishments is a way of trying to cope with the "apples and oranges" problem in comparing different mixes of tanks, ships, divisions, and so forth. This is done by estimating what it would cost *us* in dollars to produce and operate the Soviet array of forces and weapons. The latest CIA published exercise of this kind produces the dramatic results shown in Table 3. In dollars, the CIA estimates that it would cost us $146 billion to operate the 1978 Soviet forces; our actual outlay that year on our own forces was $102 billion (pensions are excluded and some other adjustments made).

Table 3

Ratio of Dollar Cost of Soviet to U.S. Forces

	1968	1978
Strategic forces	2.0	2.9
General purpose forces	0.8	1.7
Support forces	0.5	1.0
Overall defense	0.7	1.45

A look at other components points up the contrast. Consider research and development. In 1968 Soviet research and development was about 70 percent of ours; it is now about 175 percent of ours. According to Under Secretary of Defense William Perry, the cumulative disparity in these estimates since 1970 is around $70 billion (in estimated 1981 dollars). In long-range nuclear (i.e., strategic) forces, the cumulative difference is estimated at around $85 billion; in general purpose forces, around $80 billion; and in military investment programs altogether, the cumulative difference is around $240 billion since 1970.

How can this swing be squared with the secretary of defense's assertion that while we need not match the Soviets in numbers of many kinds of weapons, it is necessary for us "to maintain the crucial technology advantage that gives us superiority where we need it"? Doing this with a progressively smaller relative research and development effort may be impossible.

This approach is sometimes faulted on the grounds that costing the Soviet forces in dollars makes it look larger than it really is. When Soviet weapons and the people that it has in large numbers are valued at high American prices, the difference in cost is exaggerated. This problem can be met by doing a similar comparison in rubles, thereby creating the opposite bias—underestimating the relative Soviet expenditures. This ruble comparison still shows substantially larger Soviet spending—25 percent more compared to 45 percent more in the dollar comparison.

How sure can we be of these estimates? The CIA judges its dollar estimate to be accurate within 10 percent. The differences within and outside the intelligence community should make nonexperts treat this claim with some reserve. We often can't estimate the cost of new American weapons within a factor of two or more (almost always on the low side), and it is doubtful that we can do much better on Soviet weapons. This is consistent with the possibility that the Soviets, in dollar terms, may have been spending a good deal more than $146 billion in 1978 and that they may be outspending us in the important investment account by a good deal more than 2:1.

DEFENSE EXPANSION

The history of U.S. defense efforts over the past thirty years shows a phenomenon that, unhappily, we may be faced with in the next several years. For example, between fiscal years 1950 and 1952 the share of GNP devoted to defense tripled from about 4.5 percent to over 13 percent. An increase of this proportion of GNP, if it were to occur today, would mean an increase of around $250 billion in the defense budget. There is a nontrivial possibility that a major Soviet move will take place that will sharply alter popular and political perceptions about threats to our security and trigger a strong response. The triggering event might be a major setback abroad, such as a major Soviet move into the Persian Gulf or into Africa or even into parts of Europe. If such an event occurs—or a series of events—there could be a demand for a massive increase in defense spending varying from, say, twice the present real defense budget to upward of the World War II allocation (40 percent of GNP, about eight times the present share).

This possibility poses several important issues: One set concerns our ability to expand the output of weapons rapidly, given current limits in production capacity. Another set concerns the management of the economy. For example, given that inflation is rising at such a high rate before the buildup, how should we manage the problem of even greater inflationary pressure? The share of resources allocated to the government is very much larger than in past defense expansions. How difficult might it be, in the boom conditions that would exist, to shift transfer payments to defense (in a sense, to restore something like the *status quo ante* distribution of the 1950s between these two sectors)? Previous defense expansions have been achieved almost entirely through expansion in total output rather than through the shift of output from civilian to military purposes (Hall 1980). Would this be feasible in an era in which a much larger proportion of women are already at work? On the other hand, large increases in effective labor imports may be feasible, given the facts that the workweek has shortened, that there are more retired people who might reenter the work force, and that there are still quite a few women and others outside of the (nominal) labor force.

HOW TO GET AND KEEP GOOD PEOPLE

A basic question for any society, one currently debated in this country, is which among three social allocation mechanisms should be used for manning the armed services: voluntary choice, universal (i.e., not necessarily limited to military) service, or a less-than-universal draft using a lottery. We now face the new issue of the participation of women in military service.

In 1973 the country made a major shift from the draft to the all-volunteer force. (Universal service has not been a politically realistic alternative.) This means of providing people for military service has the signal merit of leaving the decision to individuals, a mechanism that our society values highly. It conflicts, however, with the principle that the important social function of defending the nation should not be left largely to one or a few strata of society while others enjoy the benefits of protection without contributing directly. The all-volunteer force has this effect by drawing on not only those who serve for reasons of patriotism but those whose intelligence or skill level makes military service a less bad alternative than others.

In my view, the choice between the volunteer and compulsory alternatives should turn on the extent of perceived peril to the nation by the public at large. During times when there is no widely shared sense of peril, a respect for personal preferences as well as political realities makes the voluntary choice most appropriate; when danger looms, social cohesion supports the goal of wider participation via the draft and makes it politically feasible. There is, of course, room for disagreement about the extent of present dangers, but current political realities dictate the continuation of the volunteer system for at least the near future.

However, this system is performing badly. The services are falling short in their recruiting goals, most importantly in their ability to attract people capable of maintaining and operating modern weapons. The proportion of recruits in the lowest IQ category, corresponding to those in the 10 to 30 percent categories relative to the mix of people in the army in World War II, may be as high as 45 percent. There is much evidence from each of the services of the inability of many recruits to learn to handle or maintain their weapons competently.

Even more serious is the ability of the services to retain skilled people. Trained pilots have long been lured away by the airlines who offer two to three times the salaries, but pilot retention rates have slipped greatly in the past several years—from 50 percent to 25 percent for pilots with eleven years of experience in the U.S. Air Force. Since 1976 the services have been losing over 75 percent of those completing their first enlistment, and a disproportionate number of those leaving are, as one might expect, needed people with the most marketable skills.

A large part of the explanation for this erosion of skilled people appears to be the erosion of pay. Average military compensation has fallen by 14 percent since 1972 and, on the administration's forecast of pay and inflation, by late 1981 it will have fallen—optimistically—by 25 percent from the 1972 level. Despite slow productivity growth over this period, this also represents a decline in military versus private sector incomes. An example much cited lately is that an E−4 plane handler on the carrier *Nimitz* in the Indian Ocean makes less per hour than a cashier at McDonald's; if he has a wife and a child they live below the poverty level and are eligible for food stamps. Although there are other benefits for the military, increasingly the package offered them fails to compete with those offered in the civilian sector.

A necessary but perhaps not sufficient step is to increase military pay in real terms. The elasticity of quality of people versus price (in the form of compensation) appears to be high. Restoring the 1972 level of pay by mid−1981 appears to require about a 15 percent real pay increase over today's level. In order to get enough of the people with the skills that we need, perhaps a 20 percent real increase will be needed. An increase of 20 percent in military compensation (including allowances) would add about $6.5 billion to the defense budget (in 1980 dollars). Assuming that such an increase is made, it would not be appropriate to raise compensation by this proportion across the board. Instead, increases should be allocated to those categories where the needs and expected payoffs are highest.

Another suggestion has recently been made that seems to have merit, given our need to attract people capable of being trained to handle complex technology; this is to offer a form of the GI Bill in order to attract and keep people who want to improve themselves and who value education.

Assuming that we retain the all-volunteer force, the issue of women being drafted will recede. If it arises again, however, presumably in a national emergency, at the least we should resolve the question of women serving in combat by making the firm decision that they will not. There are profound psychological and social reasons for taking this position. Moreover, there are more than enough important jobs to be done other than those in combat.

In sum, our ability to field an effective military force is in jeopardy not because the all-volunteer force is a failure, but because we have skimped on pay and other benefits. We need to fix this immediately.

WHAT SHOULD BE DONE?

The case for a substantial defense increase is strong. The Carter administration's budget is likely to produce none at all for FY 1981, despite the president's assertion on the dangers we face.[2] The president, arguably, spoke truly; at the least, this is a dangerous period and it warrants a substantial defense increase. In the immediate future, the intense concerns about inflation and the response of our Washington politicians to be able to point to something that can be plausibly represented as a balanced budget is a strong countervailing force working against a budget increase. Nonetheless, a good case can be made for a real increase of about $30 billion by FY 1982 (beginning with an FY 1980 supplemental of around $10 billion).

The illustrative categories in which additional funds should be allocated include the following (not necessarily in order of priority):

- *Improving the overall effectiveness of our forces:*
  Incentive pay to retain skilled personnel.

- *Bolstering allies and others in or near the Persian Gulf:*
  Aid to Turkey, Israel, Egypt, Pakistan, Oman.

- *Additional steps to increase our speed of response:*
  Purchase of additional airlift immediately.
  Rapid deployment force implementation.
  Prepositioned equipment in the region (e.g., Sinai, Israel, Turkey).

- *Improving our direct capacity to project power:*
  Additional carriers, carrier aviation, and land-based tactical air.
  Creation of additional airborne divisions.
  Procurement of (mainly nonnuclear) cruise missiles.

- *Filling gaps in equipment and war consumables:*
  Ground force equipment.
  Ammunition and spare parts and other war consumables.

- *Building up our nuclear capability:*
  Emergency measures to limit increases in ICBM vulnerability (but not buying the M—X).
  Proceeding more vigorously with the theater nuclear force modernization program in Europe.
  Providing an expanded cruise missile force (with a nuclear option).
  Initiating a long-range bomber program (not the B—1).

- *Improving our command and control capabilities:*
  Improve our capability to replace satellites during a conflict.

We should also urge appropriate, parallel increases on the part of our allies, especially taking into account the "gap-filling" needs created by the diversion of U.S. forces to Middle East contingencies.

The proposed $30 billion real increase in the defense budget by FY 1982, about 20 percent over the FY 1980 level, will only begin to offset the sizable imbalance created by large Soviet military investments in the past decade. Although there are inevitably many uncertainties about the challenges we will face in the 1980s and resulting future defense budget pressures, probably at least this level of real expenditure will have to be sustained in subsequent years. If continued for five years, this level would add $150 billion in 1980 dollars to the defense account. If we were to spend this increment—$30 billion annually—over the next decade, and to devote a large proportion of it to investment account, say, $20 billion, by 1990 we would about have offset the estimated $240 billion cumulative disparity in spending on weapons by the Soviets during the 1970s. In short, we are likely to find that more than this increment is needed.

The urgent manpower needs described above suggest that we give first attention to this problem in allocating our resources. We also need to devote additional resources to filling gaps in spare parts and war consumables which keep our forces from being ready for combat. In addition to these two categories, we should give high priority to doing more to bolster our position in the Persian Gulf; if we do not, we might find the source of much of the West's oil supply interrupted or under Soviet control.

As Michael Boskin points out in Chapter 2, large impending increases in government revenues from various tax sources are programmed into our tax system. He and other contributors advance powerful arguments for returning these revenues to the private sector and for reducing government spending in the aggregate. Somehow these needs have to be reconciled with the need to protect ourselves. The data presented above, on the extent to which resources since the 1950s have been shifted out of the defense and private sectors and toward federal transfer payments and state and local governments, suggest that it will be feasible to make such a reallocation without revolutionary change in our economy *if* the political will to do so emerges.

In sum, we are in a crucial period. It is one in which either the structure of relations established among the democratic nations under American leadership in the late 1940s and early 1950s will be revived and strengthened or will fragment and progressively collapse. Much depends on American behavior in the next several years, for it is by no means clear where or how the Western democracies would find the means to cope with the Soviet challenge in the absence of a strong American role backed up by strengthened military power.

12

JAMES L. SWEENEY

Energy Problems and Policies[1]

Energy liquids and OPEC. U.S. restrictions on energy substitutes. Price and export controls on oil and gas. Pricing and marginal costs. Environmental damage. Distributional issues. International supply disruptions. Gasohol. The value of market mechanisms. Trade-offs between goals.

In the six years since the 1973 oil embargo made energy a primary national concern, no consensus on energy policy has emerged. Misunderstanding about the nature of our energy problems still abounds. This chapter describes the basic energy problems and analyzes the economic, political, social, and security difficulties related to them. It concludes with an examination of our counterproductive energy policies and suggests guidelines for formulating healthier policy.

FUNDAMENTAL ENERGY PROBLEMS

There are but three basic, pervasive, and interlinked energy problems: energy liquids (petroleum) are becoming more costly throughout the world, energy substitutes for petroleum are being restricted or made more costly in the United States, and imports of energy liquids to the industrialized world are dangerously insecure. These interlinked energy problems are real; they are not about to disappear.

Energy Liquids Have Become More Costly

After several decades of continually decreasing world costs for energy liquids, the world prices for crude oil dramatically increased from an average of $2.50 per barrel in 1972 to $11 per barrel in 1974. At the same time, members of the Organization of Petroleum Exporting Countries (OPEC) reduced production of oil about 12 percent and imposed a (basically unsuccessful) embargo on oil to the United States. These events threw the industrialized world into a frenzy of activities to address energy problems.

In succeeding years the power of the OPEC cartel declined and real prices began slowly dropping. Then in late 1978 and early 1979, with the Iranian revolution, production from that country declined from an average of 5.7 million barrels per day (mmb/d) to a low of less than 1.0 mmb/d, recovering to a 1979 average of slightly more than 3.0 mmb/d. Although production elsewhere was increased to absorb much of this loss, world oil prices leaped from $14.50 per barrel to $30.00 per barrel during the year.

The same pattern can be expected to repeat itself. The most recent price jump will be followed by a gradual decline in real price as markets adjust and as inflation reduces purchasing power. Markets will remain soft until world economic growth again brings oil demand toward world production capacity. As the slack in the world markets disappears, the next shock to the oil production system will again touch off a new price explosion. The fluctuations, however, should not be deceptive: the underlying economic forces imply a continued upward trend in the price of oil.

This would be true even if OPEC were to disappear, since OPEC as an international coalition seems to no longer fundamentally determine world oil prices. Rather, internal decisions on production capacity made by the major oil exporting countries—notably Saudi Arabia, but including Kuwait, Mexico, Iraq, and Norway—seem to be the prime determinants of the upward price trends. These decisions appear to be guided to a large extent by environmental and social considerations.

One driving force for price rises is the depletable nature of liquid hydrocarbons coupled with the increasing hydrocarbon demand as the world economy expands. While significant uncertainty exists about the extent of world resources, the supply is finite; there are definite limits. One credible estimate (Nehring 1978) of total reserves plus undiscovered remaining oil resources is between 1,300 and 1,900 billion barrels, with a heavy concentration of these resources in the OPEC countries. World demand for oil has been growing rapidly. Between 1960 and 1973 oil consumption grew at an average annual rate of 7.7 percent, with 20.4 billion barrels produced in 1973.

Continued growth in the demand for a depletable resource is possible only for a limited time before the growth in demand is reversed, normally because of increased price or improved availability of substitutes. For oil, increased prices have motivated a reduction in demand growth to the 1.8 percent annual rate between 1973 and 1979. At some time in the near future production will level off or begin to fall. Unless substitutes for oil are found and developed rapidly, continued price increases will motivate the demand reductions for this resource.

In the United States the depletable nature of petroleum is more readily apparent. We currently have reserves of 27 billion barrels (bbl) and an undiscovered resource base which could lie anywhere between 50 and 130 bbl.[2] If the United States continues to produce domestic oil at the rate of 8.5 mmb/d (3.1 bbl per year), by the end of the century we would have produced between 40 and 80 percent of our remaining resources. Incentives to produce U.S. oil more rapidly imply even fewer remaining resources. Furthermore, since most new finds are discovered in high-cost frontier areas such as the outer continental shelf or the Alaskan North Slope, the economic cost of finding and producing oil in the United States will continue to escalate.

Energy Substitutes for Petroleum Are Being Restricted in the United States

The increasing costs of petroleum liquids could be mitigated if substitutes were becoming increasingly available. However, the converse seems to be true. Other forms of energy in the United States are growing more costly and/or more restricted.

One source of cost increases is unavoidable. We are depleting our lowest-cost natural gas resources. Natural gas production (about one-third of domestic energy production) continues to decline, although exploration and development have been intensified in response to increases in regulated prices.

Domestic costs have also increased because of energy restrictions motivated by environmental concerns. For example, new coal-fired electric generating facilities are required to utilize the "best available control technologies," including scrubbers to eliminate most residuals from the exhaust gases. These technologies increase the cost of generating electricity. The ability of electric utilities to obtain approvals for constructing new coal-fired facilities in the so-called "noncompliance areas" is dubious.[3] Strip-mining regulations for Western coal increase mining cost, as do requirements protecting the market shares of high-cost Eastern Coal.[4] Restrictions on imports of liquified natural gas (LNG), as experienced in California, also increase the cost of this potential substitute for oil.

The nuclear industry has been crippled by increasingly complex regulation and by licensing procedures which allow intervenors to block or greatly retard construction and the subsequent operation of nuclear power plants. The nuclear power plant lead time has increased from 5.5 years in 1967 to 7.5 years in 1974 and to 10.0 years in 1977 (Bowers 1977). One already completed plant at Diablo Canyon, California, has yet to be issued an operating license. And following Three Mile Island, a new regulatory precedent has apparently been established: cost reductions due to nuclear power plant operation will accrue to the rate payer while cost increases associated with nuclear accidents will fall on the utility stockholder. The implications of such a precedent for the future of nuclear power are ominous.

The second fundamental problem, then, is that for a variety of reasons the potential substitutes for petroleum in the United States are being restricted or made more costly. Ready availability of inexpensive petroleum substitutes is not a near-term option for mitigating the impacts of increasing petroleum costs.

Imports of Energy Liquids
Are Dangerously Insecure

The third fundamental energy problem is that a large share

of the world's petroleum comes from the highly unstable Middle East, raising the possibility of oil supply disruptions— possibly far more extreme than those experienced to date.

Thirty-eight percent of the world crude oil production in 1979 came from the Middle East,* down from 43 percent in 1973. Excluding Chinese and Soviet oil production, 49 percent of WOCA (world outside communist areas) oil is from this region. The world as a whole is thus dangerously dependent upon highly insecure oil sources.

The U.S. problem of dependency upon insecure petroleum sources has intensified since 1973. In that year the United States imported 6.3 mmb/d of oil, or 40 percent of total use; of these imports, 18 percent came from the Middle East. By 1979 U.S. imports had risen to 8.2 mmb/d, 49 percent of consumption; of these imports, 40 percent were from the Middle East. Rather than increasing security of supply after the 1973 oil embargo, the United States has increased imports in total and as a percentage of consumption, and has more than doubled its import share from the Middle East.[5]

The United States, considered alone, faces a less threatening situation than do most of our allies, since we produce one-half of our oil demand. In contrast, Germany and Japan import virtually all their petroleum. But the United States cannot be examined in isolation. In the event of severe disruptions, our allies' problems would become our problems for at least three reasons. First, if world petroleum prices rise during disruptions so as to allocate available supplies among importing countries, then each oil importing country will face roughly the same percentage reduction in consumption since each will face the same price increase.[6] Second, the United States and the other International Energy Agency (IEA) member countries have signed international treaties to

_____
*This include Algeria, Iran, Iraq, Kuwait, Libya, Quatar, Saudi Arabia, and the United Arab Emirates.

share available oil in an emergency, although the enforceability of these treaties is questionable.

Third, in the event of major military conflicts associated with supply shortages, military treaties imply that the problems of our allies become our problems. Should such conflict involve the United States, the problem of supply insecurity may be particularly acute. Military actions generally involve a major expansion in the use of petroleum. During past major conflicts the United States produced all its own oil and, in fact, exported oil. Thus the United States could be a source of petroleum for its allies. The situation now is dramatically reversed. In the event of major military action, supplies of imported oil for us and our allies may decline at a time when additional oil is needed. This contingency is especially likely if the war involves nations of the Middle East or nations close enough to the Middle East — e.g., the Soviet Union — with the power to inhibit the transportation of oil from the Middle East.

In discussions of supply disruptions, OPEC political action such as the 1973–1974 oil embargo is often cited. This possibility is probably the least important problem. More likely and much more dangerous are supply disruptions associated with internal strife, revolution, or war. The current instability in Iran, the growing Pan-Islamic movement, factionalism within many Middle East nations, the conflicts inherent in rapid development, the striking contrasts between rich and poor, and the preponderance of Palestinians in the work force of many Middle East nations all underscore the high probability of supply-disrupting upheaval or revolution in the region. The possibility of war in the Middle East stemming from regional rivalries (Israeli-Arab, Iran-Iraq, or other conflicts) or from desires to control resources (a Soviet Union invasion of Iran) certainly cannot be discounted. Moreover, the Soviet capacity to disrupt the entire flow of Middle East oil to the West has dramatically increased, while a projected decline in its own domestic oil production will likely make the Soviet Union a major oil importer during this decade—further heightening its military interest in the region.

Summary: The Problems of Rapid Transition

The three fundamental energy problems can be viewed as manifestations of a single problem of transition: We—the United States and the world—are suddenly facing a period of rapid and basic transition in the energy system, a transition occurring during a time of increasing global interdependence in energy.

The transition involves a shift from broad utilization of inexpensive petroleum liquids towards restrictions of these fuels to such mobile usages as fuel for aircraft and automobiles. It will involve temporarily a greater usage of more abundant resources such as coal, and ultimately massive adoption of such renewable resources as solar, wind, hydropower, and biomass. The transition will also involve substitutions in the input factors for each economic sector, substitutions away from energy toward labor, capital, and advanced technologies. Input factor substitutions—popularly described as "energy conservation"—will allow all nations ultimately to use much less energy per unit of output. But profound transitions do not occur quickly or smoothly. The capital stock, both physical and human, changes only slowly and then imperfectly. In a time of major, fundamental, and rapid transitions, therefore, one can expect profound difficulties. This is what is occurring.

SOME CONSEQUENCES

The fundamental energy problems have created major problems for the United States: reduction in real gross national product (GNP), balance-of-trade deficits, increased U.S. and worldwide inflation, wealth redistributions, shifts in international political power, and an increased probability of war. In the event of a severe supply disruption these difficulties will be greatly intensified and new difficulties will be added, such as a renewed threat to the international financial system.

Energy cost[7] increases reduce the GNP of oil-importing countries by increasing the amount of goods and services they must give up in exchange, and possibly by reducing the rate of capital formation and increasing structural unemployment.

Paying more to import (or to domestically produce) the given quantity of energy produces a direct GNP loss equal to the increase.[8] The $13.80 (1980 dollars) increase in the world oil price between March 1979 and March 1980 alone reduced U.S. real GNP by a full 1.8 percent, or $41 billion. Increases in the cost of producing domestic energy similarly reduce GNP. Since energy costs constitute roughly 10.0 percent of GNP, every 1.0 percent increase in the per unit cost of energy will reduce GNP by about 0.1 percent. Thus a 5.0 percent per year growth in the per unit energy costs would reduce the GNP growth rate by roughly 0.5 percentage points per year if there are no impacts on the capital stock or labor force quantities or on technological progress.

Increased energy prices may also reduce economic growth by reducing the rate of capital formation (Berndt 1975; Hudson and Jorgenson 1978, pp. 205–30). Current evidence suggests that capital and energy are complementary inputs in industrial processes; that is, increases in energy price may lead to reductions in the demand for capital and thus in the rate of new capital formation. However, tax changes such as reductions in corporate income taxes or other incentives for capital formation could compensate for this effect.

Energy price increases will also induce early obsolescence of the capital stock. Capital stock designed to use inputs in proportions appropriate for pre-embargo prices may become too costly to continue using under high energy price conditions and may be scrapped, as with the "gas guzzler" automobile. However, these capital losses are included in the discounted sum of direct GNP losses discussed above and are not in addition to them.[9]

Sudden increases in energy price may also reduce GNP by creating transitory or structural unemployment. Changing relative prices of commodities motivates adjustments in outputs and inputs of the various sectors of the economy, with some sectors expanding (e.g., communication services) and others declining (e.g., transportation). Such adjustments are normal and necessary in a healthy economy. But adjustments imply unemployment of labor and capital equipment during the transition to employment in other sectors. Some productive factors may find new employment very quickly, while other, more specialized, factors may adjust only slowly if at all. The greater the rate of structural change in the economy, the greater this transitional unemployment of men and capital and the lower the GNP.

Increased world oil prices have harmed our balance of trade, although other factors are also important. Table 1 displays the 1973 and 1979 imports and exports for energy, for manufactured products, for agricultural, chemical, and other products, and for the U.S. total. In 1973 net imports of energy equalled 9.0 percent of total exports. The United States enjoyed a trade surplus of $1 billion. Contrast this to 1979, when net import of energy was a whopping $54 billion, 31 percent of total exports. The 1973 balance-of-trade surplus had turned into a $28 billion deficit. Growth in nonenergy exports was insufficient to compensate for the vast increase in the import cost of energy. For 1980 this situation will probably be worse. The current $30 per barrel price of imported oil implies an $89 billion 1980 expenditure on imported oil alone. This change in the world oil price could almost double the U.S. balance-of-trade deficit in 1980.

Table 1

U.S. Balance of Trade: 1973 versus 1979
(billions of current dollars)

	Energy	Manufactured Products	Agricultural Chemical, and Other	Total
1973				
Imports	8	42	19	69
Exports	2	39	30	70
Net imports	6	3	(11)	(1)
1979				
Imports	60	105	42	206
Exports	6	99	74	178
Net imports	54	5	(32)	28

Source: *Monthly Energy Review* (April 1980).

Increased oil prices have fueled world inflation problems, although the magnitude and the mechanism of the impact are open to debate. Last year's doubling of the world oil prices increased average U.S. crude oil prices by 85.0 percent, raising the U.S. oil expenditure rate from 3.4 percent of GNP to 6.3 percent and producing a one-time 3.0 percent increase in the overall price level. But this may have stimulated additional inflation as contractual escalation clauses led to further price increases in vain attempts to regain lost real income. An alternative view is that energy price increases not increasing the quantity of money had no impact on inflation. A final view holds that monetary authorities, fearing a recessionary impact on the world oil price increases, rapidly increased the money supply, thus generating inflationary pressures.

Energy price increases have redistributed wealth within the United States. Beneficiaries of U.S. oil price increases include energy-producing regions (e.g., Texas and Louisiana), stockholders of energy-producing companies (oil, coal, natural gas, uranium), and owners of other expanding firms (insulation or solar panel producers or distributors). Those harmed comprise a larger group: net energy-consuming regions of the United States (e.g., New England), owners of petroleum refineries, owners of declining firms (automobile, trucking, travel and vacation, fertilizer), and consumers whose homes are heated and cars fueled with oil or its substitutes.

International redistribution of wealth from oil-importing nations (including those in the Third World) to net oil exporters has been even more sweeping and has been accompanied by a redistribution of power to the major oil producers. For example, the influence of the Saudi Arabian government over U.S. international policies has grown considerably because their oil production decisions significantly influence our GNP, balance of payments, gasoline lines, and inflation.

Each of these consequences will be greatly exacerbated in the event of a major disruption in oil availability. For example, a 10 mmb/d cut in world oil production is quite conceivable. Even with no induced unemployment, a 16 percent drop in world production could increase the world price by a factor of four,[10] could increase the net cost of U.S. oil imports to $250 billion, and could reduce GNP by 7 percent. Induced unemployment would make matters more severe. Wealth impacts on our allies (who import greater fractions of their oil than we) could be proportionately greater. Worst-case supply disruptions would cripple more completely the economies of oil-importing countries, pushing world oil prices to unimaginable levels, transfering vast wealth among nations, and causing financial imbalances so severe as to threaten the world financial system.

These severe economic and political difficulties have not been the only harmful ramifications of increasing energy prices. Public policy actions, adopted because of or in spite of our energy problems, have created a new class of difficulties.

ENERGY PROBLEMS CREATED BY POLICY RESPONSES

The Petroleum Price Control System

Perhaps the most onerous self-imposed problem has been the system of regulations by which oil prices are controlled in the United States. This system includes price controls on crude oil production, an allocation program for crude oil and petroleum products, the entitlements program, and a process for appeals and exemptions.

The evolution of this system illustrates a basic principle: regulations beget regulations. Once a regulatory body imposes restrictions on part of the economy, new behavior patterns in response will be met by new regulations, followed by additional new responses. And so the cycle proceeds, with one regulation begetting the next. The system of crude oil price controls has followed the basic pattern.

Specific crude oil price controls[11] were initiated with President Nixon's Phase IV price controls (September 1973) and the Emergency Petroleum Allocation Act (November 1973). Under these regulations a two-tier price control system was created with "old oil" controlled at an average of $5.13 per barrel[12] and "new oil" selling at an uncontrolled price. Increases in production from oil fields above the base quantities "released" from the price controls equal amounts of old oil produced on the same property. To encourage production of oil from small wells (from property whose production did not exceed 10 barrels per day over the course of a year), "stripper-well" oil was also exempt from price controls.

A problem of this system soon came to light with rumors of tied sales of controlled and uncontrolled oil (Phelps and Smith 1977). The intent of the system could be circumvented by offering to sell 4,999 barrels of controlled oil at $5, along with one barrel of uncontrolled oil for $30,005, yielding the same revenue as selling 5,000 barrels at the world market price of $11. The regulatory response, January 1974, was to freeze supplier/purchaser relationships among producers, refiners, distributors, and retailers. The "buy/sell" program also forced refineries with greater than average access to crude oil to sell, in times of oil shortages, to refiners with less than average access.

The inequities became apparent. Refiners traditionally buying U.S. oil could, by law, purchase crude for $5.25 per barrel, while those importing crude were forced to pay $11. The regulatory response was the Entitlements Program (December 1974). Refiners of old oil were required to possess one "entitlement" for each barrel of old oil refined. A fraction of an entitlement was earned whenever any oil was refined. Thus refiners of new or imported oil earned excess entitlements which could be sold to refiners of old oil. The net effect was to allow all refiners[13] to buy oil at the average price, thus subsidizing imported oil and taxing domestic.

In 1975, with the expiration of the price control provisions of the Emergency Petroleum Allocation Act, the Energy Policy and Conservation Act (EPCA) was passed, continuing and modifying the controls by eliminating the released oil category and controlling "upper tier" oil (comparable to new oil). Why wasn't the opportunity to eliminate controls embraced? In 1975, because of controls, the refiner acquisition cost of imported oil was 66 percent higher than that of domestic crude oil. It was felt that sudden decontrol would create structural and transitional unemployment, inflation, and undesirable redistributional impacts. EPCA thus was designed to reduce these impacts of decontrol by allowing a "phased decontrol" over forty months, ending in June 1979. When the mandatory EPCA controls expired, the refiner acquisition cost of imported crude oil was 59 percent higher than that of domestic oil. President Carter continued the controls while announcing a program of "phased decontrol" of crude oil prices.

As price controls are phased out, a "windfall profits tax" is being introduced. This tax is actually an excise tax on domestic crude oil, not a profits tax at all, with different rates applied to different classes of producers (majors versus independents) and to different categories of oil depending upon the geographical location, the development time of the field, and the production technology. The regulatory nightmare will continue under different rules. Prices facing oil suppliers will remain below import costs and production will be reduced. But at least import and consumption of oil will now face the world oil price. Once the regulatory route has been chosen, there always seem to be pressures for not turning back, even when the option is available.

Product prices have also been controlled, with allowable prices based upon initial prices in 1973, profit margins, increases in product costs (crude oil and refined products used as inputs), and across-the-board increases to account for nonproduct cost rises. The specific rules have changed often. Currently, gasoline is the only major refined product remaining subject to controls. However, the clamor to recontrol product prices is still heard.

The system of price controls has predictable consequences. For one, identical commodities face widely different prices. Table 2 shows average crude oil prices for major categories, ranging from $6.17 per barrel for lower-tier oil (22 percent of domestic production) to $35.11 for stripper oil (16 percent of domestic production).

The great price diversity implies strong incentives to convert oil from one category to another. Consider, as an example, the stripper exemption. Under prices indicated above, a well producing 55 barrels of lower-tier oil per day obtains daily revenues of $339; the same well could earn more revenues ($351) if it produced only 10 barrels per day so as to qualify as a stripper well.[14] No wonder the stripper category grew from 12.9 percent of production in September 1976 to 16.0 percent in December 1979.

Table 2

Crude Oil Prices, December 1979

Category of Crude Oil	Average Price per Barrel	Percentage* of Production
Lower tier	$ 6.17/bbl	22
Upper tier	13.88/bbl	33
Alaska North Slope	13.59/bbl	16
Stripper	35.11/bbl	16
Naval petroleum reserve	29.08/bbl	2
Domestic	$16.98/bbl	50
Imported	28.91/bbl	50

Source: *Monthly Energy Review* (March 1980).

*Percentages do not add to 100 percent because there are additional catergories not listed (and not statistically summarized by the Energy Information Administration).

The vast redistributional aspect of the regulations requires an extensive system for monitoring, enforcement, appeals, denials, reappeals, exceptions, exemptions, revisions, and adjustments. And special treatment goes to small refiners receiving extra entitlement benefits and to producers of heavy crude oil in California. Benefits are conferred on importers of naphtha petrochemical feedstocks in Puerto Rico. The Amerada Hess refinery in the Virgin Islands is treated as domestic when receiving entitlement benefits and as on foreign soil for the Jones Act.[15] Entitlement benefits are awarded for import of residual fuel from foreign refiners to the East Coast market and entitlement penalties are imposed on domestic refiners producing oil above a minimum level for this market. Such provisions do not exist for other regional markets.

Price controls also consistently exacerbate our energy problems. Too much energy is consumed; too little is produced. Low oil prices make other energy sources (e.g., solar) less competitive, reducing their contribution to our energy needs. The net result is increased oil imports, higher world oil prices, increased balance-of-payments deficits, reduced GNP, and greater vulnerability to supply disruption.

Natural Gas Price Regulation

The natural gas industry has long been subject to regulation. Maximum allowable prices have been set by the Federal Power Commission (FPC) for natural gas sold in interstate commerce. No such regulations were applicable to natural gas strictly in intrastate commerce. The result was a system of cheap but unavailable regulated natural gas in interstate commerce and more expensive but available unregulated gas in intrastate commerce.

With natural gas prices much higher in intrastate than in interstate markets, by the early 1970s virtually all new natural gas reserves were going to the intrastate market. Shortages in the controlled markets led to governmentally imposed restrictions against natural gas hookups for new residential customers. Firm contracts to supply natural gas were being curtailed. A nine-tier curtailment priority schedule, based upon natural gas end use and customer size, was promulgated by the FPC. The entire system had become unworkable.

Two broad classes of options were possible when the Natural Gas Policy Act was debated in 1977 and 1978: to extend price controls to all markets or to eliminate controls altogether. The former option was selected. The compromise act increased the regulated wellhead natural gas price, although the price per Btu (British thermal unit) remains but a fraction of the imported oil cost. Great price differentials still exist. In late 1979 the purchase price by major interstate pipeline companies was $1.35 per thousand cubic feet from domestic sources and $2.85 from foreign sources. Current law mandates different prices for the numerous categories of domestic producing fields.

The extension of controls to all markets was coupled to a

plan for a "phased deregulation" of natural gas production, with regulations designed to end in the late 1980s except for some categories to be permanently controlled. Sound familiar? The phase-out provisions were designed to allow natural gas prices to gradually approach crude oil prices. When the law was passed, however, $30 per barrel crude oil prices were not foreseen. Thus, under existing law, natural gas prices will gradually approach the energy equivalent of $15 per barrel oil (1979 dollars) in the late 1980s. This will virtually assure that at the expiration of the bill there will be the same interest groups, the same arguments, and the same justifications for another long period of "phased deregulation."

Export Restrictions

One provision of the Trans-Alaskan Pipeline Act bans exportation of Alaskan oil, thereby precluding agreements with Japan to exchange Alaskan oil for Middle Eastern oil. Exchange agreements would reduce transportation costs by eliminating the costly west-to-east movement of Alaskan oil. No additional security risks are involved, as sharing of oil in situations of supply disruption is already governed by the IEA sharing agreements. Furthermore, if Japanese sources do not supply Middle Eastern oil to the United States, the obligation to supply Japan with Alaskan oil would cease.

Who benefits from the restriction? The maritime industry, at the expense of everyone else. Under the Jones Act, only American ships are allowed to transport oil from Alaska to other U.S. ports. Under exchange agreements, the oil would be shipped to Japan using the far less costly fleets from other nations.

Regulatory Morass

The U.S. energy policy evolving since 1973 has been one of progressively more governmental regulation in virtually all aspects of the energy system and, as a corollary, progressively less flexibility and private initiative. The focus of decision-making has moved from firms and consumers throughout the country to Washington and, to a lesser extent, state capitols. This centralization of decision-making has brought major reporting costs, created massive bureaucracies, reduced market uncertainty, increased regulatory uncertainty, and distorted incentives. The "regulations beget regulations" principle is clearly visible.

Energy consumption in the United States is also now highly regulated. One common justification: "The prices of energy are too low, so markets lead to overuse of energy." Federal regulations specify maximum speed limits and maximum allowable thermostat settings in commercial and industrial buildings (California even specifies unenforceable maximums in residential dwellings). Building energy performance standards, corporate average fuel efficiency standards for new automobiles, and appliance efficiency standards are but part of the regulatory maze.

Electric utilities face not only price regulation but also regulations on allowable fuels. Federal legislation prohibits the use of oil or gas for new baseload electric generating facilities. Licensing procedures discussed earlier effectively prohibit new nuclear plants. The Federal Coal Conversion Program requires many existing oil-burning facilities to reconvert to the use of coal as a fuel. Clean air regulations inhibit the licensing and construction of new coal-fired plants. Overlapping jurisdictions of federal, state, and local governmental agencies create tangles of mutually irreconcilable rules.

Regulatory costs are not known with any degree of confidence. However, one federal task force (MacAvoy 1977) estimated that as early as 1976 the annual costs to the refinery industry alone of reporting and hiring legal and accounting staffs to ensure regulatory compliance may have been as much as $570 million. Total regulatory costs must greatly exceed this figure.

SIX GUIDELINES FOR FORMULATING ENERGY POLICY

Understanding energy problems and their consequences, along with understanding our self-imposed problems, leads to a framework for formulating more appropriate energy policies. Following are six guidelines:

- allow prices to reflect marginal costs rather than average costs,
- address distributional issues,
- plan for international supply disruptions,
- create energy options, but expect no panaceas,
- utilize markets more, direct government intervention less,
- deal realistically with conflicting goals.

Allow Prices to Reflect Marginal Costs

The most basic economic principle is that economic efficiency in a decentralized economy requires that prices reflect marginal costs: where marginal cost refers to the value of *additional* goods and services foregone in order to obtain an *additional* quantity of some commodity.

Just as surely as marginal cost pricing underlies modern economic thought, *average* cost pricing underlies much of our current energy policy. Electric utilities face rate-of-return regulation which attempts to equate energy revenues with average cost. The crude oil price control system and "rolled-in" pricing provisions for natural gas cause consumers to face average costs of oil and natural gas.

The first guideline for energy policy, then, is to abandon average cost pricing whenever possible and to allow energy prices to reflect marginal costs.

Marginal cost will generally exceed average cost in production of a depletable resource such as oil or gas or in production of electricity. Input resources for production are not homogeneous: the lower cost sources normally are exploited first, with higher cost sources left for increased production. For electric generation, in addition, the accounting rules generally evaluate capital costs at historical construction costs rather than at replacement costs, which are typically much higher. Adoption of marginal cost pricing rules thus would increase energy prices in the United States (leaving costs unaltered) and would motivate demand reductions, conventional source supply increases, and expansion of new sources such as solar or biomass.

What specific policies are implied by marginal cost pricing? First is the complete decontrol of oil and gas prices. Market forces in such workably competitive industries as coal, oil, or gas will equate price to marginal cost facing individual firms. Decontrol will also return some flexibility to the energy system, will undercut the political forces supporting rationing and allocation systems, and will reduce the need for a massive bureaucracy.

Oil and gas price decontrol is a necessary foundation for sensible energy policy, but it is only the first step. Decontrol is not sufficient, because the marginal cost of oil to the economy exceeds the world oil price while the latter price represents the marginal cost facing individual firms. The difference between marginal oil import cost and the world oil price—the "import premium"—will include two components: an "insecurity premium" and a "market power premium." These must somehow be reflected in U.S. energy prices.

The greater our oil imports, the greater the expected cost imposed on our economy by supply disruptions. The insecurity premium is like an insurance premium: we should be willing to pay modest costs now to protect against larger costs in the event of a disruption. Since individual firms deciding to import or use oil bear only part of this "insecurity premium," unless explicit policy actions are undertaken only part of the premium will be reflected in retail prices.

Marginal U.S. costs of oil imports also exceed world oil prices because of the U.S. collective market power as a large importer of oil. This difference will be termed the "market power premium."[16] As long as import increases lead to world oil price increases, the market power premium will be positive.[17]

The appropriate value of the market power premium is under debate. Estimates ranging from several dollars to over $70 per barrel have been suggested.[18] The appropriate value depends on factors such as the price elasticity of demand for oil, the availability of alternative energy supplies, and the production response by the oil-exporting nations. In fact, if world oil prices were set to achieve revenue targets for oil exporting countries, then demand increases would lead to price *decreases*; the market power premium would be negative. Since this possibility seems inconsistent with recent events (e.g., world prices did not fall but rose sharply when Iranian production dropped), it will be disregarded in what follows.

The logic of the import premium suggests opportunities for international cooperation among oil importing countries, since the benefits from reducing oil imports will be enjoyed by all oil importers. The import premium calculated by considering the United States alone will be smaller than the premium calculated including the interests of other importing countries.[19] Collective action by oil importing countries could pay great dividends.

A policy of allowing prices to reflect marginal costs implies that the U.S. oil price should exceed import price by the entire import premium. This will not occur unless steps above and beyond price decontrol are undertaken. Potential policy actions which would cause prices to reflect the import premium include imposition of tariffs or quotas on oil imports or of taxes on all oil consumption.

Price should reflect marginal cost for other energy sources as well. Typically, natural gas is priced on a "rolled-in cost" basis, with price equal to the weighted average of costs from all gas sources. The incremental costing provisions of the Natural Gas Policy Act provide steps in the right direction. Future policy should stress incremental cost pricing for all gas.

Rate-of-return pricing of electricity leads to prices less than marginal cost, and therefore to overconsumption of electricity. This problem is particularly severe in the Pacific Northwest, where hydropower resources supply much low-cost electricity. For example, in 1978 the marginal electricity price for large industrial users was 1.22 cents per kilowatt-hour in the State of Washington and 1.18 cents for large residential users.[20] Marginal costs were 0.04 and 0.06. Therefore, the Washington price was less than 30 percent of marginal cost.[21]

Costs of environmental damage associated with energy production and use are also not included in market prices. The buildup of atmospheric carbon dioxide from the burning of fossil fuels may change world climate and therefore the world agricultural system. Acid rains associated with sulfate and nitrate emissions have a variety of detrimental effects, including reductions in the productivity of agricultural land.[22] Marginal cost pricing requires that these environmental costs be included in energy prices, perhaps through taxes on the specific energy production.

Allowing energy prices to equal marginal costs will strongly promote energy conservation by influencing the type of capital equipment purchased and the intensity of equipment utilization. U.S. and international empirical studies suggest long-run aggregate price elasticity of demand for energy to be between 0.4 and 0.7 at the secondary level (at the busbar or refinery gate. Energy Modeling Forum 1980). In the long run, therefore, every 10.0 percent increase in energy price will motivate a 4.0 to 7.0 percent reduction in aggregate energy demand as capital and/or labor inputs are substituted for energy.

In summary, a comprehensive strategy of allowing energy prices to reflect marginal costs begins with eliminating all oil and gas price control and includes import taxes or quotas as well as incentives to reduce environmental damages. Such a program can launch the United States into an effective energy policy.

Address Distribution Issues

In a market economy, prices play two major roles. The first, discussed in the previous section, is to allocate resources. But prices also have another role—that of distributing income and wealth. Owners of a commodity are made wealthier as its price increases, while buyers are made less wealthy.

Price changes and associated wealth changes are normal and accepted in our economic system. Few people have demanded a windfall profits tax on currently developed California coastal real estate even though its value has soared because California has restricted new coastal development. But energy price changes touch virtually every member of the economy. With no price controls, for example, the $28 per barrel increase in world oil price since 1973 would annually transfer more than $1,000 per household from oil consumers to domestic suppliers and a similar amount to foreign suppliers. A major portion of the former revenues would go to the government through taxes and hence to the general population. The remainder would represent a net transfer from the general population to its members who owned oil leases or stock in oil companies. Transfers to foreign suppliers account for the GNP losses discussed previously. Along with the potential for large transfers of wealth among members of the U.S. population has come intense administrative and legislative effort to override the distributional function of prices and to reshape the wealth transfer patterns.

Some of the distributional concerns are important under commonly held notions of equity. Increasing energy prices have posed real problems for the poor, the retired, or others on fixed incomes or having few options for earning income. These problems must be addressed as energy and other economic policies are formulated, even at the expense of some economic efficiency losses.

But many distributional consequences of our programs cannot be justified from a national perspective under most notions of equity and should not continue to dominate our policy deliberations. For example, crude oil price controls transfer income from domestic oil producers to oil refiners and foreign oil suppliers, and from stockholders of oil companies to stockholders of other corporations. These transfers cannot be viewed as beneficial from a national perspective.

The standard answer for meeting the important distributional goals—using income taxes and transfer programs—is incomplete, since these other instruments also entail adverse consequences. Furthermore, a legislator desiring to change income distribution can be expected to pursue distributional goals as policies are evaluated as long as he or she believes that these other instruments will not be utilized sufficiently.

Distributional concerns can be expected to remain central to the process of energy policy formulation. Failure to address distributional issues thus is a recipe for ineffectuality. Conversely, a focus primarily on distributional issues will assure continued failure to improve our energy and economic situation. A major challenge is to develop mechanisms which satisfy distributional goals without exacerbating energy and economic problems.

One difficult area for balancing distributional goals with energy goals is in pricing policies for electric utilities. Allowing all electricity prices to equal marginal cost seems politically infeasible. Two closely related pricing approaches have been tried: inverted block rates and lifeline rates. Both rate structures incorporate low prices for small quantities of electricity and higher prices for large quantities. Once allowable revenues and average prices are set for a utility, the rate structure determines the cost distribution among ratepayers and the marginal prices that each faces. Lifeline pricing can benefit the lowest income consumers (more precisely, those who purchase little electricity) and increase the marginal electricity price, thus serving both distributional and energy goals.

Distributional and energy goals can both be served by tax policy. Bringing energy prices into line with marginal costs would require large energy taxes which will raise revenue. These additional revenues would allow corporate and personal income taxes to be cut and possibly restructured. This tax shift would be consistent with the first two guidelines for energy policy and would contribute to solutions of problems discussed elsewhere in this book—insufficient capital formation and lowered productivity growth.

Plan for International Supply Disruptions

As discussed, imports of petroleum are dangerously insecure. U.S. energy policy therefore must accommodate the near certainty that severe supply disruptions will, in fact, occur. Flexibility required for response to supply shocks can be developed by increasing the available stockpiles of energy, increasing the energy efficiency of equipment, developing opportunities for fuel switching from oil to its substitutes, and diversifying sources of supply. Flexibility must be the watchword.

Stockpiles. The first step must be development of strategic oil and gas stockpiles. Already legislated is a strategic petroleum reserve scheduled ultimately to hold 1 billion barrels of oil, enough to supply one-third of our imports for a year. If anything, the legislated goals are too modest. However, implementation towards even these modest goals has been pathetic. In two and a half years, only 91 million barrels have been stored, less than 10.0 percent of the goal; only 24 million barrels were stored in 1979. At this rate, the goal would be met in forty years. The capability for removing oil from the reserve and distributing it to refineries must be demonstrated. Whatever the reasons for halting the strategic petroleum reserve program—be they to reduce world oil demand, to meet the Saudi objections to the stockpile, or to balance the federal budget—the reserve should be an important part of our plan for disruption.

The government, however, is not the only body that can hold stockpiles. Stores of crude oil and petroleum products can be held by producers, refiners, distributors, and consumers of oil. This occurs to some extent now, but should be encouraged more.

To encourage private stockpiles, government policies must change. Past governmental actions have shown that those firms holding private petroleum stockpiles will be allowed to reap little benefit since stockpiles will be subject to price controls and governmentally determined allocations in the next oil emergency. As long as the power to control prices and allocate oil remains with the government, private stockpiles of petroleum will be discouraged. In addition, programs of mandated stockpiles have been tried by other nations and perhaps should be explored in the United States.

Natural gas also can be stockpiled. Currently, natural gas available in underground storage (excluding that which may not be available for withdrawal) varies seasonally between 1.5 and 3.0 trillion cubic feet, the energy equivalent of 250 million to 500 million barrels of oil. Expansion is probably possible. Some of this natural gas could be substituted for oil—say, in dual-fired electric generating facilities—in the event of an oil disruption, if sufficient advance plans were developed.

Energy conservation. Motivating transition to a more fuel-efficient capital stock should be a second element in planning for disruptions. Such capital stock changes would reduce our pre-disruption imports of oil but would leave flexibility for further rapid reduction in energy use at the time of supply disruption. Several existing "energy conservation" programs support this objective by accelerating the transition: corporate average fuel efficiency standards for new cars, new building energy performance standards, appliance efficiency standards, residential "weatherization" programs, tax credits for installation of insulation, thermal glass, and solar equipment.[23]

In contrast, many "energy conservation" measures alter capital stock utilization and reduce the slack in consumption. Such measures, while reducing oil imports, in no way reduce vulnerability to supply disruptions because they simply preempt opportunities to reduce consumption once the disruption occurs. Examples include incentives to eliminate discretionary driving, the 55 mile per hour speed limit, and gasoline taxes, in addition to the mandatory corporate average fuel efficiency standards (Sweeney 1979c, pp. 105–33; 1979a).

The crucial difference between these two classes of measures relates to the speed of adjustment.[24] Capital stock composition changes can occur only very slowly; little adjustment is possible within the short time span of a sudden disruption. Demand reduction associated with capital stock composition thus can occur only if the appropriate actions are taken well before a disruption. Utilization changes, on the other hand, generally can occur within the time span of a disruption. Thus, changes (e.g., turning down thermostats) which are implemented before a disruption simply preexempt the opportunities for response during the disruption and do not reduce vulnerability.

Supply diversification. Planning for disruption also involves reducing the degree of exposure to disruption by discouraging imports from unstable areas and encouraging imports from such nations as Mexico, Canada, and Venezuela.

This is generally recognized as being desirable. However, shifts in purchase patterns alone are not sufficient. If production patterns remain unchanged and the United States shifts purchases from Middle Eastern sources, other countries will then end up shifting purchases toward these sources. To the extent that available oil will be allocated by competitive markets or by the IEA sharing agreements during a disruption, such pre-disruption shifts are illusionary.

Reducing exposure to disruption requires exploration for energy sources in more stable areas of the world and their development. For example, the World Bank currently provides loans for oil development in Africa and South America. All restrictions on oil exploration and production technology could be eliminated, and U.S. tax laws for investment abroad could reflect the high risks involved.

Contingency plans. Finally, there is a need to develop contingency plans to cushion the shocks of supply disruptions. These may involve international cooperative efforts well beyond the current IEA sharing rules.

Supply disruptions can lead to large oil price increases and attendant massive wealth transfers from oil importing to oil exporting countries. Reducing this wealth transfer will require international cooperation. For example, if each oil importing country were to impose a large "disruption tax" on oil imports, the wealth transfer could be greatly reduced. If each were to impose a $30 per barrel tax on imports, then world oil would be forced downward by $30 per barrel; consumer prices would remain unchanged. The tax revenues would accrue to the treasuries of the oil importing countries rather than being transferred to the exporter. The large wealth transfers would be avoided.[25]

One contemporary plan authorized under current law is gasoline rationing. Such a plan has obvious political appeal, but it is unworkable. The administrative burden would be overwhelming. Counterfeiting can be expected, particularly in early phases while the ration coupons are relatively unfamiliar, and coupons will undoubtedly be pilfered in the distribution system. Exemptions will ultimately be granted to those with the greatest ability to further disrupt the economy (remember the truckers' strike during the recent gasoline shortage?) and to special interest groups: farmers, those commuting long distances, doctors, fire departments, truckers, etc. Lines at coupon distribution centers will rival the gasoline lines.

Rather than rationing, a disruption tax could be applied to gasoline to assure that revenues would end in the federal treasury and not in the coffers of gasoline suppliers. Tax revenues could be redistributed to consumers. Such a plan could accomplish the same ends as gasoline rationing without requiring an unworkably complex, corruption-prone system.

Create Energy Options—but Expect No Panaceas

Future energy supplies, demands, and costs remain highly uncertain, even though extensive modeling and analysis activities have reduced the degree of uncertainty. Under imperfect foresight, we must adopt policies which assure that a range of energy options will be available to deal with the prominent possibilities. Creating only options appropriate for the most likely situation is a sound strategy when there is little uncertainty and when the costs of being wrong are small. For energy, however, such a strategy invites disaster, since neither condition holds. Incentives for creation of many options must be a part of a prudent energy policy package.

Investment in basic research and development (R&D) related to energy options should be intensified. We should continue to encourage research efforts in developing energy from solar, biomass, coal combustion, nuclear, and wind resources, and to support energy conservation and technologies which reduce environmental impacts. But along with these sensible research strategies, a limited amount of basic R&D into seemingly nonsensical ideas, such as satellites to collect solar energy, is probably prudent. We must balance R&D costs against the probable high costs which occur with insufficient options if unexpected contingencies do occur. The great uncertainty associated with the energy future implies that the *range* of possible futures must be considered rather than simply the most probable future.

Creating options is different, however, from forcing specific technologies into the energy system. Requiring solar energy in new homes or authorizing the construction of uneconomic solar energy satellites should not be confused with creating options. Premature widespread implementation of technologies reduces options for the uncertain future by draining resources which could be used more constructively elsewhere, by locking obsolete or inappropriate technologies into the energy system, and by risking unknown safety or environmental hazards.

A case in point is gasohol—a blend of 10 percent alcohol and 90 percent gasoline. Gasohol provides an option for supplying liquid fuels from a domestically available renewable resource. But the production of anhydrous alcohol may use up more energy than it produces (Hopkinson and Day 1980, pp. 302–4), including liquid fuels for harvesting and transporting organic materials and for providing heat to distill the alcohol. The cost per barrel of *net* energy liquid production may be too high to justify widespread implementation. Yet massive subsidies have been legislated. The current gasohol exemption from the $0.04 per gallon federal gasoline tax translates to a $0.40 per gallon subsidy on the *gross* output of alcohol and far more on the *net* output.[26] If the proposed $0.10 per gallon gasoline tax increase were passed, then the federal subsidy would become $1.40 per gallon of gross production. This is in addition to the state subsidies.

Our current gasohol programs provide an illustration of

what *not* to do. Creating options should not imply offering massive subsidies to force implementation of highly uneconomic technologies.

In supporting new technologies, no single option should be counted as a panacea for the short run and probably none for the long run. Moreover, creating options should include not destroying old options before new ones are proven. For example, many opponents to nuclear energy argue vociferously that energy conservation, solar energy, or biomass will provide new options. Probably so. But will these be proven safe and will they soon be available economically in sufficient quantities to obviate the need for nuclear energy? Probably not. Even if they were, conservative planning implies that the nuclear option should be retained until alternatives are proven to be adequately available, safe, and economic under the possible energy futures. Solar energy and biomass may be the solutions, just as nuclear energy was once thought to be. But should we destroy old options under that hope?

International spillovers are important also in decisions to create options. The availability of energy options anywhere in the world can benefit all oil importing nations by holding down world energy prices and by reducing the impact of supply disruptions. An R&D effort which is optimal for one consuming country will be smaller than optimal for all taken together. Recognizing this, international cooperative efforts and information sharing on energy options are also important.

Utilize Markets More—Direct Government Intervention Less

The degree of federal intervention in energy markets is staggering. One fact is clear: this massive intervention has been a failure for solving energy problems. It's now time to use markets more and direct government intervention less.

In some areas government should withdraw completely—

eliminate all price controls, avoid rationing or allocating energy, avoid discouraging private stockpiling, etc. But complete withdrawal is not always appropriate: unaided markets will not supply enough R&D, market prices will not include environmental costs or the import premium, and so on.

Even when intervention is needed, markets can be utilized more, direct intervention less. For example, markets can be utilized by taxing energy import or energy use to reduce consumption, while maintaining flexibility and requiring far less governmental information than does direct intervention. Taxes which raise the price of all energy liquids would automatically subsidize those gasohol technologies which produce positive net liquid fuels and penalize those that produce negative net output. Net production would be increased without the need for federal regulations to determine the allowable gasohol technologies.

When it is desirable to impose efficiency standards on new energy-using equipment, market-like mechanisms can be used. For example, existing law imposes a standard on the minimum corporate *average* fuel efficiency of new automobiles sold by each manufacturer. Such a standard allows flexibility to sell some cars with fuel efficiency below the standard and others above it. This average standard allows maximum flexibility for competition and consumer choice consistent with a given average efficiency. Such flexibility is preferable whenever standards are desired.

To reduce opportunities for direct intervention, energy tax revenues should not be earmarked for energy programs. Earmarking revenues to support energy technology development reduces flexibility and places control of innovation in public rather than private hands. Earmarking encourages considerations of distribution among congressional districts in technology development decisions: e.g., if shale oil development is subsidized in Colorado, then there will be pressure to give California a share by subsidizing windmill development by the aerospace industry. Using energy tax revenues to reduce other taxes is more desirable—encourage greater use of markets, less of government intervention.

Deal Realistically with Conflicting Goals

Much energy policy debate involves tradeoffs between alternative goals—finding solutions to energy problems, protecting the environment, and influencing income distribution.

Energy-environment policy provides several notorious examples of failure to deal realistically with conflicting goals. Many oil-fired electric generating facilities at one time were coal fired but were converted from coal to oil. Soon after the oil embargo, however, federal legislation demanded conversion back to coal. But the environmental and other regulations making such conversions impractical were not relaxed. Thus, several sets of rules preclude conversion to coal while others mandate such a conversion. Coal conversion has not occurred.

Another blatant example involves new electric generating facilities. New baseload facilities legally cannot be fueled by oil or gas. Little untapped high-rise hydropower potential remains. Nuclear development has been blocked. This leaves coal. But in noncompliance areas, areas in which ambient levels of residuals violate national standards, a new plant can be built only if emissions from other nearby stationary sources are reduced by *120 percent* of the emissions from the new source. New coal-burning facilities thus are not allowed in noncompliance areas if the net offset is to keep emissions constant, but are allowed only if the net effect is to reduce emissions. The requirement of a 120 percent offset (rather than a simple 100 percent) can be thought of as an environmental tax on changes from the status quo distribution of energy sources. The result is a bias toward oil and against coal. One result is a delay in retiring old oil-fired facilities and an increase in oil imports.

Trade-offs between distributional goals and energy goals

require creative alternatives and difficult choices. Currently, the implicit goal of maintaining the status quo wealth distribution seems to predominate, although this goal is difficult to justify.

The tradeoffs between current and future costs must be addressed more appropriately than has occurred to date. Avoiding the crippling future costs of international supply disruptions, for example, requires the United States to bear increased costs now. However, the U.S. political system does not seem to deal effectively with tradeoffs involving increased costs borne now in order to avoid uncertain, although large, costs occurring several congressional elections in the future. Yet mechanisms must be found to facilitate realistic tradeoffs of this type.

Another tradeoff to be addressed may be that between appropriate energy-pricing and inflation policies. Increased energy prices may exacerbate inflation problems. A choice must be made.

The appropriate choices, given these and other such tradeoffs, are far from obvious. Yet without clear delineation of the value conflicts and alternative possible choices, there is little hope of satisfactory resolution. Without courage to consistently choose, we will continue to stumble, creating mutually inconsistent rules which assure that no goals are met adequately.

CONCLUSION

The decade of the 1980s will be another beset with energy problems. The three fundamental energy problems—increased world cost of petroleum, increased cost of domestic petroleum substitutes, and increased vulnerability to supply disruptions—can be expected to worsen rather than improve during the decade. The difficulties posed by these energy problems are not limited to a few industries, sectors, or consuming groups. Rather, the energy problems fundamentally influence virtually every aspect of our economy: capital formation, economic growth, inflation, income distribution, balance of payments, international distribution of political power, and the likelihood of war.

We cannot expect these problems to disappear, but we can and must demand policy responses which reduce rather than exacerbate the difficulties. This expectation now only hints at fulfillment. With courage to face hard choices realistically in the 1980s, we must lay a firm foundation to solve our energy problems.

DISCUSSION

McKINNON: Jim Sweeney seems to think that OPEC is going to last forever and that the real price of oil is going to rise 10 percent per year. If all countries in the world continued to treat their producing enterprises foolishly in the way they tax them, then I would agree with Jim; but there is no reason why countries have to tax oil producers in this way, and once we rationalize taxation in the oil industry, I don't see how OPEC can survive through the 1980s.

KOTLIKOFF: The idea of having simultaneously an oil depletion allowance—which presumably subsidizes depletion—and the windfall profits tax, taxing marginal production at 30 percent (I think that is the number), is just crazy. You are doing opposite things and twisting around the wind. If we want to reduce our dependency on foreign oil—which seems essential—we must stop taxing our own production, which only makes us more oil-import dependent. The important point is that we must ask the question out loud—what do we really want to do in the short term? Do we really want to import more now? Or less? There is a real confusion here on objectives. What we are doing now is contradictory in many ways, and unclear.

ROWEN: While Congress has no problem focusing on distributional issues, it should be focusing also on these other issues. The international dimension is particularly important, not only with regard to the Persian Gulf and OPEC, but also because in very basic respects the world market for energy—certainly, for oil—affects *all* policies, virtually all of the policy instruments that you mentioned. The effectiveness of tariffs, quotas (which is a less satisfactory instrument) and damage-limiting emergency measures—all of these are much more effective if they are done in a coordinated way among at least the major importing countries. It doesn't require everybody in the world, but at least the big countries should harmonize their policies in this respect.

KOTLIKOFF: You seem to assume that our basic policy should be directed towards reducing our imports of oil. I am just wondering whether that doesn't send a signal to the Soviets or to other unstable forces in that area that we are less likely to respond to a military move in that area. It is not clear to me that we shouldn't be using as much imported oil as we can right now, while developing and capping our reserves so they can come on line in event of a crisis. But the idea of using *our* oil now and then having to use theirs later—or the alternative of just forgetting about their oil completely and using much more expensive resources—just doesn't seem reasonable. I think a more reasonable alternative is to make a very strong statement militarily in that area—that we are not going to let that area go down the drain.

SWEENEY: I am not opposed to making strong military statements, but it is difficult for me to analyze fully the signals we are now giving the Soviet Union. Furthermore, reducing our supply vulnerability does not preclude military measures to protect our access to oil imports in the face of Soviet projection of military power. I do believe, however,

that the higher the world price of oil, the higher the probability of Soviet moves to take over the oil fields when they
get to the point of importing oil. For example, the CIA has
forecast that the Soviets will be importing about a million
barrels a day of oil in the mid-1980s. This forecast is disputed, but at current prices the cost of those imports to them
would be about $11 billion per year, which is a large share of
their hard currency earnings. It is not clear how the Soviet
economy could stand that financial drain. It seems quite
likely that they will not be averse to expanding their land
area in order to obtain the resources they need from a client
state on concessionary terms or on a barter basis. I believe it
is reasonable to link oil prices to an increased probability of
war in the Middle East.

CUDDINGTON: I have a comment on Jim Sweeney's
suggestion that monopsony power of the United States can
be used to offset OPEC monopoly power. I suspect that the
United States' monopsony power as a *purchaser* of oil is extremely limited. What's behind the bargaining strength of
OPEC versus the United States? If OPEC doesn't export oil,
how much does it really suffer? It's getting to the point now
where most of the OPEC countries have a very limited or
relatively limited ability to absorb imports. If the United
States restricted trade in oil, OPEC would have to reduce
their imports somewhat. But the question is how severe
would be the damage to their economy from that, compared
to the damage inflicted on us—meaning the United States
and its major allies—if we lost the oil that comes from the
Middle East? Now, of course, part of the U.S. bargaining
power depends on whether it acts jointly with all other oil importers. But let's take an extreme position and say that all oil
importers act together and agree not to send *anything* to
OPEC countries unless they reduce oil prices. That *might*
reduce OPEC strength somewhat, but I suggest that to get
that sort of coordinated policy by oil importers would be very
difficult. So what's at issue is that OPEC is in an extremely

strong position because they have a fairly low absorptive capacity for imports from the rest of the world.

SWEENEY: Two responses to that. You and I have two fundamentally different models. You seem to have a model of OPEC as a monolithic cartel. I don't think OPEC as an organization is particularly relevant any more in setting oil prices. I think the *Saudis* are relevant, as are some of the other major exporting countries, but OPEC as an organization is not.

Second, if you utilize the empirical evidence on the responsiveness of oil prices to world demand for oil (or what economists call the "price elasticity" of demand for oil), and you ask what would be the price premium for reducing imports by a million barrels a day, different answers are obtained, depending on which elasticity estimates and which models of OPEC behavior you use. For most models, the estimated import premium is on the order of $10 to $20 a barrel above and beyond the price of imported oil. This occurs because of the market power of the United States, but it depends also on an assumption that OPEC does not respond by changing production. Your absorptive capacity argument is that the OPEC countries have certain revenue goals and that they set prices just to meet them. Under this theory you would get the opposite answer. But then you would have to explain why it was that when the Iranian cutback in oil production occurred, world oil market prices didn't fall. They went up rapidly in response to the increased demand facing the remainder of the OPEC countries. This observation is absolutely opposite to the price changes to be expected if the absorptive capacity theory were valid.

OLSEN: Government intervention into the energy field, in my view, has been extremely detrimental in a variety of ways. One is that they have, through the windfall tax, in a sense called into question the legitimacy of private capital and the rights of private investors to the fruits of capital investment. That, coupled with subsidizing alternative sources of energy, acts to intimidate private initiative, which may not benefit from those subsidies. If you can imagine for a moment—which is actually going on—people who are doing independent research and development in the energy field for energy substitutes. They must look over their shoulder at competitors who may be subsidized by the government. This, in effect, will discourage a much more pervasive effort on the part of the private market to come up with new technology and alternative sources of energy. And this is true despite the fact that many businesses applaud these subsidies, which are allocated by bureaucratic fiat on which forms of R&D should be supported.

13

PATRICIA DRURY

ALAIN ENTHOVEN

Competition and Health Care Costs

Projected increases in medical costs. Insurance systems. The uncertainties in medical care. Cost-increasing incentives. Attempts at government regulation. The value of a competitive market. The Consumer Choice Health Plan.

High and rising health care costs pose a major problem for the United States economy. In 1965 total spending for health care inthe United States was $43 billion, or about 6.2 percent of the gross national product (GNP); by 1978 the total was

$192.4 billion, or about 9.1 percent of GNP. In real (i.e., inflation-adjusted) dollars, per capita spending on health services doubled during that period.

Even more dramatic has been the growing share of national health care expenditures borne by government, predominantly by the federal government. In 1965, before the enactment of the Medicare and Medicaid programs to finance services to the elderly and poor, federal, state, and local government spending on health was only $11 billion, about 25 percent of total health care spending. In 1978 the government share had risen to $78 billion, or more than 40 percent of total spending, with the federal government alone paying nearly $54 billion. Recent projections by the Health Care Financing Administration, assuming no major institutional changes in the health sector, are for total 1990 health care expenditures of $758 billion representing 11.5 percent of the projected 1990 GNP. The combined federal, state, and local government share by 1990 is projected to be over $325 billion or 43.0 percent of total expenditures (Freeland 1980).

The sheer size of these increases will create a serious burden on the federal budget over the next ten years. In fact, it is clear that this rate of growth in federal health expenditures simply cannot continue. There are growing pressures for increases in other areas of the federal budget, particularly for defense, while taxpayer resistance and the demands of sound fiscal policy are creating pressure to reduce the federal share of the GNP.

We believe that the government must—and inevitably will—act to bring health care costs under control. The question is which strategy will be adopted, rather than whether the status quo can somehow be preserved. Although powerful interests are intent on preserving today's health care financing system, pressures on the federal budget will almost certainly force changes during the 1980s that would not have been politically feasible during the 1970s.

The problem is not simply that a higher percentage of the

GNP is going to health care. There is a question of the appropriate mix of public and private expenditures, but there is no reason to prefer any particular total percentage of the GNP spent on health care services. However, there is evidence of waste, and evidence that a great deal of costly care is being provided with little or no apparent marginal health benefit. While it is difficult to say how much of our health care spending falls in this category, evidence suggests that it is something on the order of 20 to 25 percent. Furthermore, few forces now operating offer any hope of reversing this trend, while many forces are operating to perpetuate and even accelerate it. Health care resources are not being used efficiently, and the choices that will necessarily be made soon will depend on why we think that is and what we think we can do about it.

UNDERSTANDING THE PROBLEM

During the years when the present health care system was established, mainly from 1945 to 1965, the goal was seen almost entirely as one of providing financial protection for individuals whose costs of care could be large and distributing those costs equitably among income groups. The mechanisms created showed little concern for the total costs to society of such services.

That lack of concern in part resulted from the fact that the total costs of health services were low, at least by today's standards, and they were not increasing rapidly relative to the GNP. Health care services in 1950 accounted for 4.5 percent of the GNP; by 1960, only 5.3 percent. It also resulted in part from an apparent belief that total costs would not be significantly affected by the kind of mechanisms chosen to achieve financial protection and equity.

The Financing System Today: Health Insurance

The health care financing system was based on one or another form of health insurance, whether publicly or privately funded, which pays retrospectively for the services rendered to the beneficiaries. Health insurance is generally modeled on other forms of casualty insurance, with the need for medical care treated as a casualty loss —as an event arising from circumstances beyond the control of the insured and for which there is a specific treatment. The insurer is at risk for the cost of that treatment; the insured is at risk only for coinsurance amounts, deductibles, or copayments.

Tax laws have encouraged the growth of health insurance for the employed population. The amount an employer contributes toward premiums for employee health insurance is not included in an employee's taxable income. Health insurance thus is commonly purchased through employment groups, with premiums based on the medical cost experience of the group. As a result, premium costs are virtually invisible to the beneficiaries, the individual employees. Excluding this one part of compensation from taxes motivates both employers and employees to purchase increasingly comprehensive insurance, more than would be purchased with after-tax dollars. (In covering such things as routine dentistry, health insurance has gone far beyond "insurance" in the sense of risk reduction and has become a means of paying for routine, predictable expenses with pretax dollars.)

In 1965 Congress enacted the Medicare and Medicaid programs, Titles XVIII and XIX of the Social Security Act. Medicare covered 27 million elderly and disabled persons in 1978. Medicaid, a joint federal/state program that pays for health care services for welfare recipients and other low-income people, had nearly 23 million beneficiaries in 1978. With these programs, casualty-insurance financing for medical services was extended to millions of citizens who did not belong to employment groups.

The record shows that by 1965 casualty-insurance financing based on fees for service and cost reimbursement was widely considered to be the only legitimate way to pay for health care services. In order to overcome political resistance to such public insurance programs as Medicare and Medicaid, the programs were based on prevailing payment methods. Most people did not believe that this was a serious problem.

The Congressional Budget Office (1979) estimated that 92 to 95 percent of the population by 1976 had some health insurance. (This is a difficult estimate to make because it is nearly impossible to identify the extent of duplicate coverage; the definition of "covered" also varies for different programs.) Viewed from the provider side, over 90 percent of hospital services and 66 percent of physician's services were paid for in 1978 by one or another insurance program or other third-party payor; for very costly care, the percentage is often much higher. Once a patient has satisfied deductibles, insurance often covers 100 percent of the costs, particularly those of the hospital. Virtually all of this insurance is based on the casualty-insurance model.

Incentives

Consider the incentives created in this casualty-insurance system of financing health care.

The fee-for-service payment is the insurance mechanism for reimbursing individual physicians. Insurers pay physicians separately for each service rendered to an insured beneficiary. To increase income, a physician has only to provide more numerous or more costly services. There is therefore a fairly strong incentive to do so, and certainly no economic incentive to be conservative. This is not to say that clearly superfluous services are being rendered; it is more a question of how uncertainty is resolved. The frequency of follow-up or monitoring visits, the number and frequency of tests ordered, the extent to which screening tests are administered, tend to push toward the upper limit of what a physician perceives to be responsible care. The threat of malpractice suits has tended to raise that perceived standard.

For hospitals, the normal insurance payment mechanisms are cost reimbursement or third-party payment of charges. Medicare, the various state Medicaid programs, and Blue Cross have developed numerical standards for the "reasonableness" of routine hospital costs. "Reasonable" usually means "not far from the average," yet even the average is a disputed standard. Each hospital tries to demonstrate why its unique circumstances mean that it should not be held to an average.

With cost reimbursement, a hospital receives increased revenue for providing more services or for having the capacity to provide them. Any uncertainty about developing a new hospital service or buying new equipment is likely to be resolved in favor of doing so, for the costs will generally be reimbursed regardless of use. Streamlining of services or other efficiency improvements, on the other hand, will mean reduced revenues. The economic consequences of third-party payment of charges are discussed later.

In 1976 medical services rendered to Americans consisted of about 278 million short-term care hospital days, 190 million hospital outpatient visits, and 1 billion private doctor visits. Thus it should not be surprising that only extraordinary cases draw the attention of the payors. Claims that fall within certain statistical norms tend to be handled and paid routinely and uncritically. Claims processors or payors cannot attempt to second-guess provider decisions in the majority of cases. This system must presume most medical care to be necessary and standard.

A Basic Misunderstanding

There seems to be a misconception about the nature of medical care that persists into today's national health policy debate. That misconception is that medical need and the care provided to meet that need are solely or largely *technical* matters and not *economic* ones. In other words, there is an assumption that clear criteria exist for what constitutes medical need and that there are established standards for medical treatment. These standards and criteria, based on medical science, are presumed to be free from economic considerations. If this view were accurate, the incentives created by the financing system would not be important. Such a view, however, ignores some basic facts about medical care.

It ignores the almost all-pervasive uncertainty in medicine. The diagnosis of a patient's symptoms is often uncertain even after extensive testing. Not all physiological processes are well understood, and most tests are not 100 percent accurate. Tests produce changes in the probability that a diagnosis is correct, but not clear answers. The efficacy of many treatments is uncertain, and doctors often do not know which patient characteristics determine efficacy. Good randomized clinical trials have not been done for most procedures. Taking the whole spectrum of medical care, the emergency room doctor who knows exactly what to do for the patient with a clear-cut problem is by far the exception and not the rule.

It also ignores the variety and complexity of patients. A sick patient presents more than a technical problem and there is rarely an unambiguous "best" standard treatment. The treatment that is best depends on a wide range of variables that make up each particular set of circumstances. The values, preferences, lifestyles, beliefs, and unique physical characteristics of a patient make up a major part of those circumstances. For example, what inconveniences one patient may mean that another's career is altered. High-quality care will often differ for different patients. In every case, it consists of subtle judgments and the balancing of a wide array of values and technical considerations.

Finally, this view ignores the fact that certain conditions will not respond to any known treatment. Some physical symptoms may manifest complex physical/psychological processes which scientific medicine is ill-prepared to address. In some cases the best of doctors may not be able to determine what is wrong or be able to help much. And because of the uncertainties, a large amount of resources may be expended on a particular case before the doctor and patient conclude that a cure will not result.

To the extent that Congress assumed medical decisions were made on technical grounds alone and would continue to be so, it did not anticipate the role that economic incentives would soon play. It was generally considered safe to introduce the cost-increasing incentives described above in order to achieve financial protection and an equitable distribution of costs. The result, however, was to insulate all the decision-makers—doctors, patients, hospital administrators, and other professionals—from responsibility for the economic consequences of their decisions. And this, we believe, is at the center of today's health care cost problem.

Consequences of Today's Financing Mechanisms

Faced with uncertainty and little economic constraint, doctors have every reason to order tests and treatments whose costs exceed the value of their marginal benefits. Why be only 90 percent certain of a diagnosis if another $200 test could increase the certainty to 95 percent and if a third party will pay? To be sure, doctors respond to many incentives and considerations, including a humanitarian wish to help their patients as well as a desire to achieve technical excellence.

But they inevitably respond to economic incentives as well. Doctors who know that their patients are well insured and who are acting in their individual patient's best interests surely feel more free to order additional services and recommend the use of more elaborate technology than are doctors concerned about the financial burden their decisions will inflict on their uninsured patients.

Cost-increasing incentives have had large-scale effects. Randomized clinical trials done in recent years document examples where large expenditures of health care resources yielded essentially no discernible marginal health benefit. A study at Nottingham General Hospital (Hill 1978, pp. 837–41) looked at treatment for 350 suspected heart attack victims. Of these, 24 percent were hospitalized because of other complications or lack of a suitable home environment; the rest were assigned at random to home or hospital care. Investigators found no significant difference in results, even though hospital care was more intensive and more costly. Other studies compared different lengths of stay in the hospital for heart attack patients and were unable to demonstrate that a 21-day stay is better than 14 days or 14 days better than 7 (Hutter 1973, pp. 1141–44; McNeer et al. 1978, pp. 229–32). In the United States the national average stay following a heart attack is 14 days.

A study of 686 coronary artery disease patients treated by the Veterans' Administration found, for all but the 13 percent who had disease of the left main artery, that there was no significant difference in survival between those treated with medication and those treated with costly bypass graft surgery (Murphy et al. 1977, pp. 621–27). (This study has triggered a great deal of controversy. It deals with only one measure of "better"—three-year survival—and poses some problems of interpretation. Nonetheless, it illustrates the point that more costly care is not necessarily superior care.) By the time this study was published, bypass graft surgery had become a $1 billion per year industry.

Costly care may even yield negative marginal health benefits. This is true not only for incompetent care. Many forms of competent medical care involve substantial risks and can cause considerable pain. The risks may be justified by the expected benefits, but not necessarily always.

The problem is that nowhere in the system are there effective mechanisms operating to create cost consciousness. Employee health insurance premiums reflect the behaviors of every service provider. Changing doctors won't change an employee's premium cost. The third-party payors only enter the picture after services have been rendered and the cost-generating decisions have been made, so they are in a poor position to bring about fundamental changes. Even though the costs of employee health insurance are rising rapidly, most employers do not believe they can materially affect them. Medical care, after all, is not their area of business expertise. The increasing costs of public programs are buried in the general tax structure with most taxpayers either unaware of the amount spent on health care services or uncertain about what, if anything, should be done about it.

The cumulative effect of millions of decisions made by individual consumers and providers determines costs and the rate of their increase. The incentives and pressures affecting those consumers and providers are overwhelmingly cost-increasing.

SOLVING THE PROBLEM

Two general strategies are being considered for solving the problem of the high and rising costs of health care services. As in other policy areas, the two contenders are economic regulation and economic competition, the former relying on price and capacity controls administered by various public agencies and the latter relying on an appropriately structured private market. There has been some experience with each of these strategies.

The Regulatory Strategy

The regulatory strategy for dealing with the cost of health care services involves direct economic controls on prices and capacity. This form of regulation contrasts with regulations designed to ensure the competence of practitioners or the safety of hospitals or other institutions. There is room for debate over the specifics of safety regulations and licensure laws, but it is generally agreed that some of this type of regulation is appropriate and desirable, regardless of how we approach the cost problem.

Economic regulation, in simplest terms, is based on the view that, because the medical services industry is not cost-conscious, it is necessary to impose publicly the constraints that are not produced privately. Several such mechanisms have been proposed and implemented during the past decade. Their achievement record is poor.

One mechanism has been comprehensive health planning and certificate-of-need (CON) laws to control and limit investment in hospital facilities. The National Health Planning and Resources Development Act of 1974 mandated the creation of local Health Systems Agencies (HSAs) and state health planning agencies charged with identifying and planning for the medical service needs of their communities. Their main instrument of control is the CON program, required of states by 1980 as a condition for receiving certain federal funds. CON laws provide that, above a specified dollar threshold, hospitals may not make investments or offer additional services without first demonstrating "need" and being granted a certificate from the state health planning agency. Some states have had CON laws since the late 1960s.

The results to date have not been surprising. Several studies show either that CON laws have no effect on hospital costs or that they have a cost-increasing effect (Lewin Associates 1975; Salkever and Bice 1976, pp. 185–214; Hellinger 1976, pp. 187–93; Sloan and Steinwald 1980). HSAs have no authority to close "unneeded" or inefficient facilities. The need for a proposed new facility is necessarily judged in relation to existing facilities. As an illustration, in a hypothetical community with many low-quality or inefficiently run hospitals it would be next to impossible to demonstrate a "need" for another hospital even if there were every reason to believe that the new hospital would be very well run. And the issues are never this clear. Certificates of need effectively protect existing facilities from competition.

CON laws reduce the ability of institutions to adapt to change and tend to protect them from any need to do so. Hospitals also tend to keep doing those things they have been authorized to do, regardless of changing conditions. Once a service is discontinued, a hospital would generally require a new CON to reopen it.

CON laws are based on the assumption that uniform numerical standards are feasible and desirable in medical services. Any criterion for the number of hospital beds a community *should* have, for example, must be based on some model of anticipated hospital use. This in turn presupposes that there are—or at least, should be—standard treatment patterns. However, a committee of members of the Institute of Medicine of the National Academy of Sciences was not able to agree on a numerical standard for even this simplest measure of hospital capacity. The problem for specialized service capacities is much more difficult.

A second regulatory mechanism that has been tried is the Professional Standards Review Organization (PSRO). PSROs are independent, nonprofit associations of physicians, again with local jurisdiction, created under authority established by the 1972 amendments to the Social Security Act. The task of a PSRO is to review services provided to Medicare and Medicaid beneficiaries for necessity and adherence to professional standards. This is partly for quality control, but the record shows that the most important goal is clearly cost control.

The results of PSRO activities have not been encouraging. A review conducted by the Health Care Financing Administration (1979), the agency responsible for Medicare and Medicaid, concluded that PSROs had a small effect on reducing hospital use, on the order of 1.5 percent. The net savings generated were small, equal only to about one-tenth of one percent of the total costs of Medicare. The Congressional Budget Office concluded in its study that savings resulting from PSRO activities were less than the cost of the PSRO program (Ginsburg and Koretz 1979). Once again, such an approach to the problem could only work if standard treatments existed or if standards could be easily developed. Even more important, this sort of review identifies only the outliers, the nontypical patterns of practice. It does not offer any effective mechanism for altering the average. Coupled with professional incentives to do as much as is possible, PSRO reviews may serve to encourage the more conservative (less costly) practitioners to increase the number of services they provide up to the norm.

Hospital cost-containment legislation was proposed twice by the Carter administration and was twice defeated. Controls on hospital prices were implemented by the Nixon administration. Several states have also enacted hospital price controls. This regulatory mechanism seeks to limit hospital prices or total revenues to a fixed percentage annual increase. Even with a system of "penalties" and "bonuses" for more and less-costly hospitals (compared to a peer group median, as in the second Carter proposal), such a mechanism necessarily allows more flexibility in the form of higher allowed increases to the least efficient hospitals and punishes the most efficient with less revenue. There are considerable incentives to build in and keep as much fat as possible. Such a mechanism attempts, in the words of one congressman, to "outlaw high costs," and it does so without much regard for the services and incentives that result.

In the eight states where there was sufficient political will to create mandatory hospital price controls, the results have not been spectacular. One of the eight later repealed its law, four of the other seven substantially improved their positions relative to the national average of hospital expenditures per capita, two showed essentially no change, and one deteriorated. Two of the four that improved were New York and Massachusetts, yet they nevertheless remained the two most costly states.

Because hospital cost containment measures necessarily control some sort of average cost (per day or per case), these measures have unintended side effects. They create incentives to hospitalize patients who might otherwise be treated on an outpatient basis and to keep patients in the hospital longer, thereby adding more low-intensity care days to the total days of care provided. These actions reduce average costs but increase total costs. Hospitals are only one part of the system; controlling their unit prices does not change how well the system works as a whole.

The story is much the same for controls on physicians' fees. The Council on Wage and Price Stability found that even though physicians' fees rose more slowly than the consumer price index (CPI) during the 1972 and 1973 price controls, the median net income of physicians rose at about the same rate as the CPI (Dyckman 1978). The reason was that use of physicians' services increased. During that period the Urban Institute studied physician charges to the Medicare and Medicaid programs in California and found significant increases both in the number of physician visits performed and in the intensity (measured as procedures per visit) of those visits (Holahan and Scanlon 1979). These phenomena have led some economists to conclude that physicians have target incomes and sufficient influence over the demand for their own services to be able to achieve those targets, even under fee controls. (Recall that their insured patients, unlike consumers in normal markets, have very little economic incentive to question the need for recommended services or their value.)

From these experiences and from what we understand about the dynamics of this industry, we conclude that regulatory control over prices cannot achieve the goal of making good quality, affordable care available to all.

THE COMPETITION STRATEGY

What Market?

Today's medical services economy is *not* economic competition. To assert, as some do, that all of today's cost and allocation problems occurred in a competitive market misrepresents what has really happened. It is true that services are provided predominantly in the private sector and that there are multiple independent producers. But the existence of public and private insurance *removes consideration of cost from virtually all of the relevant transactions in this industry.* With no consciousness of cost, there can be no *economic* competition. Medical services are unique in this respect, and the application of economic analysis to this industry must take this characteristic into account.

Consider the relationship between insurance and medical services. Each insurance plan pays for *virtually any services rendered* to its beneficiaries, *by whatever provider the beneficiary (or the beneficiary's doctor) chooses.* The insurer is not a party to either of these cost-determining choices. The medical profession has insisted, in fact, that insurance plans place no restrictions on their beneficiaries' free choice of doctor or other provider.

There are hundreds of insurance plans, to be sure, but they

all finance the same set of providers making the same
choices. The basic payment mechanisms of fee-for-service
and cost-reimbursement or third-party payment of charges
are common to all traditional insurance plans. In most communities there really is only one game in town.

Recall that insurance is most commonly purchased by
employers on behalf of their employees. The premium price
is therefore often unknown to beneficiaries. The price of
public programs is part of the general tax rate. Physicians,
who control the majority of costs in this system, do not even
know—let alone have any incentive to care about—the cost
consequences of their choices. Premium prices operate in the
market between insurance companies and employers, while
health services are produced in a separate "market," one
almost entirely without a dollar price mechanism. Insurance
companies can pass on to employers any increases in the
costs of the services they finance. Employers, in turn, allow
health benefits to become a larger percentage of total
employee compensation. Neither they nor their employees
stand to gain very much by changing insurance companies.
Competition among insurance companies thus does not produce economic competition in health services.

Alternative Delivery Systems

If costs are to receive consideration by providers, we believe
that a new market based on a different concept of "product"
needs to be created. As long as the market is structured
around individual services, it will be difficult to introduce
economic constraints. Patients have little technical clinical
knowledge and are frequently in distress when they seek
medical services. They are therefore not in a good position to
exercise economic judgment in purchasing individual medical services. Key decisions are inevitably made by the physicians.

A better notion of product around which to create an economically competitive market is that of comprehensive care. Defined differently in different settings, comprehensive care is the "product" offered by the alternative financing and delivery systems that have grown in several areas of the United States. Health Maintenance Organizations (HMOs) are the best known of these alternatives. Individual services—doctor visits, lab tests, hospital days—are treated as components of comprehensive care, able to be combined differently to meet the needs and values of different patients.

Patients can select a comprehensive care organization at a time when they are not in immediate need of services, when they can evaluate the philosophy and propensities of competing organizations against their costs. In other words, in such a market patients *can* exercise economic judgment.

Comprehensive care can be priced and marketed meaningfully. Alternative financing and delivery systems enroll a defined population. They also have a limited set of providers affiliated with them. Most important, they set their price prospectively. This completely changes the incentives found in the traditional system. When an alternative delivery system renders a greater number of services or more costly ones, it does not receive higher revenues as a result. The financing and service functions are merged in a single organization. The cost consequences of the decisions made by an organization's providers are fully reflected in the prospective fee.

In order to have a competitive economic market in medical services, traditional insurance plans with their payment mechanisms must compete with other plans. The incentives in alternative financing and delivery systems lead to different decisions, different ways of resolving uncertainty, and hence different costs. Studies of some alternatives to traditional insurance plans have shown that they can deliver comprehensive care for 10 to 40 percent lower total costs per capita (Luft 1977).

Alternative financing and delivery systems have existed for decades, yet traditional insurance has so dominated the financing of medical services that many people cannot seriously imagine any other way of structuring things. This conceptual limit is the greatest barrier to implementing the competition strategy.

There are several types of alternative delivery systems. Two are described in the Health Maintenance Organization Act of 1973—prepaid group practices (PGPs) and individual practice associations (IPAs). In the former, the physicians practice in a group and may be salaried or paid a per capita amount for each of their patients plus a share of the organization's net income. Some PGPs own hospitals, while others contract for the use of community hospitals. Examples of PGPs are the Kaiser Foundation Health Plans and the Group Health Cooperative of Puget Sound, Washington.

In individual practice associations, as the name suggests, physicians practice independently in private offices. As members of the association they accept its rules and controls, and even though they are generally paid fees for service, they share in the risk borne by the organization. The total revenue to the system does not increase with increased services. Examples of IPAs are the Physician's Association of Clackamas County, Oregon, and Physician's Health Plan in Minnesota.

A third type of alternative system—not technically an HMO—is the primary care network (PCN) in which the individual primary care physician contracts with the network and assumes responsibility for providing primary care to enrollees for a fixed per capita periodic payment. This physician, contracting with the network, arranges and supervises all referrals for other services—specialists, hospitalization, or tests—services paid for by the network from an account established for each physician. The money paid into the account is based on the number of enrollees under the care of each physician and on indicators of their medical risk status.

The primary care physician shares in any surplus or deficit in this account. Examples of PCNs are Northwest Healthcare established by SAFECO Life Insurance Company in Washington and California, and the Wisconsin Physicians Service Health Maintenance Program.

These three types are by no means the only possibilities. The many legitimate ways to provide high quality medical care and the different preferences, values, and needs of different patients call for the creation of other alternatives if the market is to encourage desirable innovation.

The Essentials of Competition

There is some economic competition among existing alternative delivery systems. The results in these communities, notably Minneapolis—St. Paul and Hawaii, *are* encouraging. Costs are not rising as rapidly as in other areas, care is of high quality, and patient satisfaction with the medical service is high. The systems have adapted to competition by establishing conveniently located clinics or offices, operating during evening hours, and otherwise accommodating their members.

Even in these two areas, however, and in most other areas where there is some competition, the contest has often been unfair. In economic competition, price becomes part of the decision equation and is balanced against other values and perceptions as purchases are made. Access to alternative delivery systems, however, is generally through employment groups, and the majority of employers who offer a choice of health benefit plans nearly always subsidize the selection of more costly plans by contributing more to pay higher premiums. An alternative system with a relatively low premium because it is effective in controlling costs has no marketing advantage if employers will pay the extra cost of less effective systems.

Beneficiaries of Medicare and Medicaid programs have no access or extremely limited access, under economically unfair terms, to alternative financing and delivery systems. Those programs have been unable to pay prospectively for "comprehensive care"; they are based on the retrospective service-by-service payment mechanisms and subsidize the traditional way of doing business.

Fair economic competition among alternative financing and delivery systems and traditional health insurance plans would have to be based on the following principles:

Periodic multiple choice.   Each consumer should have the opportunity to enroll in any system meeting certain uniform standards and operating in his or her area, and should be able to change systems periodically.

Fixed dollar subsidies.   The amount of financial help a consumer gets toward the purchase of health insurance or alternative health care system membership should be the same regardless of the system chosen. Nonpoor consumers who pay the extra cost of more expensive systems will then balance cost against other attributes at the margin.

Equal rules for all competitors.   Workable, fair competition will require some rules to ensure that plans do not compete in undesirable ways by enrolling only low-risk members or by selling deceptive or inadequate coverage. The same rules must apply equally to all systems and plans, and should govern enrollment procedures, premium-setting practices, minimum covered services, and information disclosure.

Not all doctors in all plans.   Today's financing system separates cost considerations from physician decisionmakers. Alternative financing systems are not merely new ways of paying for the same services, but are systems that reintroduce cost consciousness by producing different mixes of services and by changing the practice styles and patterns of their providers. "Limited provider plans," each involving only some of the providers in a community, would accomplish this, and the results would be reflected in premiums.

Traditional insurance restricts a beneficiary's choice of doctor only to the extent of ruling out the choice of a "limited provider" system. The price of that freedom of choice, however, has been quite high, for it is the wedge that separates physicians and other decision-makers from cost concerns.

Proposals

In 1977 Alain Enthoven, a special consultant to then HEW Secretary Califano, proposed the Consumer Choice Health Plan, a program for universal comprehensive care based on the principles of competition (Enthoven 1977). The plan would replace today's tax subsidies for the non-aged, nonpoor with a refundable tax credit usable only as a premium contribution toward a qualified health care financing and delivery plan. Traditional insurance plans would be included in the choices. Plans would be available to anyone, independent of job status and without regard for age, sex, race, religion, national origin, or prior medical condition.

Medicare, which is today a large and unwieldy traditional insurance plan, would be replaced by a system of premium subsidies in fixed dollar amounts. Medicare beneficiaries would be able to join the comprehensive care organization of their choice or to retain traditional insurance. If they chose an organization that was effective in controlling costs, they would benefit in the form of reduced copayments or deductibles or broader coverage. Similarly, Medicaid would be replaced by a system of premium subsidies inversely related to income. Low-income persons outside the welfare categories would be eligible for the same income-related premium subsidies as welfare recipients.

In 1979 Senator David Durenberger of Minnesota and Congressman Al Ullman of Oregon each introduced legislation designed to reform health care financing in line with the principles of competition. Both of their proposals would leave health benefits linked to employment for the employed population, but would continue favorable tax treatment only if employers offered choices on an economically fair basis. Senator Durenberger's bill requires that employees be given a choice of three or more distinct plans. Congressman Ullman's bill also requires choices and specifies that the choices must include health maintenance organizations or, if none exist in the area, a low-cost insurance option. Both bills limit the amount of employer contribution that can be excluded from employee taxable income, and require that the contribution be the same whichever plan an employee chooses. The maximum exclusion would be about $120 per month per family in 1980 dollars. Both bills specify rules that apply to choices offered by employers; these rules require that all plans provide "catastrophic expense" coverage (limit beneficiary or member out-of-pocket expenses) and cover or provide at least certain specified basic benefits.

The changes these bills would introduce would expand the market for alternative financing and delivery systems. More such plans would be developed.

Congressman Ullman's bill includes provisions to allow each Medicare beneficiary to join an alternative system and to direct that his average cost to the Medicare program (calculated as the "adjusted average per capita cost" for people in his actuarial category who are not members of alternative systems) be paid, as a premium contribution on his behalf, to that alternative system. Ullman's bill would also mandate demonstration projects to study the feasibility and effectiveness of a competitive system to serve Medicaid beneficiaries such as Project Health already in operation in Multnomah County, Oregon.

PROSPECTS FOR THE FUTURE

The Health Care Financing Administration now projects that total national health care expenditures will rise to $438 billion by 1985 and to $758 billion by 1990. These figures are 10.5 percent and 11.5 percent, respectively, of the projected GNPs. We expect that if a program such as the Durenberger or Ullman proposals were enacted in the early 1980s and the dominant economic incentives in medical care were changed, the total costs by 1990 could be 15 to 20 percent lower than HCFA's projections; the potential savings for the year 1990 are on the order of $115 billion to $150 billion. In the longer run, with a comprehensive system of fair economic competition such as Consumer Choice Health Plan, we believe costs would be at least 25 percent less than they would be under today's system.

There is no natural constituency for competition proposals and they face difficult political obstacles. The burden of rising health care costs is spread through every industry and across both the public and private sectors.

Organizations that represent physicians and hospitals would prefer to maintain the status quo. Physicians tend not to believe that fundamental change is inevitable. Hospitals have, however, experienced some direct regulatory controls and have found them extremely burdensome. Hospital industry leaders are increasingly supportive of competition proposals as an alternative to more regulatory controls.

Commercial insurance companies and organized labor both support regulatory cost control. Organized labor tends to distrust competitive market mechanisms in general and has supported the regulatory proposals of Senator Kennedy. Some commercial insurers have actively developed alternative delivery systems, but most commercial insurance companies support price and capacity controls, apparently as a means of ensuring that one third-party payor does not gain an advantage over another.

Finally, business leaders, though sympathetic to the principles of competition, are unable to make health care competition one of their top legislative priorities. No single employer sees itself as bearing a disproportionate share of the escalating costs.

As the fiscal pressures created by those costs intensify, the inevitability of fundamental change should become increasingly clear. We hope and expect that many of these interested groups will then support the competition strategy as the best chance for achieving cost control while preserving flexibility and responsiveness to consumers in this vital industry.

DISCUSSION

BOSKIN: When I think about the health care problem, I keep coming back to one potentially great gain we all hope will happen which can cause a tremendous disaster if it is not handled properly. That is, gains in the life expectancy of the elderly. The elderly life expectancy went up between two and three years between 1960 and 1980. I don't think we know yet whether those are enjoyable or painful years at the end of life. It is a fact that those years consume a vastly disproportionate share of health expenditures—especially of those that are federally financed. If we, by virtue of research or luck or some other way, start to come up with cures for certain types of cancer and things like that, and we enable ourselves to expand the life-expectancy of the elderly still further—something we all think of as desirable barring extreme agony and pain at the end of life—the pressures for increased health expenditures implied by these advances may potentially swamp all income gains we can achieve, and the social tension between the working taxpayers and the elderly will greatly intensify.

DRURY: I think you have raised an important point. As average life expectancy increases, we can expect to spend more on health services. However, there does seem to be a biological limit on life expectancy, and that limit is now estimated to be about eighty-five years on average. There have been big gains in life expectancy for several centuries as causes of premature death have been reduced or eliminated. But we obviously can't expect to eliminate death altogether. There are not likely to be more large gains in life expectancy, but there may be some improvements that create financial pressures in the direction you are suggesting.

I think we want to establish financing structures that will achieve the most with the dollars we can allocate to this industry. High-technology care in the last year of life is not necessarily the best medical care to buy. We want to create incentives, to identify individuals for whom high technology, costly care, is not best. For some diseases there are low-technology humane forms of care that by many definitions are superior. Today's financing structures, however, provide no incentives to develop and apply lower-cost alternatives. More total dollars may need to be spent, but I also think we can do better with the dollars we have.

WEINBERGER: One reason for the explosion of health costs is that malpractice suits have been allowed to run wild, and the defensive medicine costs are enormous. This is not only because a doctor or a hospital knows that when a particular service is called for it is all right to furnish it, even if it is unnecessary, because insurance will pay for it. These services are also furnished to build an anticipatory defense against a malpractice suit. I think substantial revisions ought to be made in the tort laws of the various states to eliminate such things as the fees that are charged based upon successful outcome and on virtually unlimited statutes of limitations.

VIII

Summary and Conclusion

14

MICHAEL J. BOSKIN

An Overview

The current economic situation. General goals to be pursued. A package of recommended policies. The future.

The decade of the 1970s has been a time of trouble for the U.S. economy. Inflation and sluggish economic growth as well as waste and inefficiency in a variety of economic sectors challenge policymakers in the decade ahead and beyond. The opportunities to restore a healthy economy, however, are enormous.

While the authors in this volume differ on some specifics, there is a strong consensus about what has happened to our economy and what can and should be done to improve its performance. The U.S. economy has veered off course, and much of this malfunction can be traced to man-made disincentives to produce income and wealth and to allocate resources efficiently. There is also a clear consensus that our major economic goal for the 1980s must be to restore healthy noninflationary economic growth and that this can only be accomplished in an environment with a more stable, predictable, and slower rate of monetary expansion, a slower rate of growth in government spending, and a concerted effort to remove disincentives that obstruct working, saving, investing, and innovating.

In short, we must remake our monetary policy and the government's spending, tax, and regulatory policies. If we do not begin to control inflation and promote our economic growth, the myriad of untoward consequences created by the present situation will exacerbate as the years of sluggish activity drag on. We must begin to reverse this process soon or suffer even graver economic and social consequences in the future.

Our major need is for a steady, coherent, coordinated, long-run series of goals and for a general policy framework to achieve these goals. Without abandoning government's substantial accomplishments, such as greatly mitigating the economic distress attributable to unemployment and poverty, we must make government spending much more cost-conscious and target-effective. Without deluding ourselves about the possibilities of rapidly reducing inflation or instantly promoting our rate of growth, we must begin to unravel the disincentives for capital formation that high inflation, high and rising taxes, and government regulatory policy have created.

Without forgetting the genuine desires of many in our population, as they become wealthier, for more leisure time and more nontraditional goods and services, we must begin to sift through the regulatory morass that hinders the country's economic progress and, in doing so, strike a more effective balance between traditional economic needs and desires and those for less-traditional goods and services. Without ignoring our own national interest, we must resist the lure of protectionism and work to liberalize trade throughout the world. Without neglecting the fact that markets sometimes do not work very well, we must recognize that this is also sometimes true of governments. Perhaps the pendulum has swung too far, and it is time to restore increased reliance on market mechanisms to allocate resources, especially in such large and growing sectors as energy and health.

We cannot cure all the economy's problems instantly. With the wisdom and political courage to adopt the longer view of our economic and social welfare, we must begin to design and implement short-run economic policies with longer-term implications in mind. Rather than giving in to short-term political expediency, we must have a coherent and logical course of action in all of the spheres of economic policy. Those general goals must consist of:

1. A slower and more predicatable growth of the money supply by the Federal Reserve;

2. A slower growth rate in nondefense government spending and a more cost-effective and target-effective revision of spending programs;

3. A reduction in overall relative tax burdens heavily geared towards removing the severe obstacles taxes and high inflation have placed in the way of saving, investment, and innovation, but only in the context of an overall fiscal policy which takes some of the pressure off the Federal Reserve in this anti-inflation fight—i.e., a policy of budget balance or modest surpluses;

4. A more reasonable balance of economic and social priorities in the government regulatory process;

5. Increased reliance on market mechanisms in energy, health, and the economy in general;

6. Increased recognition of world economic interdependence, the U.S. role in it, and the need to promote genuine world trade liberalization.

Obviously this set of policies must form a package implemented steadily and continuously over a long period—certainly over many years, perhaps decades. The gains from doing so will be enormous: restoration of noninflationary steady economic progress, improved efficiency in the economy, decreased reliance on government in areas where the private economy can do better, and the substantially reduced social and economic tension among different population groups that will ensue from a growing rather than a stagnant economy.

A useful first series of policies, in addition to the general policy prescription for the Federal Reserve, might well include the following package:

1. Budget reforms such as those in the Budget Reform Act discussed in Chapter 9, which would enhance the prospects for slowing government spending growth and making spending more efficient;

2. Gradually phased-in tax cuts moving partway to the complete integration of the corporate and personal income tax and shifting to an expenditure tax; this might include simplification and acceleration of depreciation, reduction of the corporate tax rate, and gradually phased-in tax cuts in the personal income taxes' marginal tax rates; perhaps indexation for inflation, and certainly *only* in the context of a tight overall fiscal policy of budget balance or surpluses;

3. A moratorium on new nondefense spending programs (unless financed by cost savings in current ones), if necessary to provide budgetary restraint and the resources for noninflationary tax cuts;

4. A rapid reevaluation of existing government regulatory policy, heavily focused at the start on removing regulation in the energy sector and on rationalizing implementation of many overlapping health, safety, and pollution regulations confronting individuals and firms.

A new course of economic policies for the 1980s and beyond must be developed and implemented if we are to restore that spirit of vitality, creativity, productivity, and resourcefulness with which we so often described our nation and its economy, its possibilities and its accomplishments, in the past. These policies will not be easy to implement because they must overcome severe political obstacles, especially those concerning the short-run bias of political decision-making.

We have the economic capability of reversing the downward trend of our economy; whether we have the political will and the capability of doing so remains to be seen. It is clear that the costs of not surmounting these political obstacles extend well beyond our own economic well-being and that of our children and grandchildren. They include the threatened loss of political, diplomatic, and military leadership in the free world as the important example set for the mass of mankind—living on the brink of subsistence, tottering between relatively free societies and dictatorship—becomes extinguished. Our economic success stands as an important symbol of the compatibility—indeed, perhaps the correlation—of free political institutions, free markets, and rapid economic progress. Thus, how we respond to our economic challenge may influence decisively the evolution of many of the world's economic and political systems.

NOTES

1. Michael J. Boskin: "U.S. Economy at the Crossroads"

1. Two types of issue are raised by the current and future world energy problem. The first relates to questions concerning efficient energy use. The second relates to the threat of short-run disruption to the United States—indeed, world—economy from a substantial reduction in world oil production. Since our energy bill has grown from a fraction of 1 percent of GNP to over 4 percent, price changes or supply cutoffs are much more disruptive than they were in the past. Substantial price increases could handle a disruption of the sort that occurred in Iran (5 million barrels a day) without drastic disruption, but a shutdown of the oil fields in Saudi Arabia or of several smaller producers simultaneously would seriously disrupt our economy. The important point is that this would happen only with a large reduction in world oil production, *not* from an embargo by some countries on sales to the United States. The latter, without a slowdown in production, would simply permit us to buy more from other countries, and would let Japan, Germany, France, etc., buy more from the countries refusing to sell to us.

2. Michael J. Boskin: "Economic Growth and Productivity"

1. Put simply, we are growing too rapidly if the opportunity cost of foregoing current consumption today in order to increase our capacity to produce goods and services in the future does not yield a return sufficient to make future increases in the standard of living, discounted to the present, worth more than the foregone consumption. Conversely, we would be growing too slowly if, on average, the opportunity cost of the foregone consumption today was much less than the value of the increased consumption we could have in the future by diverting some resources today away from current consumption to investment.

2. In the year from the first quarter of 1979 to the first quarter of 1980, the after-tax, after-inflation average earnings in the United States declined by 7.9 percent; this decline was so large that it exceeded the personal saving rate.

3. The number of new patents granted in 1979 was a recent low, and an historically high percentage was granted to foreigners.

4. Consider a simple example. In a world with no inflation and a nominal interest rate to savers of 4 percent, a person in the 50 percent tax bracket would receive a 2 percent after-tax return. With no inflation this would also be the net-of-tax-and-inflation rate of return. If the inflation rate increases to 12 percent, however, much empirical

evidence suggests that on average the nominal before-tax interest rate will increase about point for point with the inflation rate, so in this case it would rise by 12 percentage points from 4 percent to 16 percent. Even without considering the possibility that our saver will be driven into a higher tax bracket, the 50 percent tax rate reduces the after-tax return to 8 percent; with a 12 percent inflation rate the after-tax, after-inflation rate of return is now −4 percent. Thus, the inflation, combined with our unindexed tax system which taxes nominal interest, has reduced the after-tax-and-inflation return from +2 to −4 percent. The tax-induced disincentives to save thus are worsened substantially as our inflation rate increases.

5. For example, we obtain more than one-third of our tax receipts from taxes on investment income; the corresponding figure for Germany is one-sixth, and for France, one-ninth.

6. Such as is sometimes argued in support of large tax rate cuts independent of curtailing spending growth.

7. The treasury set of estimated service lives and asset depreciation range bears little relation to true economic depreciation and is highly complicated. Something like the 10−5−3 Bill would be a great improvement.

3. John L. Scadding: "Inflation: A Perspective from the 1970s"

1. The figures in Table 1 use changes in the deflator for gross national product (GNP) to measure inflation. Another popular measure of inflation is to use changes in the consumer price index (CPI). Until recently these two measures gave roughly the same answers. Starting in 1979, however, the two measures began to diverge. Thus from December 1978 to December 1979 the CPI rose by 13.3 percent; the yearly increase in the GNP deflator, on the other hand, was only 9.0 percent.

By and large, economists tend to view changes in the GNP deflator as the better measure of inflation. The deflator is more broadly based than the CPI because it includes the cost of investment goods and government output as well as the cost of consumer goods and services. It also takes into account the fact that people reduce purchases of commodities whose prices have risen more rapidly than the average. The CPI, on the other hand, calculates the cost of a fixed basket of goods, and therefore does not reflect this substitution. Consequently the CPI tends to overstate the cost of living when the price of an important commodity rises significantly. This is what happened in 1979, of course, with the sharp rise in the price of oil, and it goes part of the way to explaining why the CPI rose faster than the deflator.

The CPI also does not treat the cost of housing in an entirely satisfactory way. The CPI includes what it costs to *buy* a house when the theoretically correct measure is the cost of owning and maintaining a house—the cost of housing *services*, in other words. The importance of this difference, however, has been overdramatized in popular discussion. Estimates by the Bureau of Labor Standards (which is responsible for compiling the CPI), for example, indicate that a theoretically "purer" treatment of housing costs would have knocked only 1 percentage point off the CPI in 1979. Moreover, the treatment of housing costs in the GNP deflator leaves something to be desired as well. The GNP deflator measures housing costs by their rental equivalent—by what it would cost to rent equivalent housing. This has probably led the deflator to understate the rise in the cost of housing because rents have tended to lag behind other prices.

2. This shift away from cash balances, incidentally, remains something of a puzzle. Fundamentally, it is a reaction to the higher tax rate on money which the current high rate of inflation represents. But relatively high inflation rates have been with us since the late 1960s. Some reduction in people's willingness to hold money was then observed, and again in the early 1970s as the high inflation rates persisted. However, neither of these experiences would have allowed one to predict the sharp break in people's behavior that occurred after 1974.

3. This focus allows us to sidestep the issue of whether government deficits are to blame for inflation. If inflation is a monetary phenomenon, deficits can be said to cause inflation only to the extent that they lead to excessive money growth. It is not obvious from the evidence that this has been the case. However, to the extent that it is true, the more interesting question is why monetary policy allowed it to happen.

4. By 1980, however, personal saving had fallen precipitously. Further, many changes such as those in the age and household structure of the population, labor force participation of women and elderly workers, life expectancy, government programs potentially substituting for private saving, had changed in the quarter-century and each of these potentially affected private savings in addition to the effects of taxes and inflation.

4. John H. Pencavel: "The Nature of the Contemporary Unemployment Problem"

1. I am indebted to John Cogan for his comments on a preliminary draft and for sharing with me some results from his ongoing research on youth employment. I also benefited from comments by Michael Boskin and Lawrence Chickering. The regression equations whose results are reported in the appendix were estimated by Kathy Krumm.

2. See, for instance, the references in Toikka (1974, pp. 62–72).

3. These results on schooling and unemployment are contained in Nickell (1979, pp. 117–31) and in Ashenfelter and Ham (1979, pp. 99–116).

4. "A crucial factor in the streetcorner man's lack of job commitment is the overall value he places on the job. For his part, the streetcorner man puts no lower value on the job than does the larger society around him. . . . Neither the streetcorner man who performs these jobs nor the society which requires him to perform them assesses the job as one 'worth doing and worth doing well.' Both employee and employer are contemptuous of the job" (Liebow 1967, pp. 57–58).

5. See, for instance, the arguments of Killingsworth (1963). The best response to the "structuralist" case is Solow (1964).

5. David J. Teece: "The New Social Regulation: Implications and Alternatives"

1. I wish to thank Lee Bach, Michael Boskin, Lawrence Chickering, Robert Flanagan, Victor Goldberg, Carsten Kowalczyk, Almarin Phillips, and Garth Soloner for many helpful comments. The views expressed, however, are entirely those of the author.

2. To construct these estimates, Robert DeFina surveyed the available literature and extracted estimates of the costs of specific regulator programs in 1976. This data

was made as consistent as possible and then aggregated. Weidenbaum (1979, p. 23) has subsequently applied the 1976 multiplier (20) of administrative to compliance costs to come up with the estimates for 1977, 1978, and 1979.

3. I am indebted to Michael Boskin for this comparison.

4. Other contributing factors may include slower growth in the amount of capital per laborer, the decline in R&D expenditures, the changing composition of the work force, and higher energy prices. The Council of Economic Advisors estimates that the diversion of resources to comply with government regulation may have accounted for as much as 0.3 of a percentage point of the decline. The council also recognizes that an increasing proportion of R&D has been aimed at compliance with regulatory require-ments (*Economic Report of the President 1980*, p. 87).

5. The median estimated social return was about 56 percent, while the median pri-vate rate of return was about 25 percent (Mansfield et al. 1977, p. 234).

6. A "public good" is defined as any commodity or service whose benefits are not depleted by an additional user and for which it is generally difficult or impossible to ex-clude people from its benefits, even if they are unwilling to pay for it.

7. An activity is said to generate beneficial or detrimental externalities if activity causes incidental benefits or damages to others, and no offsetting compensation is pro-vided to those who generate the externality or are paid by them.

8. In the case of waste discharge standards, for example, economic efficiency would be achieved if one succeeded in establishing a series of differential standards suited to the special conditions of each firm; but this, of course, involves obtaining comprehen-sive data on the costs of each firm.

9. Administrative procedures are often superior to market processes when intensive coordination and adjustment is needed. See, for example, Chandler (1977).

10. The low levels of liability neutralize incentives to take precautions against poten-tially serious accidents.

11. Gross benefits are ordinarily taken as the area under the demand curve.

12. A well-known example is that of Lave and Seskin (1970).

13. For a methodological statement, see, for example, Polinsky and Rubinfeld (1977).

6.   John T. Cuddington, Ronald I. McKinnon: "The United States and the World Economy"

1. The discussion of postwar trade legislation contained in this section draws exten-sively from Kreinin (1979, Chapter 14) and Root (1978, Chapter 7).

2. For a more detailed empirical and analytical discussion of the ideas in this sec-tion, see McKinnon (1979).

7.   John B. Shoven: "Federal Government Taxes and Tax Reform"

1. There are some exceptions—taxes that actually improve economic efficiency, such as the one on cigarettes. One could argue that because cigarette smoke bothers nonsmokers, the tax brings the individual's interests and society's interests closer together rather than farther apart. Unfortunately, it is generally conceded that effi-ciency-improving taxes alone are not numerous enough to raise all government revenue.

2. These and other ideas were more thoroughly examined less than three years ago in Boskin (1977).

3. Economists have not reached complete agreement on the answer to this question, although the consensus is that the tax is borne in the long run by all owners of capital.

9. Michael J. Boskin: "Federal Government Spending and Budget Policy"

1. The budget balance or surplus, as opposed to deficit, either will directly reduce inflationary pressure by curtailing demand or at least reduce the federal government's borrowing pressure on interest rates and hence allow the Federal Reserve to slow money growth without large interest rate increases. Further, the tax cuts themselves will *not* have much direct effect on inflation; they will increase capital formation and hence productivity (and future real income), but these productivity gains mostly will go into higher wages, not lower unit labor costs.

2. Since we have largely eliminated poverty (see Chapter 1) in an absolute sense, we have the opportunity to slow transfer payment growth as a fraction of GNP by targeting transfers more specifically to the poor and decreasing the growth of transfers to the nonpoor. A relativist definition of poverty would obviously make this much more difficult.

3. Some argue for increasing the costs while continuing to discount at the after-tax rate of return earned by savers; others would prefer a weighted average of this return and the marginal product of capital of the private sector, the opportunity costs to society for foregoing some private investment, the weights reflecting the proportions of foregone investment and consumption in order to make funds available for the government project.

4. Essentially, the size of a project should be enlarged to the point where its marginal benefits equal its marginal, or incremental, costs; a project should be built or undertaken in a period in which the discounted present value of benefits minus costs is maximized; the projects should be undertaken if, and only if, the present value of benefits exceeds the present value of costs, each discounted appropriately to the present.

5. It seems clear that in most advanced economies the citizenry has opted through the government to provide various forms of transfer payments to individuals which are in part intended to ameliorate extreme destitution. Many of these programs now provide commodities or their subsidization rather than income directly. It may well be that for certain types of goods and services, society as a whole is willing to pay more than the individual recipients of the services were able to buy. This may well lead to a case for a "basic needs" approach to social cost-benefit analysis as opposed to explicit distributional weighting of benefits and costs (see Harberger 1980).

6. Since each individual cost-benefit analysis proceeds as if it were the marginal or additional program, there must be some place in the overall evaluation of budgetary policy where the combined effects of the entire budget package—spending, tax, and debt—on the overall economy must be assessed.

7. Again, it cannot be overemphasized that the differences in interpretation about the high employment level and differences concerning the possibilities of increasing *real* GNP by expansion of government spending, except in times of extreme sustained

unemployment, suggest that we may well be deluding ourselves in using the estimated current budget deficit or surplus, or a corresponding high employment level by comparison as a measure of the overall countercyclical fiscal impact of the federal government.

8. Examination of the current deficit is itself misleading; because of inflation, the real value of previously issued debt has fallen. If we took the difference in the real value of the government debt between 1979 and 1980, the government "paid off" $12 billion. Of course, the additional new debt off-the-books is not included in this total.

9. While I shall not go into this issue here, it is worth noting that the Congressional Budget Office (CBO) also presents estimates of the potential changes in the next fiscal year's current law revenues, outlays and deficits caused by changes in the economy such as a higher or lower employment rate, inflation rate, or interest rate. For example, the CBO estimates that a 1 percentage point higher inflation rate would reduce revenues by approximately $20 billion and add about $5 billion to outlays, thereby increasing the deficit by $25 billion or so. Similarly, a 1 percentage point higher inflation rate than estimated would add about $5 to $7 billion in incremental revenues and $1 or $2 billion to outlays, thereby reducing the deficit by about $5 billion.

10. The basic point is that for capital items any excess of expenditures over receipts on capital account does not change the net asset position of the government since the new debt is matched by a new government asset. In the capital account, the purchase of assets would be included as expenditures and sales of government assets and funds transferred from the current account to cover depreciation receipts would be counted as receipts. Depreciation charges or government assets would appear as an expenditure in the current account. If the rate of purchase of government assets continued at a constant rate over time, eventually depreciation charges would equal new outlays for depreciable assets and the size of the current account deficit would be the same as that in the unified capital and current account. The current account of the divided budget would show smaller deficits than the unified budget when the capital outlays were increasing over time and a larger deficit when capital outlays were falling. The difference between the deficits or surpluses in the current account of the divided budget and in a unified budget would be smaller, the higher the depreciation rate on government assets or the shorter their useful life, for then the depreciation charges will show up more rapidly as a charge in the current budget. Maintaining a separate capital account is particularly important, since we are almost certainly drastically underestimating spending and the deficit by failing to account for the sharp reduction in government investments.

11. Even if we do not go to separate capital accounting, there ought to be a place in the budget where we can get a notion of when the budget deficit is being reduced by postponing repairs, maintenance, and replacement of government capital.

12. Some modest steps in this direction have recently been undertaken.

10. Laurence J. Kotlikoff: "Social Security and Welfare: What We Have, Want, and Can Afford"

1. I am grateful to Michael Boskin, Lawrence Chickering, Tom Gustafson, Tom Seale, and Jon Skinner for very helpful discussions.

2. *Economic Report of the President, 1980,* p. 288. These figures do not include off-budget items. See Boskin, Chapter 9, for a discussion.

3. These figures do not correct for possible selection bias that could arise if those familiar with greater taste for food are more likely to apply for food stamps.

4. The earnings test applies between ages 62 and 65 as well, but at these ages it does not, on average, mean a reduction in lifetime benefits due to work because of social security's "actuarial" reduction in benefits at these ages.

5. Peter Diamond (1977) provides an argument for the earnings test; namely, that social security benefits can be thought of as insurance paid to workers who unexpectedly discover they can no longer continue to work. My own view is that this is a minor function of social security and that its principle function is to force people to save for their old age. Under this view, each individual should receive benefits in his old age, independent of whether or not he continues to work.

6. One would want to adjust the New York figure for the higher cost of living in New York City.

7. The earnings test applies from the ages of 62 to 72, but the actuarial reduction of benefits for early retirement between 62 and 65 constitute a work incentive that, on average, offsets the implicit tax on earnings.

8. This calculation assumes that for every dollar earned, 40 cents is claimed as a working expense under AFDC. This lowers the AFDC nominal 67 percent tax rate to an effective 40.2 percent. See Lurie (1974) for a discussion of effective AFDC tax rates.

9. U.S. Department of Labor 1979a, p. 113. These figures are for 1975, a recession year, and are probably an underestimate of the average employment rates of AFDC mothers.

10. The revenue maximizing formula for a proportional tax, t, on earnings is t = 1/1+B where B is the elasticity of labor supply. Hausman (1979, p. 53) reports a B of roughly 0.5.

11. Henry S. Rowen: "Defense Spending and the Uncertain Future"

1. A peculiar feature of the politics of SALT II is that most European heads of government have supported it. My belief is that they have done so because of their heightened sense of vulnerability, the tangible payoffs from detente, political pressure from the left, and reduced confidence in U.S. strength and leadership. In short, this support is a manifestation of what has been called the "Finlandization" of Europe.

2. The FY 1981 budget assumes that inflation in calendar years 1980 and 1981 will be 9.0 and 8.6 percent, respectively (using the GNP deflator; for the consumer price index it assumes 10.4 and 8.6 percent, respectively). This estimate of inflation appears much too low. If FY 1981 turns out to be 3.0 percent higher than estimated in the budget, then the perceived real increase in defense outlays will have vanished.

12. James L. Sweeney: "Energy Problems and Policies"

1. I would like to thank, without implicating, Michael Boskin, Lawrence Chickering, Steve Powell, Ralph Samuelson, Dorothy Sheffield, and John Weyant for their helpful comments, and Henry Rowen for providing so many of the ideas adopted here.

2. Based upon USGS *Circular 725* mean estimate, updated for discoveries since 1974.

3. Noncompliance areas are those regions whose ambient concentrations of gaseous residuals exceed the federal standards.

4. In particular is the requirement for 90 percent sulfur removal from coal even if low-sulfur Western coal is burned. This regulation removes some of the competitive advantage of this lower-cost, lower sulfur-content coal.

5. These statistics exclude imports intended for the Strategic Petroleum Reserve.

6. This assumes that the elasticity of demand for oil is roughly the same in each country. Differences in these demand elasticities will lead to differences in the percentage cutbacks, with those countries which are most flexible facing the greatest proportional consumption reduction.

7. The terms "cost" and "price" should not be confused. The cost of energy is the quantity of goods and services used up by the society to produce or import a given quantity of energy. The price is the buying power an individual must give up to gain access to the given quantity. Taxes can increase price above costs, while price controls can reduce prices below costs. The average cost to the United States of importing a barrel of oil is equal to the price per barrel paid to the exporting country plus any shipping costs, even if the production cost in the exporting country is less than the price charged.

8. See Sweeney (1979*b*) for a more complete justification.

9. This assertion follows because the energy price-induced reduction in the value of capital equipment cannot exceed the discounted sum of energy used multiplied by the change in energy price.

10. This assumes a short-run crude oil price elasticity of 0.05, a figure consistent with current evidence, an insignificant short-run supply response in the United States, and an original world oil price of $30/barrel. With a short-run elasticity of 0.10, a 4.5 percent GNP loss is obtained, prices triple, and the net cost of imports is $180 billion.

11. See Sweeney (1977) for more complete discussion of the system of price controls.

12. The specific prices equalled the posted prices as of 1973, plus $1.35. Old oil was defined as that quantity produced in the specific field during corresponding months in 1972.

13. "All" is, in fact, a euphemism. Small refineries were given a disproportionate share of entitlement benefits which compensated for the fact that these refineries were in general not economically viable.

14. The production rate must be reduced for a full year before the property qualifies as a stripper property. However, from then on it is exempt from price controls.

15. The Jones Act prohibits foreign-flag ships to transport cargo between two American ports.

16. This "market power premium" is a pure wealth transfer effect, associated with avoiding a wealth transfer from the United States to the oil-exporting nations. The basic theory of such a premium is developed in literature on "optimal tariffs."

17. To illustrate, assume that a 0.1 mmb/d increase in the U.S. oil imports would increase world price by $0.20 per barrel. The daily cost of importing 8 mmb/d would be $240 million ($30 × 8 mmb/d); the daily cost of importing 8.1 mmb/d would be $244.62 million ($30.20 × 8.1 mmb/d). The additional expenditure to import an additional 0.1 mmb/d is $4.62 million/day: the marginal expenditure per barrel is $46.20. In this case, the "market power premium" is $16/barrel.

18. For example, rough estimates in *Energy Future* (Stobaugh and Yergen 1979) cite market power premium ranging from $20 to $70 per barrel. This issue is being addressed in the current Energy Modeling Forum Study (1980 "World Oil Study Design.")

19. In the example above, the $0.20/barrel increase in world oil price imposes costs on the non-U.S. oil importers of $10.80 million per day ($0.20 × 54) and increases OPEC revenues by $12.40 million/day ($0.20 × 62). Thus, if the interests of all oil importers were considered, the appropriate market power premium would be $124 per barrel, with 87 percent of the benefit being conferred on other countries. If the interests of the OPEC nations were included, this premium would be reduced to zero.

20. Marginal prices based upon Federal Energy Regulatory Commission, "Typical Electric Bills."

21. Marginal costs for electricity vary widely by time of use, with high costs in peak demand periods and lower costs in off-peak periods. To make prices reflect marginal costs, time-of-use pricing should be adopted wherever practical. Such pricing will partially level electric loads and will reduce average costs of electricity generation.

22. In addition, health effects of trace metals in coal may be important. Synthetic fuels may lead to a variety of environmental insults.

23. Some of these programs do contribute to the regulatory morass. Thus while their goals are laudable, the methods for achieving the goals are questionable.

24. The distinction helps sharpen the concept of "insecurity premium." This premium is associated with characteristics of the capital stock rather than with the rate of oil imports. Reductions in oil imports associated with capital stock changes reduce insecurity more than do equal reductions associated with changing capital stock utilization. This implies that energy prices alone cannot be sufficient to guide markets to the correct energy efficiency of the capital stock and to its correct utilization. Additional mechanisms such as credits, taxes, and standards on new capital equipment are required.

25. International cooperation is critical. If some oil importers imposed the tax while others did not, the world oil price would be reduced by less than the tax, participating nations would be harmed, and the nonparticipants would benefit.

26. A hypothetical example will illustrate how the subsidy on gross production translates to a larger subsidy on net production. Assume that every gallon of alcohol production uses 0.6 gallons of gasoline as an input; the output alcohol is perfectly substitutable for gasoline; costs of alcohol production are $1.50 gallon in addition to the gasoline cost. In this case, a *gross* output of one gallon translates to a net output of 0.4 gallon of alcohol. Costs to the producer are: $0.78 for input gasoline (assumed to be priced at $1.30 per gallon) plus $1.50 for other costs, equaling $2.28 per gallon. Revenues are $1.30 for the alcohol plus $1.40 subsidy, equaling $2.70 per gallon. Thus, production is profitable. The total subsidy of $1.40 was paid for a net production of 0.4 gallon, translating to a $3.50 per gallon of net production, or $147 per barrel subsidy.

REFERENCES

Aaron, Henry J. 1973. *Why Is Welfare So Hard to Reform?* Washington, DC: Brookings Institution.

Anderson, M. 1979. *Welfare.* Stanford, CA: Hoover Institution.

Antos, J., Mellow, S., and Triplett, J. E. 1979. "What Is a Current Equivalent to Unemployment Rates of the Past?" *Monthly Labor Review* 102, 3 (March).

Ashenfelter, Orley, and Ham, John. 1979. "Education, Unemployment, and Earnings." *Journal of Political Economy* 87, 5 (October), Part 2.

Barro, Robert J. 1974. "Are Government Bonds Net Wealth?" *Journal of Political Economy*, No. 82 (November-December).

———. 1978. "The Impact of Social Security on Private Savings—Evidence from the U.S. Time Series." Washington, DC: American Enterprise Institute.

Barth, Michael C., Carcagno, George J., and Palmer, John L. 1974. *Toward an Effective Income Support System: Problems, Prospects, and Choices.* Madison, WI: Institute for Research on Poverty, University of Wisconsin-Madison.

Baumol, William J., and Oates, Wallace E. 1979. *Economics, Environmental Policy, and the Quality of Life.* Englewood Cliffs, NJ: Prentice Hall.

Becker, Gary S. 1975. *Human Capital.* 2d ed. Cambridge, MA: National Bureau of Economic Research.

Berndt, Ernest R., and Wood, David O. 1975. "Technology, Prices and the Derived Demand for Energy." *Review of Economics and Statistics* 57 (August).

Blackhurst, Richard, Marian, Nicolas, Tumlir, Jan. 1977. *Trade Liberalization, Protectionism and Interdependence.* GATT Studies in International Trade No. 5. Geneva, Switzerland: GATT.

Boskin, Michael J., ed. 1977. *The Crisis in Social Security: Problems and Prospects.* Rev. 1978. San Francisco, CA: Institute for Contemporary Studies.

———. 1978. "Taxation, Saving and the Rate of Interest." *Journal of Political Economy* 86 (April).

———, Arvin, Mary, and Cone, Kenneth. 1980. "Alternative Solutions to the Long-Run Social Security Funding Crisis." Mimeo (March).

————, and Shoven, John B. 1980. "Issues in the Taxation of Capital Income in the United States." *Proceedings of the American Economic Association* 70, 2 (May).

Bowers, H. I. 1977. "Capital Investment Cost Estimates for Large Nuclear and Coal-Fired Power Plants." Oak Ridge, TN: Oak Ridge National Laboratory.

Cagan, Phillip. 1978. "The Reduction of Inflation by Slack Demand." In *Contemporary Economic Problems*, edited by William Fellner. Washington, DC: American Enterprise Institute.

————, and Lipsey, Robert E. 1978. *The Financial Effects of Inflation*. Cambridge, MA: National Bureau of Economic Research.

Campbell, Rita Ricardo. 1977. *Social Security: Promise and Reality*. Stanford, CA: Hoover Institution Press.

Carter, Jimmy. 1980. "State of the Union Message, 23 January 1980." *Presidential Documents*.Washington, DC: Government Printing Office.

Central Intelligence Agency. 1977. "The Impending Oil Crisis, 1977." ER 77–10147U.

Chandler, Alfred D. 1977. *The Visible Hand: The Managerial Revolution in American Business*. Cambridge, MA: Harvard University Press.

Cogan, John R. 1980. "Racial Differences in Youth Employment and the Demand for Agricultural Labor: 1950–1970." Mimeo (March).

Congressional Budget Office. 1979. "Profile of Health Care Coverage: The Haves and Have-Nots" (March). Washington, DC: Congressional Budget Office.

Council on Environmental Quality. 1980. *Environmental Quality—1979*. Washington, DC: Government Printing Office.

Denison, Edward F. 1974 *Accounting for U.S. Economic Growth, 1929–1969*. Washington, DC: Brookings Institution.

————. 1969. *Accounting for U.S. Economic Growth*.Washington, DC: Brookings Institution.

————. 1979*b*. "Effects of Selected Changes in the Institutional and Human Environment upon Output per Unit of Input." *Survey of Current Business* (January).

Diamond, Peter. 1977. "A Framework for Social Security Analysis." *Journal of Public Economics*.

Dyckman, Zachary Y. 1978. "A Study of Physicians' Fees" (March). Washington, DC: Council on Wage and Price Stability, Executive Office of the President.

Economic Report of the President, 1980. Washington, DC: U.S. Government Printing Office.

Energy Modeling Forum. 1980*a*. "Aggeegate Elasticity of Energy Demand." Stanford, CA: Stanford University.

————. 1980*b*. "World Oil Study Design." EMF 6.1. Stanford, CA: Stanford University.

Enthoven, Alain C. 1977. *Consumer-Choice Health Plan.* A National Health Insurance Proposal prepared for the Secretary of the Department of Health, Education, and Welfare Joseph Califano (22 September).

Feldstein, Martin S. 1974. "Social Security, Induced Retirement, and Aggregate Capital Accumulation." *Journal of Political Economy,* No. 82 (September-October).

———. 1979. "The Welfare Cost of Permanent Inflation and Optional Short-Run Monetary Policy." *Journal of Political Economy* 89 (August).

———, and Horioka, C. 1979. "Domestic Savings and International Capital Flow." NBER Working Paper No. 310. Cambridge, MA: National Bureau of Economic Research.

———, and Summers, Lawrence. 1978. "Inflation, Tax Rates and the Long-Term Interest Rate." *Brookings Papers in Economic Activity* (1). Washington, DC: Brookings Institution.

Fischer, S., and Modigliani, F. 1978. "Aspects of the Costs of Inflation." *American Economic Review.*

Fisher, I. 1942. *Constructive Income Taxation.* New York: Harper Publishing Company.

Freeland, Mark, et al. 1980. "Projections of National Health Expenditures, 1980, 1985, and 1990." *Health Care Financing Review* (Winter). Washington, DC: Health Care Financing Administration.

Fullerton, D.; King, A. T.; Shoven, John B.; Whalley, J. 1979. "Tax Integration in the U.S.: A General Equilibrium Approach." NBER Working Paper No. 337R. Cambridge, MA: National Bureau of Economic Research.

Fullerton, D., Shoven, John B., and Whalley, J. 1979. "Dynamic General Equilibrium Impacts of Replacing the U.S. Income Tax with a Progressive Consumption Tax." NBER Working Paper. Cambridge, MA: National Bureau of Economic Research.

Ginsburg, Paul B., and Koretz, Daniel M. 1979. "The Effects of PSROs on Health Care Costs: Current Findings and Future Evaluations." Washington, DC: Congressional Budget Office.

Gordon, Robert J. 1980. "A Consistent Characterization of a Near-Century of Price Behavior." NBER Working Paper No. 455 (February). Cambridge, MA: National Bureau of Economic Research.

Griffin, James. 1974. "An Econometric Evaluation of Sulfur Taxes." *Journal of Political Economy* 82 (July-August).

Hamermech, Daniel S. 1977. *Jobless Pay and the Economy.* Baltimore, MD: Johns Hopkins University Press.

Harberger, Arnold. 1980. " Notes on Comparing the Basic Needs and Distributional Weights Approach to Social Cost-Benefit Analysis." Mimeo. University of Chicago.

Hausman, H.A. 1979. "The Effect of Taxes on Labor Supply." Paper prepared for Brookings Conference on Taxation, 18–19 October.

Health Care Financing Administration. 1979. "Professional Standards Review Organization 1978 Program Evaluation." HEW Publication No. (HCFA) 03000 (January). Washington, DC: U.S. Department of Health, Education, and Welfare.

Heffernan, W. Joseph, Jr. 1973. "Variations in Negative Tax Rates in Current Public Assistance Programs: An Example of Administrative Discretion." *Journal of Human Resources* 8 (supplement).

Heller, Walter W., and Boskin, Michael J. 1979. "Two Perspectives on Carter's Anti-Inflation Policy." *Taxing & Spending* 2, 1 (February).

Hellinger, Fred J. 1976. "The Effect of Certificate-of-Need Legislation on Hospital Investment." *Inquiry* 13, 2 (June).

Hill, J. D. , et al. 1978. "A Randomized Trial of Home versus Hospital Management for Patients with Suspected Myocardial Infarction." *The Lancet* (22 April).

Hill, Martha S., and Corcoran, Mary. 1979. "The Incidence and Consequences of Short-Run and Long-Run Unemployment." In *Five Thousand American Families—Patterns in Economic Progress*, edited by Greg J. Duncan and James N. Morgan. Vol. 7. Ann Arbor, MI: University of Michigan Survey Research Center.

———. 1979. "Unemployment among Family Men: A 10-Year Longitudinal Study." *Monthly Labor Review* 102, 11 (November).

Holahan, John, and Scanlon, William. 1979. "Physician Pricing in California: Price Controls, Physician Fees, and Physician Incomes from Medicare and Medicaid." HEW Publication No. (HCFA) 03006 (September). Washington, DC: Department of Health, Education, and Welfare.

Hopkinson, C. S., Jr., and Day, J.W., Jr. 1980. "Net Energy Analysis of Alcohol Production from Sugarcane." *Science* 207, 18 (January).

Hudson, Edward A., and Jorgenson, Dale W. 1978. "The Economic Impact of Policies to Reduce U.S. Economic Growth." *Resources and Energy* 1, 3 (November).

Hutter, Adolph M., Jr., et al. 1973. "Early Hospital Discharge after Myocardial Infarction." *New England Journal of Medicine* 288, 22 (31 May).

International Settlements, Bank of. 1977. *Annual Report.* Basle, Switzerland: Bank of International Settlements.

Johnson, Ralph, and Brown, G. 1976. *Cleaning Up Europe's Water: Economics, Management, and Policies.* New York: Praeger.

Kaitz, Hyman B. 1970. "Analyzing the Length oif Spells of Unemployment." *Monthly Labor Review* 93 (November).

Kaldor, N. 1957. *An Expenditure Tax.* London: Allen and Unwin.

Keeley, M.C.; Robins, P.K.; Spiegelman, R. G.; West, R. W. 1978. "The Labor Supply Effects and Costs of Alternative Negative Income Tax Programs." *Journal of Human Resources* 13, 1 (Winter).

Kendrick, J. 1979. *The Formation and Stocks of Total Capital.* Cambridge, MA: National Bureau of Economic Research.

Killingsworth, Charles C. 1963. "Automation, Jobs, and Manpower." *Nation's Manpower Revolution*. U.S. Senate Subcommittee on Employment and Manpower of the Committee on Labor and Public Welfare. Hearings. 88th Congress, 1st Session. Washington, DC: Government Printing Office.

Kneese, Allen V., and Schultz, Charles L. 1975. *Pollution, Prices, and Public Policy*. Washington, DC: Brookings Institution.

Kosters, Marvin, and Welch, Finis. 1972. "The Effects of Minimum Wages on the Distribution of Changes in Aggregate Employment." *American Economic Review* 62, 3 (June).

Kotlikoff, Laurence J. 1978. "Social Security—Time to Reform." In *Federal Tax Reform: Myths and Realities*, edited by Michael J. Boskin. San Francisco, CA: Institute for Contemporary Studies.

———, Spivak, Avia, and Summers, Lawrence H. 1979. "The Adequacy of Savings for Retirement." Mimeo.

Krauss, M. 1978. *The New Protectionism: The Welfare State and International Trade*. New York: New York University Press.

Kreinin, M. 1979. *International Economics: A Policy Approach*. 3d edition. New York: Harcourt Brace Jovanovich, Inc.

Kunreuther, Howard, and Stovic, Paul. 1978. "Economics, Psychology, and Protective Behavior." *American Economic Review* 68, 2 (May).

Kursunoglu, Behram, and Perlmutter, Arnolds, eds. 1979. *Directions in Energy Policy*. Cambridge, MA: Ballinger Publishing Company.

Lave, Lester, and Seskin, Eugene. 1970. "Air Pollution and Human Health: The Quantitative Effect of Air Pollution on Human Health and an Estimate of the Dollar Benefit of Pollution Abatement." *Science* 169 (21 August).

Leighton, Linda, and Mincer, Jacob. 1979. "Labor Turnover and Youth Unemployment." NBER Working Paper No. 378 (August). Cambridge, MA: National Bureau of Economic Research.

Lewin Associates. 1975. "Evaluation of the Efficiency and Effectiveness of the Section 1122 Review Process" (September). Washington, DC: Lewin Associates.

Liebow, Elliot. 1967. *Tally's Corner: A Study of Negro Streetcorner Men*. Boston, MA: Little Brown and Company.

Lilley, William, and Miller, James. 19 . "The New Social Regulation." *The Public Interest*.

Luft, Harold S. 1978. "How Do Health Maintenance Organizations Achieve Their 'Savings'?" *New England Journal of Medicine* 298, 24 (15 June).

Lurie, Irene. 1974. "Estimates of Tax Rates in the AFDC Program." *National Tax Journal* 27.

MacAvoy, Paul W., ed. 1977. *Federal Energy Administration Regulation: Report of the Presidential Task Force*. Washington, DC: American Enterprise Institute for Public Policy Research.

————. 1979. *The Regulated Industries and the Economy.* New York: W. W. Norton.

McKinnon, R. I. 1980. "Dollar Stabilization and American Monetary Policy." *American Economic Review* (May).

————. 1979. *Money in International Exchange: The Convertible Currency System.* New York: Oxford University Press.

————. 1974. "A New Tripartite Monetary Agreement or a Limping Dollar Standard?" Princeton Essays in International Finance No. 106. Princeton, NJ: Princeton University Press.

McNeer, J. Frederick, et al. 1978. "Hospital Discharge One Week after Myocardial Infarction." *New England Journal of Medicine* 298, 5 (2 February).

Mansfield, Edwin; Rapoport, John; Romeo, Anthony; Wagner, Samuel; Bearsley, George. 1979. "Social and Private Rates of Return from Industrial Innovations." *Quarterly Journal of Economics.*

Mendeloff, John. 1980. "Using Taxes in Place of Regulation: OSHA and the Political Problem" *Taxing and Spending* (forthcoming).

Michael, Robert T., Fuchs, Victor R., and Scott, Sharon R. 1978. "Changes in Household Living Arrangements, 1950–1976." Working Paper 262 (June). Cambridge, MA: National Bureau of Economic Research.

Miller, James C., and Yandle, Bruce. 1979. *Benefit Cost Analysis of Social Regulations.* Washington, DC: American Enterprise Institute.

Moy, Joyanna. 1979. "Recent Labor Market Trends in Nine Industrial Nations." *Monthly Labor Review* 102, 5 (May).

Murphy, Marvin L., et al. 1977. "Treatment of Chronic Stable Angina: A Preliminary Report of Survival Data of the Randomized Veterans Administration Cooperative Study." *New England Journal of Medicine* 297, 12 (22 September).

Musgrave, Richard, and Musgrame, Peggy. 1973. *Public Finance in Theory and Practice.* New York: McGraw Hill.

Nehring, Richard. 1978. *Giant Oil Fields and World Oil Resources.* R–2284–CIA (June). Santa Monica, CA: The RAND Corporation.

Nichols, Albert L., and Zeckhauser, Richard. 1977. "Government Comes to the Workplace: An Assessment of OSHA." *Public Interest* (Fall).

Nickell, Stephen. 1979. "Education and Lifetime Patterns of Unemployment." *Journal of Political Economy* 87, 5 (October), Part 2.

Olson, Mancur. 1977. "The Treatment of Externalities in National Income Statistics." In *Public Economics and the Quality of Life,* edited by London Wingo and Alan Evons. Baltimore, MD: Johns Hopkins University Press.

Parsons, Donald O., and Munro, Douglas R. 1978. "Intergenerational Transfers in Social Security." In *The Crisis in Social Security,* edited by Michael J. Boskin. San Francisco, CA: Institute for Contemporary Studies.

Perry, George L. 1978. "Slowing the Wage-Price Spiral: The Macroeconomic View." *Brookings Papers in Economic Activity* (2). Washington, DC: Brookings Institution.

Phelps, Charles E., and Smith, Rodney T. 1977. *Petroleum Regulation: The False Dilemma of Decontrol.* R–1951–RD. Santa Monica, CA: The RAND Corporation.

Polinsky, Mitchell, and Rubinfeld, Daniel. 1977. "Property Values and the Benefits of Environmental Improvement: Theory and Measurement." In *Public Economics and the Quality of Life,* edited by London Wingo and Alan Evans. Baltimore, MD: Johns Hopkins University Press.

Public Social Services, Los Angeles County Department of. 1979. *Fact Sheets* (January). Los Angeles, CA: County of Los Angeles.

Robertson, A. Halworth. 1978. "Financial Status of Social Security Program after the Social Security Amendments of 1977." *Social Security Bulletin,* No 14 (March).

Root, F. 1978. *International Trade and Investment.*4th edition. Cincinnati, Ohio: South-Western Publishing Company.

Salkever, David S., and Bice, Thomas. 1976. "The Impact of Certificate-of-Need Controls on Hospital Investment." *Health and Society, Milbank Memorial Fund Quarterly* 54, 2 (Spring).

Salmon, Richard. 1970. "Systems Analysis of the Effects of Air Pollution on Materials" (January). Kansas City, MO: Midwest Research Institute.

Scherer, F. M. 1980. *Industrial Market Structure and Economic Performance.* Chicago: Rand McNally.

Siegel, R. 1979. "Why Has Productivity Slowed Down?" *Data Resources Review* (March).

Sloan, Frank A., and Steinwald, Bruce. 1980. "Effects of Regulation on Hospital Costs and Input Use." *Journal of Law and Economics* (forthcoming).

Solow, Robert M. 1964. *The Nature and Sources of Unemployment in the United States.* Wicksell Lectures.

Sorrentino, Constance. 1975. "Methodological and Conceptual Problems of Measuring Unemployment in OECD Countries." Parts I and II. Paris: Organization of Economic Cooperation and Development.

Stobaugh, Robert, and Yergen, Daniel, eds. 1979. *Energy Future.* New York: Random House.

Sweeney, James L. 1979a. "Effects of Federal Policies on Gasoline Consumption." *Resources and Energy* 2 (September).

———. 1979b. "Energy and Economic Growth: A Conceptual Framework." In *Directions in Energy Policy,* edited by Behram Kursunoglu and Arnold Perlmutter. Cambridge, MA: Ballinger Publishing Company.

———. 1977. "Energy Regulation—Solution or Problem?" In *Options for U.S. Energy Policy.* San Francisco, CA: Institute for Contemporary Studies.

———. 1979c. "New Car Efficiency Standards and the Demand for Gasoline." In *Advances in the Economics of Energy and Resources*. Vol. 1 of *The Structure of Energy Markets*, edited by Robert Pindyck. Greenwich, CT: JAI Press, Inc.

Thurow, L. 1978. "The U.S. Productivity Problems." *Data Resource Review* (August).

Tiffany, D. W., Cowan, J. R., and Tiffany, P. M. 1970. *The Unemployed: A Social-Psychological Portrait*. New York: Prentice Hall.

Tobin, James. 1980. "A Rejoinder." *Taxing & Spending* (Winter).

———, Pechman, Joseph A., and Mieszkowski, Peter. 1967. "Is a Negative Income Tax Practical?" *Yale Law Review* 77, 1 (November).

Toikka, R. S. 1974. "The Economics of Information: Labor Market Aspects." *Swedish Journal of Economics* 76, 1 (March).

U.S. Department of Commerce. 1977. "Projections of the Population of the United States: 1977 to 2050." *Current Population Reports*, Series P−25, No. 704 (July).

———. 1979. *Statistical Abstract of the United States*. 100th ed. Washington, DC: Government Printing Office.

U.S. Department of Energy. Random years. *Monthly Energy Review.* Washington, DC: Government Printing Office.

U.S. Department of Health, Education, and Welfare. 1979a. "Critical Analysis of the Welfare System." Mimeo. Washington, DC: Department of Health, Education, and Welfare.

———. 1978. *Data on the Medicaid Program: Eligibility, Services, Expenditures Fiscal Years 1966*–78. Washington, DC: Institute for Medicaid Management.

———. 1977. "The Low Income Population: What We Know about It: A Statistical Profile." Mimeo. Washington, DC: Department of Health, Education, and Welfare.

———. 1978. "An Overview of the Income Security System." Mimeo. Washington, DC: Department of Health, Education, and Welfare.

———. 1979b. "President Carter's Proposal for Welfare Reform, Summary Fact Sheet." Mimeo. Washington, DC: Department of Health, Education, and Welfare.

———. 1979c. *Social Security Bulletin* 42, No. 9 (September). Washington, DC: Department of Health, Education, and Welfare.

———. 1980. "Statement by John L. Palmer before the Subcommittee on Public Assistance of the Senate Finance Committee." Washington, DC: Department of Health, Education, and Welfare.

U.S. Department of the Interior. 1976. *Energy Perspectives 2* (June). Washington, DC: Government Printing Office.

U.S. Department of Labor. 1979b. *Employment and Training Report of the President*. Washington, DC: Government Printing Office.

———. 1979a. *Handbook of Labor Statistics 1978*. Washington, DC: Government Printing Office.

————. 1979*c*. "WIN—1968–1978: A Report at 10 Years" (June). Washington, DC: Government Printing Office.

U.S. Ex-Im Bank. 1978. *Annual Report.* Washington, DC: U.S. Government Printing Office.

U.S. Geological Survey. 1974/1975. *Circular 725.* Washington, DC: U.S. Geological Survey.

U.S. Office of Technology Assessment. 1979. *Gasohol.* Washington, DC: Government Printing Office.

Weidenbaum, Murray L. 1979. *The Future of Business Regulation.* New York: Amacom.

Welch, Finis. 1978. *Minimum Wages: Issues and Evidence.* Washington, DC: American Enterprise Institute.

Williamson, Oliver. 1979. "The Anguish of Saccharin: The Decision Process Approach and Its Alternatives." Discussion Paper No. 53 (August). Center for the Study of Organizational Innovation, University of Pennsylvania.

Yeager, L. B. 1976. *International Monetary Relations: Theory, History, and Policy.* 2d ed. New York: Harper and Row.

ABOUT THE AUTHORS

MICHAEL J. BOSKIN, Professor of Economics at Stanford University and Director, Program on Social Insurance Research, National Bureau of Economic Research, is an authority on taxation and public finance and former consultant to the Department of Health, Education, and Welfare and to the U.S. Treasury. He has written extensively on taxation, social security, econometrics, and labor economics, and is editor of two previous institute publications—*The Crisis in Social Security* and *Federal Tax Reform.*

GEORGE F. BREAK, Professor of Economics at the university of California—Berkeley, was chairman of the Department of Economics from 1969 to 1973. He is author of *Federal Lending and Economic Stability* and *Intergovernmental Fiscal Relations in the United States*, both published by The Brookings Institution, and is coauthor with Joseph A. Pechman of *Federal Tax Reform: The Impossible Dream?* He has written extensively on taxation and economic matters for government publications and for various journals of economics and public finance, and wrote the chapter on corporate tax integration in the institute's book on federal tax reform.

JOHN T. CUDDINGTON, Professor of Economics at Stanford University and coauthor with Ronald McKinnon of the chapter on free trade and protectionism in the institute's book, *Federal Tax Reform: The Politics of Protectionism*, concentrates his interests on international trade and finance, macroeconomics, money, and economic growth. His writings included "Estimating the Impacts of Property Tax Reform" in *Land Economics* and, among other articles, "Estimating the Impacts of Property Tax Reform" in *Land Economics.*

PATRICIA DRURY, Research Associate at the Graduate School of Business, Stanford University, is a former management specialist in the Office of Program Evaluation of Alameda County, California.

ALAIN ENTHOVEN is Marriner S. Eccles Professor of Public and Private Management, Stanford Graduate School of Business, and Professor of Health Care Economics and the Department of Family, Community, and Preventive Medicine at the Stanford School of Medicine. His experience in economics and public health care policy includes MIT, The RAND Corporation, The Brookings Institution, and ten years spent in research analysis at the Department of Defense. His writings include the chapter on the politics of national health insurance in the institute's book *New Directions in Public Health Care: A Prescription for the 1980s*, several journal articles on the Consumer-Choice Health Plan proposal, and the forthcoming *Health Plan: The Only Practical Solution to the Soaring Cost of Medical Care.*

LAURENCE J. KOTLIKOFF is Assistant Professor of Economics at Yale University and a Research Associate, National Bureau of Economic Research. He wrote the chapter on social security in the institute's publication *Federal Tax Reform: Myths and Realities*, and is the author of a number of articles in the *Quarterly Journal of Economics*, *The Journal of Political Economy*, and the *American Economic Review.*

RONALD I. McKINNON, Professor of Economics at Stanford University and coauthor with John T. Cuddington of the chapter on free trade and protectionism in the institute's book on federal tax reform, has been economic consultant to the governments of Uruguay, Chile, Kuwait, Colombia, and to the Organization of American States. The author of many articles on international trade, his latest book is *Money in International Exchange: The Convertible Currency System.*

JOHN H. PENCAVEL, Professor of Economics at Stanford University, focuses his attention on industrial and labor economics. His many journal articles include, most recently, "Income Tax Evasion, Labor Supply, and Nonlinear Tax Schedules" in *Journal of Public Economics*, "The American Experience with Incomes Policies" in *Incomes Policy and Relative Pay*, edited by R. F. Elliot and J. F. Fallick, and the forthcoming "The Frequency and Size of Wage Changes in a Collective Bargaining Setting," *Journal of Labor Research.*

HENRY S. ROWEN is Professor of Public Management at the Graduate School of Business, Stanford University, and Director of the Stanford International Energy Program. A former president of the RAND Corporation, he is Chairman of the Executive Panel, Office of the Chief of Naval Operations, and a member of several international security councils, the Council on Foreign Relations, and the International Institute for Strategic Studies. He wrote the initial chapter in the institute's *Options for U.S. Energy Policy* and the chapter on "The Threatened Jugular: Oil Supply of the West" in its *National Security in the 1980s: From Weakness to Strength*. His many published articles include the forthcoming "American Security Interests in Northeast Asia" (*Daedalus*).

JOHN L. SCADDING, economist at the Federal Reserve Bank of San Francisco and former Assistant Professor of Economics at Stanford University, held the position of Senior Staff Economist on the Council of Economic Advisors. In this position his duties included writing the money, credit, and monetary policy sections of *The Economic Report of the President*, analyzing and commenting on legislation affecting areas of responsibility, acting as council representative on interdepartmental and interagency task forces, and drafting, together with treasury and OMB representatives, the report for the administration's task force on financial regulation.

JOHN B. SHOVEN, Professor of Economics at Stanford University, is experienced in microeconomics and public finance. His many articles on taxation, inflation, and government policies include "Inflation and Income Taxation" in the institute's *Federal Tax Reform: Myths and Realities*, and the coauthorship of a number of *Brookings Papers on Economic Activity*.

JAMES L. SWEENEY is Professor of Engineering-Economic Systems at Stanford University and serves as Director of the Energy Modeling Forum, a national activity headquartered at Stanford University. He was Director of the Office of Energy Systems Modeling and Forecasting at the Federal Energy Administration while *The National Energy Outlook* was being written and while the supporting energy policy models were being developed. He is author of "Energy Regulations—Solution or Problem?" in the institute's *Options for U.S. Energy Policy*, and his articles have appeared in many journals and books, including *Econometrica, Journal of Economic Theory*, and *Journal of Urban Economics*.

DAVID J. TEECE is Associate Professor of Business Economics, Graduate School of Business and Department of Economics, Stanford University. He is author of a number of monographs including *The Multinational Corporation and the Resource Cost of International Technology Transfer* and the forthcoming *Technology*

Transfer, the Multinational Firm, and Engineering Manpower written with E. Mansfield et al. His articles are published in such journals as *Management Science, Economic Journal,* and *Economica.*

INDEX

PUBLICATIONS LIST*

THE INSTITUTE FOR CONTEMPORARY STUDIES

260 California Street, San Francisco, California, 94111

Catalog available upon request

BUREAUCRATS AND BRAINPOWER: GOVERNMENT
REGULATION OF UNIVERSITIES
>$6.95. 171 pages. Publication date: June 1979
>ISBN 0−917616−35− 9
>Library of Congress No. 79−51328

Contributors: Nathan Glazer, Robert S. Hatfield, Richard W. Lyman,
Paul Seabury, Robert L. Sproull, Miro M. Todorovich, Caspar W.
Weinberger

THE CALIFORNIA COASTAL PLAN: A CRITIQUE
>$5.95. 199 pages. Publication date: March 1976
>ISBN 0−917616−04−9
>Library of Congress No. 76−7715

Contributors: Eugene Bardach, Daniel K. Benjamin, Thomas E.
Borcherding, Ross D. Eckert, H. Edward Frech III, M. Bruce Johnson,
Ronald N. Lafferty, Walter J. Mead, Daniel Orr, Donald M. Pach,
Michael R. Peevey

THE CRISIS IN SOCIAL SECURITY: PROBLEMS AND PROSPECTS
>$6.95. 214 pages. Publication date: April 1977; 2d ed. rev.,
>1978, 1979
>ISBN 0−917616−16−2/1977; 0−917616−25−1/1978
>Library of Congress No. 77−72542

Contributors: Michael J. Boskin, George F. Break, Rita Ricardo Campbell,
Edward Cowan, Martin S. Feldstein, Milton Friedman, Douglas R.
Munro, Donald O. Parsons, Carl V. Patton, Joseph A. Pechman,
Sherwin Rosen, W. Kip Viscusi, Richard J. Zeckhauser

DEFENDING AMERICA: TOWARD A NEW ROLE IN THE
POST-DETENTE WORLD
>$13.95 (hardbound only). 255 pages. Publication date: April 1977 by
>Basic Books (New York)
>ISBN 0−465−01585−9
>Library of Congress No. 76−43479

*Prices subject to change.

Contributors: Robert Conquest, Theodore Draper, Gregory Grossman,
Walter Z. Laqueur, Edward N. Luttwak, Charles Burton Marshall,
Paul H. Nitze, Norman Polmar, Eugene V. Rostow, Leonard Schapiro,
James R. Schlesinger, Paul Seabury, W. Scott Thompson, Albert
Wohlstetter

THE ECONOMY IN THE 1980s: A PROGRAM FOR GROWTH AND STABILITY

$7.95, (paper). 462 pages. Publication date: June 1980.
ISBN 0−917616−39−1
Library of Congress No. 80−80647
$17.95 (cloth). 462 pages. Publication date: August 1980.
ISBN 0−87855−399−1. Available through Transaction Books,
Rutgers−The State University, New Brunswick, NJ 08903

Contributors: Michael J. Boskin, George F. Break, John T. Cuddington,
Patricia Drury, Alain Enthoven, Laurence J. Kotlikoff, Ronald
I. McKinnon, John Pencavel, Henry S. Rowen, John L. Scadding,
John B. Shoven, James L. Sweeney, David Teece

EMERGING COALITIONS IN AMERICAN POLITICS

$6.95. 524 pages. Publication date: June 1978
ISBN 0−917616−22−7
Library of Congress No. 78−53414

Contributors: Jack Bass, David S. Broder, Jerome M. Clubb, Edward H.
Crane III, Walter De Vries, Andrew M. Greeley, S. I. Hayakawa,
Tom Hayden, Milton Himmelfarb, Richard Jensen, Paul Kleppner,
Everett Carll Ladd, Jr., Seymour Martin Lipset, Robert A. Nisbet,
Michael Novak, Gary R. Orren, Nelson W. Polsby, Joseph L. Rauh,
Jr., Stanley Rothman, William A. Rusher, William Schneider, Jesse
M. Unruh, Ben J. Wattenberg

FEDERAL TAX REFORM: MYTHS AND REALITIES

$5.95. 270 pages. Publication date: September 1978
ISBN 0−917616−32−4
Library of Congress No. 78−61661

Contributors: Robert J. Barro, Michael J. Boskin, George F. Break,
Jerry R. Green, Laurence J. Kotlikoff, Mordecai Kurz, Peter
Mieszkowski, John B. Shoven, Paul J. Taubman, John Whalley

GOVERNMENT CREDIT ALLOCATION: WHERE DO WE GO FROM HERE?

$4.95. 208 pages. Publication date: November 1975
ISBN 0−917616−02−2
Library of Congress No. 75−32951

Contributors: George J. Benston, Karl Brunner, Dwight M. Jaffe, Omotunde
E. G. Johnson, Edward J. Kane, Thomas Mayer, Allen H. Meltzer

NATIONAL SECURITY IN THE 1980s: FROM
WEAKNESS TO STRENGTH
> $8.95 (paper). 524 pages. Publication date: May 1980
>   ISBN 0−917616−38−3
>   Library of Congress No. 80−80648
> $19.95 (cloth). 524 pages. Publication date: August 1980
>   ISBN 0−87855−412−2. Available through Transaction Books,
>   Rutgers−The State University, New Brunswick, NJ 08903
Contributors: Kenneth L. Adelman, Richard R. Burt, Miles M. Costick,
>   Robert F. Ellsworth, Fred Charles Iklé, Geoffrey T. H. Kemp,
>   Edward N. Luttwak, Charles Burton Marshall, Paul H. Nitze,
>   Sam Nunn, Henry S. Rowen, Leonard Sullivan, Jr., W. Scott
>   Thompson, William R. Van Cleave, Francis J. West, Jr.,
>   Albert Wohlstetter, Elmo R. Zumwalt, Jr.

NEW DIRECTIONS IN PUBLIC HEALTH CARE: AN EVALUATION
OF PROPOSALS FOR NATIONAL HEALTH INSURANCE
> $6.95. 277 pages. Publication date: May 1976
>   ISBN 0−917616−00−6
>   Library of Congress No. 76−9522
Contributors: Martin S. Feldstein, Thomas D. Hall, Leon R. Kass, Keith
>   B. Leffler, Cotton M. Lindsay, Mark V. Pauly, Charles E. Phelps,
>   Thomas C. Schelling, Arthur Seldon

NEW DIRECTIONS IN PUBLIC HEALTH CARE: A PRESCRIPTION
FOR THE 1980s
> $6.95 (paper). 290 pages. Publication date: May 1976; 3d ed.
>   rev., 1980
>   ISBN 0−917616−37−5
>   Library of Congress No. 79−92868
> $16.95 (cloth). 290 pages. Publication date: April 1980
>   ISBN 0−87855−394−0. Available through Transaction Books,
>   Rutgers—The State University, New Brunswick, NJ 08903
Contributors: Alain Enthoven, W. Philip Gramm, Leon R. Kass, Keith B.
>   Leffler, Cotton M. Lindsay, Jack A. Meyer, Charles E. Phelps,
>   Thomas C. Schelling, Harry Schwartz, Arthur Seldon, David A.
>   Stockman, Lewis Thomas

NO LAND IS AN ISLAND: INDIVIDUAL RIGHTS AND
GOVERNMENT CONTROL OF LAND USE
> $5.95. 221 pages. Publication date: November 1975
>   ISBN 0−917616−03−0
>   Library of Congress No. 75−38415
Contributors: Benjamin F. Bobo, B. Bruce-Briggs, Connie Cheney, A.
>   Lawrence Chickering, Robert B. Ekelund, Jr., W. Philip Gramm,
>   Donald G. Hagman, Robert B. Hawkins, Jr., M. Bruce Johnson, Jan
>   Krasnowiecki, John McClaughry, Donald M. Pach, Bernard H.
>   Siegan, Ann Louise Strong, Morris K. Udall

460

NO TIME TO CONFUSE: A CRITIQUE OF THE FORD
FOUNDATION'S ENERGY POLICY PROJECT *A TIME TO
CHOOSE AMERICA'S ENERGY FUTURE*
> $4.95. 156 pages. Publication date: February 1975
> ISBN 0–917616–01–4
> Library of Congress No. 75–10230

Contributors: Morris A. Adelman, Armen A. Alchian, James C. DeHaven,
George W. Hilton, M. Bruce Johnson, Herman Kahn, Walter J. Mead,
Arnold B. Moore, Thomas Gale Moore, William H. Riker

ONCE IS ENOUGH: THE TAXATION OF CORPORATE
EQUITY INCOME
> $2.00. 32 pages. Publication date: May 1977
> ISBN 0–917616–23–5
> Library of Congress No. 77–670132

Author: Charles E. McLure, Jr.

OPTIONS FOR U.S. ENERGY POLICY
> $5.95. 309 pages. Publication date: September 1977
> ISBN 0–917616–20–0
> Library of Congress No. 77–89094

Contributors: Albert Carnesale, Stanley M. Greenfield, Fred S. Hoffman,
Edward J. Mitchell, William R. Moffat, Richard Nehring, Robert
S. Pindyck, Norman C. Rasmussen, David J. Rose, Henry S. Rowen,
James L. Sweeney, Arthur W. Wright

PARENTS, TEACHERS, AND CHILDREN: PROSPECTS FOR CHOICE
IN AMERICAN EDUCATION
> $5.95. 336 pages. Publication date: June 1977
> ISBN 0–917616–18–9
> Library of Congress No. 77–79164

Contributors: James S. Coleman, John E. Coons, William H. Cornog,
Denis P. Doyle, E. Babette Edwards, Nathan Glazer, Andrew
M. Greeley, R. Kent Greenawalt, Marvin Lazerson, William
C. McCready, Michael Novak, John P. O'Dwyer, Robert Singleton,
Thomas Sowell, Stephen D. Sugarman, Richard E. Wagner

THE POLITICS OF PLANNING: A REVIEW AND CRITIQUE OF
CENTRALIZED ECONOMIC PLANNING
> $5.95. 367 pages. Publication date: March 1976
> ISBN 0–917616–05–7
> Library of Congress No. 76–7714

Contributors: B. Bruce-Briggs, James Buchanan, A. Lawrence Chickering,
Ralph Harris, Robert B. Hawkins, Jr., George W. Hilton, Richard
Mancke, Richard Muth, Vincent Ostrom, Svetozar Pejovich, Myron
Sharpe, John Sheahan, Herbert Stein, Gordon Tullock, Ernest
van den Haag, Paul H. Weaver, Murray L. Weidenbaum, Hans
Willgerodt, Peter P. Witonski

PUBLIC EMPLOYEE UNIONS: A STUDY OF THE CRISIS IN
PUBLIC SECTOR LABOR RELATIONS
> $6.95. 251 pages. Publication date: June 1976; 2d ed. rev., 1977
>   ISBN 0–917616–08–1/1976; 0–917616–24–3/1977
>   Library of Congress No. 76–17444

Contributors: A. Lawrence Chickering, Jack D. Douglas, Raymond
D. Horton, Theodore W. Kheel, David Lewin, Seymour Martin
Lipset, Harvey C. Mansfield, Jr., George Meany, Robert A. Nisbet,
Daniel Orr, A. H. Raskin, Wes Uhlman, Harry H. Wellington,
Charles B. Wheeler, Jr., Ralph K. Winter, Jr., Jerry Wurf

REGULATING BUSINESS: THE SEARCH FOR AN OPTIMUM
> $6.95. 260 pages. Publication date: April 1978
>   ISBN 0–917616–27–8
>   Library of Congress No. 78–50678

Contributors: Chris Argyris, A. Lawrence Chickering, Penny Hollander
Feldman, Richard H. Holton, Donald P. Jacobs, Alfred E. Kahn,
Paul W. MacAvoy, Almarin Phillips, V. Kerry Smith, Paul H.
Weaver, Richard J. Zeckhauser

TARIFFS, QUOTAS, AND TRADE: THE POLITICS
OF PROTECTIONISM
> $6.95. 330 pages. Publication date: February 1979
>   ISBN 0–917616–34–0
>   Library of Congress No. 78–66267

Contributors: Walter Adams, Ryan C. Amacher, Sven W. Arndt, Malcolm
D. Bale, John T. Cuddington, Alan V. Deardorff, Joel B. Dirlam
Roger D. Hansen, H. Robert Heller, D. Gale Johnson, Robert O.
Keohane, Michael W. Keran, Rachel McCulloch, Ronald I.
McKinnon, Gordon W. Smith, Robert M. Stern, Richard James
Sweeney, Robert D. Tollison, Thomas D. Willett

THE THIRD WORLD: PREMISES OF U.S. POLICY
> $5.95. 332 pages. Publication date: November 1978
>   ISBN 0–917616–30–8
>   Library of Congress No. 78–67593

Contributors: Dennis Austin, Peter T. Bauer, Max Beloff, Richard E. Bissell,
Daniel J. Elazar, S. E. Finer, Allan E. Goodman, Nathaniel H. Leff,
Seymour Martin Lipset, Edward N. Luttwak, Daniel Pipes, Wilson E.
Schmidt, Anthony Smith, W. Scott Thompson, Basil S. Yamey

UNION CONTROL OF PENSION FUNDS: WILL THE NORTH
RISE AGAIN?
> $2.00. 42 pages. Publication date: July 1979
>   ISBN 0–917616–36–7
>   Library of Congress No. 78–66581

Author: George J. Borjas

WATER BANKING: HOW TO STOP WASTING
AGRICULTURAL WATER
  $2.00. 56 pages. Publication date: January 1978
  ISBN 0—917616—26—X
  Library of Congress No. 78—50766
Authors: Sotirios Angelides, Eugene Bardach

TAXING & SPENDING
 · $15/one year, $25/two years, $4/single issue. For delivery outside the
    United States, add $2/year surface mail, $10/year airmail
A quarterly journal that analyzes the immediate and long-range effects of
    the tax limitation movement as well as the broad issues of national
    and local taxing and spending policy.